VIOLENCE
AND SERIOUS
THEFT

VIOLENCE

AND SERIOUS THEFT

DEVELOPMENT AND PREDICTION FROM CHILDHOOD TO ADULTHOOD

ROLF LOEBER   DAVID P. FARRINGTON

MAGDA STOUTHAMER-LOEBER   HELENE RASKIN WHITE

Routledge
Taylor & Francis Group
New York   London

Routledge
Taylor & Francis Group
270 Madison Avenue
New York, NY 10016

Routledge
Taylor & Francis Group
2 Park Square
Milton Park, Abingdon
Oxon OX14 4RN

© 2008 by Taylor & Francis Group, LLC
Routledge is an imprint of Taylor & Francis Group, an Informa business

Printed in the United States of America on acid-free paper
10 9 8 7 6 5 4 3 2 1

International Standard Book Number-13: 978-0-8058-5222-6 (0)

Library of Congress Cataloging-in-Publication Data

Violence and serious theft : development and prediction from childhood to adulthood / Rolf Loeber ... [et al.] ; with assistance of Darrick Jolliffe ... [et al.].
   p. cm.
Includes bibliographical references and index.
ISBN 978-0-8058-5222-6 (alk. paper)
   1. Juvenile delinquency--Pennsylvania--Pittsburgh--Longitudinal studies. 2. Criminal behavior--Pennsylvania--Pittsburgh--Longitudinal studies. 3. Criminal behavior, Prediction of--Pennsylvania--Pittsburgh--Longitudinal studies. I. Loeber, Rolf. II. Jolliffe, Darrick.

HV9106.P55V56 2008
364.3609748'86--dc22
          2007027549

Visit the Taylor & Francis Web site at
http://www.taylorandfrancis.com

and the Routledge Web site at
http://www.routledge.com

This book is dedicated to the late Evelyn Wei, her scholarship, and her major contribution to the Pittsburgh Youth Study.

Contents

Part III
Prediction of Violence, Serious Theft, and Desistance

Part IV
Conclusions

List of Figures

List of Tables

Preface

JAMES C. HOWELL

Twenty years ago, the U.S. Office of Juvenile Justice and Delinquency Prevention launched the Program of Research on the Causes and Correlates of Delinquency. It represented the most comprehensive prospective studies of the causes and correlates of juvenile delinquency in the world. Three landmark studies were funded simultaneously. Participants in the Pittsburgh Youth Study (PYS)—on which this book reports—were boys randomly selected from the first, fourth, and seventh grades of public schools. This unique research design permitted a three-cohort study of subjects covering ages 7–25. For each grade cohort, the top 30% (about 250) of boys with the highest rates of predelinquent or delinquent behavior were selected, along with an equal number of boys randomly selected from the remaining 70% for comparison purposes. This resulted in a total sample of 1,517, with approximately 500 boys from each grade.

Participants in the Rochester Youth Development Study (1,000 boys and girls) were randomly drawn from the seventh and eighth grade cohorts of Rochester, New York public schools. Subjects in the Denver Youth Survey (1,527 children and adolescents, both boys and girls) were randomly selected from households in high-risk Denver neighborhoods. Subjects were ages 7, 9, 11, 13, and 15 when the Denver study began. Subjects in all three studies are now in their 20s and 30s; thus, studies from two of the sites marked the transition from childhood to adolescence and, in all three sites, from adolescence to adulthood.

The three research teams have collaborated to use a common measurement package, collecting data on a wide range of variables that make possible cross-site comparisons. Indeed, several publications feature cross-site comparisons of similarities and differences. This is a historic first in longitudinal delinquency research throughout the world—instant replication of study results.

In addition to the Pittsburgh Youth Study, the Pittsburgh Life Studies History Program that Rolf Loeber and Magda Stouthamer-Loeber expertly direct includes the Developmental Trends Study (of 177 clinic-referred boys), and the Pittsburgh Girls Study. The latter is a recently launched communitywide longitudinal study of 2,451 girls between 5 and 8 years of age who were randomly selected from households in the city of Pittsburgh. For interested readers, an earlier book on the Pittsburgh Youth Study covers many other topics (Loeber, Farrington, Stouthamer-Loeber, & Van Kammen, 1998). In addition, 143 empirical papers have been published on the PYS, a truly remarkable record of research scholarship.

The scholarship shown in this book is phenomenal not only in the literature reviews and analytical work but in brilliant conceptualizations that provide guidance for future research. For example, the PYS researchers make a distinction between promotive factors (that reduce delinquency and promote desistance) and traditionally defined protective factors, and they demonstrate in the analyses how promotive factors have main effects in the same way that risk factors have been studied for decades. They also make the important distinction between two types of risk factors: aggravating risk factors (that predict later offending) and hindering risk factors (that influence desistance from offending). These conceptualizations add enormous precision to research in these immensely important areas.

This book itself is a treasure trove of findings from the PYS, providing answers to such provocative questions as:

- What number and types of developmental trajectories best describe young men's violence and theft?
- Is there an association between ethnicity and serious offending and how can it be explained?
- Are there unique predictors of either violence or theft?
- How does self-reported offending compare with arrest and conviction data?
- Are there developmental sequences in behavior among gang membership, gun carrying, and violence and theft?

In the limited space allowed me here, I must highlight the significance of the findings on just one of these important subjects: pathways to juvenile delinquency. This is sure to be one of the most enduring contributions of the PYS. This theoretical model is grounded in a developmental approach to criminology that focuses on changes in offending patterns that come with age, and marks changes in risk and promotive factors to which offenders and nonoffenders are exposed from childhood to adulthood.

Loeber and his colleagues have made a seminal contribution to the justice practice with their delinquency pathways model. They have discovered three empirically charted pathways that youngsters typically follow in a remarkably orderly progression from less to more serious problem behaviors and delinquency from childhood to adolescence. The PYS study and several other replications of this research show that development from antisocial behaviors to serious delinquency best fits a model of three incremental pathways: the *authority conflict pathway* (generally disruptive behavior), the *overt pathway* (marked by aggression and violence), and the *covert pathway* (consisting of property crimes). The model describes a selective process (a winnowing of subgroups of delinquents) that accounts for the most serious property and violent forms of delinquency in offenders who persist in offending and advance in the overt and covert pathways. The three-pathway model accounted for the majority of the most self-reported high-rate offenders and court-reported delinquents. (Readers who are interested in more detailed information on this pioneering explanation of delinquent careers should consult Loeber, Slot, & Stouthamer-Loeber, 2006.)

Most of the chapters in this book are devoted to illuminating the developmental sequences among offense types to increase understanding of the extent to which individuals with a prior form of offending are likely to escalate to the next higher form of offending. As the authors note, information about this type of forward probability is very scarce in the literature. Most published information focuses on backward probabilities—that is, the extent to which individuals who have reached a serious level of offending have displayed less serious forms of offending earlier in life. The PYS researchers argue in chapter 4 that "knowledge of forward probabilities is in two ways important for tertiary prevention." First, forward probabilities tend to identify a group of youth that is at a high risk of escalating to serious offending. Second, this information constitutes one of the building blocks for screening devices to identify high-risk offenders at an early age. Also, "forward probabilities reveal that many offenders do not progress further in criminal careers."

Another seminal contribution of this book to the criminology literature is on offender specialization in these pathways. The PYS research team was able to classify offenders on the basis of self-reported delinquency and court convictions. This unique combination of data permitted them to examine offense specialization more closely than have prior studies that have been based on either self-reports or official records of offending. In a major discovery, the researchers debunk a long-held notion that juvenile offenders are not selective, that their offense pattern is commonly "cafeteria-style," as proposed to the theories of Malcolm Klein (1984) and others. Notably, serious violent offenders were more likely than theft offenders to specialize in offense patterns. One-half of the serious violent offenders in both cohorts were specialized offenders, compared to one-third of the serious theft offenders.

Readers will also be pleased to know that important policy and program implications of research findings such as these are expertly drawn by the PYS research team in the final chapter. Unlike most researchers who, at best, are able to suggest an appropriate intervention point or a particular treatment approach, Loeber and colleagues are able to draw policy and program implications for the entire juvenile justice apparatus. Their approach is not an empty promise. Research findings from the PYS, the Cambridge Study in Delinquent Development (headed by David Farrington) and other studies in the Pittsburgh Life History Studies Program have already undergirded a highly successful early intervention program in Toronto, called the Under 12

Outreach Project (See Augimeri, Farrington, Koegl, & Day, in press). It is currently being replicated internationally.

I happily extend an invitation to all scholars with an interest in the development of juvenile delinquency and related problem behaviors to enjoy this volume. It will not disappoint in any respect.

Acknowledgments

In the preparation of this volume, we owe much to the Pittsburgh Youth Study (PYS) participants, their parents, and the teachers who repeatedly cooperated over many years to provide us with the detailed information on which this book is based. We always considered them experts whose knowledge is essential for furthering science. We are also greatly indebted to many individuals who have worked on this project, have given advice, or have sponsored it. First, we owe many thanks to the efforts of a large and highly professional data collection team, particularly the numerous interviewers and their supervisors: Rosemary Constanzo, Rose Jarosz, and Dianne Miller. Also, we are greatly indebted to the data management team, especially Matthew Cronin, Barbara Kumer, and Rebecca Stallings; and the secretarial staff, particularly Celia Nourse Eatman, JoAnn Fraser, Susan Jones, and, more recently, Deborah Anthony (who very effectively assisted with the preparation of this book), while Kayla Stalma, Lacey White, and Jen Wilson assisted with the compilation of the references. We are very grateful to two individuals who played key roles in the execution of the study, Welmoet B. Van Kammen and the late Evelyn H. Wei. We also received valued advice from our informal advisory board, consisting of Alfred Blumstein, Dante Cicchetti, Malcolm Klein, Lloyd Ohlin, and Lee Robins, and many other colleagues over the years. We are particularly grateful to Alfred and Dolores Blumstein for welcoming David Farrington to their house on his many visits to Pittsburgh. Moreover, we received excellent support and advice from a number of other researchers, including Adrian Angold, Rico Catalano, Jacqueline Cohen, Pat Cohen, Jane Costello, Deborah Gorman-Smith, David Hawkins, Alison Hipwell, Marc Le Blanc, Akiva Liberman, Friedrich Lösel, the late Joan McCord, Howard Snyder, Patrick Tolan, Richard Tremblay, Norman White and P.-O. H. Wikström. In addition, we are indebted to James (Buddy) C. Howell and Alex Piquero for their valuable comments on an earlier draft of this book. Much of the volume was written during our stays at the Institute of Criminology in Cambridge, England, and we are grateful for the sympathetic and most helpful support of the staff of the institute.

The yield of the PYS has been greatly enhanced by the linkage of the main study to 21 independently funded substudies. We are very indebted to the following investigators of the substudies for their inspiration, efforts, and skills in executing them and producing papers on the results: Avshalom Caspi, Jacqueline Cohen, Lisa Gatzke-Kopp, Hans Heiner, Timothy O. Ireland, Benjamin B. Lahey, Don Lynam, Terrie Moffitt, Herbert L. Needleman, Adrian

Raine, N. Wim Slot, Terence P. Thornberry, and Brandon Welsh. (The remaining substudies have been initiated by ourselves.)

In addition, we are enormously indebted to the enthusiasm and expertise of a whole range of scholars who analyzed the data for the many papers resulting from the PYS (see the appenidix at the end of this volume). We are very grateful to the following colleagues who contributed papers as first authors: Adrian Angold, Jennifer M. Beyers, Lisa Broidy, Kathy Browning, Jeff Burke, Avshalom Caspi, Tony Fabio, Horatio Fabrega, Michele Fung, Rachel Gordon, Catharina A. Hartman, Paul Hirschfield, Machteld Hoeve, David Huizinga, Oliver John, Larry Kalb, Kate Keenan, Barbara T. Kelley, Dacher Keltner, Roos Koolhof, Robert F. Krueger, Benjamin B. Lahey, Alan J. Lizotte, Don Lynam, Eugene Maguin, Barbara Maughan, Keith McBurnett, Steven F. Messner, Terrie E. Moffitt, Herbert L. Needleman, Kathy Pajer, Faith Peeples, Richard W. Robins, Mary F. Russo, Carolyn A. Smith, Wes Thompson, Terence P. Thornberry, Welmoet B. Van Kammen, Anton Van Wijk, Laurie Wakschlag, the late Evelyn H. Wei, Jennifer L. White, Per-Olof Wikström, Eric Youngstrom, and Quanwu Zhang; in addition, a multitude of coauthors made important contributions to the papers.

In the course of this study we were also inspired by the advice and collaboration from our two "sister" studies, the Denver Youth Study and the Rochester Youth Development Study, and their principal investigators, David Huizinga and Terence P. Thornberry, respectively, and their colleagues. We are also grateful to James Rieland for facilitating access to the juvenile court records of the Pittsburgh boys. Further, we received wonderful cooperation from the Pittsburgh Board of Education and staff of the Pittsburgh public schools (of which we especially must mention Jack Garrow), and from Children and Youth Services for Allegheny County, which opened its archives to provide us with information about the families.

Finally, the study would never have been initiated without the encouragement and sponsorship of the Office of Juvenile Justice and Delinquency Prevention of the U.S. Department of Justice (96-MU-FX-0020 and OJJDP 2005-JK-FX-0001). In particular, we are extremely grateful to Barbara T. Kelley and Pam Swain for initiating the program of research, and to Betty Chemers, James (Buddy) C. Howell, Donnie Le Boeuf, Michael Shader, and Irving Slott for their valuable support and assistance. In more recent years, the funding for the study has been primarily from the National Institute of Mental Health (MH73941 and MH 50778), and we are particularly grateful to Peter Jensen, Doreen Koretz, LeShawndra Price, John Richters, Susan E. Swedo, and Farris Tuma for their counsel and support. During a gap in federal funding, we received financial support from the Pew Charitable Trusts. In addition, we received funding from the National Institute on Drug Abuse (DA 411018), and we are especially grateful to the Institute's Kevin Conway, Meyer Glantz, and Naimah Weinberg for their support and advice. Points of view or opinions in this document are those of the authors and do not necessarily represent the official position or policies of the U.S. Department of Justice, the National Institute of Mental Health, or the National Institute on Drug Abuse.

Contributors

Véronique Dupéré is a doctoral student in psychology at the University of Montreal, Montreal, Quebec, Canada.

David P. Farrington is professor of psychological criminology, Cambridge University, Cambridge, UK.

Darrick Jolliffe is a senior lecturer in criminology at the University of Leicester, UK.

Eric Lacourse is assistant professor of sociology at University of Montreal and researcher at the research unit on children's psychosocial maladjustment, Ste-Justine Hospital Research Center, Montreal, Quebec, Canada.

Rolf Loeber is distinguished university professor of psychiatry, professor of psychology and epidemiology at the University of Pittsburgh, Pittsburgh, Pennsylvania, and professor of juvenile delinquency and social development, Free University, Amsterdam, Netherlands.

Dustin A. Pardini is assistant professor of psychiatry at the University of Pittsburgh, Pittsburgh, Pennsylvania, USA.

Rebecca Stallings is data manager of the Pittsburgh Youth Study, responsible for maintaining raw data, building construct variables, and making data available to investigators, Pittsburgh, Pennsylvania, USA.

Magda Stouthamer-Loeber is associate professor of psychiatry at the University of Pittsburgh, Pittsburgh, Pennsylvania, USA.

Helene Raskin White is a professor of sociology with a joint appointment in The Center of Alcohol Studies and Sociology Department at Rutgers, the State University of New Jersey, Piscataway, New Jersey, USA.

Part I
Introduction and Methods

One
Introduction and Key Questions

ROLF LOEBER, DAVID P. FARRINGTON, MAGDA
STOUTHAMER-LOEBER, AND HELENE RASKIN WHITE

Over the past century, the United States has had a much higher rate of violence than most European countries. What is far less known is that this does not apply to all forms of violence. Figures 1.1 and 1.2 compare police reports of the rate per 100,000 inhabitants for homicide and rape in the United States and a few European countries for the years 1982–1999 (Farrington & Jolliffe, 2007). The data clearly shows that the rate of homicide and rape is substantially higher in the United States compared to that of England and Wales, Switzerland, and the Netherlands. Figures 1.3–1.4 also indicate that the rates of robbery and burglary in the United States, based on victim surveys, were similar when compared to several European countries, especially since the 1990s.

Figures 1.1–1.4 also reveal that crime rates between 1981 and 1999 have varied a great deal (Farrington & Jolliffe, 2007). Major increases and decreases in crime have taken place. There are decreases in homicide, rape, robbery, and burglary in the United States; increases in burglary and rape in England and Wales; and an increase in robbery in the Netherlands. Over a longer period of observation, the rate of homicide in Europe after 1200 was much higher than the rate of homicide in the United States in the twentieth century, but the European rate has decreased dramatically since the Early Middle Ages (see Figure 1.5). The current rate of homicide in the United States is similar to the rate that was common in Europe around the year 1700 (Eisner, 2004), and the question remains whether the United States can significantly reduce its levels of homicide and general violence within the near future rather than over the next 300 years. Violence and serious theft continue to inflict widespread harm on citizens. Certainly, crime continues to be featured on a daily basis in the media and contributes to people's fear for their own and others' personal safety. Even though the media occasionally feature case histories of the most spectacular offenders, the general public is offered very little information to increase its awareness of the causes of violence and theft. This volume documents the life course of offending and other problem behaviors of 1,009 boys between the ages of 7 and 25 in Pittsburgh. It presents new information

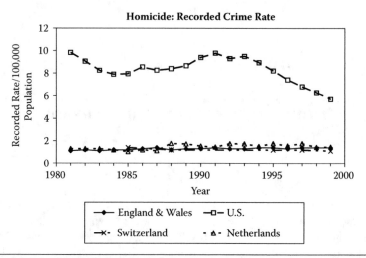

Figure 1.1 Rate of Homicide According to Police Data in the United States; England and Wales; Switzerland; and the Netherlands

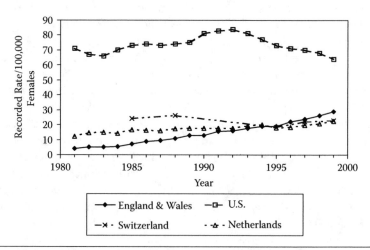

Figure 1.2 Rate of Rape According to Police Data in the United States; England and Wales; Switzerland; and the Netherlands

on individuals' delinquency careers and the putative causes of individuals' offending from childhood to early adulthood. Such knowledge is relevant to understanding age cohort differences in offending, which in turn constitutes building blocks to understanding changing crime waves over time.

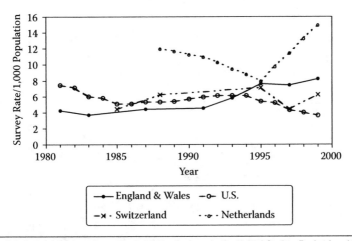

Figure 1.3 Rate of Robbery According to Victim Surveys in the United States; England and Wales; Switzerland; and the Netherlands

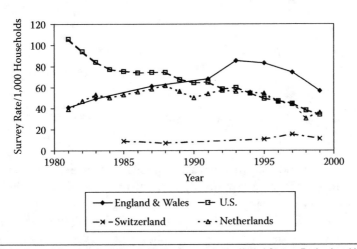

Figure 1.4 Rate of Burglary According to Victim Surveys in the United States; England and Wales; Switzerland; and the Netherlands

The Life Course Perspective

This volume extends earlier conceptualizations of the development of offenders and offending in a life course perspective (Elder, 1998; Farrington, 2003; Le Blanc & Loeber, 1998; Loeber & Le Blanc, 1990; Lösel & Bender, 2003; Piquero, Farrington, & Blumstein, 2003). The developmental approach to criminology focuses on changes in offending patterns with age and changes in risk and promotive factors to which offenders and nonoffenders are exposed from

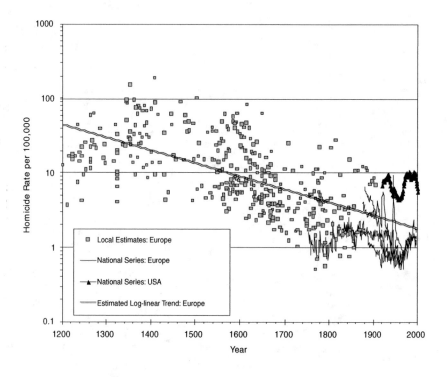

Figure 1.5 Homicide Rates in Europe (1200–2000) and the United States (1920–2000) (Eisner, 2004)

childhood to adulthood. This approach assumes that some of the propensity for delinquent offending may already be formed in early childhood, but that this propensity is maintained and modified through personal characteristics (e.g., psychopathic features) and exposure to risk and promotive factors in the person and his social environment. Definitions of these and other terms used in this volume can be found in Table 1.1. For example, the terms *offending* and *offenses* will include delinquent acts committed during the juvenile years (under age 18) and criminal acts committed during adulthood (from age 18 onward). We will use the following terms: *middle childhood* will denote ages 7–9, while *late childhood* will cover ages 10–12. *Early adolescence* will refer to ages 13–15, while *late adolescence* will be defined as ages 16–19. Finally, *early adulthood* will refer to ages 20–25.

This volume tackles major topics that are current in the empirical literature. Specifically, we will focus on the following broad questions: How widespread is violence and serious theft in two cohorts of inner-city boys between the ages of 7 and 25? Are some generations of youth more seriously delinquent than

Table 1.1 Definitions of Terms

Delinquency Career Terms

Age Cohort	Individuals who are about the same age and whose progress is followed up over time.
Age-Crime Curve	A curve showing that the prevalence of offenders is low in late childhood and early adolescence, peaks in middle to late adolescence, and decreases subsequently.
Age of Onset	Youngest age at which offending is recorded, either through self-reports or official records.
All-Source Measure of Offending	Combined measure of self-reported offending, delinquency reported by parent and teacher, and official records of conviction.
Antisocial Behavior	Behavior that inflicts harm on others, which includes minor and moderate nondelinquent problem behaviors and delinquent offenses.
Arrest	Arrest by the police.
Cohort	See Age Cohort.
Conviction	Sentenced in court for committing a crime.
Cumulative Onset	The cumulative percentage of persons starting to offend up to a certain age.
Delinquency	The act of breaking one or more criminal laws when a minor (under age 18).
Desistance	Cessation or stopping of offending forever or for a long period of time. See also Early Desistance, Intermediate Desistance, and Late Desistance.
Developmental Pathway	Pattern of development in offending from less serious problem behaviors to more serious offenses.
Developmental Sequence	Order of occurrence of different problem behaviors.
Drug Dealing	Selling marijuana or other illegal drugs.
Duration	The number of years that individuals offend.
Early Desistance	The presence of offending in late childhood (ages 10–12) followed by desistance by early adolescence (ages 13–16), and continuing desistance through late adolescence (ages 17–19).
Escalation	The increasing severity of offenses committed by individuals over time.
Forward Probability	The probability that individuals escalate over time from less serious to more serious forms of offending.

Table 1.1 Definitions of Terms (continued)

Delinquency Career Terms

Frequency	The annual rate of offending.
Gang Membership	Self-report of being a member of a gang during the assessment period.
Gun Carrying	Self-report of the carrying of a gun during the assessment period.
Intermediate Desistance	For the youngest cohort this is defined as offending in late childhood (ages 10–12) and early adolescence (ages 13–16), followed by desistance in late adolescence (ages 17–19). For the oldest cohort, intermediate desistance is defined as offending in early adolescence (ages 13–16), followed by desistance in late adolescence (ages 17–19), and continued desistance into early adulthood (ages 20–25).
Late Desistance	Offending in early and late adolescence (ages 12–16, and 17–19, respectively) followed by desistance in early adulthood (ages 20–25).
Minor Theft	Stealing outside the home, or shoplifting.
Moderate Theft	Stealing a bicycle or skateboard, stealing things worth more than $5, joyriding in a stolen vehicle, purse snatching, dealing in stolen goods, or stealing from a car.
Moderate Violence	Gangfighting.
Offending/Offenses	Delinquent acts committed during the juvenile years (under age 18) and criminal acts committed during adulthood (from age 18 onward).
Official Offending	Offenses measured by means of information from the police or the criminal court.
Oldest Sample	Boys in the Pittsburgh Youth Study who were first studied in grade 7 (age 13).
Pathway	See Developmental Pathway.
Persistence	The proportion of offenders who continue to offend over different age blocks.
Prevalence	The proportion of a population (expressed as a percentage) who engage in illegal offenses or other problem behaviors.
PYS	The Pittsburgh Youth Study.
Reported Offending	Offending as measured by means of boys' self-reports, and reports by parents and teachers.

Table 1.1 Definitions of Terms (continued)

Delinquency Career Terms

Self-Reported Offending	Offending as measured by means of boys' self-reports only.
Specialization	The tendency for individuals to commit some types of offenses disproportionally and repeatedly.
Serious Theft	Breaking and entering, or auto theft.
Serious Violence	Forcible robbery, attacking with intent to injure, sexual coercion, or rape.
Substance Use	Use of alcohol, tobacco, marijuana, or other psychoactive substances.
Theft	See Minor Theft, Moderate Theft, and Serious Theft.
Trajectories	Classification of individuals according to their pattern of offending over time.
Violence	See Moderate Violence and Serious Violence.
Youngest Sample	Boys in the Pittsburgh Youth Study who were first studied in grade 1 (age 7).

Processes that Influence Offending

Aggravating Risk Factors	Factors that predict a high likelihood of later offending in the general population.
Hindering Risk Factors	Factors that predict a low likelihood of desistance from offending among those who had previously offended.
Preventive Promotive Factors	Factors that predict a low probability of offending in the general population.
Promotive Factors	Factors that predict a low probability of serious offending in either the general population or among offenders. See Preventive Promotive Factors and Remedial Promotive Factors.
Protective Factors	Factors that predict a low probability of offending among youth exposed to risk factors.
Remedial Promotive Factors	Factors that predict cessation of offending among those who had previously offended.
Risk Factors	Factors that predict a high likelihood of offending either in the general population or among offenders. See also Aggravating Risk Factors and Hindering Risk Factors.

Table 1.1 Definitions of Terms (continued)

Age Blocks/Life Stages	
Middle Childhood	Ages 7–9.
Late Childhood	Ages 10–12.
Early Adolescence	Ages 13–15.
Late Adolescence	Ages 16–19.
Early Adulthood	Ages 20–25.

other generations? To what extent are violence and serious property offenses related to drug dealing, gang membership, gun ownership, and substance use? What is the forward probability of individuals' escalating from less serious to more serious forms of delinquency? Can individuals be classified according to their trajectories of offending? Among risk and promotive factors evident in childhood, which best predict violence and serious property crime, and what is the contribution of risk and promotive factors that emerge in adolescence?

Our Conceptual and Theoretical Orientation

Theories explain why phenomena occur. The number of theories of antisocial and criminal behavior is large (see overviews in Cullen, Wright, & Blevins, 2006; Dodge & Pettit, 2003; Farrington, 2005; Lahey, Moffitt, & Caspi, 2003; Thornberry & Krohn, 2003; Wilson & Herrnstein, 1985). Some major examples are Patterson's (1982) combined antisocial trait and social learning theory, problem behavior theory (Jessor & Jessor, 1973), social cognitive theory (Dodge, Murphy, & Buchsbaum, 1984), psychiatric theories of comorbidities (Caron & Rutter, 1991; Hinshaw, 1992), learning theory (Akers, 1973), general strain theory (Agnew, 1992), social control theory and its modifications (Elliott, Huizinga, & Ageton, 1985; Elliott, Huizinga, & Menard, 1989; Gottfredson & Hirschi, 1990; Hirschi, 1969), the social development model (Catalano & Hawkins, 1996), the moral developmental theory (Kohlberg, 1969), Farrington's motivational theory, recently updated in his developmental/life course theory (Farrington, 1993, 2003), and more biologically oriented theories (Moffitt, 1993; Raine, 1993).

Our approach to the study of crime is guided by a developmental-ecological model that is much inspired by the works of Bronfenbrenner (1979), Catalano and Hawkins (2002), Szapnocznik and Coatsworth (1999), and Tolan, Guerra, and Kendell (1995). Our model (Loeber, Slot, & Stouthamer-Loeber, 2006) stresses the interplay among risk, promotive, and protective factors in influencing the propensity to engage in antisocial acts and to commit offenses. We also assume that individual development is influenced by the ongoing structure of the social situations in which the individual lives or interacts. We conceptualize individual development of behavior as nested in different social environments (e.g., family, school, peer group, neighborhood). These different contexts exert different influences on offending as young males grow up, with family factors predominating early in development and peer and neighborhood factors becoming important later. Alongside these developments, the emergence of persistent substance use by young males, their gang membership, and their drug dealing are seen as pivotal life events that can change the developmental course to serious offending.

Our analytic strategy focuses primarily on individuals and their development over time, and secondly on relationships between different constructs. We chose a person-oriented approach over a dimensional orientation of delinquency, substance use, and other negative life outcomes. Advantages of the person-oriented approach have been articulated by several researchers (e.g., Magnusson, 2003; Von Eye & Bergman, 2003) and are relevant for practitioners and policy makers who deal with individuals rather than with measurement constructs.

Developmental Pathways and Trajectories

This volume addresses key issues raised by several prominent researchers. One of the important questions is the number and nature of developmental typologies of offenders. For instance, Moffitt (1993) distinguishes between two major developmental types: early-onset, life-course persistent offenders, and late-onset, adolescence-limited offenders. Moffitt's typology is very close to our own distinction, published years ago (see Loeber, 1988, especially p. 108), between individuals on an aggressive/versatile life course (corresponding to Moffitt's early-onset, life-course delinquents), and a nonaggressive path typical for adolescence (similar to Moffitt's late-onset, adolescence-limited offenders). Until now, for several reasons we did not further pursue typological work (other than escalation models in the form of overt, covert, and authority conflict pathways; Loeber, DeLamatre, et al., 1998; Loeber, Wei, et al., 1999; Loeber, Wung, et al., 1993). Part of the reason was that developmental types tend to be unstable and incomplete when based on data sets that lack information during high-risk periods of offending, which was the case for the Pittsburgh Youth Study (PYS) in its earlier years. This lack of long-term data also applied to the Dunedin Multidisciplinary Health and Development Study, which partly formed the basis of the Moffitt (1993) analyses. Now that she has collected data beyond adolescence, Moffitt (2006) has revised her typology, which now features additional types of low-level chronic offenders and adult-onset antisocial individuals. The present work, based on regular assessments in the PYS for the youngest cohort (between ages 7 and 19), and for the oldest cohort (between ages 13 and 25), is in a strong position to shed substantive light on both escalation models and typologies of offenders.

In our earlier work on the PYS, we identified three empirically charted pathways that youngsters typically follow in a remarkably orderly progression from less to more serious problem behaviors and delinquency from childhood to adolescence (Loeber, Keenan, & Zhang, 1997; Loeber, Wung, et al., 1993). The PYS study and several other replications of this research show that development from antisocial behaviors to serious delinquency best fits a model of three incremental pathways: (1) an authority conflict pathway prior to the age of 12 that starts with stubborn behavior, has defiance as a second stage, and authority avoidance (e.g., truancy) as a third stage; (2) a covert pathway prior to age 15 that starts with minor covert acts, has property damage as a second stage, and moderate to serious delinquency as a third stage; and (3) an overt pathway that starts with minor aggression, has physical fighting as a second stage, and more severe violence as a third stage.

The pathways model has been validated in the Denver Youth Survey and Rochester (New York) Youth Development Study samples (Loeber, Wei et al., 1999), and also in a Chicago study and the National Youth Survey (Tolan & Gorman-Smith, 1998). In addition, Tolan, Gorman-Smith, and Loeber (2000) have replicated the triple-pathway model in a sample of African American and Hispanic adolescents in Chicago and in a nationally representative U.S. sample of adolescents. The pathway model is also applicable for antisocial girls (Gorman-Smith & Loeber, 2005).

The above studies showed that with age, a proportion of children progressed on two or three pathways, indicating an increasing variety of problem behavior over time (Kelley et al., 1997; Loeber, Keenan, & Zhang, 1997; Loeber, Wung et al., 1993). Also, Loeber, Wung, et al. (1993) have found evidence that development in multiple pathways was not interchangeable, in that boys who were escalating in the overt pathway were more likely to escalate in the covert pathway as well, compared to a lower probability of boys in the covert pathway escalating in the overt pathway. Thus, aggressive boys were particularly at risk of also committing covert acts, while boys engaging in covert acts were less likely to develop aggressive behaviors. Further, escalation in either the overt or covert pathway was often preceded by boys' escalation in the authority conflict pathway (Loeber, Wung et al., 1993). In other words, conflict with authority figures was either a precursor or a concomitant of boys' escalation in overt or covert acts. Also, an early age of onset of problem behavior or delinquency, compared to an onset at a later age, was more closely associated with boys' escalation to more serious behaviors in the pathways (Tolan et al., 2000). The pathway model accounted for the majority of the most seriously affected boys, that is the self-reported high rate offenders (Loeber, Keenan, & Zhang, 1997; Loeber, Wung et al., 1993) and court reported delinquents (Loeber, Keenan, & Zhang, 1997). Further, we found two major qualitative developmental changes toward serious offending that often take place during childhood and adolescence: from disruptive behavior in the home to delinquency outside the home, and from infliction of harm on close relatives and peers to infliction of harm on strangers.

In summary, developmental pathways in antisocial behavior/delinquency and developmental transitions between different disruptive diagnoses share a conceptualization of escalation in the severity of antisocial behaviors with development in certain individuals but not in others. The pathway model also represents selection processes in that increasingly smaller groups of youth become at risk for the more serious behaviors, comparable to a successive sieving process.

It should be kept in mind that the formulation and testing of the above pathway model was limited in that it used retrospective information prior to age 7, which is known to be not reliable. Keenan and Shaw (2003) formulated a dual-stage escalation model for the preschool period. One pathway, called *pathway to reactive antisocial behavior*, consists of the development of reactive antisocial behavior, which starts with irritable behavior during infancy. Children displaying persistent irritability were at risk of developing emotional difficulties as toddlers (low frustration tolerance, overactivity, and being demanding) and in turn were at risk of developing disruptive angry behavior as preschoolers. A second pathway, called *pathway to proactive antisocial behavior*, starts with children displaying under-arousal (i.e., they are under-responsive to stimulation) who then appear at risk of developing behavior difficulties as toddlers (as demonstrated by persistent unresponsiveness to punishment, and high sensation seeking) and who in turn are at risk of developing callous, unemotional behavior as preschoolers (demonstrated by stealing, lying, deliberate fighting, and violation of rules). The two pathways in early childhood postulated by Keenan and Shaw (2003) clearly need substantiation, but can eventually be linked to the first two steps in the authority conflict pathway (stubborn behavior, and defiance/disobedience) and are likely to enhance a future, improved model of the development of antisocial behavior from early childhood to early adulthood.

The specification of developmental pathways can be contrasted with the identification of developmental trajectories, which are defined as the classification of individuals according to their pattern of offending over time. The assumption is that a population of individuals "is composed of a mixture of groups with distinct developmental trajectories" (Nagin & Tremblay, 2001a, p. 21). Typically, trajectory analyses have been based on repeated measurements of a single indicator of problem behavior. Usually, the results of trajectory analyses identify young males whose problem behavior remains high over time; those whose problem behavior remain low, those whose problem behavior increases, and those whose problem behavior decreases between childhood and early adulthood (e.g., Broidy et al., 2003; Bushway, Thornberry, & Krohn, 2003; Lacourse et al., 2003; Piquero, 2007). The trajectory models are valuable, but they do not represent escalation processes from minor to more serious offenses in a proportion of youth. This is the additional value of our three-pathway model.

The approach we take in this volume is to further investigate escalation models of antisocial behavior, including, for the first time, presenting forward probabilities within developmental pathways to serious forms of delinquency. In addition, we present new information about persistence and desistance in offending from childhood to early adolescence. We also present findings on the longitudinal classification of individuals in their offending according to their membership of developmental trajectories.

The Roles of Substance Use, Drug Dealing, Gang Membership, and Gun Carrying

Individuals' likelihood of progression on developmental pathways can be influenced by other problem behaviors. For example, it has long been known that delinquents use drugs more than nondelinquents, and that a significant proportion of delinquents deal drugs, become gang members, and carry guns. Although much has been published on these topics (Blumstein, 1995; Fagan & Chin, 1990; Howell & Decker, 1999; Thornberry, Krohn, et al., 2003; Lipton & Johnson, 1998; White & Gorman, 2000), there are relatively few longitudinal studies documenting the prevalence, onset, and duration of these behaviors between ages 7 and 25. Thus, we know little about the developmental sequences among substance use, drug dealing, gang membership, and gun carrying and violence and serious property offenses. Other major questions addressed in this volume concern the persistence and duration of these problem behaviors and how this persistence compares to serious violence and theft. Not all generations of young males are equally involved in these problem behaviors, and we address the question of cohort differences in the onset, prevalence, frequency, and duration of substance use, dealing, gang membership, and gun carrying and their relationship to violence and serious theft. Further, in order to fill a gap in the literature, we examine the extent that the use of alcohol, tobacco, marijuana, and hard drugs; dealing drugs; gang membership; and gun carrying predict serious violence and serious theft over time, and whether some problem behaviors are more predictive for violence than for serious theft, and vice versa.

Risk Factors, Promotive Factors, and Protective Factors and Processes

A key element in developmental criminology is the search for explanatory factors that can account for an individual's escalation to serious forms of delinquency, aid in the prediction of persistence and desistance, and the predictor of membership in specific developmental trajectories. Following the example of Sameroff et al. (1998), we are making a distinction between *promotive factors* and *protective factors*. *Promotive factors* are defined as factors that either (1) predict a low probability of later offending in the general population and, possibly, have a direct ameliorative effect on prosocial behavior (Luthar, Cicchetti, & Becker, 2000), which we call *preventive promotive factors*; or (2) predict desistance from offending in populations of known delinquents, which we call *remedial promotive factors*. In this volume we are particularly interested in the study of the main effects of the two types of promotive factors in the same way that the main effects of risk factors have been studied for decades (for some unexplained reason, the main effects of promotive factors have not been intensely studied).

A distinction is also being made herein between two types of risk factors: *aggravating risk factors* and *hindering risk factors*. *Aggravating risk factors* are factors that predict a high probability of later offending. *Hindering risk factors* are factors that have a hindering influence on desistance from offending, and are restricted to those factors that negatively predict desistance.

In this volume we will also investigate interactions between preventive promotive and aggravating risk factors (in Chapter 7). When interaction terms reach statistical significance, there is mention of *protective factors*, a term used by Masten and Garmezy (1985) and Rutter (1979) to examine interaction effects explaining why individuals who are exposed to high levels of risk factors do not become deviant.

Among the questions addressed in this volume are: In the general population, what are promotive factors that contribute to the prediction of serious offending and do such factors buffer the impact of risk factors? Are some risk and promotive factors more predictive of either violence or serious property crime? And, which risk and promotive factors predict desistance from serious forms of offending?

The Pittsburgh Youth Study

Answers to the above questions come from extended follow-up data in the PYS. At the time of their recruitment into the study, the boys were enrolled in public schools in Pittsburgh. The sample is almost evenly distributed between African American and Caucasian boys. The young males have been regularly followed-up over a period of 13 years. The study consists of three age cohorts of boys, who were in the first, fourth, or seventh grades at the time of the first assessment in 1987–88 (called the youngest, middle, and oldest cohorts). The present volume is about the youngest ($N = 503$) and oldest ($N = 506$) cohorts, for whom the longest-term follow-up information is available. The youngest cohort has been assessed 18 times between ages 7 and 19, while the oldest cohort has been assessed 16 times between ages 13 and 25. In contrast, the middle cohort was discontinued after seven assessments and had a single follow-up assessment at about age 24, and hence is not included in this volume.

When we started the PYS in 1987, we had no idea to what extent boys in the study (between ages 7 and 13 for the youngest and oldest cohorts, respectively) would engage in violence and serious property crime and to what extent the level of crime in the community would change over time (see Loeber, Farrington, Southamer-Loebert, & Van Kammen, 1998, which summarizes the findings at the beginning of the PYS). By age 16, just over one in four of the young men in the youngest cohort (28%) had committed serious offenses (based on self-reports and official records), while this was true of 4 out of 10 of the young men in the oldest cohort (40%). At the time that the young men in the study had reached adulthood, 33 had been convicted for killing someone. Another 31 had been accused of homicide, and were awaiting trial or had not been convicted because of lack of evidence. The figures for violence and property crime indicate the high degree to which these boys were swept up into crime.

During the first few years of the study, crime in the city of Pittsburgh increased dramatically, and was worst in the most disadvantaged neighborhoods where many of the young males were living. Figure 1.6 shows the distribution of the highly disadvantaged neighborhoods in Pittsburgh, based on an index of community socioeconomic status (SES) derived from census information in 1990 (Wikström & Loeber, 2000; the SES index is explained in Chapter 3). The SES index was moderately strongly correlated ($r = .59$) with reports to the police of violence in the disadvantaged neighborhoods. Thus, the higher the SES neighborhood disadvantage index, the more likely that there was violence in neighborhoods. For the period 1980 to 1992, Allegheny County—and Pittsburgh within that county—experienced a gradual increase in violence (part 1 index crimes: murder, rape, robbery and aggravated assault; see Figure 1.7). The picture of escalating violence in certain neighborhoods during the study period is reinforced by the fact that the city saw the emergence of gangs in the latter part of 1991 (Hsia, 1997; Tita, Cohen & Engberg, 2005).

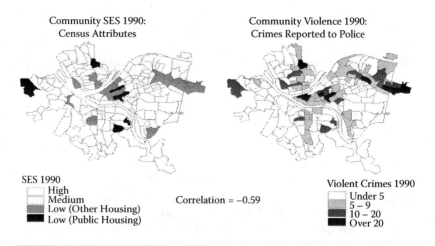

Community SES 1990:
Census Attributes

Community Violence 1990:
Crimes Reported to Police

SES 1990
High
Medium
Low (Other Housing)
Low (Public Housing)

Correlation = –0.59

Violent Crimes 1990
Under 5
5 – 9
10 – 20
Over 20

Figure 1.6 The Association between Community Disadvantage (According to an SES Index Based on Census Information) and Police Reports of Violent Crime in Pittsburgh in 1990

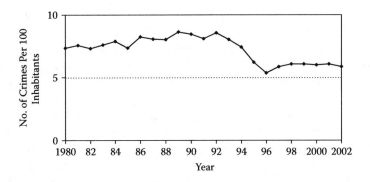

Figure 1.7 Index Crimes Known to the Police per 100 Inhabitants in Allegheny County

However, the changes in crime that the city experienced over time varied tremendously from one neighborhood to another. On average, however, a major decrease in community violence took place after 1992 (see Figure 1.7). Thus, the two age cohorts of the PYS intersected at different ages with community level changes in crime.

Compared to most longitudinal studies, the data on the youngest and oldest cohorts are unique because of the large number of uninterrupted measurements, extending from middle childhood to late adolescence for the youngest cohort, and from early adolescence to early adulthood for the oldest cohort. The uninterrupted sequence of assessments makes it possible to study the onset *and* desistance of serious forms of offending during important life periods when some youth became serious chronic delinquents while other youth began to outgrow these behaviors.

The long time interval covered by the multiple assessments in the PYS permits a reassessment of the merits of the criminal career paradigm (see e.g., reviews in Loeber, Farrington, & Waschbusch, 1998; Piquero et al., 2003; Piquero, Farrington & Blumstein, 2007; Thornberry & Krohn, 2003). Particularly needed is better knowledge on the development of violence and property crime from childhood to early adulthood in terms of onset, prevalence, frequency, persistence, desistance, and duration of offending. The PYS's measurements are strong and can shed light on each of these parameters.

Another strength of the PYS is the availability of multiple informants (including parents and teachers) to enhance the validity of measurements. Some previous researchers have presented criminal career information based on self-reports only (e.g. Elliott et al., 1989). However, in the PYS, combined reports by boys, parents, and teachers predicted later court petitions better than did self-reports by the boys, and hence had higher predictive validity (Farrington, Loeber, et al., 1996). No previous researchers have presented criminal career information based on combined reports by boys, parents, and teachers from childhood through late adolescence. Most knowledge about criminal careers is derived from official records of arrests, court referrals, or convictions (e.g., Farrington, 1997; Wolfgang, Figlio, & Sellin, 1972). We will report information about official records of arrest and conviction in Chapter 5, which also illustrates the combined prevalence of reported offending and officially recorded offending.

It can be argued that longitudinal studies often do not present more information than cross-sectional studies (see, e.g., Gottfredson & Hirschi, 1987). However, a major strength of repeated longitudinal follow-ups is that the measurements allow us to examine an individual's changes in offending over time, particularly during the periods in which offending tends to increase (during adolescence) and tends to decrease (after adolescence).

Yet another special feature of the PYS is that its team of researchers conducted the study according to very high standards of data collection: there was very low attrition (detailed in Chapter 2), and there were very comprehensive assessments (detailed in Chapter 3) and linkage to other data sources, such as Allegheny County juvenile court data, state juvenile court data, adult court data, and Federal Bureau of Investigation data (detailed in Chapter 3).

The main value of the following analyses is that we can examine criminal careers not just for a single year or a few years (as in most longitudinal studies) but comprehensively from ages 7 through 19 for the youngest cohort, and from ages 13 through 25 for the oldest cohort. In addition, data on academic achievement test scores were obtained from the public schools, and data on child maltreatment from the department of Child, Youth, and Family Services in the city of Pittsburgh.

Replication is at the heart of scientific findings. This is a particularly important criterion for the social sciences, including criminology, where chance findings are common and where variations in measurement across studies make it difficult to gauge which findings are solid. One of the major advantages of the PYS is that we can repeat analyses across several different life phases (called age blocks) using identical measurements and constructs, and this provides an opportunity to replicate findings in different parts of the data. Specifically, we are able to execute three predictive analyses in the youngest cohort over four life periods, and two predictive analyses in the oldest cohort over three life periods. These five sets of independent analyses (three in the youngest and two in the oldest cohorts) provide four opportunities to replicate findings. Replication is also made possible because of the availability of two age cohorts (differing in age on average by 6 years).

This volume is unique in yet another way—namely, that it is not driven by a narrow perspective of a single discipline but instead combines the strengths of three disciplines that often attempt to explain delinquency in young people: (1) developmental psychopathology (the study of the development of deviancy and nondeviancy processes in juveniles); (2) criminology (particularly, the study of the causes of, and justice system response to, delinquency and violence), and specifically developmental criminology; and (3) public health (the study of the spread of diseases and deviant behavior in populations).

A Critical Period: Middle Childhood to Early Adulthood

In the PYS, the youngest cohort was first interviewed when the boys were in grade 1 (average age 6.7). At the time of starting the study, we were under pressure to provide results about serious offending in a few years rather than in a decade or more. This, together with funding constraints and difficulties in locating a representative sample of preschool-aged boys (preschools were not available at that time to the general public in Pittsburgh), forced us to select public schools as the best vehicle for accessing boys at a young age. On the positive side, we selected an accelerated longitudinal design for the study (Bell, 1953), starting with three overlapping cohorts. The first cohort was to be followed up from age 7 to age 10, the second from age 10 to age 13, and the third from age 13 to age 16. Although this design made it possible to study the age period 7–16 in only 4 years, the funding agencies and we eventually decided that it was important to document an individual's changes over time, and for that reason to follow up the youngest cohort (7–19) and the oldest cohort (13–25).

This design sets some restrictions on how much we can study the early causes of offending and antisocial behavior, which may be present prior to age 7 (see e.g., Shaw, Lacourse, & Nagin, 2004; Smart et al., 2003; Tremblay, 2003; Tremblay et al., 2004; Vassallo et al., 2002). However, in contrast to most other longitudinal studies on offending that start in adolescence, the PYS has the key advantage of covering possible causes of offending that are present during the elementary school-age years, adolescence, and early adulthood.

An emphasis on the elementary school years is warranted for several reasons. This is a period in which most youth will have outgrown age-normative conduct problems (such as temper tantrums) and in which a subgroup of youth, whose problem behavior originated during the preschool period and persists during the elementary school-age period, becomes apparent. The elementary school period is also important because new problem behaviors tend to emerge, such as truancy, early substance use, and theft from public places. In this period, contact with the police because of delinquent acts will be recorded. In Pennsylvania, the age of criminal responsibility is 10, so that if a child under that age becomes delinquent, this is almost always dealt with outside the juvenile justice system. Another feature of the elementary school period, compared to the preschool period, is that juveniles become active outside of the home, have more contacts with deviant and prosocial peers, and are more influenced by their neighborhood context. Although this has been little researched, we assume that some risk and promotive factors that can explain offending and desistance emerge during the elementary school period, such as attitudes favorable to delinquency, poor supervision by the parent, and so on.

Earlier Longitudinal Studies Starting with Elementary School-Age Populations

The PYS was inspired by and benefited greatly from several other projects that combined the study of the development of antisocial behavior with the study of the development of offending. Special mention should be made of the Oregon Youth Study (e.g., Patterson, Dishion, & Yoerger, 2000), in which Rolf Loeber and Magda Stouthamer-Loeber participated in its earliest stages, and the two "sister" studies of the PYS, the Denver Youth Survey (Huizinga, Weiher, Espiritu, & Esbensen, 2003) and the Rochester Youth Development Study (Thornberry et al., 2003). Many of the instruments used in the PYS were jointly developed with staff from the Denver Youth Survey and the Rochester Youth Development Study. We also received much inspiration from the Cambridge (England) Study in Delinquent Development (Farrington, 2003), which had been started in the early 1960s and therefore was ahead of our study with the formulation of key questions and the production of longitudinal results.

Also ahead of us were the Columbia County (New York) Longitudinal Study (Huesmann, Eron. & Dubow, 2002), and the Orebro Project in Gothenburg, Sweden (Klinteberg, Andersson, Magnusson & Stattin, 1993). Similarly, we learned from the late Joan McCord's Cambridge–Somerville (Massachusetts) Youth Study (McCord, 1991) and Robins's longitudinal study in St Louis (1979), which go back to the 1930s, and the Carolina Longitudinal Study started four decades later (Cairns & Cairns, 1994). Also started in the 1970s and 1980s were the Seattle Social Development Project (Hawkins et al., 2003), the Dunedin study (Moffitt, Caspi, Rutter, & Silva, 2001), and Le Blanc's studies in Montreal (Le Blanc, McDuff, & Kaspy, 1998). Important new longitudinal studies, led by colleagues and friends, emerged in the 1990s, including the Montreal Longitudinal and Experimental Study (Tremblay et al., 1992), the Durham (North Carolina) Longitudinal Study (Coie et al., 1995), and the Chicago Youth Development Study (Gorman-Smith & Tolan, 1998). The list of studies could go on, but certainly the projects mentioned here were and remain influential in steering our data collection and analyses for this volume. Collectively, longitudinal studies have become more sophisticated over time using multiple rather than single informants, using self-reports in addition to official records of offending, paying greater attention to the psychometric quality of measurements, introducing repeated measurements to better capture changes in antisocial behavior and offending over time, and using statistical tools to study developmental change.

Questions Driving the Longitudinal Analyses for This Book

There are two main areas for which we formulated questions to be addressed in this book: (1) serious offending as an outcome over time, and developmental aspects of serious offending, including desistance; and (2) preventive promotive and aggravating risk factors explaining why, with development, some young males become violent and/or commit serious property crime while others do not, and remedial promotive factors and hindering risk factors explaining why some delinquent young males desist from offending. For ease of exposition we will refer to property crime as *theft*. The two areas of interest will be addressed in Chapters 4–8; Chapters 2 and 3 lay out the basics of the study. Below we list the key questions addressed in this book for each of the two main areas.

1. Outcomes and Development

- How high are the prevalence and frequency of reported violence and theft in inner-city young males between the ages of 7 and 25? (Addressed in Chapter 4.)
- How common are arrest and conviction for violence and theft for these males? (Addressed in Chapter 5.)
- How persistent is serious offending as measured by a combination of reported offenses and conviction for delinquent acts? (Addressed in Chapter 5.)
- How common are substance use, drug dealing, gang membership, and gun carrying? (Addressed in Chapter 6.)
- To what extent are there cohort differences in offending and related problem behaviors? (Addressed in Chapters 4, 5, 6, and 9.)
- Are violence and theft developmentally distinct offenses? (Addressed in Chapters 4, 5, 7, and 9.)
- To what extent is there specialization in violence or serious theft? (Addressed in Chapter 5.)
- How does self-reported offending compare with arrest and conviction data? (Addressed in Chapter 5.)
- How much are gang membership, gun carrying, drug dealing, and substance use interrelated, and how are they related to violence and theft? (Addressed in Chapter 6.)
- Are there developmental sequences in behavior among substance use, drug dealing, gang membership, gun carrying, and violence and theft? (Addressed in Chapter 6.)
- What number and types of developmental trajectories best describe young men's violence and theft, and what can we learn about individual differences in the onset, duration, and desistance of these two criminal behaviors? (Addressed in Chapter 8.)

- How does a developmental typology of offenders based on trajectory analyses compare with a classification based on changes in offending? (Addressed in Chapter 9.)
- What proportion of young males desist from serious violence and theft between ages 10 and 25? (Addressed in Chapters 5, 8, and 9.)
- What proportion of young males desist from moderate *and* serious offenses between ages 13 and 25? (Addressed in Chapter 9.)

2. Risk and Promotive/Protective Processes

- Which variables operate as aggravating risk factors only, which variables operate as preventive promotive factors only, and which variables operate as both promotive and risk factors? (Addressed in Chapter 7.)
- Are there developmental periods in which preventive promotive factors predominate, and are there developmental periods in which aggravating risk factors predominate? (Addressed in Chapter 7.)
- Is there an association between ethnicity and serious offending, and if so, how can it be explained? (Addressed in Chapter 7.)
- Are there unique predictors of either violence or theft? (Addressed in Chapter 7.)
- Which promotive and risk factors predict membership in particular offending trajectories? (Addressed in Chapter 8.)
- Which hindering risk factors and which remedial promotive factors predict desistance from serious and moderate offending? (Addressed in Chapter 9.)
- Are there key developmental periods in which predictors of desistance operate? (Addressed in Chapter 9.)
- How similar are preventive promotive factors predicting a low probability of serious offending and remedial promotive factors predicting desistance? And how similar are aggravating risk factors predicting offending and hindering risk factors predicting desistance? (Addressed in Chapter 9.)

Although our longitudinal study did not incorporate an experimental, therapeutic manipulation, we believe that the results presented in this volume are relevant for the early identification of youth at risk and for the planning of future therapeutic intervention to prevent or reduce offending. We are of the opinion that the developmental processes associated with the onset and maintenance of delinquent acts, described in this volume, are likely to influence the outcome of interventions. Also, our results have already influenced the development of risk assessment instruments (see, e.g., Augimeri, Koegl, Webster, & Levene, 2001; Lösel & Bender, 2003). We see many opportunities for data from the PYS to buttress science-based prevention of delinquency and remedial efforts to reduce crime and youth problems (Biglan, Mrazek, Carnine, & Fly, 2003; Greenwood, 2006; Hawkins, Catalano & Arthur, 2002; Yoshikawa, 1994; Farrington & Welsh, 2007). These opportunities are discussed in Chapter 10.

We have found that the PYS is an extremely exciting and ever-changing adventure in science and a challenge to produce findings of relevance for future generations of youth. This volume is written for educated lay practitioners in juvenile justice, education, and mental health. It is also written for scholars in delinquency, developmental psychology, psychiatry, and public health; and graduate students in criminology, psychology, public health, and the social sciences in general. We hope that the present volume will transmit to these readers some of the excitement that we experienced when investigating the data from the PYS, and that the study results represented in this volume will, eventually, have an impact on practitioners and policy makers dealing with conduct problem and delinquent youth to help create safer societies.

Two
The Pittsburgh Youth Study
Its Design, Data Collection, and Early Key Findings

ROLF LOEBER, MAGDA STOUTHAMER-
LOEBER, AND DAVID P. FARRINGTON

This chapter reviews the design and data collection procedures of the Pittsburgh Youth Study (PYS). The chapter builds on the earlier volume on the PYS, which focused on the first two waves of the study (Loeber, Farrington, Stouthamer-Loeber, & Van Kammen, 1998). For that reason, some key elements of the start of the study are summarized here from that source. In addition, this volume contains new information about the ways in which we undertook the follow-ups over 16 and 18 data waves, respectively of the oldest and youngest cohorts.

Pittsburgh

Pittsburgh is largely a blue-collar city, formerly dominated by the steel industry. It is situated at the confluence of two rivers, the Allegheny and the Monongahela (see Figure 1.6), which join to form the Ohio River. In the 2000 census (in that year the participants in the youngest and oldest cohorts were on average 19 and 25 years old) the Pittsburgh metropolitan area had about 2,358,695 inhabitants and the city of Pittsburgh had about 334,563 citizens, of which 26% were African American, 72% were Caucasian, and the remaining 2% were from other ethnic groups. Pittsburgh has a very stable population: 80% of the residents had been born in the state, compared to 62% on average across the United States. Only 3% of Pittsburgh inhabitants were foreign born, compared to 8% across the United States, and only 2% of the city's population was not fluent in English. The median family income in Pittsburgh was similar to that in the United States as a whole, with 17% of the children living below the poverty level. There are 90 neighborhoods in the city, many of which—because of rivers, railways, or ravines—are geographically distinct. Most of the neighborhoods are racially divided, with African Americans tending to live in the most disadvantaged neighborhoods.

Design

The PYS is a longitudinal study consisting of repeated follow-ups on community cohorts of inner-city boys, which began in 1987 (for the successive assessments, see Table 2.1). The boys were in grades 1, 4, and 7 in the Pittsburgh public schools at the outset of the study (called youngest, middle, and oldest cohorts). As explained in Chapter 1, this volume focuses only on the youngest and oldest cohorts, for whom the most frequent follow-up assessments, and hence, the longest time window, were available. With the assistance of the Pittsburgh Board of Education, we started out with comprehensive public school lists of the enrollment of 1,631 and 1,419 male students in grades 1 and 7, respectively. From these lists we randomly selected over 1,100 boys in each of the two grades to be contacted (1,165 and 1,125 in grades 1 and 7, respectively). However, a number of the children had moved out of the school district, were girls, or were of an incorrect age. Eventually we contacted 1,004 and 1,020 families with eligible boys in grades 1 and 7, respectively.

The participation rate of boys and their parents was 84.6% and 83.9% (for the youngest and oldest cohorts, respectively) of the eligible boys. Because of the high participation rate of families at the beginning of the study, we believe that the cohorts are representative of the populations from which they were drawn—namely, boys in grades 1 and 7 in the Pittsburgh public schools. A comparison of those who participated and those who did not indicates that there were no significant differences in racial distribution and achievement test results, which were the only two variables that could be compared from school records (Loeber, Farrington, Stouthamer-Loeber, & Van Kammen, 1998). Furthermore, the cohorts are broadly representative of boys in the general population in the city of Pittsburgh because 72% of all students residing within the city limits were enrolled in the public schools (Loeber, Farrington, Stouthamer-Loeber, & Van Kammen, 1998). Although no figures could be obtained on the differences between public school students and private or parochial school students, it is a reasonable assumption that those students not enrolled in public schools were more likely to be Caucasian and of higher socioeconomic status than the public school students.

Screening

In order to increase the number of high-risk males, we used the screening assessment at wave S. On this basis of this screening, which used information from the participant, his parent, and his teacher, the 30% of the boys identified as the most antisocial were included in the follow-up cohort, together with another 30% who were randomly selected from the remaining 70%. This strategy has the dual advantages of drawing conclusions about the population by weighting the results back to the original population see (e.g., Stouthamer-Loeber, Loeber, & Thomas, 1992), while maximizing the yield of deviant outcomes.

Table 2.1 Design and Sequence of Assessments in the Pittsburgh Youth Study

Youngest Cohort

		Middle Childhood					Late Childhood							Late Adolescence		
Age	6.2	6.7	7.2	7.7	8.2	8.7	9.2	9.7	10.2	11	12	14	15	16	17	18	19
Wave	S	A	B	C	D	E	F	G	H	J	L	P	R	T	V	Y	AA

Oldest Cohort

		Early Adolescence					Late Adolescence			Early Adulthood					
Age	12.6	13.1	13.6	14.1	14.6	15.1	16	17	18	19	20	21	22	23	24	25
Wave	S	A	B	C	D	E	G	I	K	M	O	Q	SS	U	W	Z

Note: Bold lines indicate the waves that are grouped together in an age block denoting a life period. Age shown is the mean age of participants at the midpoint of the six-month or one-year period preceding assessment.

Table 2.2 Characteristics of the Cohorts at the Beginning of the Study (Wave A)

	Youngest Cohort	Oldest Cohort
Participant		
% African American	56.4	55.8
>50th Percentile CAT Reading Score	54.5	37.9
Average Age	6.7	13.1
% Held Back in School	26.1	39.2
Family		
% Living with Natural Mother	95.2	94.0
% Living with Natural Father	39.6	37.3
% Not Living with (Acting) Father	45.7	45.3
% (Acting) Mother Not Completed High School	19.3	19.6
% (Acting) Mother with College Degree	6.3	7.4
% (Acting) Father Not Completed High School	16.9	20.4
% (Acting) Father with College Degree	12.4	10.4

Source: Loeber, Farrington, Stouthamer-Loeber, & Van Kammen, 1998.
Note: $\chi2 (1, 1) = 19.61, p < .001$.

Cohort Characteristics at First Follow-Up

Table 2.2 presents the characteristics of the participants and their parents at the second wave (A) (see Loeber, Farrington, Stouthamer-Loeber, & Van Kammen, 1998).* Over half of the boys were of African American ethnicity (56.4% and 55.8% of the boys in the youngest and oldest cohorts, respectively), and almost all of the remainder were Caucasian. Over 90% lived with their natural mother (95% and 94%, respectively, for the youngest and oldest cohorts). About one-fifth of the mothers had not completed high school (19% and 20%, respectively), which was not much different than the percentages of fathers (17% and 20%, respectively). The two cohorts cover the full range of socioeconomic strata. However, one-third of the boys' families received public assistance or food stamps.

---

* The numbers in Table 2.2 vary slightly from those mentioned in Loeber et al. (1998) because of later improved cleaning of the data.

Extent of the Follow-Ups

The youngest cohort (N = 503) has been assessed a total of 18 consecutive times from middle childhood to late adolescence (ages 7–19), while the oldest cohort (N = 506) has been assessed a total of 16 consecutive times from early adolescence to early adulthood (ages 13–25). Assessments in each of the cohorts were done initially biannually (nine assessments for the youngest cohort, and six assessments for the oldest cohort) and, later, annually (Table 2.1). Each of the assessment intervals were contiguous (in other words, without gaps), which meant that the study was uniquely poised to investigate individuals' onset of delinquency and substance use and individuals' desistance from these behaviors. During the period of study, none of the participants emigrated permanently to another country.

Overlap of Assessments between the Youngest and Oldest Cohorts

One of the advantages of the design is that there is a substantive age overlap of the assessments of the youngest and oldest cohorts (Table 2.1) between ages 13 and 19. This overlap provides an excellent opportunity to examine the degree to which results on prevalence of offending and substance use (see Chapters 4, 5, and 6), predictors of offending (Chapter 7), and predictors of desistance (Chapter 9) can be replicated across the two cohorts.

Comparison between the Youngest and Oldest Cohorts at the Beginning of the Study

Although we have stressed the advantages of comparing findings between the two cohorts for the age span 13–19, it cannot be assumed that the youngest and oldest cohorts are fully comparable. Specifically, we expected that we would have more boys in the oldest cohort (drawn from grade 7) who had repeated a grade, and who would therefore be age inappropriate for the grade attended at school. Table 2.2 summarizes three key comparisons between the two cohorts. The youngest and oldest cohorts did not differ on race, but a significantly higher percentage of the oldest compared to the youngest cohort had been held back in grade (39% vs. 26%).

Measurement of Predictors and Outcomes

The results that we report in Chapters 4–9 fall into two categories. A first category of analyses uses yearly data (for that purpose, the biannual data collections at the beginning of the study were collapsed into yearly data). The yearly data is used for prevalence, onset, and duration estimates of offending (Chapters 4 and 5); the prevalence of substance use, drug dealing, gang membership and gun carrying (Chapter 6); generalized estimating equations (Chapter 7); and trajectory analyses (Chapter 8).

However, the magnitude of the data to be analyzed over 16 to 18 waves is staggering, especially because it involves the repeated measurement of outcomes and predictive factors (note that some measures—for example, on drug dealing and weapon use—were introduced in the course of the study when such behavior could be expected to emerge). Therefore, some data condensation needed to be done over waves, which was accomplished by summing constructs across multiple, yearly data waves. This was done for the annualized frequency of offending (Chapter 4); the identification of aggravating risk, preventive promotive factors, and protective factors (Chapter 7); the prediction of violence and theft (Chapters 6 and 7); and the identification of remedial promotive factors and hindering risk factors predicting desistance from serious offending (Chapter 9).

The advantages of data condensation were to facilitate analyses and to strengthen the validity of the measurement of predictors and outcomes by basing them on multiple rather than single waves. We believe that this aggregation of predictors (also called *explanatory variables*) in the present study is unique in the social sciences and likely to have contributed to the most robust measurements that we could achieve. In the same manner, in most of the prediction analyses we aggregated, the outcome variables of violence or serious theft within age blocks of assessments, thus avoiding the prediction of offending at a particular wave (or age) and instead predicting offending levels over different developmental periods from childhood to early adulthood. To achieve this, we created age blocks of assessment waves (see Table 2.1) roughly covering middle childhood (waves AB, CD, and EF in the youngest cohort; approximately ages 7–9), late childhood (waves GH, J, and L for the youngest cohort; approximately ages 10–12), early adolescence (waves N, P, R, and T for the youngest cohort, and waves SA, BC, DE, and G for the oldest cohort; approximately ages 13–16 for both cohorts), late adolescence (waves V, Y, and AA for the youngest cohort, and waves I, K, and M for the oldest cohort; approximately ages 17–19 for both cohorts), and early adulthood (waves O, Q, SS, U, W, and Z for the oldest cohort; approximately ages 20–25). The definition of age blocks may seem somewhat arbitrary, but was governed by the time window in which assessment took place (ages 7–25), and the desire to have two identical age blocks covering the overlap between the youngest and oldest cohort (ages 13–16 and 17–19).

Unfortunately, it was impossible to have the same number of waves or years in each of the age blocks, resulting in three age blocks of 3 years (middle childhood, late childhood, and late adolescence), one of 4 years (early adolescence), and one of 6 years (early adulthood). Readers should keep in mind that the age blocks were actually based on assessment waves (see Table 2.1) rather than ages. This was unavoidable because to some degree particular measurements (such as gang activity) were introduced in the study in a specific wave rather than at a

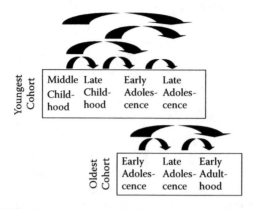

| | | Middle Child-hood | Late Child-hood | Early Adoles-cence | Late Adoles-cence |

<table>
<tr><td rowspan="3">Youngest Cohort</td><td>Middle Child-hood</td><td>Late Child-hood</td><td>Early Adoles-cence</td><td>Late Adoles-cence</td></tr>
</table>

Youngest Cohort | Middle Child-hood | Late Child-hood | Early Adoles-cence | Late Adoles-cence

Oldest Cohort | Early Adoles-cence | Late Adoles-cence | Early Adult-hood

Note: Middle Childhood = Ages 7–9; Late Childhood = 10–12; Early Adolescence = Ages 13–16; Late Adolescence = Ages 17–19; and Early Adulthood = Ages 20–25.

Figure 2.1 Prediction Analyses by Age Block (Youngest and Oldest Cohorts)

particular age. If age had been the criterion for the blocking of data, certain measures would not have been available for the maximum number of participants.

Tracking and Participant Incentives

High participation rates in longitudinal studies depend on researchers' ability to locate participants at each assessment wave and on participants agreeing to be reinterviewed. Attrition due to the inability to trace participants was low because we used procedures designed to maximize the number of participants who could be located. To facilitate tracking, each time the family was interviewed they were asked to give two names, addresses, and telephone numbers of close friends and relatives who would know their whereabouts in the event of a move. In addition, signed consent was obtained to contact schools for new addresses and telephone numbers in case of a move. Further, we used several proven techniques for tracking a boy's whereabouts (e.g., requesting address corrections from the post office, and paper and electronic telephone directories). If all of these attempts failed, program staff made a trip to the last known address in an effort to obtain information from neighbors. Other sources of information that have been used were realtors, the Department of Motor Vehicles, court records, marriage license bureaus, and electronic search options. At each postal contact, the address correction request procedure was used to inform us of any changes. Families who had moved out of a 50-mile radius of the greater Pittsburgh area were interviewed by phone.

Project staff made considerable efforts to ensure participants' continued cooperation and discourage participants' outright refusals. Interviewers were extensively trained to be professional and pleasant. Assessments took place on any day or at any time that was convenient for the participants. Monetary incentive was offered, which increased over time; the payment for the youth started at $12 and increased to $80–100 at the last assessment included in this book; the payment for the parent started at $12 and increased to $35–65 at the last assessment included in this book.

Cooperation Rates

Throughout the repeated follow-up assessments, participant retention rates in the youngest cohort have remained high, never falling below 82% of the original cohort in 18 assessments. During the 14 years of the study, 70% of participants of the youngest cohort were interviewed across all 18 assessments. Another 11% missed one assessment and 5% missed two assessments, totaling 87% with data for nearly all of the assessments. Only 6% missed more than half of the yearly assessments. The last assessment of the youngest cohort available for data analysis (the 18th assessment, at age 19) yielded a participation rate of 82.3%. The average cooperation rate for that cohort over 17 follow-ups was 92.1%. We minimized data loss even further by combining assessments into age blocks. Each age block uses the data available for all assessments a participant completed during that block. This produced the following cooperation rates for the youngest cohort: 99.8% in middle childhood (ages 7–9), 97.0% in late childhood (ages 10–12), 94.6% in early adolescence (ages 13–16), and 89.9% in late adolescence (ages 17–19). The oldest cohort ($N = 506$) has been followed-up 16 times (from age 13 to 25) covering early adolescence to mid-adulthood. The cooperation rate of the participants (young men aged 25) at the 16th wave was 83.2%. The average cooperation rate for this cohort over 15 follow-ups after the initial assessment was 89.5%. The cooperation rate by age block for the oldest cohort were as follows: 100% in early adolescence (ages 13–16), 97.6% in late adolescence (ages 17–19), and 93.7% in early adulthood (ages 20–25).

Selective Attrition

Many studies show that the most elusive and uncooperative study participants tend to be disproportionately delinquent and antisocial (see, e.g., Farrington, Gallagher et al., 1990). Hence, the loss of respondents is especially serious and likely to produce misleading and invalid results in studies focusing on delinquent or antisocial behavior. We have checked for differential participation rates across the assessment waves expressed in terms of initial risk status, race, substance use, and serious offending. No consistent pattern of selective attrition of participants was found.

Another way of examining participant loss is to compare on selected variables the participants assessed at the last age block versus those who were missing at that age block. Comparing waves A and AA for the youngest cohort and waves A and Z for the oldest cohort shows no clear trend of selective attrition by race (56% and 54% of African Americans in the youngest cohort, respectively, and 56% and 56% of African Americans in the oldest cohort). Thus, there was no clear selective attrition on the variables in these comparisons.

Data Collection Procedures

For those up to the age of 16, we routinely had three informants: the boys, their parents, and their teachers. Virtually all data collection with the child and parent was done through face-to-face interviews, usually at the family home. Care was taken to interview each informant privately and separately from the other informant. Parent interviews were continued until wave T in the youngest cohort (average age 16) and wave I in the oldest cohort (average age 17). It was not judged prudent to use teacher information from late adolescence onward, because most teachers were not sufficiently familiar with individual students in the later years of high school. Thus, teacher data were not collected beyond wave R in the youngest cohort (average age 15) and wave I in the oldest cohort (average age 17).

For the first years of the study, interviewers recorded on paper forms informants' replies to the interview questions. However, from the 6th year onward, data collection was computerized by means of laptop computers. To avoid interviewer effects, interviewers were assigned to different families at each interview.

Interviewers were trained at the beginning of each wave. Special care was taken to maximize the accuracy of each interview, which was facilitated by the structured format. We regularly contacted families after the interview to assess interviewer performance and family complaints but we rarely encountered problems in these areas. Only in a few cases were we forced to dismiss an interviewer because of poor performance.

Teacher assessments were conducted through questionnaires. Teachers filled out rating forms on each of the participants. After elementary school, this usually involved a different teacher at each of the assessments. In total, counting the three cohorts, we conducted approximately 20,000 interviews with the boys and 15,000 interviews with a parent, and we obtained 13,500 rating forms filled out by teachers.

Informed Consent

Throughout the study, we obtained and renewed informed consent from the participants for their cooperation with the assessment and for the release of other types of information (e.g., school records, juvenile court records, etc.). All procedures of informed consent were approved by the Institutional Review Board at the medical school of the University of Pittsburgh.

Confidentiality of the Information

As part of the consent procedures, we contracted with the participants that all information collected from and about them would be coded and stripped of any identifying information. For that purpose, any confidential information (such as the person's name and other personal details that could link the person's identity to the data) was stored in a locked room to which only certain staff members had access. All staff, irrespective of access to the private information, had to sign a confidentiality form promising not to communicate any details about participants to others. The consent form signed by participants stipulated that informants could not have access to information provided by another informant (this, for example, prevented parents having access to information provided by their sons, or teachers obtaining information from the parents). Participants were free to ask us to terminate their participation at any time and remove their data from the files, but this happened in only one case. Through the National Institutes of Health we obtained a certificate of confidentiality to protect the information gathered from subpoena by a judicial court. Even though many of the boys eventually were arrested and convicted for delinquent acts, none of their reported offending has ever been requested by a judge.

Data Handling, Cleaning, and Storage Procedures

The repeated measurements, with multiple informants who responded to a multitude of questions, have generated a very large data set for the PYS. At present, we have about 42 million raw data points in the data system, and over 19,000 constructs made for analyses (only a small minority of which will be used in this volume). The time-consuming aspects of analyzing complex longitudinal data sets include the effort required to access and use the kinds of data that are available on a given topic; identify the specific measures, variables, and constructs that pertain to a particular participant; and examine changes in these measures, variables, and constructs over time using multiple data waves. We have built an integrated data system to incorporate all raw data, instruments, constructs, and documentation. All of the data has been entered, cleaned, and loaded in the database for all waves. In summary, this unique data set was well collected and prepared for analyses so that it could be used to address the many questions that we raised in this volume.

A Selection of Earlier Findings from the Pittsburgh Youth Study

This volume builds upon many findings from previous analyses on the PYS data. As of May 2007, we have published 143 empirical papers on the PYS in scientific journals, to which we will selectively refer (see the appendix for a full list of PYS publications). In addition, we have published a volume on executing complex studies and retaining a very high percentage of the participants over many repeated assessments (Stouthamer-Loeber & Van Kammen, 1995), and a volume on the background and results obtained in the first two data waves of the study (Loeber, Farrington, Stouthamer-Loeber, & Van Kammen, 1998). The following are examples of key findings that have resulted so far from the PYS and its substudies.

Prevalence, Development, and Cost

- The development from antisocial behaviors to serious delinquency best fits a model of three incremental pathways: the authority conflict pathway, the overt pathway, and the covert pathway (Loeber & Wung, et al., 1993; Loeber, DeLamaire, et al., 1999), which are discussed in more in detail in Chapter 1.
- Delinquency is concentrated in some families: 5% of the families contained 30% of the offenders, and, more broadly, 12% of the families contained almost half (44%) of the offenders. These figures did not vary markedly by ethnicity (Farrington, Jolliffe et al., 2001).
- Almost 2% of the boys in the middle and oldest cohorts were convicted of homicide (Loeber et al., 2005), and 2.6% had been convicted of rape (Van Wijk et al., 2005).
- An early onset of offending prior to age 13 is about equally common in disadvantaged and advantaged neighborhoods. However, late-onset offenders (age 13 and over) are more common in disadvantaged neighborhoods, especially in public housing areas in advantaged neighborhoods (Wikström & Loeber, 2000).
- Over 90% of all victim-related costs of crime result from violence as compared to theft (Welsh et al., in press).

Risk, Promotive, and Protective Factors

- Risk, promotive, and protective factors for delinquency are situated in the domains of the individual, family, school, peer group, and neighborhood (Loeber, Farrington, Stouthamer-Loeber & Van Kammen, 1998; Stouthamer-Loeber, Loeber et al., 2002).
- The higher the number of risk domains (in the child, family, school, etc.), the higher the probability of later serious delinquency; the higher the number of promotive domains, the lower that probability. Risk and promotive factors appear to cancel each other out in influencing the long-term risk of serious delinquency (Stouthamer-Loeber et al., 2002; Wikström & Loeber, 2000).
- The higher the level of neighborhood disadvantage (as evident from census data), the more likely it is that boys will be exposed to risk factors and the less likely it is that they will be exposed to promotive factors (Stouthamer-Loeber et al., 2002; Wikström & Loeber, 2000).

- However, children and adolescents with high scores on risk factors offend in serious crime at similar high rate regardless of the socioeconomic context of their neighborhood (Wikström & Loeber, 2000).
- For most comparisons, delinquent attitudes predicted delinquency as strongly as the reverse. However, delinquent attitudes predicted delinquency better with advancing age (Zhang, Loeber, & Stouthamer-Loeber, 1997).
- Child-parent interactions tend to be stable over time, and this applies to physical punishment, communication, supervision, positive parenting, and bad parent-child relationship qualities. However, physical punishment decreased while poor supervision and low positive parenting increased during adolescence. In contrast, poor communication and a disadvantaged relationship between the parent and child did not materially change between ages 6 and 18 (Loeber, Drinkwater et al., 2000).
- Predictors of homicide among those who had committed violence are a subset of predictors of violence. However, predictors of homicide appear to be qualitatively different from the predictors of violence, in that the latter are drawn from the domain of child, family, peer, and neighborhood factors. In contrast, predictors of homicide are mainly individual factors (Loeber et al., 2005).
- Some variables (e.g., delinquent peers) only predict offending between individuals, whereas others (e.g., parental supervision) predict offending both between and within individuals (Farrington, Loeber, Yin, & Anderson, 2002).
- Predictors of desistance from persistent serious offending often are proximal to the offending, but we have also documented long-term predictors present in early and late adolescence (Stouthamer-Loeber, Wei, Loeber, & Masten, 2004).
- A comparison of the predictors in late childhood of court appearances for delinquency in adolescence (ages 10–16) in the Cambridge Study in Delinquent Development and the PYS showed major similarities across the two studies, cohorts, and locations (Farrington & Loeber, 1999).

Substance Use

- Violent offenses compared to theft are more often committed under the influence of alcohol and/or drugs (White, Tice, Loeber, & Stouthamer-Loeber, 2002).
- Over time, changes in alcohol consumption, compared to changes in marijuana use, became much stronger predictors of changes in violence in the oldest cohort (White, Loeber, Stouthamer-Loeber, & Farrington, 1999). In contrast, in the youngest cohort, frequent

marijuana use was more strongly related to later violence than was frequent alcohol use. However, the association between frequent marijuana use and violence was no longer significant when common risk factors—specifically, ethnicity and hard drug use—were controlled (Wei, Loeber, & White, 2004).

This small sample of findings does not do justice to the great variety of publications that have resulted from the PYS (see appendix 1). The current volume expands on the prior articles in several ways. First, we are now able to make use of the full data set for the analyses (18 waves for the youngest cohort, covering ages 7–19, and 16 waves for the oldest cohort, covering ages 13–25). Second, predictor variables, which in past analyses often had been restricted to a particular age or wave, are now available over multiple waves, thereby considerably extending their explanatory power. Third, the explanation of offending (and desistance in offending) will be based on risk, promotive, and protective factors.

Three
Measurement Instruments and Constructs

MAGDA STOUTHAMER-LOEBER AND REBECCA STALLINGS

This chapter reviews the structure and scope of the measurement instruments used, and then describes the data reduction procedures leading to the definition of the key constructs used in this book. Details of the protocol of data collection can be found in Chapter 2, which also contains the design of the study. Recall that several strengths of the study were: (1) the repeated assessments without time gaps between ages 7 and 19 for the youngest cohort and ages 13 and 25 for the oldest cohort; (2) repeated assessments of independent and dependent variables; (3) multiple informants on most measures; and (4) offending measures based on self-reports, parent and teacher reports, and official records. The measurement waves are labeled with letters of the alphabet; the timing and sequence of the waves are shown in Table 2.1.

An overview of the timing and number of waves in which each instrument was used can be requested from the authors. Note that some behaviors, such as gang activity and drug dealing, were not assessed at younger ages because such behaviors are highly uncommon in childhood. Because many constructs contain items from more than one measure, constructs are discussed after all measures have been described. The description of measures and constructs will cover those that survived reliability checks and checks for multicollinearity. Dropped constructs are mentioned at the bottom of the tables listing constructs (see Tables 3.3–3.7).

The measures will be described by domain, although several measures cover more than one domain. Information from caretakers and teachers was collected for the youngest cohort from screening to wave T (mean age 16) and for the oldest cohort from screening to wave I (mean age 17). Interviews with these informants then stopped because the youths had reached an age at which many of them had left school and/or begun living independently.

We assumed that the reading skills of many participants were limited. Therefore, all interviews were verbally administered to the youths. For all measurements obtained through interviews, care was taken to delimit the time window for the respondent's answers. The interviewer specified the time frame before the questions were asked, and personal events as well as dates (e.g., Christmas or the beginning of school) were used to help delineate the appropriate time period. Most questions pertained to the period between assessments (6 months or 1 year). In the first assessment (screening) lifetime questions were asked in addition to six-month questions for offending and drug-use items. Other time frames have been applied to the mental health questions, as specified below.

The organization of this chapter is as follows: (1) measurement instruments related to youth behavior, family functioning, peers, school, neighborhood, and demographics; (2) data reduction; and (3) measurement constructs.

Measurement Instruments

Youth Behavior

Youth Offending

The Self-Reported Delinquency Scale The 40-item Self-Reported Delinquency Scale (SRD), based on the National Youth Survey, has been evaluated extensively (see Elliott, Huizinga, & Ageton, 1985). The scale had been modified for the Causes and Correlates of Delinquency Program (Loeber, Farrington, Stouthamer-Loeber & Van Kammen, 1998). The youngest cohort was given this instrument from wave G on, and the oldest cohort responded to this scale from screening on. For each type of delinquent behavior, the youth was asked whether he had committed it and, if so, how many times in the assessment period (6 months or 1 year). At the first administration, the youth also was asked lifetime questions about delinquent acts "ever" committed, using a yes-or-no format.

The Self-Reported Antisocial Behavior Scale The SRD was judged to be too difficult to understand for the youngest cohort when they were first graders. Also, a number of the delinquent behaviors in the SRD were age inappropriate or would have had an exceedingly low base rate for youths under age 11. Examples of such behaviors were: being drunk in a public place, lying about one's age to get into a movie or to buy alcohol, using checks illegally, and committing rape. Therefore, a new scale was developed, which included 27 items of delinquent behaviors appropriate to younger children (Loeber, Stouthamer-Loeber, Van Kammen, & Farrington, 1989). Other changes had to do with making the items easier for young children to understand. An example is theft, which in the SRD was categorized according to value; in the Self-Reported Antisocial Behavior Scale (SRA), however, theft was categorized by where it occurred without specifying the value. Thus, the SRA was shorter and used, at times, wording slightly different from that of the SRD (e.g., "taking something that does not belong to you" vs. "stealing"). In addition, certain items (property damage, stealing, and hitting) were repeated specifying different situations or persons in order to make the content less abstract.

In the SRA, questions about certain delinquent acts were preceded by questions that hoped to ascertain whether the youth understood the meaning of the behavior. First, the interviewer read a sentence containing the behavior and asked the youth whether he knew what that meant. If he answered yes, he was asked to give an example. If the youth did not understand the behavior or had difficulty giving an example, the interviewer gave an example and then asked the youth again to give an example. If the youth still could not produce an example indicating understanding of the behavior, the question was skipped. Exceptions to this procedure were the items for smoking marijuana and sniffing glue, for which no explanation was provided by the interviewer to the youth. The explanation of these two behaviors was withheld for ethical reasons in order to avoid raising the youth's curiosity about those acts.

Like the SRD, the SRA collected information about lifetime delinquency at screening using yes-or-no questions. In addition, delinquency in the past 6 months was assessed at every wave. For the 6-month questions, the answer format was "never," "once or twice," or "more often," because reliable estimates of exact frequency were thought to be beyond the capability of most young children.

The Gang Questionnaire This questionnaire was added to the assessments at wave H for the youngest cohort and at wave D for the oldest cohort. The questionnaire (see Gordon et al., 2004) established gang membership, gang activities, and individual roles within gangs.

Court Records Four court sources of arrest (having been charged for a crime) and conviction (having been convicted in court) were used for the juvenile and adult years. Juvenile court data was obtained from the Allegheny County Juvenile Court records for offenses within Allegheny County from the participants up to 2001 (the data collection covered ages 10–18, all three sample groups). In addition, the Pennsylvania Juvenile Court Judges' Commission provided data on all participant offenses throughout Pennsylvania up to 1997 (the data covered ages 10–16 for the youngest sample and ages 10–18 for both samples). The Pennsylvania State Police Repository provided state criminal history record information up through spring 2001 (covering up to age 20 for the youngest sample and up to age 26 for the oldest sample). The Federal Bureau of Investigation (FBI) provided federal criminal history record information in spring 2001 (the data covered ages 18–20 for the youngest sample and 18–26 for the oldest sample).

With regard to official offending, Allegheny County Juvenile Court records were searched and coded for offense date, offense category, and disposition, according to the format developed by Weinrott (1975) and further improved by Maguin (1994). In addition, we instituted an official records project consisting of a compilation and integration of youths' court records collected from Allegheny County, the Commonwealth of Pennsylvania, and the FBI. The coding system follows the definitions of crimes in the FBI Uniform Crime

Reports and corresponds with the format used by the National Center for Juvenile Justice (Homish, 2002).

The Youth Self-Report   The Youth Self-Report (YSR; see Achenbach & Edelbrock, 1987) measures youth behavior problems (also containing some information on offending), as well as social and academic competence. Nine items were added to this scale to increase the overlap with the caretaker and teacher form of the Child Behavior Checklist (Achenbach & Edelbrock, 1979, 1983) and to cover covert (concealing) antisocial behaviors. The answer format was "not true," "somewhat or sometimes true," and "very true or often true." This instrument was administered to the youngest cohort from wave H on and to the oldest cohort from screening on. At wave V for the youngest cohort and at wave U for the oldest cohort this instrument was replaced by the young adult version of the YSR (Achenbach, 1997).

The Extended Child Behavior Checklist   The extended Child Behavior Checklist (CBCL; see Achenbach, 1978; Achenbach & Edelbrock, 1979, 1983; Loeber, Farrington, Stouthamer-Loeber & Van Kammen., 1998) was administered to the primary caretaker. This extended version of the CBCL is a 112-item questionnaire covering a wide range of youth behavior problems such as anxiety, depression, compulsions, oppositional behaviors, hyperactivity, and offending. The standard version has been widely used and has adequate test-retest reliability (Achenbach & Edelbrock, 1983); however, specific delinquent behaviors and concealing antisocial behaviors (e.g., various forms of dishonesty and minor forms of property infraction) were underrepresented in this scale. Therefore, we added 88 items to cover concealing antisocial behaviors, and some of the behaviors from the SRD. The answer format of all items is "not true," "somewhat or sometimes true," and "very true or often true."

Selected Problem Behaviors   Twenty-one questions with a yes-or-no answer format were administered to the caretaker at screening to assess the lifetime prevalence of selected problem behaviors (SPB) measured by the extended CBCL. These behaviors included running away from home, fire setting, and truancy.

The Teacher Report Form   Teachers completed an extended version of the Teacher Report Form (extended TRF), which is complementary to the CBCL (Edelbrock & Achenbach, 1984). Twenty-three delinquent and concealing antisocial behavior items were added to this scale to increase its comparability with the youth and caretaker reports.

Substance Use   A 16-item *Substance Use Scale*, based on the National Youth Survey (Elliott et al., 1985) was administered from wave G on for the youngest cohort and in all waves for the oldest cohort (Loeber, Farrington, Stouthamer-

Loeber & Van Kammen, 1998). In the initial waves for the youngest cohort, six questions about substances were asked as part of the SRA to ensure that the questions were age appropriate (Loeber et al., 1989).

Psychopathology and Conduct Problems

The Revised Diagnostic Interview Schedule for Children   The revised Diagnostic Interview Schedule for Children (DISC; see Costello, Edelbrock, Kalas, Kessler, & Klaric, 1982; Costello, Edelbrock, & Costello, 1985) was administered to the caretaker at wave A for both cohorts. This instrument was developed as a measure of youth psychopathology to be administered by lay interviewers in epidemiological surveys. It covers most forms of youth psychopathology contained in the Diagnostic and Statistical Manual of Mental Disorders (*DSM-III* and *DSM-III-R*; American Psychiatric Association, 1980 and 1987), as well as the age at which the problem behaviors were first noted. Not covered were anxiety and relatively rare disorders such as psychosis.

For the youngest cohort at wave P, the DISC-P was administered to the caretaker and the DISC-C (DSM-III-R) to the youth. The extended CBCL administered to the caretaker, as well as the extended TRF and the YSR, also included measures of youth psychopathology and conduct problems.

The Recent Mood and Feelings Questionnaire   Because caretakers or teachers are usually not good judges of a youth's depression, the youths were administered the Recent Mood and Feelings Questionnaire (Angold et al., 1995; Costello & Angold, 1988; Messer et al., 1995). This 13-item scale is a measure of a youth's depression to be used in epidemiological studies. The youth was asked to rate on a 3-point scale his agreement with statements such as, "You didn't enjoy anything at all" and "You hated yourself" regarding his feelings over the previous 2 weeks. This scale was administered once a year (waves A, C, E, G, and every wave from J on for the youngest cohort; waves A, C, and every wave from E on for the oldest cohort).

Competence and Cognition

The Attitude to Delinquent Behavior Scale   This measure (Elliott et al., 1985) gauged youths' attitudes on a 5-point scale about the acceptability of 15 delinquent and substance-using acts. The youngest cohort prior to wave G was administered a version of the scale with 12 items more appropriate to children. For example, the theft questions were phrased in terms of stealing from different locations rather than stealing different amounts, and questions about drug dealing and joyriding were not asked.

The Likelihood of Getting Caught Scale   Beginning at wave C for the youngest cohort and wave A for the oldest cohort, youths were administered the

Likelihood of Getting Caught Scale. This 11-item scale measures youths' perceptions of how likely it is that they would be caught by the police if they committed specific delinquent acts, and their perception of what would happen if they were caught.

The CBCL, the TRF, and the YSR contained information on competence with regard to the youth's academic competence and involvements in sports, other social activities, and prosocial behaviors.

Interviewers' Impressions of Youth Questionnaire The interviewers completed a questionnaire about their interactions with the youth. From wave I on, questions about maturity, boredom, cooperation, pleasantness, hostility, and politeness were added.

The Work/Skills Questionnaire Information about work, work skills, and general life skills was gathered starting with wave P for the youngest cohort and starting with wave G for the oldest cohort.

Physical Development

The Birth and Developmental History Questionnaire At wave C the caretaker responded to the Birth and Developmental History Questionnaire, which covered pre-, peri-, and postnatal conditions potentially influencing the youth's health and milestones (e.g., the age at which he was able to walk).

Pubertal Development Pubertal development (see Petersen, Crockett, Richards, & Boxer, 1988) was measured for the youngest cohort from waves H to T. Both caretaker and youth responded to this scale. The scale was not used with the oldest cohort because they were first studied in seventh grade, when puberty would have already begun for the majority of the youths.

Data were collected on a yearly basis from the *Family Health Questionnaire* about serious injuries and wounds (five questions). In addition, data were collected in the *Victimization Questionnaire* on various forms of victimization. This questionnaire was administered to the caretaker and to the youth, starting for both cohorts at wave G and repeated through each subsequent assessment.

Family Functioning
Child-Rearing Practices

The Discipline Scale This scale assessed the youth's perception of his male and female caretakers' discipline methods (eight items for each). The scale evolved from previous pilot work at the Oregon Social Learning Center (Loeber, Farrington, Stouthamer-Loeber & Van Kammen, 1998). Questions covered the method of discipline and the persistence and consistency with which discipline was applied. For the youngest cohort from wave A to F, a shorter form was used. Caretakers at all waves were administered a questionnaire parallel to the version given to the oldest cohort.

The Supervision/Involvement Scale Caretakers and youths were administered versions of the Supervision/Involvement Scale. The 43 questions in this scale concern the caretakers' knowledge of the youth's whereabouts; the frequency of joint discussions, planning, and activities; and the amount of time that the youth is unsupervised. Youths reported on their male and female caretakers, whereas caretakers reported only on their own knowledge of and interaction with the youth. The scale is based on a literature review of family factors related to offending (Loeber & Stouthamer-Loeber, 1986), previous pilot work, the Family Environment Scale (Moos & Moos, 1975), and Skinner, Steinhauer, and Santa-Barbara's (1983) Family Assessment Measure.

The Positive Parenting Scale This scale was administered to both youths and caretakers. For the youths it consisted of their perception of their parents' frequency of responding in a variety of positive ways to their behavior (ten items for each). Caretakers reported only on their own positive responding.

Child Maltreatment Data Child maltreatment data were collected from Allegheny County Children and Youth Services (CYS) records. Information was gathered on any referral for the families of participants made to CYS. This information covered the time span from the youth's date of birth to age 13 for the youngest cohort and to age 18 for the oldest cohort. The Maltreatment Classification System developed by Cicchetti and his colleagues (Barnett, Manly, & Cicchetti, 1993) was used for data collection.

Caretaker Characteristics

The Perceived Stress Scale This scale was administered to caretakers once a year. This 14-item scale, constructed by Cicchetti (personal communication, 1987) asked about perceived stress levels and caretakers' abilities to cope with stress in the previous month. Examples of topics included are unexpected upsets, feeling nervous and stressed, inability to cope, and feelings of anger about things that happened.

The Expectations/Aspirations Questionnaire This questionnaire was administered to the youngest cohort and their caretakers at waves G, J, N and R. The oldest cohort received this questionnaire at waves G, I, K and M, and their caretakers completed it at waves G and I. Respondents rated on a 4-point scale the importance for people in general of achieving certain goals, such as finishing high school or saving money. They also rated the likelihood that the youths themselves would meet each goal.

The Family Health Questionnaire   Based on Burns et al. (1990), this questionnaire contained questions about seeking help for caretakers' mental health problems during the previous year. At wave A it also asked about lifetime mental health problems of absent biological parents.

The Alcohol/Drugs Parent Questionnaire   This questionnaire contained 11 questions about alcohol problems and one question about drug problems experienced by the primary caretaker. The same questions were asked about the caretaker's partner. This questionnaire was given at waves E and T to caretakers of the youngest cohort and at wave E to caretakers of the oldest cohort.

Family Criminal History   Lifetime data on family arrest and conviction were collected from caretakers at wave C.

Peers

The Peer Delinquency Scale   This scale was administered to the youths, and contained 15 items corresponding to a number of items on the Self-Reported Delinquency Scale and the Substance Use Scale (Elliott et al., 1985). It asked whether "all," "most," "half," "few," or "none" of the youth's peers engaged in delinquent acts or used substances. The youngest cohort prior to wave G was administered a version of this scale asking whether "all," "some," "one," or "none" of the youth's peers engaged in 12 behaviors more appropriate to children. For example, younger youths were asked whether peers had hit an adult or gotten into a fight with other kids, whereas older youths were asked whether peers had attacked someone with a weapon or committed forcible robbery.

The Parents and Peers Scale   Both youths and their caretakers were administered this scale (Loeber, Farrington, Stouthamer-Loeber & Van Kammen, 1998). This measure consisted of 11 items measuring the number and nature of the youth's friendships, the extent to which their caretaker(s) approved of these friendships, and the reasons for disapproval.

The Child's Relationship with Caretaker/Siblings Scale   Youths were administered this scale (Loeber & Stouthamer-Loeber, 1986), which had 15 items on the youths' perception of their relationship with their mothers and 15 items on their perception of their relationship with their fathers. Separate questions covered the youths' relationships to children in the home.

The Victimization Questionnaire   This scale, administered to both caretakers and youths, starting for both cohorts at wave G and repeated through each subsequent assessment, collected data on the youth's experiences of harassment, violence, and crime.

Caretakers reported on their relationships with the youths in the *Caretaker-Child Relationship Questionnaire* and reported how well the youth got along with other caretakers or children in the household in the *Demographic Questionnaire*. Demographic information was collected at each assessment wave.

School

Information about the youth's performance in school came from the caretakers' (CBCL), teachers' (TRF), and youths' (YSR) evaluations of achievement in reading, math, writing, and spelling; caretakers and youths also evaluated youths' achievement in up to three other academic subjects, such as history, science, or geography. In addition, information was collected on the youth's feelings about and behavior in school, such as, "Do you think homework is a waste of time?" and "Do you care what teachers think of you?" These questions were asked in the introductory stage of the interview at wave A and in the School/Religion/Resources questionnaire at wave G and waves J through T for the youngest cohort, and at waves G and I for the oldest cohort.

Neighborhood

The Neighborhood Scale (Loeber, Farrington, Stouthamer-Loeber & Van Kammen, 1998) measured the caretakers' perceived quality of the neighborhood in which their families resided. This instrument contained 17 items covering the presence of prostitution, assaults, burglaries, and similar problems in the neighborhood. This scale was given to caretakers once a year using wave T for the youngest cohort and wave I for the oldest cohort, and given to the youth starting with wave N for the youngest cohort and wave K for the oldest cohort.

Demographics

The Demographics Questionnaire This questionnaire collected extensive information from the caretaker including names, aliases, birth dates, place of birth, ethnicity, education, work, and marital status of the caretaker and the caretaker's partner. Information was also collected on other persons taking care of the youth, on absent and present siblings, and on other children and adults in the household. If one or both of the biological parents did not live in the home, the caretaker answered demographic questions about the absent parent(s) and the youth's contact with them.

The Participant Demographics Questionnaire At wave G, youths in the oldest cohort who lived independently of adult caretakers began to complete their own Participant Demographics Questionnaire. Regardless of their living situation, all oldest-cohort youths completed this questionnaire beginning at wave K, and all youngest-cohort youths completed it beginning at wave V. For each member of the household, it asked the person's age, sex, relationship to the youth, and how well the youth got along with the person.

The Caretaker History Questionnaire At wave G the caretaker was administered the Caretaker History Questionnaire explaining which male adult and which female adult had been most responsible for the youth over the course of his life and the reasons for any changes in caretakers.

Data Reduction

Most constructs were made from multiple questionnaire items, to optimize psychometric quality and reduce non-construct-related variance (Wiggins, 1973). To ensure that the results of analyses could be communicated clearly to lay people as well as professionals, the items included in each construct were relatively homogeneous.

In general, constructs were created from items that had face validity and were intercorrelated. For constructs consisting of five or more items, Cronbach's (1951) alpha was calculated as a measure of internal consistency of the construct. Average correlations were used for constructs consisting of fewer than five items. Some constructs included items that belonged conceptually to the same domain but had different base rates; there was thus no reason to expect high intercorrelations. (For example, shoplifting items of low value may not correlate with breaking and entering, but both behaviors may be considered measures of theft.) Alphas were not calculated for these constructs. For this volume, alphas were calculated at the age block level (see below). Constructs with an alpha consistently below .70 were not used in the analyses.

As much as possible, a construct was formed using data from multiple informants: the youth himself, his caretaker, and his teacher. This strategy made it possible to: (1) measure behaviors occurring in multiple settings, such as home and school; and (2) use a "best estimate" algorithm to establish whether the behavior occurred at all within the assessment period. For example, if the youth reported that he had not set fires, but the caretaker reported that he had, then the construct "fire setting" reflected the fact that at least one informant reported the behavior.

As a first step, constructs were organized according to the interview wave in which the data were collected. After the constructs were completed, an additional level of constructs was created to "block" the data into just a few constructs, each of which represents a stage of development lasting several years. For the youngest cohort, waves A–F (3 years, approximate age range 7–9) constituted middle childhood, waves G–L (3 years, approximate age range 10–12) constituted late childhood, waves N–T (4 years, approximate age range

13–16) constituted early adolescence, and waves V–AA (3 years, approximate age range 17–19) constituted late adolescence. For the oldest cohort, screening and waves A–G (4 years, approximate age range 13–16) constituted early adolescence, waves I–M (3 years, approximate age range 17–19) constituted late adolescence, and waves O–Z (6 years, approximate age range 20–25) constituted early adulthood. A construct for each age block was calculated using an appropriate algorithm, as explained in the descriptions of individual constructs. The age block constructs were means if the constructs consisted of scales (i.e., mean number of thefts per year) or proportions if the scores were dichotomous (i.e., proportion of years in which the family received welfare).

Missing Data

Answers to some questions were missing. This occurred because the informant was not interviewed at that wave, because he refused to answer, because he did not know the answer, or because the interviewer accidentally skipped the question or there was a computer error. Most constructs were coded as missing in a wave if more than 30% of the raw data items making up the construct were missing; if there were missing items but less than 30%, the mean of the available responses was substituted for the missing items. Where this method was not appropriate, a construct was coded as missing if any raw data item was missing and none of the items was positive. Age block constructs were calculated using those waves for which data were available (called applicable valid waves) and were set to missing only if all of the waves in the age block were missing.

For this volume we considered 87 independent constructs. However, we reduced the number by calculating intercorrelations and removing constructs that were highly intercorrelated within a domain. In general, we kept the construct with the highest alpha or with the fewest intercorrelations. In addition to those constructs with low internal consistency, we also deleted some constructs that depended on having two caretakers present in the family because of the reduction in number. The deleted constructs are listed at the bottom of Tables 3.3–3.7.

Many age block constructs of the independent variables were trichotomized, separating the 25% of participants with the most antisocial scores and the 25% with the most prosocial scores from the middle 50%. This process achieved comparability and compensated for skewed distributions. In addition, this division allowed us to check separately for risk and promotive effects (see Chapter 7).

Age Transformation

For certain constructs in the offending and drug domains, an additional level of constructs was created, independent of the age block constructs, to organize the data according to youths' age at the time of interview. For example, some individuals in the youngest cohort were 13 years old at wave J, and others were not 13 until wave R; some individuals in the oldest cohort were 13 at screening, and others were not 13 until wave D. Thus, the construct "fire setting at age 13" includes data about fires set at the wave when a youth was 13, regardless of which wave that was. The age of each youth at wave A was calculated by subtracting his birth date from his interview date and subtracting an additional three months to obtain his average age during the six-month period covered by the interview. Age at screening was calculated by subtracting six months from age at wave A. Age at each subsequent wave was calculated by adding six-month increments to age at wave A. All ages then were rounded down to integers. This resulted in a smooth progression of age, such that no youth had the same integer age for more than two consecutive six-month waves or more than one consecutive one-year wave. Data from two six-month waves at which a youth was the same integer age were combined into a single construct; the procedures for combining are explained in the descriptions of individual constructs. Age-of-onset constructs were made by noting the age at which a youth first reported a behavior. These scores were formed cumulatively, such that in the final year the construct's value was equal to the age at which the behavior first appeared.

In order to minimize collinearity, we examined the intercorrelations among the predictor constructs. As a result, we excluded the following constructs from analyses in this book: countercontrol, caretaker drug problem, relationship with caretaker, close to caretaker, and caretaker/child communication. In addition, because of absent fathers and a consequent lowering of the available number for analyses we removed the following constructs: marital happiness, marital involvement, marital agreement, and caretakers disagree on discipline. Further, the tables in the following sections listing the predictor constructs do not show these constructs in the outcome period—that is, late adolescence for the youngest cohort and early adulthood for the oldest cohort.

Constructs

Youth Behavior Constructs

Offending Table 3.1 summarizes offending constructs derived from youth (self-reported), caretaker, and teacher reports (youth, caretaker, and teacher combined is called *reported*), and constructs made from court records (official records). When official records and reported sources of offending are combined the construct is called *all-source*. Some reported constructs could not be made for middle childhood because some questions about serious violence were not asked and because frequency data were not collected. With regard to violence, two levels are defined: *moderate violence* is gang fighting and *serious violence* is forcible robbery, defined as attacking with intent to injure, sexual coercion, or rape. Three levels of theft are defined: *minor theft* is stealing less

Table 3.1 Offending Constructs

	Childhood		Adolescence		Adulthood
	Middle	**Late**	**Early**	**Late**	**Early**
Average Ages	7–9	10–12	13–16	17–19	20–25
		Violence			
Violence Seriousness Classification	—	Y	Y/O	Y/O	O
	MODERATE/SERIOUS VIOLENCE PREVALENCE				
Reported*	Y	Y	Y/O	Y/O	O
Arrest, Official Records	—	Y	Y/O	Y/O	O
Conviction, Official Records	—	Y	Y/O	Y/O	O
All-Source (Reported and Conviction)†	—	Y	Y/O	Y/O	O
	MODERATE/SERIOUS VIOLENCE FREQUENCY				
Self-Reported	—	Y	Y/O	Y/O	O
Arrest, Official Records	Cumulative				
Conviction, Official Records	—	Y	Y/O	Y/O	O
	MODERATE/SERIOUS VIOLENCE AGE OF ONSET				
Reported	Cumulative				
Arrest, Official Records	Cumulative				
Conviction, Official Records	Cumulative				
		Theft			
Theft Seriousness Classification	Y	Y	Y/O	Y/O	O
	MINOR THEFT				
Minor Theft Prevalence (Reported)	Y	Y	Y/O	Y/O	O
Minor Theft Frequency (Reported)	Y	Y	Y/O	Y/O	O
Minor Theft Age of Onset	Cumulative				
	MODERATE/SERIOUS THEFT PREVALENCE				
Reported	Y	Y	Y/O	Y/O	O
Arrest, Official Records	—	Y	Y/O	Y/O	O
Conviction, Official Records	—	Y	Y/O	Y/O	O
All-Source (Reported and Conviction)†	—	Y	Y/O	Y/O	O

Table 3.1 Offending Constructs (continued)

	Childhood		Adolescence		Adulthood
	Middle	**Late**	**Early**	**Late**	**Early**
MODERATE/SERIOUS THEFT FREQUENCY					
Self-Reported	Y	Y	Y/O	Y/O	O
Arrest, Official Records	—	Y	Y/O	Y/O	O
Conviction, Official Records	—	Y	Y/O	Y/O	O
MODERATE/SERIOUS THEFT AGE OF ONSET					
Reported	Cumulative				
Arrest, official records	Cumulative				
Conviction, official records	Cumulative				
ALL-SOURCE SERIOUS THEFT/VIOLENCE PREVALENCE					
Reported and Conviction	—	Y	Y/O	Y/O	O
Drug Selling					
Prevalence (Reported)	—	Y	Y/O	Y/O	O
Frequency (Reported)	—	Y	Y/O	Y/O	O
Age of Onset (Reported)	Cumulative				
Other Constructs					
Gun Carrying (Reported)	—	Y	Y/O	Y/O	O
Age of Onset (Reported)	Cumulative				
Gun carrying (reported)	Y	Y	Y/O	Y/O	O
Prison time	—	Y	Y	Y/O	O

Notes: Y = youngest cohort; O = oldest cohort; reported = youth, caretaker, teacher information; official records = court records; *not for serious violence in middle childhood; †only for serious violence and serious theft prevalence.

than $5 outside the home or shoplifting; *moderate theft* is stealing a bicycle or skateboard from the street, stealing things worth more than $5, joyriding, purse snatching, dealing in stolen goods, or stealing from a car; *serious theft* is breaking-and-entering or auto theft.[1]

Official records yielded information on arrest and conviction using approximately the same levels as for reported offending, but some adjustments were necessary because the offense categories did not match exactly. *Moderate violence* is simple assault. *Serious violence* is robbery, homicide, rape, aggravated assault, involuntary deviate sexual intercourse, aggravated indecent assault, or spousal sexual assault. *Moderate theft* is larceny or dealing in stolen property; because it was impossible to classify court-reported acts of larceny in as much detail as self-reported thefts, it was assumed that any theft serious enough to result in criminal charges was equivalent to moderate theft. *Serious theft* is burglary or motor vehicle theft. Finally, three additional constructs were made combining information from reported constructs with official records of convictions (all-source), as well as a construct measuring the average number of weeks per year in prison.

Violence

Violence Seriousness Classification This construct categorizes youths according to the most serious level of violence committed. Those who did not commit violence were scored 0. Data is taken from the youth (SRD and YSR) and the caretaker (CBCL and, at screening, SPB). This construct was not made for the youngest cohort prior to wave G because the SRA and CBCL did not provide data on serious violence. Six-month waves were combined into yearly constructs by placing a youth at the highest level attained across the two 6-month assessments. The score for each age block was set to the highest level attained by a youth across the years within the block.

Reported Moderate/Serious Violence Prevalence Each of these constructs is positive if a youth or his caretaker reported that the youth engaged in violence at that level. Full-year and age block constructs were scored positive if any applicable wave was positive.

Prevalence of Moderate/Serious Violence Arrest/Conviction Each of these constructs is positive if there is an official record of arrest/conviction for moderate/serious violence. Age block constructs were created by determining each youth's age during the waves in the block and setting the block construct to positive if he was arrested/convicted at any age in the age block.

All-Source Serious Violence Prevalence This construct combines reported serious violence and serious violence conviction. Serious violence (all-source) is considered present if either source is positive (see Chapter 5 for details).

All-Source Moderate or Serious Violence Prevalence This construct is positive if there was any reported moderate violence, reported serious violence, official record of moderate violence conviction, or official record of serious violence conviction.

Self-Reported Frequency of Moderate/Serious Violence Each of these constructs measures the number of incidents of reported violence at each level.

These constructs could not be made for the youngest cohort prior to wave G because these behaviors are not in the SRA, and the CBCL does not measure frequency. Annual constructs were created by summing the frequency from two 6-month waves. If a youth reported more than 50 incidents in one year, his score was rounded down to 50. Age block constructs were created by calculating the mean of all valid years within each age block.

Frequency of Moderate/Serious Violence Arrest/Conviction   Each of these constructs counts the number of times an arrest/conviction for moderate/serious violence is found in official records.

Reported Age of Onset of Moderate/Serious Violence   Each of these constructs measures the age at which the youth or his caretaker first reported his involvement at that level of violence. If the reported age was younger than 5, the construct was coded 5.

Age of Onset of Moderate/Serious Violence Arrest/Conviction   Each of these constructs measures the age at which the youth was first mentioned in official records as being arrested or convicted for moderate or serious violence. Data from official records were available for the span of the study.

Theft

Theft Seriousness Classification   This construct categorizes youths according to the most serious level of theft committed. Those who did not commit theft scored 0. Data were taken from the youth (SRA or SRD, and YSR where available) and the caretaker (CBCL and, at screening, SPB). Six-month waves were combined by placing a youth at the highest level attained across the two. Age block constructs were set to the highest level attained across the waves in each block.

The following constructs each have a version for moderate theft and one for serious theft. Reported constructs also have a version for minor theft.

Reported Prevalence of Minor/Moderate/Serious Theft   Each of these constructs is positive if a youth or his caretaker reported that he engaged in theft at the given level. Full-year and age block constructs were assigned a positive score if any applicable wave was positive.

Prevalence of Moderate/Serious Theft Arrest/Conviction   Each of these constructs is positive if there is an official record of arrest/conviction for moderate/serious theft.

All-Source Serious Theft Prevalence   This construct combines reported serious theft and serious theft conviction. Serious theft (all-source) is considered present if either source is positive (see Chapter 5 for details).

All-Source Moderate or Serious Theft Prevalence   This construct is positive if there was any reported moderate theft, reported serious theft, official record of moderate theft conviction, or official record of serious theft conviction.

Reported Frequency of Minor/Moderate/Serious Theft   Each of these constructs measures the total number of incidents of self-reported theft at that level. Six-month constructs were combined by summing the incidents from the two waves to create an annual frequency. If a youth reported more than 50 delinquent acts in 1 year, his score was rounded down to 50. Age block constructs were created by calculating the mean of all valid waves in each block.

Reported Age of Onset of Minor/Moderate/Serious Theft   Each of these constructs measures the age at which the youth or his caretaker first reported his involvement in theft at the given level. If the reported age was younger than 5, the construct was coded 5.

Age of Onset of Moderate/Serious Theft Arrest/Conviction   Each of these constructs measures the youth's age the first time he was arrested/convicted for moderate/serious theft.

All-Source Prevalence of Serious Violence and Theft   This construct combines serious violence and serious theft and was made using reported and official conviction data (see Chapter 5 for details).

Drug Selling

Prevalence of Drug Selling   This construct is positive if a youth reported selling marijuana or hard drugs. This construct was not made for SRA waves because the relevant questions were not asked. Full-year and age block constructs were scored positive if any wave was positive.

Frequency of Drug Selling   This construct measures the number of times a youth sold illicit drugs during the assessment period, according to his self-report. This construct was not made for SRA waves because the relevant questions were not asked. Six-month constructs were combined by summing the incidents from the two waves. If a youth reported more than 50 incidents in 1 year, his score was rounded down to 50. Age block constructs were created by calculating the mean of all valid waves in each block.

Age of Onset of Drug Selling   This construct measures the age at which the youth first reported selling any illicit drug.

Other Constructs

Gang Membership　This construct is positive if a youth reported being a member of a gang. The Gangs Questionnaire was not administered until wave H for the youngest and wave D for the oldest cohort. Full-year and age block constructs were scored positive if any applicable wave was positive.

Age of Onset of Gang Membership　This construct measures the age at which the youth first reported being a member of a gang. When the Gangs Questionnaire was given for the first time, youths who had ever been gang members were asked the age at which they first joined. For youths who reported their first gang membership at a subsequent wave, the age of onset is the age at that wave.

Gun Carrying　This construct is positive if the youth (SRA/SRD) reported carrying a gun during the assessment period. Full-year and age block constructs were assigned a positive score if any applicable wave was positive.

Prison Time　This construct combines interview data with official records data to calculate the average number of weeks in prison per age block.

Youth Substance Use

Table 3.2 summarizes the youth substance use constructs. Data for the constructs in Table 3.2 came from the SRA or Drug Consumption Questionnaire. Note that no questions about hard drugs were asked of the youngest cohort prior to wave G.

Prevalence of Alcohol Use　This construct is positive if a youth reported drinking beer, wine, or liquor during the assessment period. Alcohol use was excluded from consideration if caretakers knew about it, the reason for drinking was "special occasion or religious ritual" or "with adults at dinner," and the youth had no prior onset of drinking that type of alcohol. Full-year and age block constructs were scored positive if any wave was positive.

Frequency of Alcohol Use　This construct sums up a youth's self-reported number of sessions of uses of beer, wine, and liquor during the assessment period. Alcohol use excluded under the above criteria was not counted. Six-month waves were combined by summing the incidents from the two waves. If a youth reported more than 365 incidents in one year, his score was rounded down to 365. Age block constructs were set to the highest frequency reported in any year in the block.

Age of Onset of any Alcohol Use　This construct is based on the youth's self-reported age when he first drank beer, wine, or liquor, not counting incidents

Table 3.2 Youth Substance Use

	Childhood		Adolescence		Adulthood
	Middle	Late	Early	Late	Early
Average Ages	*7–9*	*10–12*	*13–16*	*17–19*	*20–25*
Prevalence of Alcohol Use	Y	Y	Y/O	Y/O	O
Frequency of Alcohol Use	Y	Y	Y/O	Y/O	O
Age of Onset of any Alcohol Use	Cumulative				
Prevalence of Tobacco Use	Y	Y	Y/O	Y/O	O
Frequency of Tobacco Use	Y	Y	Y/O	Y/O	O
Age of Onset of Tobacco Use	Cumulative				
Prevalence of Marijuana Use	Y	Y	Y/O	Y/O	O
Frequency of Marijuana Use	Y	Y	Y/O	Y/O	O
Age of Onset of Marijuana Use	Cumulative				
Prevalence of Hard Drug Use	—	Y	Y/O	Y/O	O
Frequency of Hard Drug Use	—	Y	Y/O	Y/O	O
Age of Onset of Hard Drug Use	Cumulative				

Notes: Y = youngest cohort; O = oldest cohort.

excluded under the above criteria. If he had used alcohol prior to screening, he was asked how old he was when he first drank. If he began drinking at a later wave, age of onset was his age at that wave. If the reported age was younger than 5, it was recoded to 5.

Prevalence of Tobacco Use This construct is positive if a youth reported smoking cigarettes, pipes, cigars, or chewing tobacco during the assessment period. Full-year and age block constructs were scored positive if any applicable wave was positive.

Frequency of Tobacco Use This construct counts a youth's self-reported number of uses of any form of tobacco during the assessment period. Six-month waves were combined by summing the incidents from the two waves to create an annual frequency. If a youth reported more than 365 incidents in one year, his score was rounded down to 365. Age block constructs were set to the highest frequency reported in any year in the block.

Age of Onset of Tobacco Use   This construct is based on the youth's self-reported age when he first smoked or chewed tobacco. If he had used tobacco prior to screening, he was asked how old he was when he first used it. If he began using tobacco at a later wave, age of onset is his age at that wave. If the reported age was younger than 5, it was recoded to 5.

Prevalence of Marijuana Use   This construct is positive if a youth reported using marijuana during the assessment period. Full-year and age block constructs were scored positive if any applicable wave was positive.

Frequency of Marijuana Use   This construct counts a youth's self-reported number of days of using marijuana during the assessment period. Six-month waves were combined by summing the incidents from the two waves. If a youth reported more than 365 incidents in one year, his score was rounded down to 365. Age block constructs were set to the highest frequency reported in any year in the block.

Age of Onset of Marijuana Use   This construct is based on the youth's self-reported age when he first used marijuana. If he had used marijuana prior to screening, he was asked how old he was when he first used it. If he began using it at a later wave, age of onset was his age at that wave.

Prevalence of Hard Drug Use   This construct is positive if a youth reported that during the assessment period he used any of ten illicit drugs: hallucinogens, powder cocaine, crack cocaine, heroin, barbiturates, amphetamines, tranquilizers, codeine, other prescription drugs, or PCP. Drugs prescribed by a doctor were excluded. Full-year and age block constructs were scored positive if any applicable wave was positive.

Frequency of Hard Drug Use   This construct counts a youth's self-reported total number of days of using, without a prescription, any of the ten illicit drugs mentioned above. Six-month waves were combined by summing the incidents from the two waves. If a youth reported more than 365 incidents in one year, his score was rounded down to 365. Age block constructs were set to the highest frequency reported in any year in the block.

Age of Onset of Hard Drug Use   This construct is based on the youth's self-reported age when he first used, without a prescription, any of the ten illicit drugs listed above. If he had used these drugs prior to the first wave when he was asked (wave G for the youngest cohort and screening for the oldest cohort), he was asked how old he was when he first used them. If he began using hard drugs at a later wave, age of onset was his age at that wave.

Youth Psychopathology

Table 3.3 summarizes the youth psychopathology constructs.

ADHD Symptoms This construct is made from information gathered at waves A (oldest and youngest cohort, based on caretaker information only) and P (youngest cohort, based on caretaker and youth information). Because of the time of the measurement, only DSM-III-R diagnoses could be made (American Psychiatric Association, 1987). This construct was based on the DISC-P questions used in diagnosis of ADHD. Each of 14 symptoms was scored positive if the informant answered "often" to any question measuring the symptom and the construct was the total number of symptoms scored positive.

Physical Aggression (Parent, Teacher) This construct includes physically aggressive behaviors, such as picking fights and hitting people. The behaviors were measured by seven items from the primary caretaker (CBCL) and five items from the teacher (TRF). If either informant said a behavior occurred often, the youth received a positive score for that behavior. The behaviors were then counted to create the final construct. Six-month waves were combined by assigning a positive score to any behavior reported at either wave and then counting the behaviors.

Table 3.3 Youth Psychopathology

	Childhood		Adolescence	
	Middle	**Late**	**Early**	**Late**
Average Ages	*7–9*	*10–12*	*13–16*	*17–19*
DISRUPTIVENESS				
ADHD Symptoms	Y	—	Y/O	—
OTHER DISRUPTIVE PROBLEMS				
Physical Aggression (Parent, Teacher)	Y	Y	Y/O	—
Physical Aggression (Child)	Y	Y	Y/O	O
Psychopathic Features	Y	Y	Y/O	—
Truancy	Y	Y	Y/O	—
Running Away	Y	Y	Y/O	—
DEPRESSION AND ANXIETY				
Depressed Mood	Y	Y	Y/O	O
Anxiety	Y	Y	Y/O	O
Shyness/Withdrawal	Y	Y	Y/O	O

Notes: Y = youngest cohort; O = oldest cohort.

Physical Aggression (Child) This construct is made from the youth's self-report of his tendency to hit people (SRA waves) or to attack people or get into many fights (SRD and YSR waves). Six-month waves were averaged to create one-year constructs.

Psychopathic Features This construct includes 32 behaviors considered representative of childhood psychopathy (Frick, O'Brien, Wootton, & McBurnett, 1994; Lynam, 1997) assessed by the caretaker (CBCL) and teacher (TRF). Items included "lying or cheating," "sudden changes in mood or feelings," and "behaving irresponsibly." Full-year and age block constructs were created by calculating the mean of all applicable valid waves.

Truancy This construct is based on youth (SRA or SRD and YSR), caretaker (CBCL), and teacher (TRF) reports of the youth's truancy. A youth was considered truant if any informant reported that he had been truant. Full-year and age block constructs were scored positive if any applicable wave was positive.

Running Away This construct is based on youth (SRA or SRD) and caretaker (CBCL) reports of whether the youth had run away from home. The construct was positive if either informant gave a positive report. Full-year and age block constructs were scored positive if any applicable wave was positive.

Depressed Mood This construct is the sum of 13 items on the Recent Mood and Feelings Questionnaire administered to the youth. The items covered criteria for a diagnosis of major depression according to DSM III-R. This construct was made only once a year during the six-month assessments. Age block constructs were created by calculating the mean of all valid waves in each block.

Anxiety This construct measures the youth's anxious behaviors. It included seven items from the caretaker (CBCL), eight items from the teacher (TRF), and seven items from the youth (YSR) relating to eight behaviors such as "clings to adults" and "nervous, high-strung, or tense." If any informant answered "sometimes" or "often," the youth was scored positive for that behavior. The behaviors were then counted to create the final construct. Age block constructs were created by calculating the mean of all valid waves in each block.

Shyness/Withdrawal This construct measures the youth's withdrawn and shy behaviors. It included seven items from the caretaker, seven items from the teacher, and seven items from the youth relating to seven behaviors such as "likes to be alone" and "refuses to talk." If any informant answered "sometimes" or "often," the youth scored positive for that behavior. The behaviors were then counted to create the final construct. Age block constructs were created by calculating the mean of all valid waves in each block.

Youth Competence

Table 3.4 summarizes the youth competence constructs.

The following constructs were removed because of low reliability: religious observance; number of organizations belonged to; and jobs and chores competence.

Prosocial Behavior This construct is based on nine items from the YSR, such as being "pretty honest," being willing to help others, and so on. This construct was made for the youngest cohort beginning at wave H and for the oldest cohort at all waves. Full-year and age block constructs were created by calculating the mean of applicable valid waves.

Interaction with Interviewer This construct is made from six items of the Interviewers' Impressions of Youth Questionnaire. The interviewer rated on a 3-point scale the maturity, boredom, cooperation, pleasantness, hostility, and politeness expressed in the youth's behavior toward the interviewer. This construct was not made until wave I because the questions were not asked earlier. Age block constructs were created by calculating the mean of all valid waves in each block.

Table 3.4 Youth Competence

	Childhood		Adolescence	
	Middle	**Late**	**Early**	**Late**
Average Ages	*7–9*	*10–12*	*13–16*	*17–19*
Prosocial Behavior	—	Y	Y/O	O
Interaction with Interviewer	—	Y	Y/—	O
Self-Aspirations	—	Y	Y/O	O
Attitude toward Delinquency	Y	Y	Y/O	O
Likelihood of Getting Caught	Y	Y	Y/O	O
Age Left Home	Cumulative			
Life Skills	—	—	O	O
Liking of Adults	—	—	O	O
Job Skills	—	—	O	O
Getting a Job	—	—	O	O
Attitude toward Substance Use	Y	Y	Y/O	O

Notes: Y = youngest cohort; O = oldest cohort.

Self-Aspirations   This construct is based on the Expectations/Aspirations Scale questions about the importance of 11 life goals for people in general. Goals included "finishing high school" and "having a good reputation in the community." This construct was made only at waves G, I, J, K, M, N, and R. Age block constructs were created by calculating the mean of all valid waves in each block.

Attitude to Delinquency   This construct is based on the Attitude Toward Delinquency Scale and made from nine items for the youngest cohort at waves A, C, and E, and from 11 items for the youngest cohort at waves G through T and the oldest cohort at waves A, C, E, and G through M. Age block constructs were created by calculating the mean of all valid waves in each block.

Likelihood of Getting Caught   This construct is made from the scale of the same name, consisting of ten questions asking the youth to judge the likelihood that he would be caught by the police if he committed specific delinquent acts. This construct was made for the youngest cohort at waves C, E, G, J, L, N, P, and R, and the oldest cohort at waves A, C, E, G, and M. Age block constructs were created by calculating the mean of all valid waves in each block.

Age Left Home   This construct indicates the age at which youths in the oldest cohort first lived independently from parents or other adult caretakers. Those who were living independently at wave K or M were asked how old they were when they first moved out of the parental home.

Life Skills   This construct is made for the oldest cohort from wave G on. It includes four items from the Work/Skills Questionnaire about the youth's ability to cook, repair clothing, do laundry and fix electrical things. Age block constructs were created by calculating the mean of all valid waves in each block.

Liking of Adults   This construct is made for the oldest cohort from wave G on, based on the School/Religion/Resources Questionnaire item about the number of relatives he liked. The age block construct was the mean of the applicable valid waves. Age block constructs were created by calculating the mean of all valid waves in each block.

Job Skills   This construct is made for the oldest cohort from wave G on. It included items from the Work/Skills Questionnaire about the youth's skills that he felt might get him a job. Age block constructs were created by calculating the mean of all valid waves in each block.

Getting a Job   This construct sums up resources, such as family members who might give the youth a job or adults who might write letters of recommendation. Age block constructs were created by calculating the mean of all valid waves in each block.

Attitude to Substance Use   This construct is based on the youth's judgments of the acceptability of behaviors related to illicit drug use. For the youngest cohort at waves A, C, and E, it was made from three items from the Attitude To Delinquent Behavior Scale: drinking alcohol, smoking marijuana, and sniffing glue. At waves G through T for the youngest cohort and waves A, C, E, and G through M for the oldest cohort, it was made from four items from the scale: drinking alcohol, smoking marijuana, using hard drugs, and selling hard drugs. Age block constructs were created by calculating the mean of all valid waves in each block.

Youth Physical Development/Problems

Table 3.5 summarizes the youth physical development and physical problem constructs.

Perinatal Problems   This construct is made from the Birth and Development Questionnaire completed by the caretaker at wave C only. It uses questions concerning the length of labor, type of delivery, birth complications, birth weight, prematurity, and whether the baby stayed in the hospital longer than his mother did. Labor length was considered problematic if it was less than three hours or more than 20 hours. Type of delivery was considered problematic if it was breech or cesarean. Birth complications that were considered problematic were oxygen deprivation and severe jaundice. Birth weights of less than 53 ounces were considered problematic. Birth was considered premature if it occurred more than 20 days before the due date. The score was the total number of problems.

Table 3.5 Physical Development/Problems

	Childhood		Adolescence	
	Middle	Late	Early	Late
Average Ages	*7–9*	*10–12*	*13–16*	*17–19*
Perinatal Problems	Y	—	O	—
Prenatal Problems	Y	—	O	—
Mother Smoking during Pregnancy	Y	—	O	—
Mother Using Alcohol during Pregnancy	Y	—	O	—
Pubertal Development	—	Y	Y	—
Serious Injuries	Y	Y	Y/O	O
Victim of Violence (Child)	—	Y	Y/O	O
Victim of Theft (Child)	—	Y	Y/O	O

Notes: Y = youngest cohort; O = oldest cohort.

Prenatal Problems This construct is made from the Birth and Development Questionnaire completed by the caretaker at wave C only. It uses questions concerning maternal weight gain, medication use, alcohol consumption, illicit drug consumption, and cigarette smoking during pregnancy. Weight gain was considered problematic if it was more than 40 pounds. Use of medications other than vitamins, acetaminophen, or Bendectin was considered problematic. Alcohol consumption was considered problematic if it exceeded one drink per week. The score was the total number of problems.

Mother Smoking during Pregnancy This construct is positive if the youth's biological mother smoked tobacco while pregnant with the youth. It was made from a single item of the Birth and Development Questionnaire. Although this information was included in the prenatal problems construct, it was analyzed separately as well.

Mother Using Alcohol during Pregnancy This construct is positive if the youth's biological mother used alcohol while pregnant with the youth. It was made from a single item of the Birth and Development Questionnaire. Although this information was included in the prenatal problems construct, it was analyzed separately as well.

Pubertal Development This construct is based on youths' and caretakers' reports of the youths' progress in puberty. Each informant rated the youth's growth in height, growth of facial hair, growth of body hair, skin problems, and voice change, on a 4-point scale from "not yet begun" to "seems completed." This construct was made for the youngest cohort at waves H through T. The oldest cohort was not asked about puberty because they were already pubescent at the beginning of the study. Age block constructs were set to the highest value (most advanced development) reported during the waves in each block.

Serious Injuries This construct counts the total number of severe cuts, severe burns, head injuries, internal injuries, and broken bones the youth sustained during the assessment period. Data came from the Family Health Questionnaire completed by the caretaker at early waves and the Participant Health Questionnaire completed by the youth at later waves. This construct was available only once a year during the six-month assessments. Wave A was not used because it did not distinguish between injuries in the previous year and injuries earlier in life. Age block constructs were created by calculating the mean of all valid waves in each block.

Victim of Violence This construct measures the total number of times the youth reported being a victim of intentional injury during the assessment period. It was available from wave G on. Age block constructs were created by calculating the mean of all valid waves in each block.

Victim of Theft This construct measures the total number of times the youth reported being a victim of theft during the assessment period. It was available from wave G on. Age block constructs were created by calculating the mean of all valid waves in each block.

Family Functioning

For constructs concerning family functioning (see Table 3.6), the *caretaker* is the primary caretaker, the adult who has the most responsibility for the youth. This was the person who completed the caretaker portion of the interview. Most questionnaires completed by the youth asked about his mother (or female caretaker) and father (or male caretaker). When making constructs, we used the gender of the primary caretaker from the Demographic Questionnaire to determine which of the youth's responses pertained to the primary caretaker.

Persistence of Discipline This construct is made from four items from the caretaker's and five items from the youth's Discipline Scale, regarding the

Table 3.6 Family Functioning

	Childhood		Adolescence	
	Middle	Late	Early	Late
Average Ages	*7–9*	*10–12*	*13–16*	*17–19*
Family Interaction				
Persistence of Discipline	Y	Y	Y/O	—
Physical Punishment	Y	Y	Y/O	—
Child Maltreatment by Age 12	—	Y	O	—
Supervision	Y	Y	Y/O	—
Boy Not Involved	Y	Y	Y/O	—
Parental Reinforcement	Y	Y	Y/O	—
Caretaker Characteristics				
Parent Antisocial Attitude	Y	Y	Y/O	—
Parent Aspirations for Youth	—	Y	Y/O	—
Parental Stress	Y	Y	Y/O	—
Parent Alcohol Problem	Y	—	Y/O	—
Biological Father Behavior Problems	Y	—	O	—
Biological Parent Police Contact	Y	—	O	—

Notes: Y = youngest cohort; O = oldest cohort.

degree to which the caretaker persisted in disciplinary action toward the youth. Full-year and age block constructs were created by calculating the mean of all applicable valid waves.

Physical Punishment   This construct combines caretaker and youth reports from the Discipline Scale of whether the caretaker hit, slapped, or spanked the youth when he misbehaved. Full-year and age block constructs were created by calculating the mean of all applicable valid waves.

Child Maltreatment by Age 12   This construct covers all forms of substantiated maltreatment requiring the intervention of Children and Youth Services. In order to have a construct that was similar for the youngest and oldest cohort, we chose to use data up to age 12.

Supervision   This construct combines caretaker and youth reports of the extent of the caretaker's knowledge of the youth's activities. It was made from four items from each informant's Supervision/Involvement Scale. Full-year and age block constructs were created by calculating the mean of all applicable valid waves.

Youth Not Involved   This construct combines caretaker and youth reports of the degree to which the youth was involved in planning and participating in family activities. It was made from four items from each informant's Supervision/Involvement Scale. Full-year and age block constructs were created by calculating the mean of all applicable valid waves.

Parental Reinforcement   This construct combines caretaker and youth reports of the frequency of the caretaker's positive behaviors toward the youth, such as giving special privileges or compliments. It was made from the Positive Parenting Scale, using nine items from the caretaker and seven items from the youth. Full-year and age block constructs were created by calculating the mean of all applicable valid waves.

Caretaker Characteristics

Parent Antisocial Attitude   This construct summarizes the caretaker's opinions about whether it was acceptable for the youth to engage in antisocial behaviors, such as fighting and skipping school. It was made from 18 items from the Perceptions of Problem Behavior Questionnaire administered at waves A, G, P, and T. Age block constructs were created by calculating the mean of all valid waves in each block.

Parent Aspirations for Youth   This construct is based on the Expectations/ Aspirations Scale questions about the importance of 12 life goals for people in general. Goals included "finishing high school" and "having a good reputation in the community." This construct was made only at waves G, I, J, N, and R. Age block constructs were created by calculating the mean of all valid waves in each block.

Parental Stress This construct summarizes the caretakers' perceptions of their stress levels and ability to handle problems in the month prior to assessment. It was made from 14 items of the Perceived Stress Scale, such as, "You could not cope with all the things you had to do" and "You felt unable to control the important things in your life." Age block constructs were created by calculating the mean of all valid waves in each block.

Parent Alcohol Problem This construct summarizes a caretaker's behavior problems as a result of drinking, using 11 items such as "Have you lost a job due to your drinking?" and "Have you had traffic accidents due to your drinking?" If the youth had two adults in the home, the one with the more severe alcohol problem was used in this construct. It was made from lifetime retrospective data collected from the caretaker in the Alcohol/Drugs Parent Questionnaire at wave E for both cohorts and wave T for the youngest cohort.

Biological Father Behavior Problems This construct is positive if the biological father was living in the home and had ever sought help for behavior problems, or if he was not living in the home and had ever had behavior problems, as reported in the Family Health Questionnaire by the caretaker at wave A.

Biological Parent Police Contact This construct counts the total number of times the youth's biological mother and father were arrested or detained by police, using retrospective lifetime data collected from the caretaker at wave C.

Peer Behavior, School, Neighborhood, and Demographics
The first section of Table 3.7 summarizes the peer behavior constructs.
The construct, number of close friends, was removed because of low reliability. The following constructs were removed because of high intercorrelation with constructs that were retained: peer drug score, school motivation, old for grade level, and unemployed mother. The construct, unemployed father, was removed because of reduced number.

Peer Delinquency This construct, made from the scale of the same name, summarizes the participation of the youth's friends in various delinquent activities, such as stealing and vandalism. The youngest cohort rated five behaviors on a 3-point scale through wave F. The youngest cohort at later waves, and the oldest cohort at all waves, rated nine behaviors on a 5-point

Table 3.7 Peer Behavior, School, Neighborhood, and Demographics

	Childhood		Adolescence	
	Middle	**Late**	**Early**	**Late**
Average Ages	*7–9*	*10–12*	*13–16*	*17–19*
PEER BEHAVIOR				
Peer Delinquency	Y	Y	Y/O	O
Relationship with Peers	Y	Y	Y/O	—
Gets Along with Siblings	Y	Y	Y/O	O
SCHOOL				
Academic Achievement	Y	Y	Y/O	—
Attitude toward School	Y	Y	Y/O	—
Repeated Grade	Cumulative			
Youth Educational Level	—	—	—	O
NEIGHBORHOOD				
Neighborhood Impression	Y	Y	Y/O	O
Neighborhood Disadvantage (Census)	Y	—	O	—
DEMOGRAPHICS				
Participant Ethnicity	Y	—	O	—
Number of Biological Parents in Home	Y	Y	Y/O	O
Two or More Caretaker Changes by Age 10	—	Y/O	—	—
Age of Mother When Having Her First Child	—	Y	O	—
Family/Youth Socioeconomic Status	Y	Y	Y/O	O
Family/Youth on Welfare	Y	Y	Y/O	O
Family Size	Y	Y	Y/O	—
Small House	Y	Y	Y/O	—
Housing Quality	Y	Y	Y/O	—
Youth Living with Wife or Girlfriend	—	—	—	O
Youth in Military	—	—	—	O

Notes: Y = youngest cohort; O = oldest cohort.

scale. Full-year and age block constructs were created by calculating the mean of all applicable valid waves.

Relationship with Peers This construct is made from a single caretaker (CBC) item, a single teacher (TRF) item, and a single youth (YSR) item regarding the youth's tendency to get along with his peers. Full-year and age block constructs were created by calculating the mean of all applicable valid waves.

Gets Along with Siblings This construct combines youth's and caretaker's perceptions of how well the youth got along with other children in the household. Full siblings, half siblings, step-siblings, and any other children in the home (such as cousins or foster siblings) were considered. The youth rated each relationship on a 3-point scale, and the caretaker rated each on a 5-point scale. Youth ratings for all siblings were averaged together, and caretaker ratings for all siblings were averaged together. These two preliminary constructs then were adjusted to the same numerical range and combined. Age block constructs were created by calculating the mean of all valid waves in each block.

School
The second section of Table 3.7 summarizes constructs related to the youth's school performance and attitudes toward school.

Academic Achievement This construct combines the caretaker's (CBCL), teacher's (TRF), and youth's (YSR) evaluations of the youth's performance in reading, math, writing, and spelling; caretakers and youths also evaluated up to 3 other subjects. Performance was rated on a 4-point scale, ranging from "failing" to "above average." The TRF also offered the response "well above average," which was combined with "above average" before making the construct. The ratings of all subjects by all informants were averaged to create the construct. Full-year and age block constructs were created by calculating the mean of all applicable valid waves.

Attitude toward School This construct is made from seven questions related to the youth's feelings about and behavior in school, such as, "Do you think homework is a waste of time?" and "Do you care what teachers think of you?" These questions were asked in the introduction of the interview at wave A and in the School/Religion/Resources Questionnaire at waves G, I, J, L, N, P, R, and T. Age block constructs were created by calculating the mean of all valid waves in each block.

Repeated Grade This construct counts the number of grades repeated by a youth over his educational career. Youths who were older than 6 in first grade or 12 in seventh grade on September 1 of the school year when the screening interview took place were considered to have repeated one grade prior to wave A. For each subsequent school year, if a youth's teacher (TRF) gave an affirmative answer to the question, "Is he repeating a grade this year?" the construct's value increased by one. When a school year comprised two 6-month waves, the teacher's report from the first wave was used; if the first wave was missing, the report from the second wave was used.

Youth Educational Level This construct indicates the highest level of school the youth had reached: elementary school, middle school, some high school, high school diploma or some post-secondary education. This construct was made for the oldest cohort at waves K and M. The age block construct is the higher of the two scores.

Neighborhood

The third section of Table 3.7 contains neighborhood constructs derived from the participants as well as from the U.S. Census.

Neighborhood Impression This construct is a summary assessment of the quality of the neighborhood in which the youth lived at the time of the interview. It includes 17 items regarding the prevalence of abandoned buildings, unemployment, racial tension, and various criminal activities. Data came from the Neighborhood Questionnaire completed by the caretaker, except at waves K and M, when it was completed by the youth. This construct was made only once a year during the 6-month assessments. Age block constructs were created by calculating the ratio of positive scores to total valid scores across waves in each block.

Neighborhood Disadvantage (Census) This construct is made from 1990 U.S. Census data on the neighborhood in which the youth resided at screening. The youth's address was used to determine his census tract, and then the tracts were matched to neighborhoods. A factor analysis was done on census variables, forming a construct made up of single-parent households, median income, families below the poverty line, families on public assistance, unemployed adults, and percentage of African American residents (Wikström & Loeber, 2000).

Demographics

The large amount of demographic information gathered in the study is summarized in the constructs of the fourth section of Table 3.7.

Participant Ethnicity This construct is based on data from the Demographic Questionnaire completed by the caretaker at screening. The distribution of ethnicity is as follows: youngest cohort: 41.4% Caucasian, 56.3% African American, 0.4% Hispanic, 1.0% Asian, 0.8% mixed race, and 0.2%

American Indian; oldest cohort: 42.1% Caucasian, 55.5% African American, 0.2% Hispanic, 0.4% Asian, and 1.8% mixed race. The Participant Ethnicity construct divides youths into two racial groups: *Caucasian* includes those of European and Asian ancestry, and *African American* includes those of African, Hispanic, American Indian, and mixed ancestry. It should be noted that there were extremely few youth with Hispanic, American Indian, or mixed ancestry; rather than omitting these participants, they were included in the African American category.

Number of Biological Parents in Home This construct categorizes the youth's living situation according to how many biological parents lived in the home. Categories were two biological parents, one biological parent, and no biological parents at home. Full-year constructs were set to the smaller number of biological parents reported in the two six-month waves. Age block constructs were created by determining the response given in the majority of waves in each block; if there was no majority, each block construct was set to the smallest number of biological parents among the tied scores. Data came from the Demographic Questionnaire completed by the caretaker at earlier waves and the Participant Demographics Questionnaire completed by the youth at later waves.

Two or More Caretaker Changes by Age 10 This construct is positive if the caretaker reported more than one change in the people caring for the youth from the time of his birth to his 10th birthday. The female adult most involved in his care was considered the female caretaker, and the male adult most involved was considered the male caretaker. This information was taken from the Caretaker History Questionnaire at wave G.

Age of Mother When Having Her First Child This construct indicates the age of the youth's biological mother when her first child (whether or not it was the participant) was born. The mother's age was trichotomized into three categories: ages 12–17 (called *young mother*), ages 18–22, and ages 23–37 (called *older mother*). This construct was made only at wave G, the only wave at which the necessary data were collected in the Demographic Questionnaire completed by the caretaker.

Family/Youth Socioeconomic Status This construct measures the socioeconomic status (SES) of the youth's family by applying the Hollingshead (1975) index of social status to data from the Demographic Questionnaire completed by the caretaker. The scale value for occupational prestige was multiplied by 5, and the scale value for educational level was multiplied by 3; the two numbers were then added together to create one SES score for the female caretaker and one SES score for the male caretaker. The family construct was equal to the highest score attained between the two caretakers or to the score attained by a single caretaker. Six-month waves were averaged together to create one-year constructs. Age block constructs were set to the highest SES found across the waves in each block. Beginning at wave G for youths who were no longer living with a caretaker, and beginning at wave K for all youths in the oldest cohort, a Participant SES construct was made using data on the youth's own education and occupation. The age block construct is the higher of the two wave scores.

Family/Youth on Welfare   This construct is positive if anyone in the youth's household had received public assistance during the previous year. It was based on the Financial Information Questionnaire completed by the caretaker. This construct was made only once a year during the six-month assessments. Beginning at wave G for youths who were no longer living with a caretaker, and beginning at wave K for all youths in the oldest cohort, the Work/Skills Questionnaire assessed whether the youth was receiving public assistance. Age block constructs were created by calculating the ratio of positive scores to total valid scores across waves in each block.

Family Size   This construct is the youth's report of the total number of children under 18 years old, other than himself, living in his house at the time of the interview. Age block constructs were created by calculating the mean of all valid waves in each block.

Small House   This construct is positive if the number of rooms in the youth's home, including kitchen and bathrooms, was fewer than six. It is made from a single item on the Financial Information Questionnaire completed by the caretaker. Age block constructs were created by calculating the ratio of positive scores (i.e., less than six rooms) to total valid scores across waves in each block.

Housing Quality   This construct summarizes the interviewer's assessment of the youth's home. It is made from eight items related to the structural condition of the home, visible signs of deterioration, and cleanliness. Full-year and age block constructs were created by calculating the mean of all applicable valid waves.

Youth Living with Wife or Girlfriend   This construct was made from Participant Demographic Questionnaire data from the oldest cohort at waves K and M. A participant is given a positive score per age block if he had lived with a wife or girlfriend during that time.

Youth in the Military   This construct is based on the youth's address and notes made by the interviewer when attempting to locate the youth. Military enlistment first occurred in the oldest cohort at wave I. A participant was given a positive score per age block if he had been in the military at any time during the age block.

The following constructs were removed because of high intercorrelations with other constructs that were retained: conduct disorder DSM III-R diagnosis; oppositional defiant disorder DSM III-R diagnosis; oppositional defiant disorder symptom score; ADHD DSM III-R diagnosis; disruptive disorder diagnosis; hyperactivity/impulsivity/attention problems; nonphysical aggression; cruelty; unaccountability; untrustworthiness; lack of guilt; manipulativeness; and suspension from school.

Note

1. Of these, sexual coercion and rape (serious violence); stealing things worth more than $5 and dealing in stolen goods (moderate theft); and auto theft (serious theft) are available at SRD waves only.

Part II
The Epidemiology of Violence, Serious Theft, Substance Use, Drug Dealing, and Gang Membership

Four
The Age-Crime Curve in Reported Offending

DAVID P. FARRINGTON, ROLF LOEBER,
AND DARRICK JOLLIFFE

One of the most consistent findings across studies on offending in different countries is the unimodal age-crime curve (Farrington, 1986; Laub & Sampson, 2003; Tremblay & Nagin, 2005) showing that the prevalence of offenders is low in late childhood and early adolescence, peaks in middle to late adolescence, and decreases subsequently (see Figure 4.1). The age-crime curve incorporates several basic criminal career parameters (Blumstein, Cohen, Roth, & Visher, 1986), including prevalence, frequency, age of onset, duration, and age of desistance. Most of the studies on the age-crime curve have been based on official records, which often underestimate the number of delinquent individuals and the frequency of offending, and hence, the height and probably also the shape of the age-crime curve. Therefore, it is important to examine the curve in light of more comprehensive information, such as that based on self-reports of offending and, in our case, complemented by reports from parents and teachers.

The age-crime curve is not invariant, but differs depending on characteristics of offenses and offenders. For instance, serious violence tends to peak later than serious theft in adolescence, and hence there are different age-crime curves underlying each. Also, the criminal propensity of successive age cohorts is not necessarily the same, with more individuals in some age cohorts being delinquent, and over a larger number of years (i.e., with a higher duration), than individuals in other age cohorts (see, e.g., Collishaw, Maughan, Goodman, & Pickles, 2004; Cook & Laub, 2002; Farrington, 1986). This is an important topic because age-crime curves of successive age cohorts are the constituents of secular crime waves. For instance, if there are later age cohorts whose levels of offending are higher than those of earlier age cohorts, then there will likely be an increase in the community level of crime. The number of calendar years of high crime will depend partly on the number of age cohorts with above-average levels of offending. As we will see later, variations in the age-crime curve for different age cohorts are also important because they require differential explanations to account for age differences in onset

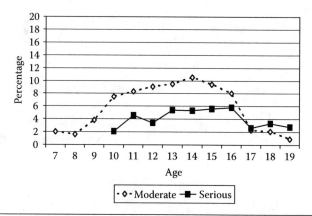

Figure 4.1 Annual Prevalence of Reported Violence (Youngest Cohort)

(i.e., the upslope of the curve) and desistance (i.e., the downslope of the curve). As Farrington (1986) has stressed, longitudinal studies have the great advantage of avoiding the problem of selection effects that often occur in cross-sectional data when different birth cohorts are studied at different ages. In this case, age differences are confounded with other differences between birth cohorts. No previous study has constructed age-crime curves based on a prospective longitudinal survey with repeated, uninterrupted measurements.

One hypothesis about the age-crime curve is that under conditions of high community crime, young people will offend at a higher rate, and on average will start their delinquency career earlier, than those exposed to lower levels of community crime. However, our earlier research (Wikström & Loeber, 2000) has shown that high- and low-crime areas are likely to differ in the proportion of late-onset offenders. Thus, we expect that the age-crime curve for those boys who grew up in a period of high community crime will be different in two ways from the age-crime curve of boys who grew up under more favorable conditions. First, the curve will reach a higher level, reflecting the higher proportion of youth engaging in offending. Second, the curve will have a broader base (increasing earlier and decreasing later) and the downward slope will be later (delinquency careers will be longer lasting) than for a cohort of boys who grew up at a time of lesser community crime.

Researchers have not been in agreement about whether the prevalence of offending is correlated over age with the frequency of offending (see, e.g., Blumstein et al., 1986), and whether as the prevalence increases so does the frequency (that is, in the upslope of the age-crime curve). Conversely, when the prevalence of offending decreases, does the frequency of offending also decrease (in the downslope of the age-crime curve)? Yet, research on the frequency of offending at different ages has been scarce (see, e.g., Barnett, Blumstein, & Farrington, 1987; Loeber & Le Blanc, 1990; Loeber & Snyder, 1990).

We are also interested in the relationships between key criminal career parameters, such as the age of onset and the duration of offending (for recent overviews, see Piquero, Farrington, & Blumstein, 2003, 2007). We particularly want to investigate the replicability of previous findings that early onset—when compared to late onset—of offending is associated with a longer criminal career (e.g., Loeber & Farrington, 2001) and later desistance from offending, and to determine whether this association applies to both violence and theft. In addition, we can examine whether there are developmental sequences in offending patterns in which one type of crime tends to precede or follow another type.

Very few studies have focused on the duration of offending (Kazemian & Farrington, 2006). This is an important topic because we need to know how long people tend to commit offenses and whether the duration of their criminal careers varies according to the presence of violence or theft, and whether it varies depending on the seriousness of delinquent acts. In a broader but related perspective we need to know whether developmental aspects of violence should be studied separately from those of theft. If the parameters of prevalence, frequency, onset, and duration are similar across violence and theft, then it is sufficient to use a total delinquency score as an outcome. However, if violence and theft differ substantially on these parameters, this will have major theoretical and practical implications (e.g., changes in the manifestations of crime with development, when violent or theft offenders are likely to outgrow offending, and offense specialization, which is reviewed in Chapter 5).

Definitions of criminal career terms can be found in Table 1.1 (see Chapter 1). For example, *prevalence* refers to the proportion of boys who commit an offense during a certain time period (herein, at each age). Frequency refers to the annual rate of offending by those who are offenders (also called *lambda* by Blumstein et al., 1986). The age of onset is the age at which the first offense is committed. Cumulative onset shows the emergence of new offenders at different ages. Here, *duration* refers to the number of years that individuals offend. *Persistence* refers to the proportion of offenders who continue to offend over different age blocks: middle childhood (ages 7–9), late childhood (ages 10–12), early adolescence (ages 13–16), late adolescence (ages 17–19), and early adulthood (ages 20–25).

As detailed in Chapter 3, self-report information was obtained in the Self-Reported Antisocial Behavior Scale (SRA) up to wave G for the youngest cohort (approximately age 10) and in the Self-Reported Delinquency Scale (SRD) for the youngest cohort after wave G, and for the oldest cohort. Information from the parents about the boy's offending was obtained from an extended version of the Child Behavior Checklist that included the SRD items. Information from the teachers about the boy's offending was obtained from an extended version of the Teacher Report Form that included the SRD items. Information about the frequency of offending was only obtained in the SRD.

Violence and theft were divided into the following levels of seriousness, which reflect steps in the overt and the covert pathways (see Loeber, Wung, et al., 1993; Loeber, DeLamaire, 1998, p. 53; and Wolfgang, Figlio, Tracy, and Singer, 1985, for justification)[1]:

Violence

Moderate: Gang fighting.
Serious: Robbery, attacking to hurt or kill, or forced sex.

Theft

Minor: Stealing outside the home, or shoplifting.
Moderate: Stealing a bicycle or skateboard from the street, stealing things worth more than $5 from the store, joyriding, purse snatching, stealing from a car, or dealing in stolen goods.
Serious: Breaking and entering, or auto theft.

Please note that to avoid cluttering the text with statistical details, we provide *p*-values only for statistically significant results. Details of individual statistical tests are obtainable from the senior author. Also, the results of the following analyses are not based on weighted data because this made very little difference to the results and allowed us to better describe the numbers of individuals with different combinations of career features (see further justification in the afterword to this chapter). Analyses of criminal career parameters that follow are based on information obtained from youths, their caretakers, and their teachers (the exception is frequency data, which are based on self-reports only). The joint report by a boy, his caretaker, and his teacher is called *reported offenses* and will focus on different seriousness levels of violence and theft, respectively, because age of onset, prevalence, frequency, and duration tend to be different for less serious—compared to more serious—forms of offenses. Much of the data reported in this chapter is based on yearly measurements, but in the case of frequency of offending it is based on age block data, which has been explained in Chapter 2 and is summarized below.

Criminal career information based on official records of offending is summarized in Chapter 5. In that chapter, we will also report on an "all-source" measure of offending, which combines information from the youth, parent, and teacher with convictions for offenses derived from court records. This chapter does not deal with individual differences in criminal careers and the extent to which empirical distinctions can be made among offenders in terms of the development of their offending (which will be the focus of Chapter 8). Instead, this chapter first focuses on the age-crime curve by describing prevalence and frequency, onset and duration, and persistence of violence and theft. It then summarizes similarities and differences between the development of violence and theft. Finally, it presents a brief summary of differences between the two age cohorts.

Prevalence and Frequency of Violence and Theft

We will address the following questions about the prevalence and frequency of violence and theft from ages 7 to 25:

What is the prevalence of different seriousness levels of violence and theft at different ages?

How does the frequency of violent and theft offending (at different levels of seriousness) vary with age?

What does the age-crime curve look like when based on longitudinal, repeated assessments?

In what respects does the age-crime curve show cohort differences?

Prevalence of Violence

Our results show that the prevalence of moderate and serious violence at each age peaks in early adolescence (ages 13–16) but, as expected, the prevalence is higher for moderate than for serious offending. This is shown in Figure 4.1 for the youngest cohort between ages 7 and 19. Reported serious violence (robbery, attacking to hurt, kill, or forced sex) peaked at ages 13–16 (5–6%), and then declined to 2% or less at ages 17–19. For moderate violence (gang fighting), the pattern of peaking and declining was broadly similar but at a higher prevalence, which was highest at ages 10–16, peaking at age 14 (11%). After that, prevalence declined to approximately 3% at ages 17–19.

How do the results compare with those of the oldest cohort, who as we pointed out in Chapter 1, grew up at a time when community crime levels were higher? Figure 4.2 shows the prevalence of levels of violence for that cohort between ages 13 and 25. Serious violence was highest at ages 18–19 (11%) but then decreased dramatically to 2% by age 22 and remained at this level through age 25. Moderate violence was also high at ages 14–15 (17%) and subsequently decreased steadily. Thus, moderate and serious violence peaked in early adolescence (as was the case for the youngest cohort), but the oldest and not the youngest cohort experienced another peak in serious violence in late adolescence, possibly indicating the prelude to a longer criminal career for the oldest cohort.

Comparisons of offending levels between the youngest and oldest cohorts can be flawed because they were not measured over the same age period. Instead, it is more useful to compare the two cohorts for the age period of measurement that they share—that is, from ages 13 to 19. A comparison of Figures 4.1 and 4.2 show substantially higher levels of violence in the oldest—compared to the youngest—cohort at similar ages. At ages 13 to 15, the prevalence of moderate violence was about two-thirds higher for the oldest

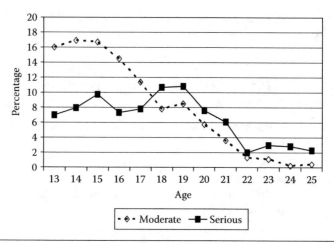

Figure 4.2 Annual Prevalence of Reported Violence (Oldest Cohort)

cohort (16–17%, versus about 10% for the youngest cohort); these differences were statistically significant for each of the ages (p = .02 to .001). Also, the prevalence of serious violence in the oldest cohort at ages 13–16 was about one-third higher for the oldest cohort (about 8% vs. less than 6% for the youngest cohort), but this was only statistically significant at age 15 (p = .02). Cohort differences in the upslope (i.e., onset) of the age-crime curve could not be examined fully due to left-hand censoring in the oldest cohort, because the assessments only started at age 13 (compared to age 7 for the youngest cohort). Data from the youngest cohort shows that the prevalence of moderately serious violence started to climb after age 8, whereas the prevalence of serious violence started to increase 2 years later, after age 10.

The downslope of the age-crime curve is more comparable between the two cohorts. The oldest cohort outgrew moderate violence at a much slower pace than did the youngest cohort, reaching a prevalence of about 2% by age 22, compared to age 17 for the youngest cohort. This 5-year delay was also evident for serious violence, which reached about 2% for the oldest cohort by age 22, compared to that level by age 17 for the youngest cohort.

We know from prior studies that the onset of less serious forms of offenses tends to precede the onset of more serious forms of offenses (see, e.g., Loeber, Wung, et al., 1993). This is reflected in prevalence data, which is most obvious for the youngest cohort (see Figure 4.1), showing that the upslope of the age-crime curve occurs earlier for moderate violence than it does for serious violence. Researchers are more in disagreement about the timing of decreases of different seriousness levels of offending. For example, Loeber and Le Blanc (1990) have hypothesized that decreases in serious forms of offenses precede decreases in less serious crime. However, our results (in Figures 4.1–4.2) show something that we have never seen referred to in the literature—namely, that the decrease in moderate and serious violence is much more synchronous (visible for the youngest and oldest cohorts; see Figures 4.1–4.2) than what we had expected. This was true for both the youngest and oldest cohorts, even though the decrease took place much earlier for the youngest cohort. We are currently following up the youngest cohort, which eventually can inform us as to whether the downslope of the age-crime curve is maintained for this cohort past age 19.

Prevalence of Theft

How do the results on the prevalence of violence compare with those on theft? First, does the prevalence of theft of different seriousness levels peak at the same age? Figure 4.3 shows the annual prevalence of levels of theft for the youngest cohort between ages 7 and 19. The prevalence of minor theft (stealing outside home or shoplifting) was stable between ages 7 and 13 at about 25%, peaked at 28% by age 14, and then decreased steadily to 5% by age 19. The prevalence of moderate theft (more serious stealing) was stable at about 7% between ages 7 and 10, after which the prevalence increased in a linear fashion to peak by ages 14–15 (19%), subsequently decreasing to 6% by age 19.

In comparison, the prevalence of serious theft (breaking and entering or auto theft) was very low (about 1%) in middle childhood (ages 7–10), after which it increased to a peak at ages 14–17, at 4–6%. Subsequently, the prevalence of serious theft decreased to 1% by age 19. As expected, the prevalence of theft varied by seriousness, with the least serious forms of theft being the most prevalent and the most serious forms of theft being the least common (which has been observed in several other studies cited; e.g., Loeber & Le Blanc, 1990). However, the differences in prevalence between the different forms of theft

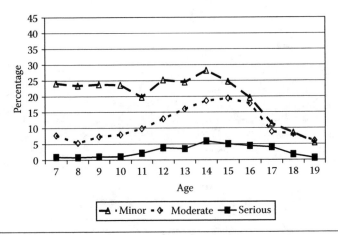

Figure 4.3 Annual Prevalence of Reported Theft (Youngest Cohort)

were greatest at younger ages (ages 7–15) but decreased afterward and became relatively small between ages 17 and 19.

Where do the results reflect the typical age-crime curve, and where do they not? The results show that the curve is most clearly visible for moderate theft and less clearly visible for serious theft (see Figure 4.3). However, minor theft does not show the typical age-crime curve. In the case of minor theft, the problem was left-hand censoring, and it was not clear when that behavior increased prior to age 7.

What can be learned from the prevalence data for theft in the oldest cohort (see Figure 4.4)? The prevalence of minor theft decreased steadily from a high at 42% by age 13 to a low of 1% by age 25. The prevalence of moderate theft increased to a peak in the oldest cohort by age 15 (32%) before decreasing gradually between ages 15 and 25, reaching a low of 4% by age 25. The prevalence of serious theft at ages 13–15 hovered around 8–11%, and then gradually decreased to 0 by age 25.

For theft, the results for both cohorts show a sequential onset of offending according to seriousness, but a synchronous decrease of different seriousness levels. This was most clearly visible for the onset of moderate compared to serious theft in the youngest cohort, which tended to occur in sequence, with moderate theft increasing prior to serious theft increasing. In contrast, much of the decrease in minor, moderate, and—to a slightly lesser extent—serious theft appeared synchronous in the same time frame for the youngest and oldest cohorts, although the decrease extended over many more years for the oldest cohort. These results suggest that processes associated with the onset of different seriousness levels of offending occur more in sequence, where processes associated with desistance across different forms of offenses and levels of seriousness occur more simultaneously.

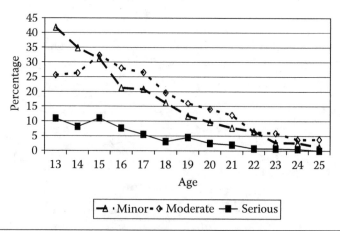

Figure 4.4 Annual Prevalence of Reported Theft (Oldest Cohort)

To what extent are there cohort differences in offending during the age period (13–19) that the two cohorts have in common? The results show that the prevalence of all categories of theft was higher for the oldest cohort, and that this was already apparent at the time of early adolescence. For instance, the prevalence of minor theft at age 13 was 42% for the oldest cohort, compared to 25% for the youngest cohort ($p < .0001$), while the prevalence of serious theft at that age was almost three times as high (11% vs. 4%; $p < .0001$). Second, the data show that the age by which the three levels of theft had all decreased to 6% or less was age 22 for the oldest cohort, compared to age 19 for the youngest cohort. Third, the decreasing prevalence slope was more gradual for the oldest cohort than it was for the youngest cohort. Specifically, decreasing prevalence of theft for the oldest cohort extended over a period of ten years (age 13 to at least age 23), while decreasing prevalence of theft for the youngest cohort took place over a time frame of only five years, concentrated in the ages 15–19.

Frequency of Violence

Trends in prevalence depend on whether individuals in a population commit at least a single offense in a measurement time frame. It is also important to investigate whether the frequency of offending changes over time, which takes into account those active offenders who commit multiple offenses in a given time frame. For this part of the results, we switch from a year-by-year presentation to age blocks (see the explanation in Chapter 2). The reason is that average offending rates by year tend to be quite variable and become somewhat clearer when aggregated across several years. The results also shed light on the controversial question of whether the age-crime curve also applies to frequency data. Note that the average frequencies are based on self-reports only, because parents and teachers were not asked to assess the frequency of offending by the boys. The average frequency of self-reported offending was obtained by dividing the number of offenses by the number of offenders in each age block, and then these frequencies were averaged over the ages included in each range to produce an annual frequency. Because frequency was derived from the SRD, it was not measured under age 10 (the SRA administered up to age 10 did not ask for frequency in numbers—only according to a categorical scale of "never," "once or twice," or "more often").

Figure 4.5 shows the average annual frequency of violent offending by those in the youngest cohort for different levels of violence and different age blocks (10–12, 13–16, and 17–19). The average annual frequency of moderate and serious violence increased over the three age blocks. A pattern more similar to the age-crime curve was observed for moderate and serious violence in the oldest cohort (see Figure 4.6), which peaked at about four offenses per offender per year during late adolescence (ages 17–19), before dropping in early adulthood (ages 20–25) to the level that was typical of early adolescence (ages 13–16).

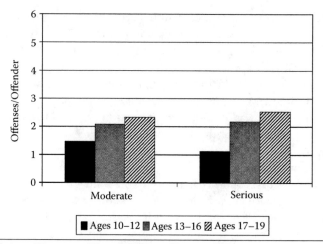

Figure 4.5 Annual Frequency of Reported Violence (Youngest Cohort)

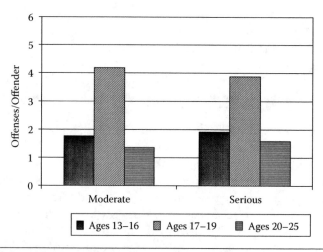

Figure 4.6 Annual Frequency of Reported Violence (Oldest Cohort)

Notably, even though the youngest and oldest cohorts demonstrated a similar frequency of moderate violence in early adolescence (2.1 vs. 1.8, n.s.), by late adolescence the frequency of moderate violence in the oldest cohort was double that in the youngest cohort (4.2 vs. 2.1, $p < .05$) and almost double for serious violence (3.9 vs. 2.5), but this did not reach statistical significance.

In summary, both cohorts committed a substantial level of violence, at a minimum average level of just under two violent offenses (either moderate or serious) per offender per year. Evidence was found for an age-crime curve in the frequency as well as the prevalence of violent offending, but only for the oldest cohort. For the comparable age blocks, the annual frequency of violence was substantially higher, especially in late adolescence for the oldest cohort. Thus, not only were there more violent offenders in the oldest cohort (see the discussion of prevalence, p. 79), but active offenders in that cohort also committed violence at a higher rate than in the youngest cohort.

Frequency of Theft

Figure 4.7 shows the average annual frequencies of different levels of theft in three age blocks (10–12, 13–16, and 17–19) for the youngest cohort. The annual frequency of theft increased up to early adolescence and then remained stable (or decreased) in late adolescence. Serious theft, surprisingly, had similar annual frequencies in early and late adolescence (about 2.1 to 2.4 offenses per offender). For all levels of theft there was evidence of an increase in frequency from late childhood to early adolescence, but this was only significant for moderate theft.

Figure 4.8 shows the average annual frequencies of theft for the oldest cohort across the age blocks. For minor, moderate, and serious theft, the frequency was highest in late adolescence (ages 17–19), at 3.5 to 5.4 offenses per offender. The frequency of serious theft was very low during early adulthood (ages 20–25), and there was only a small number of theft offenders during these ages. In summary, the annual frequency of all levels of theft increased between early and late adolescence, but not significantly. The decrease in frequency from late adolescence to early adulthood was significant for minor theft ($p < .02$) and serious theft ($p < .0001$).

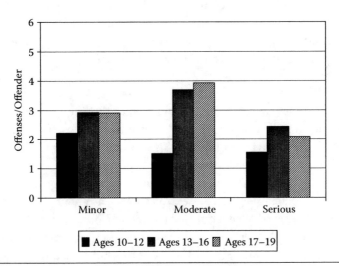

Figure 4.7 Annual Frequency of Reported Theft (Youngest Cohort)

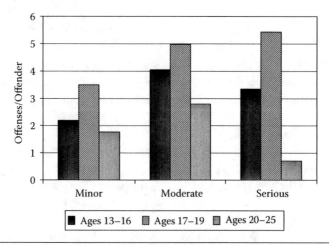

Figure 4.8 Annual Frequency of Reported Theft (Oldest Cohort)

A comparison of the oldest and youngest cohorts shows that the annual frequencies of minor and moderate theft in early adolescence were similar in both cohorts (about three offenses per offender). However, the annual frequencies of minor, moderate, and serious theft in late adolescence, and of serious theft in early adolescence, were higher in the oldest cohort than in the youngest cohort but reached statistical significance only for serious theft (5.4 vs. 2.1, $p < .01$).

Frequency of Violence and Theft Compared

A comparison of Figures 4.5 and 4.7 for the youngest cohort, and Figures 4.6 and 4.8 for the oldest cohort shows that the annual frequency of theft was slightly higher than that of violence (the exceptions were late adolescence in the youngest cohort, and early adolescence in the oldest cohort, when the annual frequencies of violence and theft were similar).

Cumulative Onset of Violence and Theft

Prevalence curves are not the best tool with which to demonstrate by what age the majority of the eventual delinquent individuals are most prone to become engaged in certain types of offenses. This issue is important because often researchers and practitioners think of onset as a dichotomy—as, for example, postulated by Moffitt (1993) in her distinction between early-onset, life-course persistent delinquents and late-onset, and adolescence-limited offenders. We propose that onset is much more gradual and much less abrupt than posited by Moffitt, and that there are more than two onset categories. In addition, we posit that what is important is the age at which the majority of the eventual offenders have started offending. Such knowledge will highlight the risk period in which most offenders emerge, which means the risk period of development on which preventive and remedial interventions should be focused.

Cumulative onset curves are also important because they may reveal differences between cohorts in the length of the time frame in which the onset of, for example, violence tends to take place. It can be expected that youth living in high-crime time periods will have a longer time frame during which onset occurs than youth living in low-crime time periods, and will make up a higher proportion of late-onset offenders (e.g., between ages 14 and 18) than those youth who grow up in relatively low-crime time periods. In addition, cumulative graphs can reveal by what age most serious offenders have emerged, indicating the risk window of the onset of serious offending.

One of the weaknesses of cumulative onset curves is that they may suggest, but not prove, that the onset of one type of offending precedes the onset of another type. A better way of addressing the sequential aspects of offense types is to ask what proportion of offenders who engaged in two types of offending had type X before type Y, compared to the reverse order or their co-occurrence within the same time frame. Earlier research on developmental pathways indicates that less serious forms of offending tend to start before more serious forms (Le Blanc, Côté, & Loeber, 1991; Loeber, Wung, et al., 1993, Loeber, DeLamaire, et al., 1999; Tolan, Gorman-Smith, & Loeber, 2000).

The exploration of developmental sequences among offense types will help us to understand better to what extent individuals with a prior form of offending are likely to escalate to the next higher form of offending. To our knowledge, information about this type of forward probability is very scarce in the literature. Instead, we and others have published much more information about backward probabilities—namely, to what extent individuals who have reached a serious level of offending have displayed less serious forms of offending earlier in life (see, e.g., Loeber, Wung, et al., 1993). Although knowledge of backward probabilities is valuable for the identification of developmental pathways, we argue that knowledge of forward probabilities is in two ways important for tertiary prevention. First, forward probabilities tend to identify a group of youth that is at a high risk of escalating to serious offending. Second, this information constitutes one of the building blocks for screening devices to identify high-risk offenders at an early age. Forward probabilities also reveal that many offenders do not progress further in criminal careers.

This section on different aspects of the age of onset of offending addresses the following questions:

What is the cumulative onset of different levels of violence and theft by age 19 (youngest cohort) and age 25 (oldest cohort)?
What is the average age of onset of different levels of violence and theft?
Are there developmental sequences in different seriousness levels of offending?

What is the forward probability of individuals progressing from less to more serious forms of offending?

Cumulative Onset of Violence

Figures 4.9 and 4.10 show the cumulative onset of moderate and serious levels of reported violence for the youngest and oldest cohorts, respectively. Moderate violence was higher in the youngest cohort up to age 13, but higher in the oldest cohort from age 14 onward. Information was obtained prospectively at all ages from the repeated assessments for the youngest cohort. Prior to age 12, this information in the oldest cohort was obtained from retrospective questions (in the screening phase). Possibly because of this, the retrospectively reported cumulative onset of violence in the oldest cohort was very low up to age 11.

By age 19, 36% of the youngest cohort had committed moderate violence, which is significantly lower ($p < .001$) than the 49% for the oldest cohort at that age (for the oldest cohort, the prevalence of moderate violence remained high, at 51% by age 25).

The cumulative onset of serious violence was similar in the youngest and oldest cohorts up to age 14 (youngest 17%, oldest 19%), but by age 19 was almost twice as common in the oldest cohort (42% vs. 23%; $p < .0001$). Serious violence in the oldest cohort increased steadily from age 11 (4%) to age 19 (39%). The peak period of onset occurred between ages 10 and 16 for the youngest cohort, but between ages 10 to 20 for the oldest cohort (and thus, four years longer).

If we consider all of those who become violent at the latest age of measurement as 100%, what is the earliest age by which *most* of the violent youth have

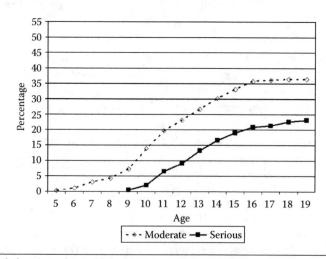

Figure 4.9 Cumulative Onset of Reported Violence (Youngest Cohort)

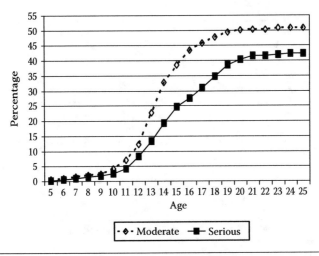

Figure 4.10 Cumulative Onset of Reported Violence (Oldest Cohort)

become apparent? By age 15 the majority of the eventually moderately violent boys had started this behavior (91% for the youngest cohort and 76% for the oldest cohort). By that same age, 82% of the eventually serious violent offenders in the youngest cohort had begun their serious violence, compared to 58% for the oldest cohort. Compared with the youngest cohort, more males in the oldest cohort started to commit moderate and serious violence between ages 15 and 18. Phrased differently, the onset window for moderate and serious violence was about three years longer (age 18 vs. age 15) for the oldest compared to the youngest cohort. The cohort difference is also shown by the fact that the proportion of late-onset offenders (defined as those with an onset between ages 14 and 18) was about twice as high in the oldest cohort.

Cumulative Onset of Theft

Figure 4.11 shows the cumulative onset of levels of theft for the youngest cohort, again based on prospective data. The results clearly show an ordering among the cumulative onset curves, with minor theft coming first, moderate theft next, and serious theft last. The cumulative onset (up to age 19) was highest for minor theft (72%), followed by moderate theft (57%) and serious theft (21%). In the oldest cohort (see Figure 4.12), the cumulative onset (up to age 25) was also highest for minor theft (79%), followed by moderate theft (76%), and serious theft (42%). As expected, the most serious level of theft was the least common.

In the youngest cohort, minor theft increased sharply (in a positively accelerating manner) from 17% at age 6 to 55% at age 10. Moderate theft increased steadily (in a linear manner) from age 6 (4%) to age 16 (53%), and serious theft increased from 1% at age 6 to 20% by age 17, after which it flattened out. The

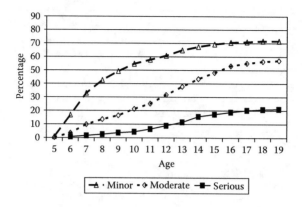

Figure 4.11 Cumulative Onset of Reported Theft (Youngest Cohort)

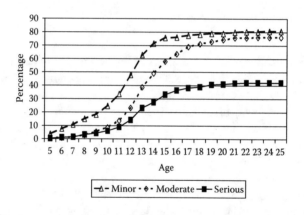

Figure 4.12 Cumulative Onset of Reported Theft (Oldest Cohort)

cumulative onset of lower levels of theft was much higher in the youngest than the oldest cohort up to age 13, probably because of the prospective information collected. Minor theft in the oldest cohort increased sharply from 18% at age 9 to 76% by age 15. Moderate theft also increased sharply in the oldest cohort from 14% at age 11 to 69% by age 17. The cumulative onset of serious theft was higher in the oldest cohort, increasing from 9% at age 11 to 36% by age 16.

The cumulative onset graphs also reveal by what age the majority of theft offenders had become apparent. In the youngest cohort, 90–93% of those who eventually committed minor theft already had become apparent by age 13. In contrast, 86–93% of the eventually moderate or serious theft offenders in that cohort had become apparent by age 16 (90% for the oldest cohort by age 17). These results show the developmental nature of increasing seriousness of theft with age, and the expanding populations of those engaged in minor, moderate, and serious theft at successive ages. The results when compared to the cumulative onset graphs for serious violence (Figures 4.9–4.10) underscore the fact that the risk window for serious theft was longer than that for violence—that is, the onset of theft started earlier and extended later, into late adolescence.

Average Ages of Onset of Violence

It might be expected that more serious levels of offenses would have later average ages of onset, and this was generally true. For violence in the youngest cohort, the mean ages of onset were 11.6 for moderate violence and 13.3 for serious violence, a statistically significantly difference ($p < .0001$). Similarly, for violence in the oldest cohort, the mean ages of onset were 13.9 for moderate violence and 15.1 for serious violence ($p < .001$).

Average ages of onset were higher in the oldest cohort, and not just because of the longer time frame. In the comparative age range (up to age 19) the mean age of onset in the oldest cohort was 13.7 for moderate violence and 14.6 for serious violence, compared with 11.6 and 13.3 in the youngest cohort. It seems likely that ages of onset were lower (and more accurate) in the youngest cohort because of the prospective questions. An alternative explanation is that, as shown above, the percentage of late-onset cases of violence (defined as those age 17 or older) was about twice as high in the oldest cohort, thereby increasing the average age of onset. Both explanations might be true.

Average Ages of Onset of Theft

As with violence, the average age of onset of theft was higher in the oldest cohort. In the youngest cohort, the mean ages of onset were 8.8 for minor, 11.7 for moderate, and 12.7 for serious theft, compared with 11.6 for minor, 13.8 for moderate, and 13.5 for serious theft in the oldest cohort. To compare the age range of the two cohorts, up to age 19 in the oldest cohort the mean ages of onset were 11.3 for minor, 13.4 for moderate, and 13.2 for serious theft. The results show that the age of onset of minor and moderate theft was earlier for the youngest cohort ($p < .0001$ and .001, respectively), but did not differ for serious theft. Again, it seems likely that ages of onset were lower (and more accurate) in the youngest cohort because of the prospective questions. On the other hand, this trend might be explained by the fact that the percentage of late-onset cases of serious theft (between ages 14 and 18) was about twice as high for the oldest cohort.

Are There Developmental Progressions in Different Severity Levels?

Violence

Table 4.1 shows how much the onset of one seriousness level coincides with, is followed by, or is preceded by the onset of the next seriousness level for boys who committed offenses of both levels of seriousness. In the youngest cohort, for boys who committed both moderate and serious violence, the mean age of onset was lower for moderate violence (11.6, compared with 13.2 for serious violence; $p < .0001$). Of 73 boys who committed both, it appeared more common for serious violence to be committed at a later age ($N = 42$; 57%) rather than at the same age ($N = 16$; 22%) or an earlier age ($N = 15$; 20%), but these differences did not reach statistical significance. Ages of onset between moderate serious violence were not significantly correlated ($r = .21$; $p = .079$).

In the oldest cohort, for boys who committed both moderate and serious violence, the mean age of onset was lower for moderate violence (14.2) compared with serious violence (15.1; $p < .01$). Of the 136 boys who committed both, it was more common for serious violence to be committed at a later age ($N = 68$; 50%) rather than at the same age ($N = 31$; 23%) or an earlier age ($N = 37$; 27%). However, the ages of onset between moderate and serious violence were not significantly correlated ($r = .15$; $p = .078$). The results on developmental progressions in different severity levels of violence further lend support to our pathway model (Loeber, Wung, et al., 1993).

Theft

Table 4.1 shows how much the onset of one seriousness level of theft coincides with, is followed by, or precedes the onset of the next seriousness level for boys who committed offenses of both levels of seriousness. In the youngest cohort, 69% ($N = 162$) of those who had committed both minor and moderate theft

Table 4.1 Onset of One Level of Offending versus Onset of Next Level of Offending (Youngest and Oldest Cohorts)

		Mean Age		Next Level (N)			
First Level	*Next Level*	*First*	*Next*	*Same*	*Earlier*	*Later*	*r*
		YOUNGEST COHORT					
Moderate Violence	Serious Violence	11.6	13.2	16	15	42	.21
Minor Theft	Moderate Theft	8.6	11.6	50	24	162	.32*
Moderate Theft	Serious Theft	11.1	12.7	27	12	53	.46*
		OLDEST COHORT					
Moderate Violence	Serious Violence	14.2	15.1	31	37	68	.15
Minor Theft	Moderate Theft	11.5	13.5	75	55	180	.37*
Moderate Theft	Serious Theft	12.7	13.4	57	38	81	.31*

Notes: N = number; *$p = .0001$.

started moderate theft after minor theft (and another 21%, $N = 50$, committed minor and moderate theft in the same time frame). Thus, the majority of boys who eventually committed minor and moderate theft followed a developmental sequence in which minor theft was a precursor to moderate theft. The figures were somewhat lower for the oldest cohort, but still in the same direction, and are more questionable because of retrospective recall of theft offenses prior to age 13. In both cohorts, only a minority (10% in the youngest cohort and 18% in the oldest cohort) showed the inverse sequence of committing moderate theft prior to minor theft.

Table 4.1 also shows whether there is a developmental sequence between moderate and serious theft. In the youngest cohort, 58% of those who eventually committed both moderate and serious theft first committed moderate theft and then followed with serious theft (46% in the oldest cohort). Another group started moderate and serious theft in the same time frame (29% in the youngest cohort and 32% in the oldest cohort). Only a modest proportion of boys showed the inverse order (serious theft followed by the onset of moderate theft), which amounted to 13% and 22% in the youngest and oldest cohorts, respectively. In summary, if boys engaged in different seriousness levels of theft, they tended to commit these offenses in a developmental sequence starting with less serious forms of theft and followed by more serious forms of theft (see also Kazemian & Farrington, 2005). Again, the results on developmental progressions in different severity levels of theft lend further support to our pathway model (Loeber, Wung, et al., 1993).

Developmental Sequences between Violence and Theft

Among the boys with reported serious violence and reported serious theft, which came first? In both cohorts, serious theft tended to occur first. Of 58 boys who committed both in the youngest cohort, 27 (47%) committed serious theft first, 19 committed serious violence first, and 12 committed serious theft and violence at the same age; for the boys who committed serious violence and serious theft, the mean age of onset was 12.7 for serious theft and 13.4 for serious violence, a nonsignificant difference. Of 108 boys who committed both in the oldest cohort, 58 (54%) committed serious theft first, 26 committed serious violence first, and 24 committed serious theft and violence at the same age; for these boys, the mean age of onset was 13.8 for serious theft and 15.0 for serious violence ($p < .006$). Thus, theft tended to precede violence, but the effect was larger for the youngest compared to the oldest cohort. We speculate that this has to do with a higher proportion of late-onset offenders in the oldest cohort who were engaged in violence but not in theft.

Forward Probability of Escalation in Seriousness of Offending

What is the likelihood that young offenders at a low seriousness level of offending escalate to more serious acts? Given that we found major cohort differences, is the forward probability of escalation higher in the oldest cohort, or is the eventual higher prevalence of serious offending in the oldest cohort more the result of a higher prevalence of low-level offenders when compared to the youngest cohort?

In the youngest cohort, the forward probability of moderately serious violent offenders progressing to serious violence was .25 (42/165), compared to .30 (68/223) in the oldest cohort, which was not a statistically significant difference. Thus, one-fourth to one-third of boys who had committed moderately serious violence progressed to serious violence later. We will discuss this finding once we have reported on the forward probabilities of different seriousness levels of theft.

Theft   What is the forward probability that youth who engaged in less serious forms of theft later committed more serious forms? There were a total of 336 boys in the youngest cohort who committed minor theft. The probability of minor thieves progressing to moderate theft was .48 (162/336). How does this compare with the oldest cohort? There were a total of 381 boys in the oldest cohort who committed minor theft. Of these, 180 progressed to moderate theft, which constitutes a very similar forward probability of .47 (180/381). Thus, despite prevalence differences in theft among the two cohorts, about half of the minor thieves in each cohort progressed to moderate theft at a later age (this was a nonsignificant difference between the two cohorts).

How do the cohorts compare in their forward progression from moderate to serious theft? There were a total of 261 boys in the youngest cohort who had an onset for moderate theft. The forward probability of these boys progressing to serious theft was .20 (53/261). The comparable forward probability for the oldest cohort was .23 (81/346). Thus, one in five of the boys with moderate theft progressed to serious theft across the two cohorts.

The results are intriguing in that the cohorts were very similar in their forward probabilities of minor thieves progressing to moderate theft, and moderate thieves progressing to serious theft. As mentioned, the cumulative onset of serious theft by age 19 was about twice as high in the oldest cohort. The cumulative onset was also higher for moderate theft. There are several reasons why such major cohort differences might occur. We can rule out forward probabilities because they were very similar across the cohorts. Another reason might be differences in the prevalence of less serious forms of theft across the cohorts. If there are more youth in one cohort who commit less serious forms of theft than in another cohort, then (given similar forward probabilities) we can expect that more youth in the first cohort will progress to serious theft. Figures 4.3 and 4.4 show that the prevalence of minor theft and of serious theft was substantially higher in the oldest cohort. Thus, prevalence differences among cohorts in serious forms of theft tend to emerge more as a result of differences in the base rate of less serious forms of theft than as a result of cohort differences in the forward probabilities of escalation from less to more serious forms of theft.

Violence   Our interpretation of the results on theft compare well with the results on the forward probabilities from moderate to serious violence. Across the two cohorts we found very similar forward probabilities for escalation from moderate to serious violence. However, by age 19, about twice as many of the young people in the oldest cohort had committed serious violence. This cohort difference could again be explained by the higher prevalence of moderately serious violence in the oldest cohort by age 13 (see Figures 4.1 and 4.2). The results suggest a cascading of different manifestations of offending over time. Once a cohort has a higher prevalence of less serious forms of offending in early adolescence, it is likely that such a cohort will end up having the highest prevalence of serious offending in late adolescence and probably into adulthood. Conclusions drawn from these findings will be summarized at the end of this chapter.

Information about the age window in which most of the violence emerged is potentially important for interventions. The results show that for the youngest cohort, the highest risk window of onset was between ages 7 and 15 for moderate violence and ages 10 and 15 for serious violence. The lower age limits of such a window could not be established for the oldest cohort, but the results show a larger risk window for the onset of moderate and serious violence in that cohort compared for the youngest cohort. This finding underscores how much violence reduction programs in the community can gain if the age-crime curve can be kept narrow (as in the youngest cohort) rather than broad (as in the oldest cohort). The results also indicate that some of the causes of emerging violence lie in childhood rather than in adolescence as is often assumed (see also Tremblay, Hartup, & Archer, 2005, who traced the onset of aggression to an earlier age). We will return to this point in Chapter 7, in which we will examine predictors of violence from middle childhood onward.

Duration and Persistence of Violence and Theft

Earlier in this chapter we demonstrated that the peak ages of violence and theft differed, but does this also imply that the duration of a violence career is longer than that of a theft career? If so, does this mean that the stability of violence is higher than that of theft? If this is the case, then it could have implications for our understanding of what drives the duration of delinquency careers, and would also have implications for theories of delinquency.

Since, as we saw, less serious forms of offending tend to emerge prior to more serious forms, does this mean that the duration of these less serious forms of offending is longer than that of more serious forms? Could it be instead that desistance takes place earlier for less serious forms, thereby making the duration of less serious forms of offending about the same as for more serious forms?

There is a consensus in the research findings that an early age of onset predicts a longer delinquency career (Farrington, Loeber, Elliott, et al., 1990; Loeber & Farrington, 2001). Does this apply to violence and theft as well? In this section we address the next set of questions that are relevant to the duration and persistence of serious offending:

What is the average duration of careers of violence and theft, and does duration differ for different offense seriousness levels?
How stable is offending?
How well does the age of onset predict the duration of theft and violence careers?

Table 4.2 shows the average duration of violence and theft careers within each level of seriousness.

Violence

In Table 4.2, duration was computed as the time period between the first and last offense (including durations of zero for those who offended in only one year). For the youngest cohort, the average career durations were 2.1 years for moderate violence, and 1.4 years for serious violence. The corresponding figures for the oldest cohort were 2.8 years for moderate violence, and 2.7 years for serious violence. Thus, the duration of moderate violence was approximately two years in both cohorts, while the duration of serious violence was about twice as long in the oldest cohort. It should be taken into account, however, that the oldest cohort had a larger window of opportunity to persist.

Was an early age of onset of violence, compared to a later age of onset, associated with a longer violence career? Table 4.2 shows that boys in the youngest cohort who first committed moderate violence between ages 7 and 9 had an average moderate violence career duration of 4.1 years, whereas boys in the youngest cohort who first committed moderate violence between ages 13 and 16 or ages 17 and 19 had an average moderate violence career duration of only 0.7 years. In general, for all seriousness levels of violence, the earlier the boy started his criminal career, the longer he continued offending.

Theft

The average duration of theft in the youngest cohort was 5.1 years for minor theft, 3.0 years for moderate theft, and 1.4 years for serious theft. The corresponding figures for the oldest cohort were 5.5 years for minor theft, 4.5 years for moderate theft, and 2.2 years for serious theft. The higher the seriousness level of theft, the shorter the duration of the theft career. This finding was similar across the two cohorts. Thus, in both cohorts, on average the duration of minor theft was the longest (about 5 years), and less serious offenses were

Table 4.2 Age of Onset versus Mean Duration (in Years) of Delinquency Careers (Youngest and Oldest Cohorts)

Age of Onset	Moderate Violence	Serious Violence	Minor Theft	Moderate Theft	Serious Theft
		YOUNGEST COHORT			
7–9	4.1	*	5.8	5.5	1.8
10–12	2.4	2.4	3.6	3.4	2.3
13–16	0.7	1.0	1.4	1.3	1.1
17–19	0.7	0.2	0.4	0.1	*
Total	2.1	1.4	5.1	3.0	1.4
		OLDEST COHORT			
7–9	9.7	8.4	9.5	9.5	7.0
10–12	4.0	5.8	5.7	6.9	3.5
13–16	2.5	2.5	3.1	4.0	1.8
17–19	1.3	1.5	1.2	1.5	0.5
20–25	0.5	0.21	0	0.5	0.5
Total	2.8	2.7	5.5	4.5	2.2

* Number too small to compute value.

characterized by longer criminal careers, probably because they had earlier ages of onset.

Was an early age of onset of theft, compared to a later age of onset, associated with a longer theft career? Table 4.2 shows the relationship between the age of onset and the average duration of theft within each level of seriousness. For example, boys in the youngest cohort who first committed moderate theft between ages 7 and 9 had an average moderate theft career duration of 5.5 years, whereas boys in the youngest cohort who first committed moderate theft between ages 13 and 16 had an average moderate theft career duration of only 1.3 years. The findings paralleled those for violence in that in general, for all seriousness levels of theft, the earlier the boy started his criminal career, the longer he continued.

We found that career duration was always longer in the oldest compared to the youngest cohort. How much was this a consequence of the longer follow-up of the oldest cohort (to age 25, compared with age 19 for the youngest)? Up to age 19 in the oldest cohort, the average career durations were 4.0 years for minor theft, 2.9 years for moderate theft, and 1.7 years for serious theft. These durations were comparable to those for the youngest cohort. Hence, controlling for time at risk (ages 13–19), theft career durations were similar for the youngest and oldest cohorts. The results show that the youngest and oldest cohorts did not differ in the duration of minor theft, but the oldest cohort had significantly longer durations of moderate and serious theft ($p < .0001$ and .005, respectively).

Summary of Key Findings

Violence and Theft

We found more differences than similarities between delinquency career parameters of violence and theft. Specifically, we found the following:

Prevalence

- In both cohorts, the prevalence of theft was much higher than the prevalence of violence. By age 19 about three-fourths of the young men in the youngest cohort had engaged in minor theft, compared to one-half who had engaged in moderate theft, and just under one-fifth who had engaged in serious theft. In comparison, violence was much less common: one-third of the boys had engaged in moderate violence and one-fifth had engaged in serious violence. Thus, only at the levels of serious theft and serious violence were similar percentages of boys involved in each, but in all other comparisons, theft was more common than violence.

The Age-Crime Curve

- Onset curves of violence and theft offending are gradual rather than abrupt, indicating a gradual emergence of offenders with age.
- The age-crime curve for prevalence could be best studied in the youngest cohort, and the results show that the age-crime curve applied to both violence and theft (the exception is minor theft, which is already high in childhood and early adolescence).
- The results show that violence and theft in the youngest cohort differed in the upslope of the age-crime curve (theft preceding violence), but overlapped much more in the downslope. The latter finding was replicated in the oldest cohort. Thus, the onset of theft and violence was much more in sequence (i.e., spread over time), whereas the decrease in theft and violence was much more synchronous (i.e., similar in time).

Frequency of Offending

- The annual frequency of theft was higher than that of violence for most of the age periods in both cohorts.
- In the youngest cohort, the annual frequency of serious violence doubled between ages 10 and 12 and between 17 and 19, and the annual frequency of moderate theft increased to a lesser extent. In contrast, the frequency of serious theft remained relatively stable.

Thus, the data show an increased frequency of serious violence in the age period 17–19, but not for serious theft. In the oldest cohort, the annual frequency of serious violence doubled between ages 13 and 16 and ages 17 and 19, while the frequency of serious theft also increased somewhat during that period, but fell sharply at ages 20–25. Compared to the age period 16–19, the proportional decrease was lower for violence than for theft in the age period 20–25. In summary, in the oldest cohort a shift took place, with frequent theft being more common in the early part of criminal careers, while frequent violence became more common in the later part of criminal careers.

- The frequency of offending largely followed an age-crime curve in the oldest but not in the youngest cohort.

Developmental Sequences in Offending
- Theft tended to precede violence, but the pattern was more common for the youngest cohort.
- The probability of progression to the next level of seriousness decreased with increasing seriousness. About half of the young men who committed minor theft progressed to moderate theft, and this was similar across the two cohorts. About one-fifth to one-quarter of young males who committed moderate forms of violence or theft progressed to serious violence or theft, respectively, and this was similar across the two cohorts. Thus, these forward probabilities did not indicate that escalation to serious forms of violence and theft was more common in the oldest cohort. Instead, it is likely that cascading toward a higher prevalence of serious offending in the oldest cohort was the result of a higher prevalence of the precursors of minor and moderate offending. Put differently, it is likely that the higher prevalence of moderate offending (either violence or theft) in the oldest cohort "set the stage" for more of the youth in the oldest cohort to progress to serious offending than those in the youngest cohort.

Persistence and Duration
- An early onset of offending predicted a long duration of offending careers in violence and theft (also found in Loeber & Farrington, 2001).
- Although serious violence was less prevalent than serious theft, the persistence of serious violence tended to be higher than for serious theft. Also, in the oldest cohort, twice as many of the "new" violent offenders during late adolescence persisted into early adulthood than was the case for serious theft. In addition, more than six times as many of the violent offenders compared to theft offenders persisted from early adolescence into early adulthood. However, the higher persistence of violence was much clearer in the oldest cohort than

in the youngest cohort. For the youngest cohort, similar percentages persisted in serious violence and serious theft from early to late adolescence. In summary, conclusions about the relative persistence of violence and theft were partly a function of cohort differences.

- The average duration of serious violence was similar to the average duration of serious theft in the youngest cohort (about 1.5 years) and the oldest cohort (over 2 years). However, minor and moderate theft had a longer duration in both cohorts than did moderate violence. Thus, there was a tendency for theft, compared to violence, to be associated with a longer duration of offending. However, at the most serious level, the duration of offending was similar for violence and theft.

Summary of Cohort Differences

The results show that, for the comparable age period 13–19, the oldest cohort was more involved in serious violence and serious theft. Specifically:

- The oldest cohort showed a higher prevalence and frequency of more and less serious forms of offending.
- The oldest cohort showed a higher cumulative onset of violence and theft.
- The proportion of late-onset offenders was about twice as high in the oldest cohort, suggesting a much larger onset window, and a later average age of onset.
- The duration of offending for the age period 13–19 was the same across the two cohorts. However, the oldest cohort was engaged in serious offending over a larger age window and their persistence in offending was higher, especially in terms of violence.
- The downslope of the age-crime curve was more gradual in the oldest cohort, indicating a slower outgrowing of serious offending in this cohort.

It has long been known that one needs to distinguish among period, age, and cohort effects. Separate analyses undertaken by Fabio et al. (2006) indicate that period effects may have operated for the youngest and oldest cohorts, although the precise nature of such effects is not clear. Period effects are effects that have an impact on all age cohorts during a specific period of time. (However, period effects, such as a crack cocaine "epidemic," are often temporary). The present analyses clearly show age effects in that there are systematic changes for each cohort in the age-crime curve. In addition, the analyses show major cohort differences in the shape of the age-crime curve. In Chapter 7 we will address the question of which factors in boys' lives can help to explain the major differences in violence and theft between the youngest and oldest cohorts.

Afterword: The Weighting of Data

It might be argued that indicators of prevalence, including cumulative onset, are affected by the screening method that we applied at the beginning of the study to increase the number of high-risk boys in each cohort. However, the cumulative onset figures were usually only slightly lower when they were reweighted back to the original cohort at screening (which is more representative of boys in the Pittsburgh public schools). For moderate and serious violence in the youngest cohort, the weighted figures were 35% and 21%, respectively, compared with the unweighted figures of 36% and 23%, respectively. For moderate and serious violence in the oldest cohort, the weighted figures were 44% and 37%, respectively, compared with the unweighted figures of 51% and 42%, respectively (see Figure 4.9).

The cumulative onset figures were higher in the oldest cohort even up to the same age as the youngest cohort (19). Up to age 19, for moderate and serious violence in the oldest cohort, the weighted figures were 43% and 33%, respectively, compared with the unweighted figures of 49% and 39% (see Figure 4.10), respectively. The results indicate that weighted data produced lower prevalence rates of violence. However, because the differences were small, there was little reason to weight the data in all subsequent analyses of violence.

We repeated earlier analyses done for violence to compare whether weighting the theft data would affect prevalence. For moderate and serious theft in the youngest cohort, the weighted figures were 55% and 20%, respectively, compared with the unweighted figures of 57% and 21% (see Figure 4.11), respectively. For moderate and serious theft in the oldest cohort, the weighted figures were 65% and 33%, respectively, compared with the unweighted figures of 73% and 42% (see Figure 4.12), respectively. Up to age 19, for serious theft in the oldest cohort the weighted figure was 31%, compared with the unweighted figure of 41%. As with violence, we found that weighting reduced the prevalence of theft. The decrease was very small in the youngest but not in the oldest cohort.

In general, all the trends shown in the Figures and Tables were similar in weighted and unweighted data. We have chosen to use unweighted data because we can then more easily compare numbers of individuals (e.g., committing both violence and theft, or committing moderate violence before serious violence). Most notably, bivariate and regression analyses produced very similar results with weighted and unweighted data (for details, see Loeber, Farrington, et al., 1998).

Note

1. Only behaviors that could lead to criminal prosecution were included in the analyses for this book. For that reason, seriousness levels of violence and theft studied in the present volume only partly overlap with severity levels in the developmental pathways, and excluded nondelinquent antisocial behaviors that

were part of the pathway model (see Loeber, Wung, et al., 1993). The current analyses extent earlier analyses on developmental progressions by including the full time frame available for the youngest and oldest cohorts (ages 7–19 and 13–25, respectively).

Five
Comparing Arrests and Convictions with Reported Offending

ROLF LOEBER, DAVID P. FARRINGTON,
AND DARRICK JOLLIFFE

Knowledge of delinquency careers depends greatly on the type of information on which the career parameters are based. Most knowledge is based on official records (often arrest; see e.g., Blumstein, Cohen, Roth, & Visher, 1986; Sampson & Laub, 1993; Tracy, Wolfgang, & Figlio, 1990). This is understandable because such records are often available without the considerable cost of contacting individuals to obtain self-reports of offending. Also, many justice services concerned with youth—the police, the courts, and probation and parole services—assess their work load, community impact, and efficacy in terms of the volume of known offenders and the volume of documented offenses. Addressing the criminal career parameters through arrest records is important, because justice officials need to know whether crime as monitored by them peaks at a certain age and whether and how quickly it then tends to decrease through adolescence and early adulthood. Also important for them is to know whether there are cohort differences in the downslope of the age-crime curve (see Chapter 4), and whether some cohorts have extended criminal careers while other cohorts have shorter careers.

Possibly the most important question about official delinquency records (such as arrest and court petition) is the extent to which they underrepresent self-reported offending (also addressed for the Pittsburgh Youth Study [PYS] by Farrington, Jolliffe, Loeber, & Homish, 2007; see also Farrington, Jolliffe et al., 2003). In addition, it is critical for justice personnel to know whether the ratio of arrest to self-reported offending varies with the age of offenders, which may indicate that police detection of offending is better at some developmental periods.

Another reason for studying official records of offending lies in the relative inability of self-reports to measure certain crimes. Specifically, self-reports may underrepresent certain forms of offending, such as homicide and rape. All of these are good reasons for us to focus on official records of offending by youth in the PYS as well as unofficial measures. Thus, whereas Chapter 4 dealt with offending reported by the boys, their parents and teachers, this chapter documents delinquency career parameters based on official records of offending, including arrest and conviction. To deal with the relative strengths and weaknesses of different measures of offending, this chapter will also focus on an "all-source" measure of offending based on reported delinquency and convictions for delinquent acts.

Scholars have been interested for a long time in specialized offending as compared to versatile, nonspecialized offending, and have not been in agreement about whether offense specialization occurs (Brame, Mulvey, & Piquero, 2001; Deane, Armstrong, & Felson, 2005; Farrington, Snyder, & Finnegan, 1988; Klein, 1984; Loeber, 1982; Piquero, Farrington, & Blumstein, 2007). We define *specialized offending* as the tendency for individuals to commit some types of offenses disproportionally and repeatedly. For example, Klein (1984) has concluded that a generalized "cafeteria style" of offending prevailed in empirical studies. However, it can be argued that generalized offending is most common when less serious offenses are included, and less common when the focus is on more serious offenses (as is the focus of the present volume). Moffitt (1993) assumed that adolescent-limited offenders mostly engage in nonviolent offenses, while life course offenders are more violent. Lynam, Piquero, and Moffitt (2004) have pointed out that specialization is more evident in self-reports than in official records. Researchers (see, e.g., Morizot & Le Blanc, 2007; Piquero, 2000; Piquero et al., 1999; Stander, Farrington, Hill, & Altham, 1989) have also postulated that offense specialization increases with age, leading to some offenders becoming, for example, professional burglars or bank robbers. This development often occurs with a decrease in co-offending between adolescence and adulthood (Reiss & Farrington, 1991). A limitation of past studies, however, is that most analyses have been based on official records (see e.g., Farrington et al., 1988; Piquero et al., 1999; Piquero et al., 2007; Stander et al., 1989) rather than on self-reports of delinquency. We have not found studies that combined self-reports and official records to quantify specialization.

Researchers attempting to quantify specialization are often hampered by the fact that many longitudinal studies have time gaps in assessment. Hence, it is risky to classify individuals on less than complete data, because the classification status can be affected by missing information on the life course of offending (see, e.g., Moffitt, 1993, which classifies individuals on their offending in adolescence when self-reported delinquency data are only available intermittently). Data from the PYS, because of the comprehensiveness of the assessments, allows us more clearly to classify violent (or theft) offenders over many years (i.e., ages 10–19 for the youngest cohort, and ages 13–25 for the oldest cohort) on the basis of the all-source measure of reported delinquency *and* conviction. This will permit us to examine offense specialization better than in prior studies that have been based on either self-reports or official records of offending.

To obtain official records of offending, the names of all boys were searched in nationwide Federal Bureau of Investigation records as well as in the Allegheny County and Pennsylvania state records (see details in Chapter 3). No boy in the youngest or oldest cohorts emigrated permanently from the United States. One boy in the youngest cohort died before age 16 and for that reason was excluded from the analyses. One other boy in that cohort also died before age 16, but had been arrested, and hence is included in the analyses. No boy in the oldest cohort died before age 18. Thus, all boys in that cohort were included in the analyses. As far as possible, similar levels of seriousness, violence and theft were studied, as in Chapter 4:

Violence

Moderate: Simple assault.

Serious: Robbery, aggravated assault, aggravated indecent assault, homicide, forcible rape, involuntary deviate sexual intercourse, or spousal sexual assault.

Theft

Moderate: Larceny or possession of stolen property.

Serious: Burglary or auto theft.

No attempt was made to classify minor theft (or physical aggression, as rated by parents or teachers) on the assumption that theft or aggression leading to an official record were likely to be on the moderate or serious levels.

Specifically, this chapter reports on the prevalence and frequency of arrest, and on the age of first conviction. It also reveals "hidden delinquency" by comparing arrest (and conviction) with reported offending. Conversely, the chapter shows the degree to which reported offending fails to identify youth who eventually are convicted for serious delinquent acts. For that reason, we report on an all-source measure of offending based on reported offending and conviction information. Based on this all-source measure, we investigate the extent to which there is specialization in either violence or theft, and the extent to which violent and theft offenders desist from offending and by what age. To streamline the chapter, we will review the weighing of data and cohort arrest differences in afterwords 1 and 2 respectively at the end of this chapter.

Arrests and Convictions for Violence and Theft

Questions addressed in this section are:

Is the age-crime curve known from reported offending (see Chapter 4) also evident from arrest data? And is the age-crime curve displayed in both prevalence and frequency of arrest data?

What is the age of first conviction for violence and theft, and how many young men are eventually convicted of violence or theft, respectively?

In presenting answers to these questions, we discuss in this chapter's first after-word the reasons why we did not apply weighting to the arrest or conviction data.

Prevalence and the Age-Crime Curve of Arrest

Violence   Figure 5.1 shows the annual prevalence of arrests for violence for the youngest cohort. The prevalence of serious violence increased from less than 1% by age 9 to peak at age 16 (7%), and then decreased to just over 5%. The prevalence of moderate violence showed two peaks, by ages 14 (4%) and 18 (4%), and then a decrease to 2% at age 19. How do these figures compare with those for the oldest cohort? The oldest cohort was first studied at age 13. In Chapter 4, which was based on reported offending, we saw that the oldest cohort continued offending into early adulthood and that the prevalence of their offending then decreased (see Figure 4.2). Figure 5.2 shows that the annual prevalence

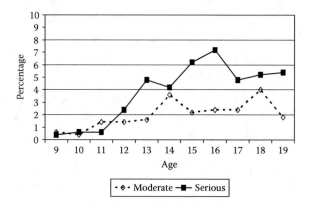

Figure 5.1 Annual Prevalence of Arrests for Violence (Youngest Cohort)

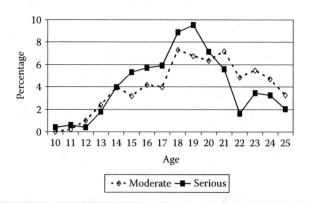

Figure 5.2 Annual Prevalence of Arrests for Violence (Oldest Cohort)

of arrests for serious violence increased to a peak (10%) by age 19, while the prevalence of moderate violence showed two peaks, by ages 18 and 21 (7%). The prevalence of moderate and serious violence subsequently decreased to 3% and 2%, respectively.

Theft   How do these results on violence compare with theft? In the youngest cohort (see Figure 5.3), the prevalence of arrests for moderate theft increased from 0, at age 9, to two peaks—one by age 16 (10%) and the other by age 18 (9%)—and then decreased to about 4% by age 19. The prevalence of arrests for serious theft was 0 by age 10, peaked by age 16 (5%), and then decreased gradually to 2% at age 19. Figure 5.4 shows the annual prevalence of theft arrests for the oldest cohort. Both moderate and serious theft arrests peaked by age 16 (moderate 15%; serious 12%). The results show clearer evidence for an age-crime curve for the oldest cohort than for the youngest cohort.

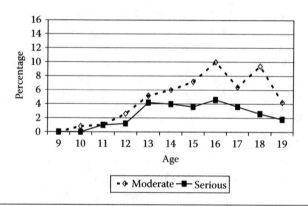

Figure 5.3 Annual Prevalence of Arrests for Theft (Youngest Cohort)

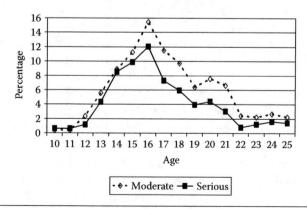

Figure 5.4 Annual Prevalence of Arrests for Theft (Oldest Cohort)

How do the prevalence curves of reported offending compare to those based on arrest? For the youngest cohort, the downslope of reported violence throughout late adolescence that was noted in Chapter 4 (see Figure 4.1) was much less clear from arrest data (see Figure 5.1). In contrast, in the oldest cohort the downslope was more visible in arrest data for violence into early adulthood (see Figure 5.2). The same applied to serious theft: the decrease of reported theft in late adolescence noted for the youngest cohort (see Figure 4.3) was much less apparent in the arrest data (see Figure 5.3). Again, the decrease was more visible on the graphs of reported theft and arrest for the oldest cohort (compare Figures 4.8 and 5.4).

In conclusion, the shape of age-crime curves varied depending on whether they are based on information from reported offending or arrest. This has implications for theory, estimates of community crime rates over time, and indicators of changes in offending used by justice personnel. First, a key aim of theory is the explanation of crime. However, this also means that various theories may need to be adjusted when addressing the life course of arrest when compared to data based on self-reports of offending, combined or not with parent or teacher reports. Second, since community levels of crime over time are dependent on the sum of age-crime curves of consecutive birth cohorts, it follows that methods of measuring the age-crime curve will influence the shape of community levels of crime over time. Third, such variation will influence justice personnel's ascertainment of whether there are changes in community crime rates over time.

Frequency and the Age-Crime Curve of Arrest for Violence and Theft
Does frequency-of-arrest data show a similarly peaked age-crime curve as found for prevalence of arrest? We addressed this question using age blocks rather than for each year because we were interested in comparing official and reported frequencies. Figure 5.5 shows the average annual frequency of arrests for violence committed by active offenders in the youngest cohort, in the age blocks 10–12, 13–16, and 17–19. The average annual frequency was calculated in the same way for arrests as for reported violence (see Chapter 4). The annual frequency of arrests for moderate violence in the youngest cohort was stable from late childhood to late adolescence (0.4 to 0.5). The annual frequency of arrests for serious violence was similar to that of moderate violence, and was also stable from late childhood to late adolescence (0.5 to 0.6).

Figure 5.6 shows the average annual frequency of arrest for violence for the oldest cohort, in the age blocks 13–16, 17–19, and 20–25. For both levels of violence, annual frequency was highest during late compared to early adolescence (ages 17–19; at 0.6 arrests for moderate violence and 1.0 arrests for serious violence per offender per year; $p < .0001$ and $p < .0001$). Both moderate and serious violence decreased during early adulthood (ages 20–25).

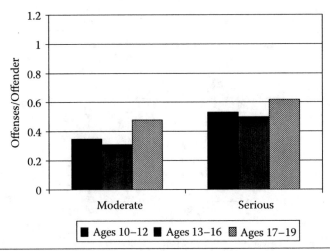

Figure 5.5 Annual Frequency of Violence Arrests (Youngest Cohort)

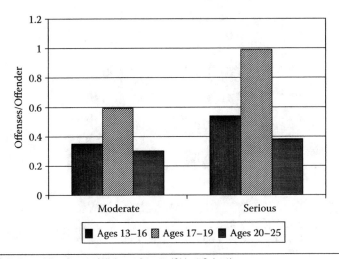

Figure 5.6 Annual Frequency of Violence Arrests (Oldest Cohort)

Figure 5.7 shows the average annual frequency of theft arrests per offender for active offenders in the youngest cohort. The frequency of moderate theft increased in a linear fashion from late childhood to late adolescence (to 0.87 arrests in late adolescence), but there was much less of an age trend for serious theft (to 0.57 arrests in late adolescence).

How frequent is theft from middle childhood through early adulthood? Figure 5.8 shows the average annual frequency of theft arrests for the oldest cohort. Frequency was highest for moderate theft during early and late adolescence (at about 0.9 to 1.0 arrests per offender per year). Serious theft also

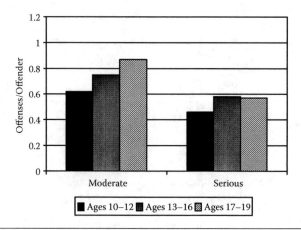

Figure 5.7 Annual Frequency of Theft Arrests (Youngest Cohort)

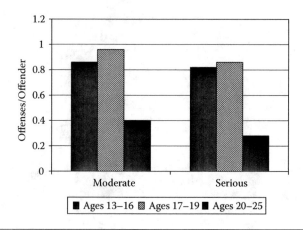

Figure 5.8 Annual Frequency of Theft Arrests (Oldest Cohort)

peaked during early to late adolescence (at about 0.8 to 0.9 arrests per offender per year), and decreased significantly from adolescence to early adulthood ($p < .0001$). In conclusion, the frequency of arrest did not clearly follow an age-crime curve for the youngest cohort, and varied for violence and theft in the oldest cohort. Thus, arrest data in contrast to the reported offense data did not consistently reveal an age-crime curve.

Cumulative Onset

This section addresses three questions pertaining to the age of first arrest:

What is the cumulative age of onset of arrest for moderate and serious violence and theft by age 19 (youngest cohort) and age 25 (oldest cohort)?

What is the average age of first arrest of moderate and serious violence and theft?

What is the relationship between age of first arrest and the duration of the offending career?

Cumulative Age of Onset of Arrests for Violence

Figure 5.9 shows the cumulative onset of arrests for violence for the youngest cohort. The cumulative onset of arrests for moderate and serious violence increased linearly at different slopes from age 11 to age 19. By age 19, 17% of the boys had been arrested for moderate violence and 26% for serious violence.

Figure 5.10 shows the cumulative onset of arrests for violence for the oldest cohort. Again the cumulative onset increased in an almost linear

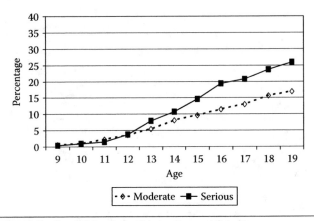

Figure 5.9 Cumulative Onset of Arrests for Violence (Youngest Cohort)

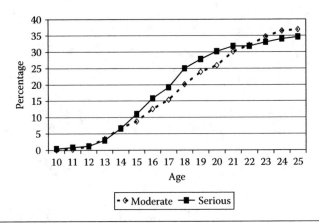

Figure 5.10 Cumulative Onset of Arrests for Violence (Oldest Cohort)

manner between ages 13 and 22. By age 19, 24% had been arrested for moderate violence, and 28% for serious violence. By age 25, 37% had been arrested for moderate violence, and 35% for serious violence. The problem of retrospective information prior to age 13 (noted in Chapter 4) did not apply to the oldest cohort in this chapter, because all arrests were based on official records.

Cumulative Age of Onset of Arrests for Theft

Figure 5.11 shows the cumulative onset of arrests for theft for the youngest cohort. For moderate and serious theft, the cumulative onset increased linearly from age 12 to age 18. By age 19, 30% of the youngest cohort had been arrested for moderate theft and 17% for serious theft.

Figure 5.12 shows the cumulative onset of arrests for theft for the oldest cohort. The cumulative onset curves were not linear for both moderate and

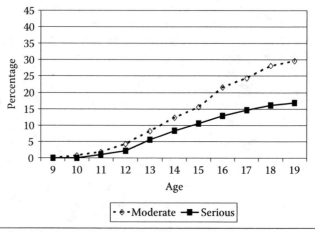

Figure 5.11 Cumulative Onset of Arrests for Theft (Youngest Cohort)

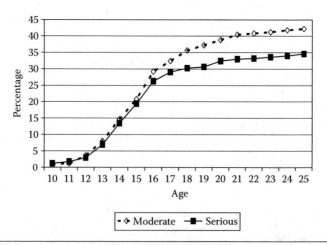

Figure 5.12 Cumulative Onset of Arrests for Theft (Oldest Cohort)

serious theft. They increased sharply between ages 12 and 17 and then more slowly. By age 19, 37% had been arrested for moderate theft, and 31% for serious theft. By age 25, 42% had been arrested for moderate theft and 35% for serious theft.

Average Age of First Arrest for Violence

It might be expected that the more serious levels of offenses would tend to have older average ages of onset, but this was not true for arrests. For the youngest cohort, the mean age of first arrest was 15.2 for moderate violence, and 15.0 for serious violence. For the oldest cohort, the mean age of first arrest was 18.4 for moderate violence, and 17.3 for serious violence.[1]

Average Age of First Arrest for Theft

Table 5.1 shows that for the youngest cohort, the mean age of onset was 14.1 for moderate theft, and 14.7 for serious theft, which was not significantly different. For the oldest cohort, the mean age of onset of arrest was 14.8 for moderate theft, and 15.2 for serious theft, which also was not significantly different. Thus, average ages of onset were only slightly higher in the oldest cohort than in the youngest cohort. When the follow-up period was the same for both cohorts (i.e., up to age 19), the difference between the two cohorts was no longer evident for theft. For arrests of the oldest cohort up to age 19, the mean age of onset was 15.0 for moderate theft, and 14.7 for serious theft. In summary, for the most part, the mean ages of onset for different severity levels of theft were similar.

Table 5.1 Onset of One Level of Arrest versus Onset of Next Level of Arrest for Offenses (Youngest and Oldest Cohorts)

		Mean Age			Next Level (N)		
First Level	*Next Level*	*First*	*Next*	*Same*	*Earlier*	*Later*	*r*
		YOUNGEST COHORT					
Moderate Violence	Serious Violence	15.1	14.6	16	23	15	.29*
Moderate Theft	Serious Theft	14.1	14.7	43	7	25	.71*
		OLDEST COHORT					
Moderate Violence	Serious Violence	17.3	17.1	30	50	39	.51*
Moderate Theft	Serious Theft	14.8	15.2	102	17	34	.68*

Notes: N = number; r = correlation coefficient; *p = .0001.

Table 5.1 also shows the degree to which the onset of arrest for moderate delinquency preceded the onset of arrest for serious delinquency. For both cohorts, there were trends for moderate violence to precede serious violence, but this was not uniformly the case. Serious theft had a strong probability of being preceded by moderate theft in the youngest cohort, but this was not the case in the oldest cohort. In summary, in contrast to data based on reported offending, developmental sequences in the seriousness of delinquency were not uniformly strong when based on arrest data.

Duration of the Arrest Career

Table 5.2 shows the average duration of arrest careers within each level of seriousness. The duration is simply the time between the first and last arrest. Note that the data are right-hand censored in that the maximum duration is limited by the availability of official records (up to age 19 for the youngest cohort, and age 25 for the oldest cohort). Average career durations were slightly but significantly longer for serious violence than for moderate violence (youngest cohort: 0.7 years for moderate violence, compared with 1.4 years for serious violence; oldest cohort: 2.0 years for moderate violence compared with 2.5 years for serious violence). The opposite was found for theft: the average career durations were slightly but significantly longer for moderate than for serious theft (youngest cohort: 1.4 years for moderate theft compared with 1.1 years for serious theft; oldest cohort: 3.0 years for moderate theft, compared with 2.2 years for serious theft).

To what extent does the duration of offending depend on the measurement mode? A comparison of the reported offending (Table 4.2; see Chapter 4) with

Table 5.2 Age of Onset versus Mean Duration (in Years) of Careers Based on Arrest Records (Youngest and Oldest Cohorts)

Age of Onset	Violence		Theft	
	Moderate	Serious	Moderate	Serious
	YOUNGEST COHORT			
10–12	2.7	3.9	3.2	1.9
13–16	0.3	1.4	1.5	1.2
17–19	0.1	0.0	0.2	1.0
Total	0.7	1.4	1.4	1.1
	OLDEST COHORT			
10–12	5.8	4.7	7.1	5.1
13–16	3.4	4.2	3.7	2.5
17–19	2.1	1.5	0.7	0.8
Total	2.0	2.5	3.0	2.2

arrests (Table 5.2) shows that the duration of serious violence was similar across reported offending and arrests (averages of 1.4 years vs. 1.4, and 2.7 vs. 2.5, in the youngest and oldest cohorts, respectively). However, the duration of moderate violence was shorter when measured by arrests compared to reported offending. These results are likely to be affected by a higher probability of arrests for serious, compared to moderate, violence.

Table 5.2 also shows the relationship between the age of onset and the average duration of criminal careers within each level of seriousness of arrests. As expected, the earlier the boy started his criminal career, the longer he continued. For example, in the youngest cohort, the boys who engaged in serious violence during late childhood (ages 10–12) had a duration of violence that was three times longer than the boys who first engaged in that level of violence during early adolescence (ages 13–16; duration of 3.9 years vs. 1.4 years). The comparable figures for the oldest cohort were 4.7 years versus 4.2 years, while an onset during ages 17–19 was associated a much shorter average duration of offending (1.5 years).

Age of First Conviction

In Pennsylvania the minimum age of criminal responsibility is 10, which means that juveniles are not convicted prior to that age (although they may be arrested). This is indeed clear for both cohorts (see Figures 5.13 and 5.14). However, from about age 12 onward the cumulative onset of convictions tends to increase linearly with age (at least up to age 16). Up to age 19, 9% of the youngest cohort was convicted for moderate violence, and 12% for serious violence. New cases of conviction for moderate or serious violence increased most between ages 12 and 16, and were much less common after that. Figure 5.14 shows the cumulative onset of convictions for violence for the oldest

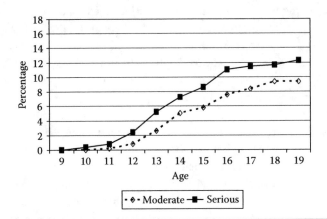

Figure 5.13 Cumulative Onset of Convictions for Violence (Youngest Cohort)

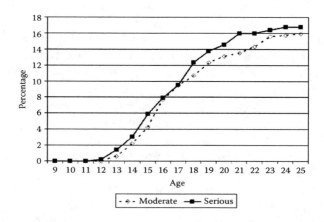

Figure 5.14 Cumulative Onset of Convictions for Violence (Oldest Cohort)

cohort. By age 19, 12% had been convicted for moderate violence, and 14% for serious violence, which was not statistically different from the figures in the youngest cohort. Most of the increase in convictions for violence took place between ages 13 and 20, and less so afterward. By age 25, 16% had been convicted for moderate violence, and 17% for serious violence.

Turning to theft, Figure 5.15 shows the cumulative onset of convictions for theft for the youngest cohort. Up to age 19, 15% of the boys had been convicted for moderate theft, and 9% for serious theft. The peak period for the onset of convictions for serious theft was ages 13–17, after which few new cases emerged. Figure 5.16 shows the cumulative onset of convictions for theft for the oldest cohort. Up to age 19, 26% of the boys in the oldest cohort had been convicted of moderate theft, and 22% for serious theft. These results were statistically higher for the oldest compared to the youngest cohort ($p < .0001$, and $p < .0001$ for moderate and serious theft, respectively). Up to age 25, 28% of boys had been convicted for moderate theft, and 22% for serious theft. The peak period for conviction for moderate and serious theft was ages 13–17, after which few new cases emerged.

In summary, taking conviction (i.e., proven guilt) as a criterion, 1 in 10 boys in the youngest cohort were convicted for violence between ages 12 and 19, and 16% of the oldest cohort were convicted between ages 12 and 25. The figures for conviction for theft were either similar or somewhat higher. Given the total number of boys involved in the community, this constitutes a heavy burden on the justice system. Moreover, this burden varies between age cohorts and, therefore, can put additional strain in some years on the justice system. We will reexamine the figures for offending later in this chapter when

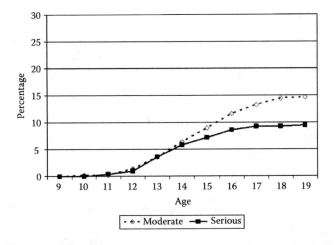

Figure 5.15 Cumulative Onset of Convictions for Theft (Youngest Cohort)

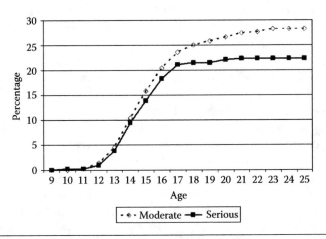

Figure 5.16 Cumulative Onset of Convictions for Theft (Oldest Cohort)

we review the prevalence of an all-source measure of offending based on a combination of reported offending and conviction.

Comparisons among Reported Offending, Arrest, and Conviction

The data from the PYS are unusual in that they allow a comparison between different types of delinquency career data—particularly, reported offending, arrests, and convictions (see also Farrington et al., 2007; Huizinga & Elliott, 1987; Piquero et al., 2007; West & Farrington, 1977). Overall, one would expect that, because the police do not apprehend every offender for every offense committed, reported offending would be higher in prevalence and frequency, earlier in onset, and longer in crime duration (see Farrington & Welsh, 2003; Kirk, 2006). However, the verification of these hypotheses may depend on the type of offense (violence vs. theft) and on cohort differences. Important in this respect is the proportional difference between reported offending and arrest/conviction, because this shows how effective the justice system is in detecting and prosecuting offenders.

Reported Offending versus Arrest

Overall, the data show that the prevalence of reported serious offending was higher than the prevalence of arrests for serious offending (a finding that is generally observed in the literature; see, e.g., McCord, Widom, & Crowell, 2001). The only exception was that the peak prevalence of reported serious violence in the youngest cohort was slightly lower than the peak prevalence of arrests for serious violence (reported peak 6%, arrest peak 7%), but this was not a statistically significant difference. Otherwise, the prevalence of reported offending was higher than the prevalence of arrests in all other comparisons. For example, a comparison of Figures 4.2 and 5.2 for the oldest cohort shows that the peak for reported violence (17% for moderate violence and 11% for serious violence) was higher than the peak for arrests for violence (7% for moderate violence and 9% for serious violence). The difference between reported and arrests for violence was largest for moderate violence.

For moderate theft, the peak prevalence of reported offending in the oldest cohort was about twice as high as the peak prevalence of arrest (33% vs. 15%). Also, the peak for reported moderate theft was 2 years later than that of arrests for moderate theft. The magnitude of the difference between the prevalence of reported serious theft and arrests for serious theft was much smaller than for moderate theft. Thus, even though the prevalence of reported serious offending tended to be higher than that of arrest, the difference was lower when the most serious acts—of either violence or theft—were considered. This was observed in both the oldest and the youngest cohorts in the prevalence and the cumulative onset data (compare, e.g., Figures 4.5 and 5.5, and Figures 4.6 and 5.6). We interpret this finding as showing that the justice system is more effective in arresting more serious than less serious offender. The majority of serious violent offenders (robbers, rapists, and individuals committing aggravated assault) and the majority of serious theft offenders (car thieves and burglars) were arrested sooner or later (but their arrest might have been for less serious forms of offending).

This last statement implies that there is a narrowing with age in the gap between the prevalence of reported offending and arrest, with a larger proportion of undetected boys committing serious crime around, for example, age 13, compared to age 17. This is clearly apparent for both cohorts. For instance, at age 13 the prevalence of reported serious theft of the oldest cohort was 11%, compared to a 4% prevalance of arrest; this difference had narrowed down by age 17 to 5.5% for reported serious theft versus 7% for arrests for serious theft. A similar trend was observable for serious violence at ages 13 and 17.

In summary, the findings indicate that a larger proportion of the boys engaged in serious offenses during early adolescence without being arrested than during later adolescence. Although, in general, official records of arrests underestimated actual offending, this was more acutely the case during early adolescence than during late adolescence. This may mean that active offenders have a few years of offending in which the justice system appears to treat them more leniently, after which they are more likely to be convicted (a "catch-up" process). This also means that age-crime curves for arrests occur several years later than age-crime curves based on reported offending, which was more obvious for the oldest cohort.

Annual frequencies of arrests also underestimated annual frequencies of self-reported offending. For example, the annual self-reported frequency of serious violence in the oldest cohort during late adolescence was three times higher than that according to arrests (compare Figures 4.4 and 5.4; averages of 6.8 vs. 2.1). A similar proportional difference was found for serious violence in the youngest cohort (compare Figures 4.3 and 5.3). Thus, arrest records were less adequate in assessing the frequency of offending (as apparent from self-reports) and more adequate in ascertaining the prevalence of offending in late adolescence and young adulthood.

In contrast to the prevalence and frequency measures, the mean duration of serious careers was similar according to arrests and reported offending. However, the mean duration of careers of moderately serious forms of offending was longer according to reports than according to arrests. This may reflect more effective official response to serious offenses than moderate offenses. Analyses not reported here indicate that the results held true when prison time was taken into account. These results are contrary to those reported by Piquero et al. (2001) on incarceration results up to age 33.

In addition, the results show that developmental sequences of theft or violence (i.e., from moderately serious to serious forms of theft, and from moderately serious to serious forms of violence) were more evident from reported offending data (shown in Chapter 4) than from arrest data. This finding has direct implications for justice policy in that information about a currently arrested offense (compared to knowledge derived from reported offending) is less likely to inform justice personnel about the risk of that individual escalating to more serious forms of offending (see also Farrington et al., 2007). For such a determination, clearly other information is needed, such as the number of offenses, and the presence of risk and promotive factors (which will be reviewed in Chapter 7).

Arrests versus Convictions

Only a proportion of arrested serious offenders are convicted. We know that arrests do not always lead to prosecution, let alone to conviction. In principle, we could repeat all of the above analyses for arrests with convictions as the outcome. Because of space limitations, we focus on the cumulative onset of convictions. Figure 5.13 shows the cumulative onset of convictions for violence for the youngest cohort. Up to age 19, 12% of boys were convicted for serious violence, and 9% were convicted for moderate violence. These figures were about half of the corresponding percentages for arrests (26% for serious violence and 18% for moderate violence; see Figure 5.9). Similar results were found for the oldest cohort. Up to age 25, 16% of men in the oldest cohort were convicted for serious violence, and 16% were convicted for moderate violence (see Figure 5.14), which were less than half of the corresponding percentages for arrests (34% for serious violence and 37% for moderate violence; see Figure 5.10).

Do the same results apply to theft? Figure 5.15 shows the cumulative onset of convictions for theft for the youngest cohort. Up to age 19, 10% of boys were convicted for serious theft, and 15% for moderate theft. These figures were about half of the corresponding percentages arrested (18% for serious theft and 30% for moderate theft; see Figure 5.3). Figure 5.16 shows the cumulative onset of theft convictions for the oldest cohort. Up to age 25, 22% of boys were convicted for serious theft, and 28% for moderate theft. This compares to 42% arrested for serious theft, and 35% arrested for moderate theft (see Figure 5.4).

Thus, in seven of the eight comparisons, the prevalence of convictions was about half of that of arrests. The percentage difference between arrests and convictions did not vary by crime type (theft vs. violence) and did not clearly differ by age cohort (the only exception was a smaller percentage difference for moderate theft). It is unclear to what extent this reduction resulted from the arrest of innocent people, weak evidence to secure a conviction, or diversion as an alternative to conviction.

Age of Onset of Reported Offending, Arrest, and Conviction

Remarkably, the mean age of onset of arrests was slightly higher than that for convictions. In the youngest cohort, the mean age of onset of arrests and convictions were 15.0 and 14.2 for both serious violence and serious theft (compared with 13.3 for reported serious violence and 12.7 for reported serious theft). In the oldest cohort, the figures for the mean age of onset of arrests and convictions were 17.3 and 17.0 for serious violence (compared with 15.0 for reported offending) and 15.5 and 15.0 for serious theft (compared with 13.4 for reported offending). Thus, although reported serious offending (either violence or theft) on average occurred prior to arrests and conviction, the mean age of onset of arrests was slightly higher than for convictions in all comparisons. These results may be partly explained by the fact (shown above) that about half of all arrests do not result in conviction, and the age-of-conviction data are based only on the sample who were convicted. Thus, the convicted boys are probably more serious offenders who began offending at an earlier age.

In fact, when the analysis was restricted to boys with all three onsets (reports, arrests, and convictions), the onset of reported offending always appeared first, followed by the onset of arrests, and finally the onset of conviction. In the youngest cohort, the means were 13.4, 13.6, and 14.3, respectively, for serious violence and 13.1, 14.0, and 14.1, respectively, for serious theft. In the oldest cohort, the means were 15.4, 15.9, and 16.7, respectively, for serious violence and 13.7, 14.6, and 15.1, respectively, for serious theft. However, almost all of these differences were nonsignificant (the exception was for theft in the oldest cohort, where reported theft was significantly earlier than arrests for theft, $p < .02$). It should be taken into account, however, that deviancy processes often take much longer to emerge. Loeber, Farrington, & Petrechuk (2003), using data from the PYS, have shown that on average there was a 7.5-year interval between the emergence of minor problem behavior and a court appearance for an index offense.

Among the boys with an official record for both serious violence and serious theft, which occurred first? This was investigated for arrests because the number of boys with convictions for both serious violence and serious theft was very small (20 in the youngest cohort and 44 in the oldest cohort). In both cohorts, serious theft tended to occur first: 23 theft first, versus 17 violence first, and 13 same, in the youngest cohort; and 61 theft first, versus 27 violence first, and 23 same, in the oldest cohort. For boys who committed both serious theft and serious violence, the mean age of onset was lower for serious theft: 14.6 compared with 15.0 in the youngest cohort, and 15.4 compared with 17.0 in the oldest cohort. Thus, on average, in arrest data, serious theft emerged first, followed by serious violence. This result had also been evident in reported offending data (see Chapter 4).

The Measurement of Offending, Revisited

Traditionally, self-reported (and other-reported) measures of offending and official records of offending are studied separately in criminology. It is well known that arrest or conviction data underestimate actual offending when measured through self-reports (Farrington et al., 2006). It is therefore important to compare these different types of measures not just because of measurement accuracy, but also because the information can shed light on the efficacy of the justice system in dealing with offenders. To return to the measurement side, reported offending based on self-reports, parent reports, and teacher reports, although valid (Farrington, Loeber, et al., 1996), may have limitations

because offenders may suppress information about their engaging in delinquent acts. For these reasons, we address the following questions:

What proportion of reported delinquents are arrested and/or convicted?
What proportion of convicted serious delinquents are not identified
from reports of offending?
Can a more comprehensive measure of serious offending be constructed
based on the combination of reported offending and convictions
(called *the all-source measure of offending*)?

The Proportion of Reported Delinquents Who Are Arrested or Convicted

Table 5.3 investigates how frequently the boys who had reported serious violence or theft also had arrests or convictions for serious violence or theft. In
the youngest cohort, 53% of boys with reported serious violence were arrested,
and 31% were convicted for serious violence. In the oldest cohort, 55% of boys
with reported serious violence were arrested, and 30% were convicted for serious violence. Thus, about 70% of the serious violent offenders in the youngest
and oldest cohorts were not convicted for their violence. This high percentage of serious offenders not being convicted in court also applied to the serious theft offenses in the youngest cohort (43% of boys with reported serious
theft were arrested, and 32% were convicted for serious theft, meaning that
68% of the serious theft offenders were not convicted). This gap was somewhat
lower in the oldest cohort (61% of the reported serious theft offenders were

Table 5.3 Arrests and Convictions Compared to Reported Offending (Youngest and Oldest
Cohorts)

	Not Reported as Delinquents		Reported as Delinquents		%	%
	Yes	No	Yes	No	(O/NR)	(O/R)
			YOUNGEST COHORT			
Violence Arrests	70	288	54	47	20	53
Theft Arrests	43	334	38	50	11	43
Violence Convictions	26	332	31	70	7	31
Theft Convictions	18	359	28	60	5	32
			OLDEST COHORT			
Violence Arrests	63	234	103	83	21	55
Theft Arrests	74	255	92	59	22	61
Violence Convictions	23	274	56	130	8	30
Theft Convictions	29	300	78	73	9	52

Notes: Serious offenses only; O = official offender (arrested or convicted); R =
reported; NR = not reported.

arrested and 52% were convicted, meaning that 48% of the reported serious theft offenders were not convicted). These findings raise questions about how much we can currently rely on the justice system applying sanctions to serious offenders (see also Huizinga & Elliott, 1987; Kirk, 2006).

How valid was reported offending when compared to conviction data? Between 5% and 9% of boys with no reported violence or theft were nevertheless convicted for violence or theft. It is likely that some of these boys were deliberately concealing their serious offending. However, others may have had no reports because they were not interviewed on all occasions (lowest 0.2% at wave A, and highest 18% at wave AA), and others may have been convicted when they were in fact innocent. Other discrepancies between reports and convictions could have been caused by differences between the types of offenses covered (especially for violence).

The above findings indicate that some misclassification may occur if serious violent offenders and serious theft offenders are identified only on official records, while a modest amount of misclassification may occur when using reports of offending. As to official records, we had a choice of using arrest or conviction data. Arrests may occur when the individual has not actually engaged in delinquent acts and is falsely suspected. We chose conviction because it is based on the individual's proven guilt of having committed delinquent act(s). Therefore, we decided to construct a comprehensive index of offending based on a combination of reported serious offending and convictions for serious offending. Details of the construction of this all-source indicator of serious offending can be found in Chapter 3.

The All-Source Measure of Serious Offending

How persistent is serious offending between ages 7 and 25? To address the question, we will use the all-source measure of serious violence and theft combined as the best indication of persistence. Figure 5.17 shows the prevalence of the all-source serious offending (violence and theft combined) for the age blocks detailed in Chapter 2—that is, ages 10–12 (late childhood), 13–16 (early adolescence), 17–19 (late adolescence), and 20–25 (early adulthood).[2] For the youngest cohort, the results approximate an age-crime curve, starting with 2% of the boys being identified on the all-source measure of serious theft/violence in middle childhood, increasing to 15% in late childhood, and 27% during early adolescence, after which the prevalence dropped to 13% during late adolescence. In comparison, the results for the oldest cohort do not show an age-crime curve but instead show a decrease in offending from early adolescence through early adulthood. Specifically, Figure 5.17 shows that 40% of the boys were identified on the measure of all-source violence/theft during early adolescence, which decreased by half to 21% during early adulthood. In Chapter 8 we will return to the prevalence of the all-source measure of

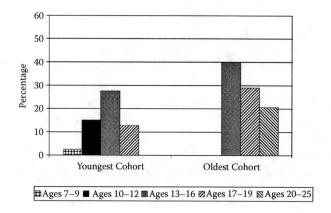

Figure 5.17 Prevalence for the All-Source Measure of Serious Violence and Theft Combined

violence and theft, where we will show the annual prevalence of this indicator for the youngest and oldest cohorts.

Are the above results, using the all-source measure of serious violence and theft combined, similar to results when serious violence and theft are considered separately? Starting with violence, the answer to this question can be gleaned from Figure 5.18, which shows that 10% of the boys in the youngest cohort were identified through the all-source measure of serious violence in late childhood; this doubled in early adolescence (20%), and then decreased during late adolescence to 8%. As expected, the level of violence for the oldest cohort substantially exceeded that of the youngest cohort for the comparable

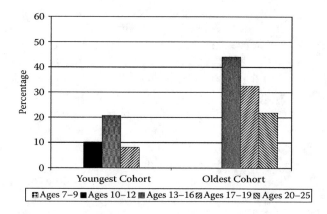

Figure 5.18 Prevalence for the All-Source Measure of Violence

age blocks: fewer than half of the boys were seriously violent during early and late adolescence (21% and 44%, respectively), decreasing to 22% during early adulthood for the oldest cohort.

Turning to prevalence of serious theft as seen through the all-source measure, Figure 5.19 shows that during middle childhood, 2% of the boys in the youngest cohort were identified, which slightly increased by late childhood (8%), doubled during early adolescence (16%), and then was reduced by two-thirds during late adolescence (7%). In the case of the oldest cohort, almost 6 out of 10 of the boys were identified through the all-source measure (57%) during early adolescence (thus, three times as many as those in the youngest cohort during that time period), decreasing during late adolescence to 43%, and further to 31% during early adulthood. In summary, the all-source measures of serious violence and theft again clearly indicate the much higher degree of delinquent involvement of the oldest over the youngest cohort.

The data represented in Figures 5.17–5.19 also shed light on persistence and desistance in moderate and serious offending, which will be discussed in Chapter 9.

Specialization in Offending

In Chapter 4 we saw that the development of reported violence was different from theft in several respects (e.g., prevalence, onset, frequency, etc.). However, we did not examine the degree to which moderate to serious violent offenders committed moderate to serious theft, or the degree that moderate to serious theft offenders committed moderate to serious violence. This is basic

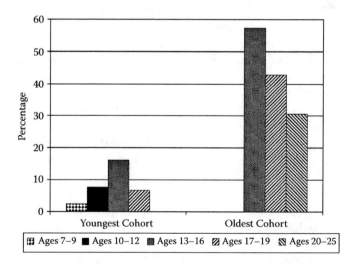

Figure 5.19 Prevalence for the All-Source Measure of Theft

information to determine the extent to which offenders are or are not specialized in their offending. We now address this question using the all-source measure of offending, which, compared to reported offending, provides the best possible test of specialization. The basic question here is, to what extent do the data show specialized offenders (i.e., those limiting serious offending to either violence or theft), and to what extent are there generalized offenders (i.e., those who commit both serious violence and theft)? The specific questions addressed in this section are:

Are violent offenders, compared to theft offenders, more likely to become specialist offenders?
Does the proportion of specialized offenders change with age?

Table 5.4 addresses the issue of specialization in either serious violence or serious theft using as a criterion the all-source measure of offending. The results show a considerable amount of specialization in either serious violence or serious theft (see Figure 5.20). For the youngest cohort, almost half (47%) of the violent offenders were specialized offenders and did not engage in serious theft, which was about the same for the oldest cohort (44%). Conversely, just over half of the violent offenders were generalized offenders in that they also committed serious theft.

Turning to serious theft offenders, Table 5.4 shows that about one-third of the serious theft offenders were specialized offenders (36% and 34% in the youngest and oldest cohorts, respectively). Conversely, the majority of the serious theft offenders were generalized offenders in that they also committed serious violence (as shown in Figure 5.20).

Table 5.4 also summarizes the overlap between serious violence and serious theft according to reports, arrests, and convictions. In the youngest cohort, 55% of the reported, 41% of the arrested, and 33% of the convicted violent offenders were also theft offenders. In the oldest cohort, 54% of the reported, 64% of the arrested, and 51% of the convicted violent offenders were also theft offenders. Thus, each data type demonstrates the presence of specialized offenders.

These results are remarkable in several ways. First, the findings are consistent for violence and theft, and are consistent across the two cohorts. Second, as shown in Table 5.4, the percentage of specialization based on the all-source measure of offending was very similar to that based on reported offending (in three out of the four comparisons) but was lower compared to specialization based on arrest or conviction data (this applied to seven out of the eight comparisons). The data contradict the notion that specialized offenders are uncommon and that generalized offending is the rule (Klein, 1984). However, it is possible that our findings apply especially to the serious end of the offense distribution and that generalized offending is more typical among the less serious offenders.

Table 5.4 Specialization in Violence and Theft (Youngest and Oldest Cohorts)

	Number (Total)	Number Violent	% Specialized Violent Offenders	% Also Theft	Number Theft	% Specialized Theft Offenders	% Also Violent	Number Both
Youngest Cohort								
Reported	456	98	45	55	87	38	62	54
Arrested	502	130	59	41	85	38	62	43
Convicted	502	61	67	33	47	57	43	20
All-Source	502	131	47	53	107	36	64	69
Oldest Cohort								
Reported	474	177	46	54	145	44	66	95
Arrested	506	173	36	64	172	45	65	111
Convicted	506	83	49	51	110	62	38	42
All-Source	506	213	44	56	183	34	66	120

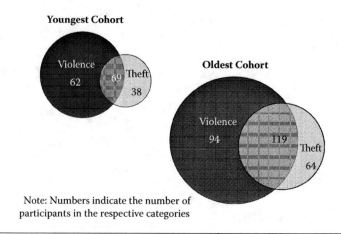

Note: Numbers indicate the number of
participants in the respective categories

Figure 5.20 Specialization in Offending as Indicated by the Nonoverlap between Violence and Theft

Age Changes in Specialization

Does specialization change with age? Several studies have commented on the emergence of more specialized offenders with age (see, e.g., Piquero, 2000). However, it is unclear whether this is equally true for serious violent and serious property offenders. Second, it remains to be seen whether increased specialization results from new cases emerging or from a change in the offense pattern of existing delinquent cases. Phrased differently, are new cases of violence emerging during adolescence of boys who are little involved with serious theft? Or does the predominant mode of offending changes for violent cases with an earlier onset in that they selectively desist from serious property offenses but not from violence?

Data shown in Table 5.5 and Figure 5.18 only partly confirm that offense specialization (based on the all-source measure of offending) increases with age. Table 5.5 shows the data for reported offending. Offense specialization for violence in the youngest cohort is curvilinear, peaking at ages 10–12 and 17–19 and lowest at ages 13–16. Specialization for theft varies in the same way, being highest at ages 10–12 and ages 17–19 and lowest at ages 13–16.

In the oldest cohort, Figure 5.21 shows that specialization in violence clearly increased with age from 53% in early adolescence (ages 13–16) to 83% in early adulthood (ages 20–25), whereas specialization in theft was curvilinear, being lowest during late adolescence (ages 17–19), but increasing during early adulthood. In summary, in three out of the four age comparisons, the results reveal curvilinear relationships between offense specialization and age, showing an increase at a later age. For the oldest cohort there was increased offense specialization during adulthood, especially for violence.

Table 5.5 Age Changes in the Specialization of Offending Based on Reported Offending (Youngest and Oldest Cohorts)

Age	Number (Total)	Number Violent Offenders	% Also Theft	% Specialized Violent Offenders	Number Theft Offenders	% Also Violent	% Specialized Theft Offenders	Number Both
				YOUNGEST COHORT				
10–12	485	39	31	69	35	34	66	12
13–16	475	72	47	53	60	57	43	34
17–19	452	29	28	72	22	36	64	8
10–19	456	98	55	45	87	62	28	54
				OLDEST COHORT				
13–16	506	108	47	53	120	43	57	51
17–19	491	95	29	71	46	61	39	28
20–25	474	65	17	83	25	44	56	11
13–25	474	177	54	46	145	66	34	95

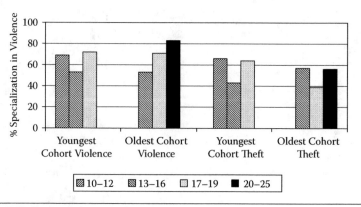

Figure 5.21 Changes in Specialization with Age

The results on offense specialization should be considered in light of the heterogeneity of the offender population. As will be discussed in Chapter 9, desistance processes operate more strongly for theft than for violence, which can help to account for increasing specialization in violence during early adulthood in the oldest cohort. In addition, the results suggest the presence of a substantial specialist theft-offender group that is highest early in the delinquency career, decreases when the age-crime curve peaks (at the time when there are more generalized offenders) and then increases at the end of the delinquency career, probably as a result of a group of generalized offenders becoming less involved in violence (or the emergence of specialist offenders with no prior involvement in violence). Clearly, there is much more to specialization that needs to be investigated in light of the fact that there are developmental changes in the heterogeneity of offender types with development. We will return to the overlap of violence and theft when discussing joint violence-theft offense trajectories in Chapter 8.

Summary of Key Findings

We now highlight several key findings from this chapter.

Arrest and Conviction

- Annual frequencies of arrests underestimated annual frequencies of self-reported offending, but the prevalence of arrest approximated the prevalence of self-reported offending.
- One-fourth of the study participants in the youngest cohort had been arrested for serious violence by age 19, and 1 in 10 had been convicted for serious violence by that age. Almost 1 in 5 had been arrested for serious theft, and 1 in 5 was convicted for serious theft.

• Arrest and conviction levels across the two cohorts were similar up to age 19. However, 1 in 3 young males in the oldest cohort had been arrested for serious violence by age 25, and 1 in 6 had been convicted of serious violence. Also, 1 in 3 of the study participants had been arrested for serious theft, and 1 in 5 had been convicted of serious theft.

• Arrest was more common for serious than for moderately serious levels of violence or theft.

• When contrasted with reported levels of offending, arrest for serious offending was proportionally less common during early adolescence than it was during late adolescence.

• Onset of offending in late childhood was a better predictor of persistence than was onset of offending in middle childhood.

Delinquency-Career Parameters Based on the All-Source Measure of Offending

• For offenders with an onset in childhood, violence and theft persisted to the same degree, but for offenders with an onset during adolescence, violence persisted longer than theft.

• Half of the serious violent offenders in both cohorts were specialized offenders, compared to a third of the serious theft offenders.

Afterword 1: The Weighting of Data

The cumulative onset figures for arrest were lower when they were reweighted back to the original cohort at screening (which was more representative of boys in the Pittsburgh public schools). For arrests for serious violence in the youngest cohort, the weighted figure was 25%, compared with the unweighted figure of 26%. For arrests for serious violence in the oldest cohort, the weighted figure was 30%, compared with the unweighted figure of 35%. For arrests for serious theft in the youngest cohort, the weighted figure was 17%, compared with the unweighted figure of 17%. For arrests for serious theft in the oldest cohort, the weighted figure was 30%, compared with the unweighted figure of 35%.

Up to age 19, for arrests for serious violence in the oldest cohort, the weighted figure was 23%, compared with the unweighted figure of 28%. For arrests for serious theft in the oldest cohort, the weighted figure was 26%, compared with the unweighted figure of 31%.

The cumulative conviction figures were also lower when they were reweighted back to the original cohort at screening. For serious violence in the youngest cohort, the weighted figure was 11%, compared with the unweighted figure of 12%. For serious violence in the oldest cohort, the weighted figure was 14%, compared with the unweighted figure of 17%. For serious theft in the youngest cohort, the weighted figure was 9%, compared with the unweighted figure of 9%. For serious theft in the oldest cohort, the weighted figure was 18%, compared with the unweighted figure of 22%.

In summary, the examples of weighted prevalence show that in most instances the weighting procedure somewhat lowered the prevalence. The magnitude of difference between the two procedures, however, was modest in the majority of instances (0% to 2% difference), and larger magnitudes were the exception.

Afterword 2: Cohort Differences

We have mentioned that the study of cohort differences is important because such differences constitute essential elements for understanding changes in community crime trends over time. To what extent are cohort differences, documented in reported offending (shown in shapter 4) also evident from official records of arrests and conviction?

Violence

We have already alluded to differences in the arrests of boys from the youngest and oldest cohorts. How large are these differences for the comparable age range, up to age 19? Figures 5.1 and 5.2 show that the prevalence of arrests for violence was two to three times higher for the oldest cohort for moderate violence ($p < .0002$) and serious violence ($p < .02$). Also, considering the full age ranges studied in each cohort, the peak for violent offending was 3 years later for the oldest compared to the youngest cohort (age 19 vs. age 16). The cumulative onset of violence arrests was greater in the oldest cohort than in the youngest cohort (Figures 5.9 and 5.10). The same applied to the cumulative onset of convictions for serious, but not for moderate, violence (Figures 5.13 and 5.14).

However, the annual frequency of arrests for violence was generally similar in the two cohorts for the age period 13–16 (Figures 5.5 and 5.6), but higher for the oldest cohort at ages 17–19 ($p < .002$).

Another way to establish whether there are cohort differences is to examine the correlation between the age of onset of different seriousness levels of offending. In the youngest cohort, the ages of onset of moderate and serious violence were weakly correlated ($r = .29$), but were more strongly correlated in the oldest cohort ($r = .51$). One interpretation of this finding is that moderate violence stimulated more serious violence in the oldest than in the youngest cohort. This effect may have been amplified by the higher prevalence of moderate violence in the oldest cohort. However, the arrest data demonstrate that there was no evidence of a developmental sequence in violence. On average the first arrest for serious violence occurred earlier than arrest for moderate violence.

Are the cohort differences also evident in the duration of offending? *Duration* is defined here as the number of years between the first and last known arrests. Table 5.2 shows that for moderate violence, the mean duration was almost three times greater in the oldest cohort (2.0 years vs. 0.7 years for the youngest cohort), but this was influenced by the fact that arrests were measured up to age 25 for the oldest cohort, compared to age 19 for the youngest cohort. Similarly, the duration of serious violence was on average almost twice as long in the oldest cohort (2.5 years, vs. 1.4 years for the youngest cohort). The results held up after equating time at risk. Table 5.2 also shows that for the age periods shared by the two cohorts (ages 13–16 and 17–19), the duration of moderate and serious violent offending was substantially longer for the oldest cohort. Thus, the results show that the oldest cohort inflicted a considerably greater burden on the justice system for both arrests and convictions for violence than did the youngest cohort. Was the same true for theft?

Theft

For the comparable age range (up to age 19), the annual prevalence of arrests for serious theft was higher for the oldest cohort (Figures 5.3 and 5.4; p = .002. Figure 5.12 shows the cumulative onset of arrests of the oldest cohort. In terms of cumulative onset of serious theft, by age 19, almost twice as many of the study participants in the oldest cohort had been arrested for serious theft (30%, vs. 17% for the youngest cohort), a difference that was statistically significant. By age 25, 41% of the participants had engaged in moderate theft and 34% had engaged in serious theft. Hence, the cumulative onset of theft arrests was greater in the oldest cohort than in the youngest cohort.

The frequency of arrests for serious theft during late adolescence (ages 17–19) was also slightly higher in the oldest cohort than in the youngest cohort (averages 0.9 and 0.6 for the oldest and youngest cohorts, respectively; p < .04). In the youngest cohort, the ages of onset of moderate and serious theft were highly correlated (r = .71), and this was also the case for the oldest cohort (r = .68). We conclude that the onset of moderate theft partially drove the onset of serious violence. We postulate that the higher prevalence of serious theft in the oldest cohort was partly driven by the higher prevalence of moderate theft in the oldest cohort. However, we cannot exclude the possibility that the correlation was spurious because it may be due to common predictors of moderate and serious theft. We will return to this issue in Chapter 7.

Did the higher prevalence and frequency of offending by the oldest cohort translate into longer delinquency careers as evident from arrest records? Results summarized in Table 5.2 show that the average career durations were longer for theft in the oldest cohort, and this applied to moderate theft (oldest cohort: 3.0 years; youngest cohort: 1.4 years), and for serious theft (oldest cohort: 2.2 years; youngest cohort: 1.1 years). However, the average durations of arrest careers were not longer in the oldest cohort when it was truncated by age 19. Unusually, in the oldest cohort, theft and violence persisted into early adulthood (even though the youngest cohort was not followed up into early adulthood, it was clear that most desistance in theft and violence occurred before age 19).

In summary, the cohort differences based on reported offending that were identified in Chapter 4 for violence and theft were also evident from arrest and conviction data. However, the age-crime curve and frequency findings from the reported offending data were less clearly seen in the arrest data.

Notes

1. Note that the figures here are different from those of Table 5.1 because that table reports on individuals who were arrested for both moderate and serious delinquency, whereas the information here does not have that restriction.
2. For the annual prevalence of the all-source measure, see Chapter 8, Figure 8.1.

Six

Substance Use, Drug Dealing, Gang Membership, and Gun Carrying and Their Predictive Associations with Serious Violence and Serious Theft

HELENE RASKIN WHITE, ROLF LOEBER,
AND DAVID P. FARRINGTON

Serious theft and violent offending have been linked to many other problem behaviors, such as substance use, drug dealing, gang membership, and gun carrying. One advantage of the Pittsburgh Youth Study (PYS) is that it has collected annual data on all of these problem behaviors. Therefore, it is possible to examine the prevalence, onset, and duration of them between ages 7 and 25. Further, the data make it possible for us to examine the onset of the problem behaviors in relation to the onset of violent and theft offending, and investigate which of the problem behaviors differentially predict violence or theft, or both.

The strong association between substance use and offending has been documented in numerous studies (for a review, see White & Gorman, 2000). In general, the research shows that delinquents—compared to nondelinquents—report higher rates of alcohol and other drug use, and drugs users report higher rates of offending than nonusers. While drug use and offending are closely related for many adolescents, there are some adolescents who use drugs but are not involved in delinquent behavior and others who are delinquent but do not use drugs (see Fagan, Weis, Cheng, & Watters, 1987; White, Pandina, & LaGrange, 1987; White & Labouvie, 1994). Furthermore, a high rate of both violent and nonviolent crime is committed under the influence of alcohol or drugs (White, Tice, Loeber, & Stouthamer-Loeber, 2002). The theoretical explanations for the observed associations between substance use and illegal activities are discussed later in this chapter.

Drug use and nondrug offending have also been linked to drug dealing. (In the present volume, we distinguish drug-related offending, such as possession and dealing, from other types of offending.) In fact, drug dealing is the major illegal activity for drug-involved criminals (Lipton & Johnson, 1998), probably because dealing provides the needed drugs and/or income to buy drugs

(Harrison, 1992). Nevertheless, rates of drug use vary considerably among dealers. Many dealers, especially those at the top of the dealing hierarchy, do not use drugs or do so only moderately (Hunt, 1990; Lipton & Johnson, 1998). During the 1990s, for many young crack cocaine dealers, selling had become an economic opportunity rather than a means of financing their own drug use (Harrison & Freeman, 1998; Inciardi & Pottieger, 1994). Many high-frequency dealers also engage in other illegal activities (Inciardi & Pottieger, 1998; Lipton & Johnson, 1998; Van Kammen & Loeber, 1994).

The violence associated with the illegal drug market has been labeled *systemic violence* (Goldstein, 1985). It is assumed that systemic violence accounts for a significant amount of drug-related violence among youths in inner cities (Fagan & Chin, 1990; Inciardi & Pottieger, 1991). Some researchers have blamed the increased violence associated with drug dealing on youth gangs. In general, however, studies show that there are numerous types of gangs, many of which do not sell or use drugs (Levine & Rosich, 1996). Further, dealing is just as prevalent among gang members as among others who do not belong to gangs, and there is no proof that drug-related activities increase gang violence (Fagan, 1989; Levine & Rosich, 1996; Moore, 1990; for greater detail on gangs, violence, drug use, and drug dealing, see also Klein, Maxson, & Miller, 1995; Moore, 1990; Thornberry, Krohn, Lizotte, Smith, & Tobin, 2003.) Yet studies show a strong link between alcohol use and violence within gangs (for a review, see Hunt & Laidler, 2001). In addition, the high rates of violence, and especially homicides, observed during the late 1980s and early 1990s have been linked to increases in gun use as well as to the increase of youths in crack distribution (Blumstein, 1995).

Because substance use, drug dealing, gang membership, and gun carrying have been linked to serious theft and violence, in this chapter we examine the prevalence, frequency, onset, and duration of these problem behaviors and compare them to those reported for serious violence and serious theft in chapters 4 and 5. We also examine the longitudinal associations between these problem behaviors and serious violence and theft. As in the earlier chapters, *prevalence* refers to the proportion of boys who engage in each behavior at each age. *Frequency* refers to the annual rate of engaging in each behavior for those who engage in the behavior. The *age of onset* is the age at which the boy first engages in the behavior. *Persistence* or *duration* refers here to the length of time between the first and last involvement in each problem behavior.

In this chapter we use the term *substance use* to cover the use of alcohol (beer, wine, and hard liquor), tobacco, marijuana, and hard drugs (including hallucinogens, powder cocaine, crack cocaine, heroin, barbiturates, amphetamines, tranquilizers, codeine, other prescription drugs, or PCP; use prescribed by a doctor was excluded). *Drug dealing* includes selling marijuana and other illegal drugs. We also assess whether the boy carried a gun (*gun carrying*) and belonged to a gang (*gang membership*) within the preceding year.

In this chapter we address the following questions:

What is the prevalence of substance use, drug dealing, gang membership, and gun carrying during the ages 7–25, and how does peak involvement in each of these behaviors compare to peak involvement in serious violence and theft?

How frequently do individuals use substances and deal drugs during the ages 7–25, and how does the frequency of these behaviors compare to the frequency of serious violence and theft?

What is the cumulative onset of these problem behaviors by age 19 (youngest cohort) and age 25 (oldest cohort) and how do cumulative onset rates compare to those for serious violence and theft?

What is the average age of onset of substance use, dealing drugs, gang membership, and gun carrying, and how do these ages of onset compare to those for serious violence and theft?

What is the sequencing of onsets of substance use, dealing, gang membership, and gun carrying, and how do onsets of these behaviors relate to the onset of serious violence and theft?

What is the persistence/duration of these problem behaviors and how does this persistence compare to that for serious violence and theft?

Are there cohort differences in the onset, prevalence, frequency, and duration of substance use, dealing, gang membership, and gun carrying?

Do substance use, dealing drugs, gang membership, and gun carrying predict serious violence and serious theft over time?

Are there cohort differences in the predictions of serious violence and serious theft?

Are some problem behaviors more predictive for serious violence than for serious theft?

Prevalence of Substance Use, Drug Dealing, Gang Membership, and Gun Carrying

Starting with the youngest cohort, Figure 6.1 shows the annual prevalence curves for the four types of substance use, and Figure 6.2 shows the annual prevalence curves for drug dealing, gang membership, and gun carrying from ages 7–19. The prevalence of all forms of substance use increased from age 7 through ages 18 or 19. The most prevalent substance used at each age was alcohol, which reached a peak of 62% at age 19, followed by tobacco and marijuana. Whereas the annual prevalence curves were similar for tobacco and marijuana through age 16, they diverged thereafter with the annual prevalence of tobacco use continuing to increase to about 50% at age 19 and the prevalence of marijuana use leveling off at around 39% at age 18. At each age from 11 on, the annual prevalence of drug dealing (Figure 6.2), which peaked at 15% at age 16, was higher than that for hard drug use, which peaked at 7%

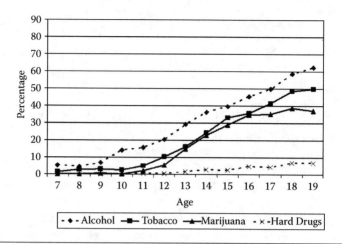

Figure 6.1 Annual Prevalence of Substance Use (Youngest Cohort)

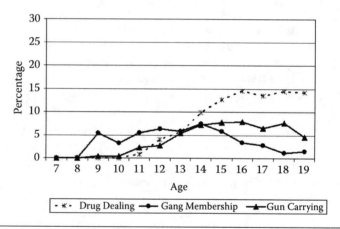

Figure 6.2 Annual Prevalence of Dealing, Gang Membership, and Gun Carrying (Youngest Cohort)

at ages 18 and 19 (Figure 6.1). In late adolescence, gang membership demonstrated the lowest annual prevalence rates; however, in late childhood annual prevalence rates were higher than for marijuana use, hard drug use, dealing, and gun carrying. In contrast to the other problem behaviors, gang membership peaked in early adolescence, reaching a peak of 7% at age 14, and declined to 2% by age 19. Gun carrying peaked at age 16 at 8% and stayed almost as high through age 18, dropping to 5% at age 19.

Figures 6.3 and 6.4 show comparable data for the oldest cohort between the ages of 13 and 25. These patterns were similar to those for the youngest cohort; however, they extend beyond age 19 to age 25. Only the annual prevalence of tobacco use continued to increase slightly through age 25 (56%), whereas for all other problem behaviors the annual prevalence declined at some point in late adolescence or young adulthood. The peak annual prevalence rates for the other problem behaviors were 81% at age 22 for alcohol, 43% at age 20 for marijuana, 10% at age 21 for hard drugs, 24% at age 19 for drug dealing, 9% at age 19 for gang membership, and 17% by age 19 for gun carrying.

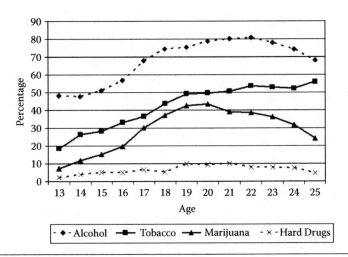

Figure 6.3 Annual Prevalence of Substance Use (Oldest Cohort)

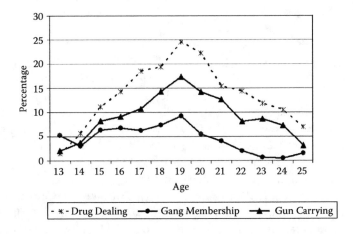

Figure 6.4 Annual Prevalence of Dealing, Gang Membership, and Gun Carrying (Oldest Cohort)

How does drug use in the PYS sample match national rates of drug use? We compared annual prevalence rates by age 18 for the PYS cohorts with those for high school seniors in the Monitoring the Future (MTF) study (Johnston, O'Malley, & Bachman, 2001) at the same time (1998 for the youngest cohort, and 1992 for the oldest cohort). MTF is based on a nationally representative sample of high-school students assessed annually, but it excludes dropouts and absentees, whose rates of drug use may be somewhat higher than their age peers who attend school. Despite its limitations, MTF is probably the most widely cited assessment of substance use among adolescents in the United States. The annual prevalence rates for marijuana (39% PYS vs. 38% MTF) and alcohol (79% PYS vs. 81% MTF) in the youngest cohort were virtually identical to the national rates. The annual prevalence rates for marijuana were somewhat higher in the PYS oldest cohort (37%) compared to the MTF sample (22%), whereas rates for alcohol were the same (74% PYS vs. 73% MTF).

Similarly, we compared rates of the other problem behaviors with those reported in other studies. A study of inner-city male adolescents reported an annual prevalence rate of 16% for drug dealing (Altschuler & Brounstein, 1991). During mid-adolescence, the prevalence rates of drug dealing in the PYS youngest and oldest cohorts were quite similar to those of the other study. In addition, annual prevalence rates for gang membership were similar to those reported for boys in a national school sample (Gottfredson & Gottfredson, 2001), although peak ages differed somewhat. In the national study, the peak was 8% at age 16, whereas the PYS youngest cohort peaked at 7% at age 14 and the oldest cohort peaked at 9% at age 19. However, gang membership rates for the PYS cohorts were lower than those reported for high-risk youth in large cities, which ranged from 14% to 30% (Thornberry, 1998).[1] In summary, for the most part, the PYS prevalence rates for substance use at age 18 and gang membership during adolescence were fairly similar to national rates at the same time.

Cohort Differences in Annual Prevalence

Are there cohort differences in the annual prevalence of problem behaviors? The prevalence data between ages 13 and 19 can be compared for both cohorts. Chapters 4 and 5 showed a higher prevalence of serious violence and serious theft offenses in the oldest cohort. Does this also apply to substance use and other risk behaviors? The results show that the oldest cohort reported a significantly ($p < .001$) higher prevalence of alcohol use at each age, especially in early adolescence. The oldest cohort also reported greater use of hard drugs at most ages than the youngest cohort, but these differences were only significant ($p < .05$) at age 15. In contrast, marijuana use was about twice as prevalent ($p < .001$) in the youngest cohort throughout early adolescence, but after that rates did not differ significantly between cohorts. Rates of tobacco use did not differ significantly between cohorts. For the most part, rates of drug dealing did not differ across cohorts, although there were significantly more dealers at ages 13 ($p < .001$), 14 ($p < .05$), and 17 ($p < .05$) in the youngest cohort. Gang membership did not decline as quickly in the oldest cohort and its prevalence was significantly higher in the oldest cohort from age 16 through age 19 ($p <.05$ at ages 16 and 17 and $p < .001$ at ages 18 and 19). On the other hand, there were significantly ($p < .05$) more gang members at age 14 in the youngest cohort. Gun carrying was significantly more prevalent at ages 13 ($p < .01$) and 14 ($p < .05$) in the youngest cohort, but the reverse was true at ages 17 ($p < .05$), 18 ($p < .01$), and 19 ($p < .001$). These differences could reflect a period effect.

Differences between the Prevalence of Serious
Offending and Other Problem Behaviors

To what extent are there developmental differences in offending compared to substance use, dealing, gang membership, and gun carrying? A comparison of the annual prevalence rates for different forms of substance use and serious violence and serious theft (see Chapter 4, Figures 4.1, 4.2, 4.3, and 4.4) shows some interesting differences. As mentioned in Chapter 4, for the youngest cohort, the annual prevalence of serious violence peaked at age 16 and declined thereafter, and the prevalence of serious theft peaked at age 14 and declined to near 0 by age 19. In contrast, the annual prevalence of alcohol, tobacco, marijuana, and hard drug use and drug dealing peaked at an older age, around age 18 or 19. The prevalence of gang membership and gun carrying followed a similar pattern to the prevalence of serious theft. Furthermore, much higher percentages of boys engaged in all the problem behaviors (except gang membership and hard drug use) than engaged in serious violence or serious theft. For example, the annual prevalence rates for alcohol, tobacco, and marijuana use peaked above 39%, compared to 6% for serious violence and 11% for serious theft.

As discussed in Chapter 4, in the oldest cohort the prevalence of serious violence peaked around ages 18–19 and declined rapidly in the 20s; the prevalence of serious theft peaked at age 15 and declined to 0 by age 25. Drug dealing, gun carrying, and, especially, gang membership followed similar patterns to serious violence in the oldest cohort. On the other hand, the annual prevalence of substance use continued to increase into the 20s, which is in marked contrast to serious theft and violence. Although alcohol, marijuana, and hard drug use showed declines by age 25, they did not decrease as steeply as either serious violence or serious theft.

Frequency of Substance Use, Drug Dealing, Gang
Membership, and Gun Carrying

Figure 6.5 shows the frequency (number of times) in the youngest cohort that substance users used substances and drug dealers dealt drugs in the previous year. This figure presents the mean of the highest frequency for active users or dealers within each age block. Note that the offending measures (i.e., dealing, serious violence, and serious theft) were truncated at 50 times per year and the substance use variables were truncated at 365 times per year, which could affect comparisons across problem behaviors. The frequency of problem behaviors increased with age, even though the annual prevalence did not, necessarily (compare Figure 6.5 with Figures 6.1 and 6.2). The most frequently used substance was tobacco, which was used almost daily (a mean of 294 times per year) by users during late adolescence (at ages 17–19) and about five times per week (259 times per year) in early adolescence (at ages 13–16). Marijuana was the next most often used substance, and it was used on average three times per week (161 times per year) by late adolescence and more than twice a week (120 times per year) during early adolescence. There were sharp increases in both tobacco and marijuana use frequencies from late childhood to early adolescence. In each age block except late childhood, marijuana was used more frequently by marijuana users than alcohol was drunk by alcohol users. The frequency of alcohol use peaked during late adolescence at under twice a week (87 times). The frequency of hard drug use doubled from early to late adolescence. At the peak (late adolescence), hard drugs were used on average less than twice a month (19 times). On average, dealing occurred more than twice a month (30 times in late adolescence), and the frequency was fairly consistent from early to late adolescence.

Figure 6.6 shows similar frequency data among users and dealers ages 13–25 for the oldest cohort. The frequency of substance use among users continued to increase into young adulthood except for tobacco use, which leveled off after late adolescence. Tobacco was used almost daily by users between late

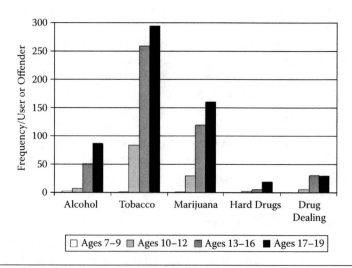

Figure 6.5 Frequency of Substance Use and Dealing (Youngest Cohort)

adolescence and young adulthood (more than 300 times per year). As in the youngest cohort, marijuana was used more frequently than alcohol during each age block, although by young adulthood both were used between three and four times a week (marijuana 181 times and alcohol 174 times, per year). Hard drugs were used about weekly in young adulthood (57 times per year) and about twice a month in adolescence (21 to 26 times per year). Dealers dealt less than once per week from young adolescence into young adulthood (between 28 and 35 times per year).

Cohort Differences in Frequency of Use and Dealing

Are there differences in the frequency of substance use and dealing between the two cohorts? A comparison of the two cohorts in late adolescence (ages 17–19) indicates that the mean frequencies of substance use for the oldest and youngest cohorts followed similar patterns, although frequency of alcohol use among users was significantly higher (by about 20%; $p < .05$) in the oldest cohort (compare Figures 6.5 and 6.6). None of the other frequencies differed significantly between cohorts in late adolescence. In contrast, during early adolescence (ages 13–16), the average frequency of alcohol, tobacco, and marijuana use was significantly higher in the youngest cohort (45%, 25%, and 120% higher, respectively; $p < .01$ for alcohol; $p < .001$ for tobacco; $p < .001$ for marijuana). The frequency of hard drug use was three times higher in the oldest cohort in early adolescence, although this difference was not statistically significant, probably due to the small number of hard drug users in both cohorts. There was no significant cohort difference in the frequency of drug dealing.

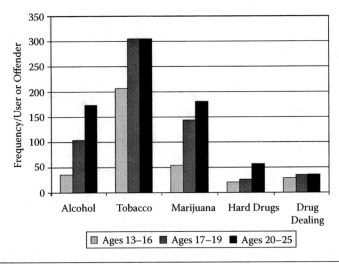

Figure 6.6 Frequency of Substance Use and Dealing (Oldest Cohort)

Differences between the Frequencies of Serious
Offending and Other Problem Behaviors

How do the frequencies of problem behaviors compare to the frequencies of offending among serious offenders? When one compares Figures 6.5 and 6.6 with Figures 4.5, 4.6, 4.7, and 4.8, it is very clear that these problem behaviors were engaged in more frequently than either serious violence or serious theft. In fact, in most age blocks, the frequencies for alcohol, tobacco, and marijuana use were more than 10 times higher and the frequency of dealing was two to three times higher than for serious offending, especially serious violence.

Cumulative Onset of Substance Use, Drug Dealing,
Gang Membership, and Gun Carrying

What are the peak periods of onset for each problem behavior? Figure 6.7 presents the cumulative onset curves for substance use, and Figure 6.8 presents the cumulative onset curves for drug dealing, gang membership, and gun carrying for the youngest cohort up to age 19. These figures differ from Figures 6.1 and 6.2 in that they add individuals cumulatively as they begin to engage in each behavior, whereas Figures 6.1 and 6.2 only count the percentage of those who engaged in each behavior at each specific age.

By age 19, 90% of the youngest cohort had drunk alcohol, 66% had used tobacco, 66% had used marijuana, and 16% had tried hard drugs. About one-third (38%) of the cohort had dealt drugs, one-fifth (21%) had been gang members, and one-fourth (25%) had carried a gun by the age of 19. (Note that those individuals who begin engaging in these behaviors after age 19 are not included in these figures. Therefore, the cumulative onset rates may not reflect the full pattern through young adulthood.)

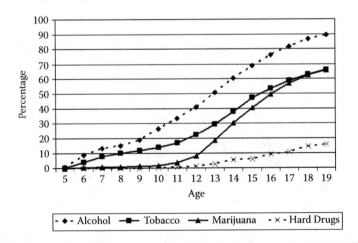

Figure 6.7 Cumulative Onset for Substance Use (Youngest Cohort)

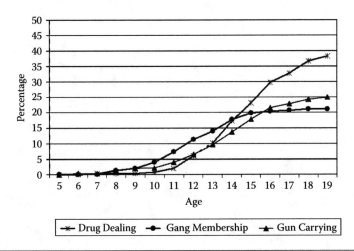

Figure 6.8 Cumulative Onset of Dealing, Gang Membership, and Gun Carrying (Youngest Cohort)

The onset of alcohol use increased gradually from age 6 onward and increased most between ages 10 and 16. The onset of tobacco use also increased gradually from age 6 with the sharpest increases occurring during the early to middle adolescence (ages 11–16). The onset of marijuana use peaked rapidly between ages 12 and 16, whereas the onset of hard drug use and gun carrying increased steadily between ages 12 and 18. The onset of drug dealing also increased most rapidly between ages 13 and 18. In contrast, the onset of gang membership increased earlier, between ages 11 and 14.

Figures 6.9 and 6.10 present these same data on cumulative onset for the oldest cohort until age 25. Because little substance use initiation occurs after age 25, it is likely that these data more accurately reflect the complete onset sequence than those for the youngest cohort. Almost all (99%) of the boys had tried alcohol, four-fifths (81%) had tried tobacco, three-fourths (74%) had tried marijuana, and one-third (34%) had tried hard drugs by age 25. By age 25, about one-half the cohort had dealt drugs (56%) or carried a gun (44%) at some point, and a little over one fourth (27%) had been gang members.

In the oldest cohort, large increases in alcohol and tobacco use onset occurred between ages 11 and 13. As was discussed in Chapter 4, these curves might be affected by retrospective reports of onset prior to age 13. No one began drinking alcohol after age 21, and almost every drinker had had his first drink by age 17. Large increases in marijuana use onset occurred from age 12 to age 18, and hard drug use onset continued somewhat later. The greatest increases in dealing and gun carrying occurred in the mid- to late teens, and onset of both behaviors was parallel. The onset of gang membership was fairly gradual from age 11 through age 20. No one first joined a gang after age 22, and very few after age 19.

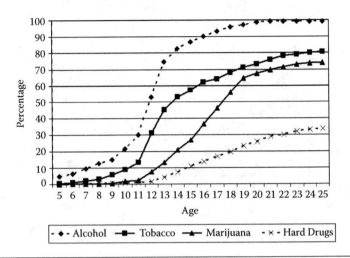

Figure 6.9 Cumulative Onset of Substance Use (Oldest Cohort)

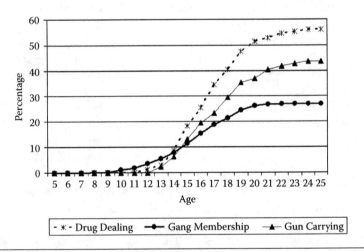

Figure 6.10 Cumulative Onset of Dealing, Gang Membership, and Gun Carrying (Oldest Cohort)

Cohort Differences in Cumulative Onset

Is the cumulative onset of problem behaviors similar across cohorts through late adolescence? A comparison of the oldest and youngest cohorts indicates that the oldest cohort was significantly more likely to have used alcohol (97%, vs. 90% for the youngest cohort; $p < .001$) and hard drugs (23% vs. 16%; $p < .01$), dealt drugs (47% vs. 38%; $p < .01$), and carried a gun (35% vs. 25%; $p < .001$) by age 19 ($p < .001$ for alcohol; $p < .01$ for hard drugs; $p < .01$ for drug dealing; $p < .001$ for gun carrying). The cumulative onset rates for the rest of the problem behaviors did not differ significantly across cohorts.

Differences between the Cumulative Onset of Serious
Offending and Other Problem Behaviors

We also compared the cumulative onset rates by age 19 for both cohorts with the cumulative onset rates for reported serious theft and serious violence measures reported in Chapter 4 (Figures 4.9 to 4.12). As was seen for annual prevalence, the age 19 cumulative onset rates for alcohol, tobacco, and marijuana were much higher than those for serious offending and rates for dealing and gun carrying were somewhat higher.

Average Age of Onset

Numerous studies have examined the sequencing of substance use and found that there is a progression from legal drugs (e.g., alcohol and tobacco), to marijuana use, and then to harder drugs (Kandel, Yamaguchi, & Chen, 1992). Our data support this stage model and also show how the other problem behaviors fit within this sequence (Table 6.1). In the youngest cohort, gang membership (mean age = 12.3) and alcohol use (12.5) were the earliest behaviors. A year later came tobacco use (13.3), followed by gun carrying (13.9), marijuana use (14.8), drug dealing (14.8), and hard drug use (15.7). Although the stage model of substance use is supported by these data, the difference in age of onset between alcohol use and tobacco is larger than found in many other studies. This finding probably reflects the nature of the PYS sample, which is more than half African American; African Americans begin smoking at older ages than do Caucasians (Juon, Ensminger, & Sydnor, 2002; White, Nagin, Replogle, & Stouthamer-Loeber, 2004). It is also interesting to note that drug dealing started approximately one year before hard drug use and that gun carrying started about one year earlier than either illegal drug use or dealing.

In the oldest cohort, the pattern of onset among the problem behaviors was similar to the youngest cohort except for the positions of gang membership and gun carrying, which had later ages of onset in the oldest cohort, which could reflect a period effect. Alcohol use (mean age = 12.2) came first, followed by tobacco use (14.2), gang membership (15.9), marijuana use (16.5), drug dealing (17.0), gun carrying (17.3), and hard drug use (17.5). As with the youngest cohort, the two-year gap between alcohol and tobacco onset is noteworthy and accounted for by the older onset of tobacco use in this sample (White et al., 2004). Also, we see a later onset for hard drug use than dealing (about six months), although dealing preceded gun carrying by several months. For these analyses again, it should be noted that the data for the youngest cohort do not include anyone who may begin a behavior after age 19. Therefore, the means for age of onset are higher in the oldest cohort because those who first

Table 6.1 Average Ages of Onset of Problem Behaviors and Serious Offending (Youngest and Oldest Cohorts)

Youngest Cohort		Oldest Cohort (through age 25)		Oldest Cohort (through age 19)	
Behavior	*Mean Age*	*Behavior*	*Mean Age*	*Behavior*	*Mean Age*
Gang Membership	12.3	Alcohol Use	12.2	Alcohol Use	12.0
Alcohol Use	12.5	Serious Theft	13.5	Serious Theft	13.1
Serious Theft	12.7	Tobacco Use	14.2	Tobacco Use	13.2
Tobacco Use	13.3	Serious Violence	15.1	Serious Violence	14.6
Serious Violence	13.3	Gang Membership	15.9	Gang Membership	15.4
Gun Carrying	13.9	Marijuana Use	16.5	Hard Drug Use	15.6
Marijuana Use	14.8	Drug Dealing	17.0	Marijuana Use	15.7
Drug Dealing	14.8	Gun Carrying	17.3	Drug Dealing	16.2
Hard Drug Use	15.7	Hard Drug Use	17.5	Gun Carrying	16.3

engaged in a problem behavior between ages 20 and 25 increased the mean for the oldest cohort.

To test for the effects of right censorship, we recalculated the mean ages of onset for each behavior in the oldest cohort only for those participants who began the behavior by age 19 (Table 6.1). Although the ages of onset were lower than when all participants were included in the analyses regardless of when they first began the behavior, the pattern was primarily the same as reported above. The one exception was that hard drug use (average age 15.6) fell between gang membership (age 15.4) and marijuana use (15.7).

Cohort Differences in Ages of Onset

Are there cohort differences in the ages of onset? A comparison across cohorts including only those who began by age 19 (Table 6.1) indicates that the age of onset for all behaviors except alcohol, tobacco, and hard drug use was significantly earlier in the youngest than oldest cohort ($p < .001$ for marijuana use; $p < .001$ for drug dealing; $p < .001$ for gang membership; $p < .001$ for gun carrying). This difference could reflect the fact that the oldest cohort relied on retrospective reports for all behaviors that began before age 13 (see discussion in Chapter 4) or, alternatively, that there was a period effect.

Differences between the Ages of Onset of Serious
Offending and Other Problem Behaviors

How do the ages of onset of these problem behaviors compare to those for serious violence and theft? Based on the data presented in Chapter 4 for the youngest cohort, the onset of serious theft (mean age = 12.7) occurred later than gang membership and alcohol use, but earlier than the other problem behaviors. The onset of serious violence (13.3) occurred at the same time as the onset of tobacco use and before gun carrying, marijuana use, drug dealing, and hard drug use. Examining the ages of onset in the oldest cohort up to age 25, we see that the onset of serious theft (13.5) occurred after alcohol use onset but before all other problem behaviors. The onset of serious violence (15.1) occurred between the onset of tobacco use and the onset of gang membership. These findings demonstrate that, for the average adolescent in the oldest cohort, serious violence preceded gang membership, dealing, and gun carrying. In the youngest cohort serious violence preceded dealing and gun carrying, but not gang membership.

Developmental Sequences in Onset

Sequencing among the Onsets of Problem Behaviors

The above data on mean ages of onset do not necessarily show the sequence of onsets among behaviors because for each behavior all individuals who engaged in a given behavior are included in the mean. Therefore, these mean ages do not assess the temporal order or sequencing between two behaviors among only the individuals who engage in both. Data on onset sequences for each pair of problem behaviors among those who engaged in both are presented in Table 6.2. The upper portion shows these data for the youngest cohort. In the first two columns are the two problem behaviors; the column on the left has a lower mean onset age than the column on the right among those who engaged in both behaviors. In the next two columns are the mean ages for the expected earlier behavior and the expected later behavior. For example, for those who both drank alcohol and used tobacco, the mean age of onset of alcohol occurred one year earlier (mean age 12.3 vs. 13.3). Of the 281 boys who used both, it was significantly ($p < .001$) more common for tobacco compared to alcohol to be used later ($N = 140$) than earlier ($N = 75$).

For ease of presentation we distinguish between two groups of substances as legal (alcohol and tobacco) and illegal (marijuana and hard drugs). Although alcohol and tobacco are not legally available for adolescents, these two substances are legal for adults and their use has different normative connotations compared with the use of illegal (also known as *illicit*) drugs.

In the youngest cohort, the use of either of the two legally available drugs (i.e., alcohol or tobacco) occurred more than three years earlier (age 11.6) than the use of marijuana (14.8) for those who used both, and a significantly

Table 6.2 Onset of One Problem Behavior versus Onset of Another Problem Behavior (Youngest and Oldest Cohorts)

		Mean Age		Next Level		Correlation	
Earlier	Later	Earlier	Later	Same (N)	Later (N)	Earlier (N)	r
		YOUNGEST COHORT					
Alcohol Use	Tobacco Use	12.3	13.3	66	140	75	.34***
Legal Drug Use	Marijuana Use	11.6	14.8	58	211	19	.34***
Marijuana Use	Hard Drug Use	14.4	15.8	19	38	5	.50***
Legal Drug Use	Illegal Drug Use	11.6	14.7	58	211	22	.34***
Legal Drug Use	Gang Membership	11.0	12.3	25	48	24	.26**
Gang Membership	Illegal Drug Use	12.3	13.7	25	46	16	.13
Gang Membership	Drug Dealing	12.5	14.4	23	45	5	.41***
Illegal Drug Use	Drug Dealing	13.9	14.8	68	69	21	.38***
Legal Drug Use	Gun Carrying	11.3	13.9	12	77	19	.25**
Illegal Drug Use	Gun Carrying	13.8	13.8	31	41	28	.29**
Gun Carrying	Drug Dealing	13.9	14.3	38	33	29	.37***
Gang Membership	Gun Carrying	12.4	13.6	24	34	7	.53***
		OLDEST COHORT					
Alcohol Use	Tobacco Use	11.9	14.1	96	213	59	.35***
Legal Drug Use	Marijuana Use	11.6	16.5	33	284	8	.27***
Marijuana Use	Hard Drug Use	15.3	17.4	19	91	14	.48***
Legal Drug Use	Illegal Drug Use	11.6	16.4	36	292	11	.26***
Legal Drug Use	Gang Membership	11.8	15.9	11	90	12	.16
Gang Membership	Illegal Drug Use	15.9	16.1	21	41	42	-.02
Gang Membership	Drug Dealing	16.0	16.4	25	43	32	.41***

Table 6.2 Onset of One Problem Behavior versus Onset of Another Problem Behavior (Youngest and Oldest Cohorts) (continued)

		Mean Age		Next Level			Correlation
Earlier	Later	Earlier	Later	Same (N)	Later (N)	Earlier (N)	r
Illegal Drug Use	Drug Dealing	15.9	16.9	60	117	50	.36***
Legal Drug Use	Gun Carrying	11.9	17.3	7	177	1	.29***
Illegal Drug Use	Gun Carrying	15.8	17.2	42	94	36	.28***
Drug Dealing	Gun Carrying	16.7	17.1	58	61	34	.53***
Gang Membership	Gun Carrying	16.1	17.0	27	36	25	.26*

Notes: N = number; r = correlation coefficient; *$p < .05$; **$p < .01$; ***$p < .001$.

($p < .001$) greater proportion of boys used legal drugs before marijuana. Marijuana was first used more than one year earlier than hard drugs, and the former drug was significantly ($p < .001$) more likely than the latter to be used first. The most consistent finding is that the onset of legal drugs occurred before the onset of illegal drugs and this sequence was significantly ($p < .001$) different from chance. These findings are consistent with a stage model of substance use, although there are still several boys who did not follow the typical sequence. The stage model has usually been applied only to substance use, but below we extend it to include the other problem behaviors.

Those who joined gangs and drank alcohol or smoked cigarettes began their use of legal drugs earliest (age 11) and more than one year earlier than they joined a gang (12.3). A significantly ($p < .01$) greater proportion of boys used legal drugs before they joined a gang. On the other hand, gang membership was significantly ($p < .001$) more likely to precede illegal drug use (12.3 vs. 13.7, respectively) and drug dealing (12.5 vs. 14.4, respectively). Illegal drug use (13.9) preceded dealing (14.8) and this pattern was significantly ($p < .001$) different from chance. Whereas a significantly ($p < .001$) greater proportion of boys first carried guns after using legal drugs and joining a gang, they were equally as likely to first carry a gun before as after first using illegal drugs and first dealing. These findings on sequencing are different from those reported in Table 6.1 when we looked at average ages of onset for the total sample rather than for boys who engaged in both behaviors.

The order of sequences found for the youngest cohort was replicated in the oldest cohort except that dealing significantly ($p < .01$) preceded gun carrying in the oldest cohort. For all other comparisons, a significantly ($p < .001$) greater proportion of boys engaged in the earlier behavior before the later behavior, except for the associations between gang membership with illegal drug use, dealing, and gun carrying, for which the ordering of behaviors was not significantly different from chance.

Cohort Differences in the Onsets of Problem Behaviors

Although the sequences of onset were similar for both cohorts, all problem behaviors (except alcohol use) appear to start later in the youngest cohort. This difference probably occurred because the age data for the youngest cohort do not extend beyond age 19. The difference in the ages of onset for gang membership, however, reflects an actual later age of onset in the oldest than youngest cohort given that virtually no one first joined a gang after age 19. The earlier age of gang membership in the youngest cohort accounts for the fact that fewer boys in the youngest than oldest cohorts were discordant for the expected sequence. In the oldest cohort there was a larger gap between the onset of alcohol and tobacco use for those who used both (two years vs. one year, respectively), which reflects the fact that more individuals started tobacco use than started alcohol use after age 19.

Correlations among the Onsets of Problem Behaviors

Table 6.2 also shows the correlations between the ages of onset of different problem behaviors (see the far right column). Ages of onset of substance use were significantly intercorrelated. Nevertheless, only the correlation between marijuana use and hard drug use ($r = .50$ [$p < .001$] in the youngest cohort and .48 [$p < .001$] in the oldest cohort) was strong and the others were moderately strong ($r = .26$ to .35, $p < .01 - .001$). The age of first dealing was also significantly related to the age of gang membership ($r = .41$ [$p < .001$] in both cohorts) and the age of onset of illegal drug use ($r = .38$ [$p < .001$] in the youngest cohort and .36 [$p < .001$] in the oldest cohort). In addition, the age of first gun carrying was significantly related to the age of onset of gang membership in the youngest cohort ($r = .53$, $p < .001$) and of dealing in the oldest cohort ($r = .53$, $p < .001$). In contrast, the correlations between ages of onset of gang membership and illegal drug use were not significant in either cohort. This finding suggests that joining a gang is not necessarily related to illegal drug use.

Sequencing of Serious Offending with Other Problem Behaviors

Table 6.3 shows the sequencing of these problem behaviors with serious violence and serious theft. For ease of presentation, the earliest age for alcohol and tobacco is counted as the onset of legal drugs and the earliest age for marijuana and hard drug use is counted as the age of onset of illegal drugs.

The upper part of Table 6.3 shows the sequencing of the onset of serious violence with the other problem behaviors. The sequence was the same in both cohorts except for gang membership. For both cohorts, serious violence followed legal drug use by 2.5 to 3.5 years and a significantly ($p < .001$) greater

Table 6.3 Onset of One Problem Behavior versus Onset of Serious Violence and Serious Theft (Youngest and Oldest Cohorts)

		SERIOUS VIOLENCE					
		Mean Age		**Next Level**		**Correlation**	
Earlier	Later	Earlier	Later	Same (N)	Later (N)	Earlier (N)	r
		YOUNGEST COHORT					
Legal Drug Use	Serious Violence	10.8	13.3	18	71	12	.31**
Serious Violence	Illegal Drug Use	13.4	13.6	20	35	39	.20
Gang Membership	Serious Violence	12.3	13.0	14	30	14	.25*
Serious Violence	Drug Dealing	13.6	14.6	15	38	19	.29*
Serious Violence	Gun Carrying	13.5	13.9	18	30	22	.24*
		OLDEST COHORT					
Legal Drug Use	Serious Violence	11.6	15.0	22	136	21	.20**
Serious Violence	Illegal Drug Use	14.9	15.5	34	66	57	.12
Serious Violence	Gang Membership	15.5	15.9	18	32	33	.23*
Serious Violence	Drug Dealing	15.2	16.3	34	59	44	.11
Serious Violence	Gun Carrying	15.3	16.9	32	58	29	.18*
		SERIOUS THEFT					
		Mean Age		**Next Level**		**Correlation**	
Earlier	Later	Earlier	Later	Same (N)	Later (N)	Earlier (N)	r
		YOUNGEST COHORT					
Legal Drug Use	Serious Theft	10.8	12.7	15	58	19	.34***
Serious Theft	Illegal Drug Use	12.9	13.7	25	33	26	.29**
Gang Membership	Serious Theft	12.2	12.6	13	18	9	.22
Serious Theft	Drug Dealing	13.0	14.3	22	34	15	.33**
Serious theft	Gun carrying	12.9	13.7	16	23	15	.20

Table 6.3 Onset of One Problem Behavior versus Onset of Serious Violence and Serious Theft (Youngest and Oldest Cohorts) (continued)

		Mean Age		Next Level			Correlation
Earlier	Later	Earlier	Later	Same (N)	Later (N)	Earlier (N)	r
		OLDEST COHORT					
Legal Drug Use	Serious Theft	11.3	13.4	35	109	37	.08
Serious Theft	Illegal Drug Use	13.4	15.5	17	107	38	.10
Serious Theft	Gang Membership	13.6	15.9	11	45	14	.18
Serious Theft	Drug Dealing	13.8	16.3	25	91	19	.16
Serious Theft	Gun Carrying	13.9	16.7	22	70	14	.22*

Notes: N = number; r = correlation coefficient; $*p < .05$; $**p < .01$; $***p < .001$.

proportion of boys first used legal drugs before they first engaged in serious violence. On the other hand, boys were equally as likely to first use illegal drugs as they were to first engage in serious violence, and the mean age of onset of serious violence preceded the mean age of onset of illegal drug use by only a few months. Therefore, developmentally, using drugs does not necessarily lead to serious violence. A significantly ($p < .05$) greater proportion of boys in the youngest cohort were first serious violent offenders (by about one year) before they first dealt drugs, whereas in the oldest cohort the sequence did not differ significantly from chance, although the mean age of violence was also about one year earlier. In the youngest cohort, gang membership preceded serious violence by less than one year, and a significantly ($p < .05$) greater proportion of boys first engaged in gang membership before engaging in serious violence. On the other hand, in the oldest cohort the mean age of onset of serious violence preceded gang membership by a few months, although boys were equally likely to first be seriously violent or first be a gang member. The onset of serious violence preceded the onset of gun carrying by only a few months in the youngest cohort, but by about 1.5 years in the oldest cohort; in the oldest cohort, a significantly ($p < .01$) greater proportion of boys were first violent before they carried a gun, whereas in the youngest cohort the sequence was not significantly different from chance.

In both cohorts, the onset of serious theft followed the onset of legal drug use, but preceded the onset of illegal drug use, dealing, and gun carrying (see the lower part of Table 6.3). All of these sequences were significantly ($p < .001$) different from chance in the oldest cohort, but only significantly different for theft with legal drugs use ($p < .001$) and dealing ($p < .01$) in the youngest cohort. As with violence, the sequencing of gang membership and serious theft differed between the cohorts. In the youngest cohort, an equal proportion of boys first joined gangs before as joined gangs after they committed their first serious theft offense, whereas in the oldest cohort three times as many boys had engaged in theft before joining a gang than had joined a gang before engaging in theft. Note the earlier age of legal and illegal drug use among those who also committed serious theft compared to those reported in Table 6.2 for boys who had only used substances.

What is the sequence of onsets for those who engage in all problem behaviors and serious offending? In the youngest cohort, 44 boys had engaged in all problem behaviors and serious violence by age 19. Their average sequence of onset was legal drugs (mean age = 11.1), gang membership (12.4), violence (13.3), gun carrying (13.5), illegal drugs (13.6), and dealing (14.0). In the oldest cohort 70 had engaged in all problem behaviors and serious violence by age 25. Their average sequence of onset was legal drugs (mean age = 12.0), violence (15.5), illegal drugs (15.8), gang membership (16.0), drug dealing (16.0), and gun carrying (16.6).

In the youngest cohort, 29 boys had engaged in all problem behaviors and serious theft by age 19. Their average sequence of onset was legal drugs (mean age = 10.4), gang membership (12.5), theft (12.8), illegal drugs (13.3), gun carrying (13.3), and drug dealing (14.0). In the oldest cohort 55 had engaged in all problem behaviors and serious theft by age 25. Their average sequence of onset was legal drugs (mean age = 11.6), theft (13.9), illegal drugs (15.3), drug dealing (15.9), gang membership (16.3), and gun carrying (16.6). The differences between the two cohorts in the sequencing of gang membership and gun carrying in relation to the other problem behaviors and serious offending is noteworthy.

Correlations of Serious Offending with Other Problem Behaviors

The onset of serious violence correlated significantly with the onset of all problem behaviors (r = .24 to .31) except illegal drug use in the youngest cohort (Table 6.3). In the oldest cohort, the onset of serious violence correlated significantly with the onset of legal drug use (r = .20), gang membership (r = .23), and gun carrying (r = .18). Therefore, the association between the onset of violence and some problem behaviors remained significant even into young adulthood.

In the youngest cohort, there were significant correlations between the onsets of serious theft and legal drug use (r = .34), illegal drug use (r = .29), and drug dealing (r = .33), but not the onsets of gang membership (r = .22) or gun carrying (r = .20). The lack of significance of these latter two correlations may reflect the small number of boys who were gang members or carried a gun and who also committed serious theft. In the oldest cohort, none of the correlations between the onset of serious theft and the onsets of the other problem behaviors were significant except for the correlation with gun carrying

($r = .22$). The difference between the two cohorts may reflect the greater variability in the age of onset of drug use, that is, the fact that some individuals first used drugs after age 19, whereas few first initiated serious theft in late adolescence or early adulthood. Overall, these data indicate that the onset of serious theft and the onset of other problem behaviors were strongly related during the adolescent years, but were not related in adulthood.

Duration/Persistence of Substance Use, Drug Dealing, Gang Membership, and Gun Carrying

How long do individuals persist in their involvement in problem behaviors? The PYS, with its repeated assessments, is in a unique position to provide information about how long the young men engaged in problem behaviors. Table 6.4 shows the mean years of duration for engagement in all problem behaviors as well as serious theft and violence for both cohorts. The number of years of duration is calculated by subtracting the age of onset from the last year in which the individual engaged in the behavior. Thus, those who began and ended their involvement in a problem behavior within the same year get a duration score of 0. Duration is only calculated for those who engaged in a behavior. For the oldest cohort, we also include the mean years of duration up to age 19 so that the two cohorts can be compared.

In the youngest cohort, alcohol and tobacco use persisted the longest, with an average of 5 and 4 years, respectively, up to age 19. Marijuana use followed next, with an average of 3 years, then gun carrying, drug dealing, and gang membership for 2 years, and finally hard drug use for 1 year. In the oldest cohort, alcohol use persisted on average for almost 11 years up to age 25, tobacco use for 9 years, and marijuana use for 6 years. Dealing came next for about 3.5 years, hard drug use and gun carrying for 3 years, and gang membership for 2 years. The longer persistence of these problem behaviors in the oldest cohort reflects the fact that the youngest cohort were only studied until age 19.

Cohort Differences in the Duration of Problem Behaviors

Are there cohort differences in persistence of problem behaviors? If we compare both cohorts up to age 19, we see that duration of alcohol use was significantly ($p < .001$) longer in the oldest cohort and drug dealing and gun carrying persisted longer in the youngest cohort ($p < .05$ and $p < .01$, respectively). There were no significant differences in duration for the other problem behaviors. Comparing the duration of problem behaviors up to age 19 and up to age 25 in the oldest cohort shows that most behaviors persist beyond age 19 except gang membership.

Table 6.4 Average Number of Years of Duration for Each Problem Behavior and Serious Offending (Youngest and Oldest Cohorts)

Behavior	Mean Duration, Youngest Cohort	Mean Duration, Oldest Cohort (through Age 25)	Mean Duration, Oldest Cohort (through Age 19)
Alcohol Use	5.0	10.9	6.2***
Tobacco Use	4.4	8.6	4.9
Marijuana Use	2.8	5.6	2.5
Hard Drug Use	1.2	3.1	1.6
Drug Dealing	2.1	3.5	1.6*
Gang Membership	1.6	2.3	1.7
Gun Carrying	2.2	3.1	1.3**
Serious Violence	1.4	2.7	1.6
Serious Theft	1.4	2.2	1.7

Notes: T-tests were conducted between the mean duration in the youngest cohort—compared to the oldest cohort—through age 19; *$p < .05$; **$p < .01$; ***$p < .001$.

Differences between the Duration of Serious Offending and Other Problem Behaviors

How does the persistence of serious violence and theft compare to persistence of other problem behaviors? Alcohol, tobacco, and marijuana use persisted two to three times longer in the youngest cohort and two to four times longer in the oldest cohort than serious offending. These differences are due to the persistence of substance use into young adulthood in combination with the maturation out of serious offending in late adolescence. Dealing and gun carrying persisted longer than serious offending in both cohorts. The similarities in the persistence of gang membership and serious offending through age 19 for both cohorts are noteworthy, although differences between cohorts might emerge if downward slopes beyond age 19 were to be examined.

The Predictive Associations of Substance Use, Drug Dealing, Gang Membership, and Gun Carrying to Serious Violence and Theft

Thus far this chapter has focused on describing patterns of problem behaviors and how they compare to patterns of serious offending. Next we examine whether these problem behaviors predict serious offending over time.

Past studies show that alcohol is the drug most often associated with violence (White & Gorman, 2000). While the rates of alcohol use by offenders at the time of an offense vary greatly across studies, in general they indicate that about half of all homicides and assaults are committed when the offender, victim, or both have been drinking (Collins & Messerschmidt, 1993; Greenfeld & Henneberg, 2001; Roizen, 1993). It should be noted that reports of use at the time of offense commission may only indicate that offenders use alcohol often, rather than that their use causes them to commit the violent act. In fact, studies indicate that violent offenders have much higher rates of daily drinking, heavy drinking, and alcohol abuse than the general population (Greenfeld & Henneberg, 2001; White & Gorman, 2000).

In addition, criminal justice statistics indicate that offenders are heavier drug users than those in the general population (Dorsey, Zawitz, & Middleton, 2002; Kouri, Pope, Powell, Oliva, & Campbell, 1997). Data from the Arrestee Drug Abuse Monitoring Program in 1999 indicate that about two-thirds of adult and one-half of adolescent arrestees tested urine positive for illegal drugs at the time of their arrest (Dorsey et al., 2002). However, data from adult arrestees and prisoners indicate that alcohol use is more strongly associated with violent crime, whereas illegal drug use (i.e., marijuana, cocaine, and heroin) is more strongly associated with property crime (Dorsey et al., 2002; Harlow, 1999; Valdez, Yin, & Kaplan, 1997). In contrast, adolescent arrestees' reports of crime commission under the influence are fairly equal for alcohol and drugs (Bureau of Justice Statistics, 1994). However, in a study of high-risk male adolescents, White, Tice, et al. (2002) found that violent acts are more often related to self-reported acute use of alcohol than marijuana (see also Huizinga, Menard, & Elliott, 1989; White & Hansell, 1998).

Goldstein (1985) has proposed a tripartite model to explain the association between substance use and violence, which may also explain the association between substance use and theft. This model postulates that there are three ways in which drug use could cause crime: (1) through psychopharmacological effects of drugs on the individual; (2) by generating predatory crime to get money to pay for drugs; and (3) because of systemic violence involved in the illegal drug market (for greater detail, see White & Gorman, 2000).

It is also possible that serious violent and theft offending increases drug use, drug dealing, gang membership, and gun carrying by exposing individuals to deviant subcultures that provide opportunities and reinforcement for such behavior (White & Gorman, 2000). Another viable and well-supported explanation for the association among these problem behaviors is the common cause model, which postulates that substance use and offending do not have a direct causal link. Rather, they are related because they share common causes (e.g., impulsivity, risk taking, abuse or rejection in family, lack of parental nurturance, early school failure, and peer rejection; see Hawkins, Catalano, & Miller, 1992; Reiss & Roth, 1993). Given that these behaviors share several common causes, the same individuals would be expected to engage in all of them. In addition, criminal offending, as well as drug use, drug dealing, gangs, and gun carrying, are often concentrated in neighborhoods that are poor, densely populated, and racially segregated and have a transient population (Bursik, 1988; Sampson, Raudenbush, & Earls, 1997; Ensminger, Anthony, & McCord, 1997), which could also explain the observed relationship among problem behaviors. It is probable that one single explanation cannot account for the associations of substance use, drug dealing, gang membership, and gun carrying with serious violence and theft, and that different models apply to different situations (White & Gorman, 2000). Below, we shed light on the tripartite model by examining whether these problem behaviors predict serious offending over time.

In the following analyses, the problem behaviors (i.e., alcohol, tobacco, marijuana, and hard drug use; drug dealing; gang membership; and gun carrying) were considered to be risk factors for serious offending and were dichotomized to reflect the top 25% in terms of maximum frequency within an age block compared to the remaining 75%. (For greater detail on risk factor development, see Chapter 7.) For alcohol use in late childhood, early and late adolescence, and young adulthood, tobacco use in early and late adolescence and young adulthood, and marijuana use in early and late adolescence and young adulthood, participants were dichotomized into the top 25% in terms of the highest frequency achieved in any year in an age block versus the remaining 75%. For the remainder of problem behaviors and alcohol, tobacco, and marijuana use at earlier ages, less than 25% of the youths engaged in the behavior within an age block. Thus, for these measures participants were dichotomized into those who had engaged in it within the age block and those who had not. We use the all-source measure of self-reports and convictions (see Chapter 5) as the outcome variable in these analyses; we control for current offending when predicting offending in the next age block, excepting predictions from the first age block. For predictions of violence from the first age block, we control for physical aggression because there is no self-reported or officially reported serious violence in the first age block. For predictions of theft from the first age block, we control for self-reported serious theft because there is no officially reported serious theft at the first age block.

Associations between Problem Behaviors and Serious
Violence in the Youngest Cohort

The left side of Table 6.5 presents the odds ratios for the associations of each problem behavior, controlling for current violence with the all-source measures of serious violence (V) in the next age block for the youngest cohort. Alcohol use significantly predicted serious violence; those who drank frequently in early adolescence had six times the risk of committing a violent offense in late adolescence than those who did not drink or drank less often. Those who drank frequently in middle childhood and early adolescence had more than twice the risk of committing a violent offense in the next age block than those who did not drink or drank less often. Those who smoked tobacco more often in one age block were about three times more likely to engage in serious violence in the next age block than those who did not smoke or smoked less often. Frequent marijuana smokers had four to five times the risk of later

Table 6.5 Odds Ratios Predicting Combined Serious Violence and Combined Serious Theft from Substance Use, Drug Dealing, Gang Membership, and Gun Carrying, Controlling for Earlier Violence or Theft (Youngest and Oldest Cohorts)

Predictor-Outcome Interval 1	Youngest Cohort								Oldest Cohort					
	Middle Childhood (7–9) to Late Childhood (10–12)		Late Childhood (10–12) to Early Adolescence (13–16)		Early Adolescence (13–16) to Late Adolescence (17–19)		Middle Childhood (7–9) to Late Adolescence (17–19)		Early Adolescence (13–16) to Late Adolescence (17–19)		Late Adolescence (17–19) to Early Adulthood (20–25)		Early Adolescence (13–16) to Early Adulthood (20–25)	
Outcome	V	T	V	T	V	T	V	T	V	T	V	T	V	T
Alcohol Use	2.54*	3.15**	2.19**	1.42	6.40***	1.37	1.58	1.06	2.31***	2.02*	1.57	1.38	2.16**	0.67
Tobacco Use	2.92*	2.63*	2.80**	2.45**	3.28**	2.99**	1.26	2.60	1.44	1.27	1.46	1.55	1.11	1.12
Marijuana Use	N/R	N/R	4.20***	2.33	5.20***	1.11	N/R	N/R	2.15**	1.71	1.38	1.59	1.49	1.01
Hard Drug Use	N/A	N/A	2.87	4.60	1.96	2.91*	N/A	N/A	1.51	1.49	0.90	2.57*	1.14	1.38
Drug Dealing	N/A	N/A	8.26***	3.49*	4.55***	0.88	N/A	N/A	4.21***	2.27*	2.56***	2.21*	1.89*	0.57
Gang Member	N/A	N/A	2.81**	1.51	2.25	0.52	N/A	N/A	3.76***	1.45	3.67***	2.19	2.40*	0.32
Gun Carrying	N/R	N/R	2.09	2.40	4.37***	0.46	N/R	N/R	3.61***	2.05*	4.46***	2.42*	3.05***	1.33

Notes: *p < .05; **p < .01; ***p < .001; V = all-source measure of serious violence; T = all-source measure of serious theft; N/R = not run because of too few cases engaging in the problem behavior; N/A = not asked in middle childhood applicable; b = The violence analyses control for the combined violence measure in the earlier age block and the theft analyses control for the combined theft measure in the earlier age block except for predictions from the first age block; for predictions from middle childhood (7–9), the violence analyses control for physical aggression and the theft analyses control for self-reported serious theft.

violence than nonusers or less frequent users. Although hard drug users were two to three times more likely to be violent in the next age block, these odds ratios were not significant, probably because of power (i.e., there were too few hard drug users in the analyses). Drug dealing and gang membership in late childhood significantly increased the risks of violent offending in early adolescence and dealing and gun carrying in early adolescence significantly increased the risk of violence in late adolescence. In fact, those who dealt drugs in late childhood had eight times the risk of violent offending in early adolescence and those who dealt drugs or carried guns in early adolescence had four to five times the risk of serious violent offending in late adolescence. Middle-childhood alcohol or tobacco use did not significantly increase the risks of violence in late adolescence. In sum, in the youngest cohort, all of the problem behaviors except gun carrying in late childhood and hard drug use in both late childhood and early adolescence significantly predicted violence in the next age block even with controls for earlier violence.

Associations between Problem Behaviors and Serious Violence in the Oldest Cohort

The findings for the oldest cohort are presented on the right side of Table 6.5. Frequent alcohol use in early adolescence doubled the risk of later violence in both late adolescence and early adulthood, although frequent alcohol use in late adolescence was not a significant predictor of later violence. Similarly, marijuana use in early adolescence significantly increased the risk violence in late adolescence, but later marijuana use did not increase the risk of violence in young adulthood. In contrast, tobacco and hard drug use were not significantly related to later violence in any age block. Drug dealing, gang membership, and gun carrying were strongly related to serious violent offending over time, including from early adolescence into young adulthood. Gang members and individuals who carried guns had about three to five times the risk of later violence even with controls for current violence.

Associations between Problem Behaviors and Serious Theft in the Youngest Cohort

Table 6.5 also shows the odds ratios for the problem behaviors predicting the all-source measure of serious theft over time, controlling for current theft. Early alcohol and tobacco use increased the risk of later theft and, in fact, frequent tobacco use was related to theft across each age block. Marijuana use was not related to later theft. Hard drug use in early adolescence predicted theft in late adolescence and dealing in late childhood significantly predicted theft in early adolescence.

Associations between Problem Behaviors and Serious Theft in the Oldest Cohort

Early adolescent frequent alcohol use doubled the risk of serious theft in late adolescence, and hard drug use in late adolescence almost tripled the risk of serious theft in early adulthood. None of the other substance use-theft associations were significant. Dealing and gun carrying in early and late adolescence were significant predictors of later theft, whereas gang membership was not.

Cohort Differences in Associations

Are there differences between cohorts in the associations between the problem behaviors and serious violence? To address this question, it is possible to compare the early adolescence to late adolescence prediction period for both cohorts using odds ratios as a criterion. Substance use was a stronger predictor of serious violence in late adolescence for the youngest than oldest cohort. Dealing and gun carrying were similarly strong in both cohorts, whereas gang membership was significantly associated with violence for the oldest cohort but not the youngest cohort.

The associations with serious theft differed across cohorts. Tobacco and hard drug use were significant predictors for the youngest cohort, whereas alcohol use, dealing, and gun carrying were significant for the oldest cohort.

Differences between Serious Violence and Theft in Associations

There were more significant associations of the problem behaviors with serious violence than serious theft, especially in the youngest cohort. Marijuana use was related to violence but not theft, whereas hard drug use was related to theft but not violence. Gang membership was only related to violence. Although dealing and gun carrying were related to both serious violence and serious theft, the odds ratios were larger for serious violence than serious theft.

Summary of Key Findings

In this chapter we have examined the prevalence, frequency, onset, and duration/persistence of substance use, drug dealing, gang membership, and gun carrying, as well as the longitudinal associations of these problem behaviors to serious violence and theft. The design of the PYS has allowed us to compare these important parameters across problem behaviors, which has not been done in such detail in previous studies. Below we highlight the key findings:

- The majority of young men used alcohol, tobacco, and marijuana, and substantial numbers of young men also belonged to gangs, dealt drugs, used hard drugs, and carried a gun by the time they reached young adulthood.
- The prevalence of substance use and gang membership within the PYS sample was comparable to national rates, which suggests that results reported in subsequent chapters may have generalizability beyond this sample.
- There were disparities between developmental patterns of substance use and patterns of serious theft and violence, with all forms of

offending following the age-crime curve (see Chapter 4), but substance use not showing the downturn typical of this. Substance use continued to escalate into young adulthood in terms of prevalence and frequency, whereas the prevalence and frequency of serious theft and violence decreased in young adulthood.

- Developmental patterns of drug dealing, gang membership, and gun carrying were comparable to serious offending, especially serious violence. However, gun carrying and drug dealing persisted longer than serious offending.
- There were cohort differences in the prevalence of problem behaviors. The oldest cohort was more likely to be involved in alcohol use, hard drug use, drug dealing, and gun carrying in late adolescence, whereas the youngest cohort was more involved in several problem behaviors at a younger age, especially marijuana use, gun carrying, and gang membership.
- Violent offending was more likely to precede than to follow illegal drug use. Thus, illegal drug use is not necessarily a precursor to serious violent offending.
- The onset of gun carrying followed the onset of both violence and theft in the oldest cohort, although gun carrying was equally likely to precede as to follow serious offending in the youngest cohort. The onset of gun carrying also followed the onset of most of the other problem behaviors in the oldest cohort. The earlier gun carrying in the youngest cohort could reflect period changes in the acceptance of guns and a greater willingness to carry them whether or not one is involved in other problem behaviors.
- Gang membership preceded serious violence and theft in the youngest cohort, but followed them in the oldest cohort. In addition, the sequencing between gang membership and several of the other problem behaviors differed between cohorts, probably because of the earlier involvement in gangs in the youngest cohort. This cohort difference could reflect a period effect.
- Hard drug use was related to theft, but not to violence. This finding could support an economic motivation model.
- Drug dealing was related to violence, but not to theft. This association could reflect the systemic violence associated with the illegal drug market, or the fact that dealing and violence were predicted by a similar set of common causes.
- Substance use—and especially tobacco use—in late childhood and early adolescence predicted later serious offending. Marijuana use was related to violence, but not theft, while alcohol use predicted violence more consistently than theft. Whereas tobacco and marijuana use are not known to pharmacologically cause violence, there

is abundant evidence that heavy alcohol use can lead to disinhibition and violence (Wei, Loeber, & White, 2004).

It is probable that the problem behaviors studied here are related to serious offending for different reasons. For many young men, individual characteristics and early parent-child interactions, in combination with socioenvironmental factors, may increase the risk for involvement in all types of problem behavior. Therefore, it is important to examine how these problem behaviors are related to serious violence and theft over time, controlling for these additional domains of risk factors. In the next chapter we examine these more complex relationships.

Note

1. The prevalence of gun carrying at age 19 for the youngest cohort was similar to that found in the Rochester Youth Development Study (RYDS; see Bjerregaard & Lizotte, 1995), but was much higher for youth in the oldest cohort of the PYS. The prevalence of gang membership in the PYS was lower than that in the RYDS (Bjerregaard & Smith, 1993).

Part III
Prediction of Violence, Serious Theft, and Desistance

Seven
Promotive and Risk Processes at Different Life Stages

DAVID P. FARRINGTON, ROLF LOEBER, DARRICK JOLLIFFE, AND DUSTIN A. PARDINI

One of the strengths of the Pittsburgh Youth Study (PYS) is its ability to demonstrate which factors predict serious violence and serious theft from different life stages, starting from middle childhood and ending with early adulthood. Recall that the life stages are divided into the following age blocks: middle childhood (ages 7–9), late childhood (ages 10–12), early adolescence (ages 13–16), late adolescence (ages 17–19), and early adulthood (ages 20–25).

Most of the literature on the prediction of serious offending and recidivism (Cottle, Lee, & Heilbrun, 2001; Hawkins et al., 1998; Lipsey & Derzon, 1998; Loeber & Dishion, 1983) has focused on risk factors, defined as factors that increase the probability of later delinquency, rather than on promotive factors associated with a decreased probability of later delinquency (for exceptions, see Pollard, Hawkins, & Arthur, 1999; Lösel & Bender, 2003). This chapter focuses on both risk and promotive factors. *Preventive promotive factors* are defined as factors that predict a low probability of later delinquency in the general population (discussed in this chapter) while *remedial promotive factors* predict desistance from offending in populations of known delinquents (discussed in Chapter 9). The aim of identifying preventive promotive factors is to enable main effects to be detected, as has been done for risk factors.

Following the example of Sameroff, Bartko, Baldwin, Baldwin, and Seifer (1998) we distinguish between promotive and protective factors. *Protective factors* differ from promotive factors in that they are only those promotive factors that in interaction analyses are statistically significant in buffering or nullifying the impact of risk factors. For example, if poor supervision by the parent increases the risk of offending for children from low-income families but not for children from high-income families, high income could be classified as a protective factor. In this chapter we will also focus on aggravating risk factors predictive of later delinquency, whereas in Chapter 9 we will review hindering risk factors that negatively predict individuals' desistance from offending.

Most research on promotive factors has focused on factors that scholars on an a priori basis assigned to operate in a desirable manner (e.g., Arthur, Hawkins, Pollard, Catalano, & Baglioni, 2002; Werner, 2005). Hence, the scientific basis for the identification of promotive factors that actually operate in a positive way is very slim. Thus, for us the key issue was to empirically demonstrate which possible preventive promotive factors actually predict a low probability of serious offending.

How is such empirical demonstration done? We use the term *risk factor* to refer to a case when the probability of offending is greater in the "worst" category of a variable (e.g., poor supervision by the parent) than in the middle category (explained below). Conversely, we use the term *promotive factor* to refer to a case when the probability of offending is less in the "best" category of a variable (e.g., good supervision) than in the middle category (explained below). In order to investigate risk and promotive factors independently, variables need, at a minimum, to be trichotomized, although we could also compare the worst, middle, and best ranges of scores on a variable. As mentioned, we reserve the term *protective factor* for variables that interact with a risk factor to buffer or nullify its effects. Thus, our approach is to first establish which factors principally operate as risk or promotive factors (basically the study of main effects of each), and then study interaction effects between risk and protective factors.

Several scenarios are possible, each of which can have profound implications about mechanisms and processes that operate between predictors and later serious offending. In one scenario, results from analyses in this volume may confirm the commonly held assumption that most variables operate as risk factors that encourage offending and that there are few promotive factors that discourage offending. In another scenario, the results may show that risk and promotive effects occur in about equal proportions. In a third scenario, the research may show that promotive effects outnumber risk effects, but which may vary by age period.

It is likely that the processes that operate between predictors and outcomes are vastly different in each of the three scenarios. In the first scenario, serious offending would largely result from the presence of multiple negative events in children's lives (e.g., poor supervision, poor parent-child relations, school failure, etc.). In the second scenario, serious offending would depend on the balance between multiple negative events in children's lives and multiple positive events (such as good supervision, good parent-child relations, etc.). In the third scenario, positive events (such as good supervision) would be the more important factors predicting low rates of serious offending.

Scientific evidence for each of these scenarios has different and profound implications for conceptualizations about how children develop to become serious delinquents or avoid such an outcome, and how positive change can be optimized through interventions (Arthur et al., 2002). In the first scenario, in which risk factors dominate, positive development mostly depends on the removal or reduction of risk factors. In the second scenario, positive change depends on both the removal or reduction of risk factors and the increase or enhancement of promotive factors. In the third scenario, most of the behavioral change to a positive outcome would result from the introduction of new promotive factors in children's lives and/or the enhancement of existing promotive factors.

This chapter addresses several major questions. The first set of these are:

Which variables operate as aggravating risk factors only, which variables operate as preventive promotive factors only, and which variables operate as both promotive and risk factors?

Are there developmental periods in which preventive promotive factors predominate, and are there developmental periods in which aggravating risk factors predominate?

On average, is the strength of relationships between aggravating risk factors and the later high probability of violence or theft similar to the strength of relationships between preventive promotive factors and the later low probability of serious violence or theft?

The next set of questions examines the independent contribution of aggravating risk and preventive promotive factors in multivariate analyses to the prediction of serious violence and theft.

What are the most important independent preventive promotive and aggravating risk factors for violence and theft from middle childhood to early adulthood?

Do preventive promotive factors continue to predict a low probability of violence or serious theft even if risk factors are taken into account?

Among the best predictors of violence and theft, are there factors that are potentially modifiable and that can be incorporated in primary prevention programs? (Factors relevant to tertiary prevention—that is, the reduction of violence and theft in known offenders—will be discussed in Chapter 9.)

Are the preventive promotive and aggravating risk factors that predict violence the same as those that predict theft?

Are there preventive promotive factors that buffer the impact of aggravating risk factors?

In the following set of analyses, serious violence and serious theft were measured using the all-source measure combining convictions and reported offenses (as described in Chapter 5). Any offense within an age block was counted. For ease of exposition, we will refer to *violence* and *theft* rather than *serious violence* and *serious theft*.

Studying Risk and Promotive Effects

As mentioned, in order to study both risk and promotive effects separately, trichotomized variables are needed as a minimum. In contrast, with dichotomized variables, a comparison of the risk category with the promotive category, and a comparison of the promotive category with the risk category, produce identical results, making it impossible to distinguish between risk and promotive effects. For that reason, we have chosen trichotomization of a continuous variable to identify which part of the distribution is related to serious offending, and whether risk or promotive effects prevail. Trichotomization allows the tests for preventive promotive or aggravating risk factors to be conducted separately (Stouthamer-Loeber et al., 1993; Stouthamer-Loeber, Loeber, Wei, Farrington, & Wilkström, 2002; Stouthamer-Loeber, Wei, Loeber, & Masten, 2004).

Variables were trichotomized as close as possible to the lower 25% the middle 50%, and the upper 25% of the distribution. The test for preventative promotive factors was based on the comparison between the lower 25% and the middle 50%, while the test for aggravating risk factors was based on the comparison between the upper 25% and the middle 50%. Most of the factors listed in Chapter 3 could be examined in this way. However, some factors (such as one vs. two biological parents, a small house, truancy, running away, and repeating a grade) were inherently dichotomous, and for that reason were excluded from the analyses aimed at identifying risk and promotive effects. For these variables we had to make a decision about whether to label them as *risk factors* or *promotive factors*. Using prior research (Hawkins et al., 1998; Lipsey & Derzon, 1998; Loeber & Dishion, 1983) as a guide, we decided to label all dichotomous variables as risk factors (i.e., truancy, running away, mother's alcohol use during pregnancy, child maltreatment by age 12, parent alcohol problems, repeating a grade, low educational level, violence victimization, theft victimization, high serious injuries, fewer than two biological parents at home, two or more caretaker changes by age 10, family on welfare, and small house). However, we must stress that this is an arbitrary decision and that we cannot be sure that these variables have risk effects rather than promotive effects.

Testing for Nonlinear Effects

The identification of risk and promotive factors is facilitated through the testing of nonlinear effects. Figures 7.1–7.3 distinguish three important possibilities (based on hypothetical data). Figure 7.1 shows a linear relationship between a predictor (classified into low, medium, and high values) and offending. The percentage who become delinquents is 32% of those with low values, 50% of those with medium values, and 68% of those with high values of the predictor. In this example, the predictor has both a risk effect (because the percentage of individuals who become delinquents significantly increases from medium to high values) and a promotive effect (because the percentage who become delinquents significantly decreases from medium to low values). The logarithm of the odds of offending (+.75 at 68% and -.75 at 32%) shows the symmetry of these percentages.

We can quantify these effects by calculating odds ratios (ORs) comparing (1) high values and medium values—the risk effect; and (2) medium values and low values—the promotive effect. In our analyses, we identified the highest quarter of the boys (about 120 in each cohort) as high risk, the middle half (about 240) as medium risk, and the lowest quarter (about 120) as low risk. With these numbers, Figure 7.1 would have a risk OR of 2.11 (95% confidence interval 1.65–2.57, $p < .05$) and an exactly equal promotive OR of 2.11.

Figure 7.2 shows a nonlinear association between the predictor and the outcome, representing a risk effect only. The percentage who become

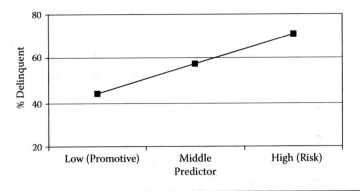

Figure 7.1 Linear Relation between a Predictor and Delinquency (Both Risk and Promotive Effects)

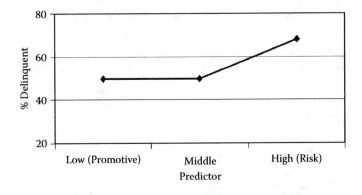

Figure 7.2 Nonlinear Relation between a Predictor and Delinquency (Risk Effect)

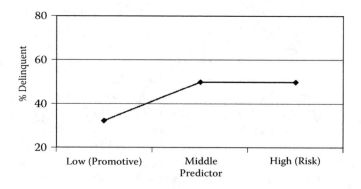

Figure 7.3 Nonlinear Relation between a Predictor and Delinquency (Promotive Effect)

delinquents increases from medium to high values of the predictor (from 50% to 68%, with the same OR of 2.11), but does not decrease from medium to low values (with a promotive OR of 1.00).

Figure 7.3 shows a promotive effect only. The percentage who become delinquents decreases from medium to low values of the predictor (from 50% to 32%, with the same OR of 2.11), but does not increase from medium to high values (with an OR of 1.00). Hence, the relative sizes of the risk and promotive ORs indicate whether there are risk or promotive effects, or both. In Figures 7.2 and 7.3, the two ORs were significantly different ($z = 3.26$, $p = .001$).

These percentages were not chosen arbitrarily. The statistical significance of nonlinear trends can be measured using the Cochran-Armitage linear trend test (Agresti, 1990, pp. 100–102). This partitions the overall chi-squared value (here, based on a 3 x 2 table) into linear and nonlinear components. The size of the nonlinear component (with 1 d.f.) tests whether there is a significant nonlinear relationship. Setting 50% of the delinquents out of 240 in the middle category and 50% of the delinquents out of 120 in one extreme category, the other extreme category has to be 38.62 out of 120 (32.2%), or equivalently 81.38 out of 120 (67.8%) for the size of the nonlinear component of chi-squared to equal 3.84 ($p = .05$, two-tailed) and hence, to be statistically significant. These percentages, therefore, are shown in Figures 7.1–7.3.

The Identification of Risk and Promotive Factors

First, we examined which variables had risk effects (called *aggravating risk factors*). Second, we examined which variables had promotive effects (called *preventive promotive factors*). Third, we examined which variables in some cases had risk effects and other cases had promotive effects (called *mixed factors*). Figure 2.1 (in Chapter 2) shows that the prediction analyses could be done in a proximate manner between contiguous age blocks (e.g., middle childhood to late childhood) or long-term between nonadjacent age blocks (e.g., middle childhood to late adolescence). We had multiple ways of investigating predictors (six comparisons for the youngest cohort, and three comparisons for the oldest cohort) for violence, and the same number of comparisons for theft (and thus, a total of 18 comparisons).

If a particular variable repeatedly showed as a promotive factor (and never or hardly ever as a risk factor) we regarded this as a pervasive preventive promotive factor. In the same manner, if a specific predictor repeatedly showed as a risk factor (and never or hardly ever as a promotive factor), this would provide us with evidence that we were dealing with a pervasive aggravating risk factor. Specifically, a promotive effect was only noted if most (i.e., over 70%) of the effects were promotive. Along the same lines, a risk effect was only noted if most (i.e., over 70%) of the effects were risk effects. In all other instances, the effects were deemed mixed.

Table 7.1 shows the results of the analyses. The criterion for identifying a promotive or risk effect was an odds ratio that was significant at the $p <$ .05 level or was 2.0 or larger (considered by Cohen, 1996, to be a substantial effect) in comparisons of upper versus middle (risk) and middle versus lower (promotive) values of the variable. An odds ratio of 2.0 or larger was usually statistically significant, so we will refer to *significant effects*. We used two indicators to demonstrate how clearly the distinction between risk and promotive factors could be made. First, we calculated the proportion of significant effects out of total effects examined across the two cohorts, which we call the pervasiveness index. The maximum number of comparisons was 18 (12 for the youngest cohort and 6 for the oldest cohort). Note that because of the maximum number of 18 comparisons, we would expect by chance ($p < .05$) that there would be one statistically significant effect (0.9 to be exact). Note that some predictors were not measured or available for certain age blocks; this is indicated by a dash (—) in Table 7.1. The higher the pervasiveness index, the higher the degree of replication across development and the higher the consistency of the findings. Second, we calculated a consistency index, which shows the percentage of observed associations that indicated risk as opposed to promotive effects.

Preventive Promotive Factors

The results certainly were different from what we had expected. For instance, we had assumed for years that ADHD symptoms, physical punishment, and several other child-rearing practices by parents tended to operate mostly as risk rather than promotive factors (see also Gershoff, 2002). The results, however, proved us wrong, since the effects were mostly promotive. For example, Table 7.1 shows that low ADHD symptoms acted as a promotive factor, reducing the likelihood of later serious offending (rather than high ADHD symptoms increasing the probability of serious offending). Of the significant comparisons, 5 out of 12 were promotive (42% pervasiveness [P]), and all of

Table 7.1 Results of Initial Analyses to Identify Promotive, Risk, and Mixed Predictors of Violence and Theft (Youngest and Oldest Cohorts)

Predictor-Outcome Interval	Youngest Cohort						Oldest Cohort												Risk, Promotive, or Mixed Effect	% Pervasive	% Consistent
	From Middle Childhood to Late Childhood		From Late Childhood to Early Adolescence		From Early Adolescence to Late Adolescence		From Middle Childhood to Early Adolescence		From Middle Childhood to Late Adolescence		From Late Childhood to Late Adolescence		From Early Adolescence to Late Adolescence		From Late Adolescence to Early Adulthood		From Early Adolescence to Early Adulthood				
Outcome	V	T	V	T	V	T	V	T	V	T	V	T	V	T	V	T	V	T			
PARTICIPANT PSYCHOPATHOLOGY																					
Truancy	R	R	R	R	R	R	R	R	R		R		R	R	—	—	R	R	Risk (d)	—	—
Running Away	R	R	R	R	R	R	R	R	R		—	—	R	R	—	—	R		Risk (d)	—	—
ADHD Symptoms	P		—		P		P		—				P	P					Promotive (Violence)	42	100
Psychopathic Features	P	P*	B	P*	B	P	P		B		B		P		—		B	B	Mixed (Violence) / Promotive (Theft)	— / 63	— / 83
Depressed Mood	B	R			R		P		P		P	P	R						Mixed	—	—
Anxiety		P	P		P						P	P							Promotive	17	100
Shyness/Withdrawal									P		P	P	P		P				Promotive	17	100
PARTICIPANT COMPETENCE																					
Prosocial Behavior	—				P	P	—	—	—	—	P		P	R	P	R	—		Promotive	33	80
Interaction with Interviewer	—	—	P		R	P	—	—	—	—	R				B	P	—		Mixed	—	—
Self-Aspirations	—				R		R		—		—		R				R		Risk	25	75
Attitude Toward Delinquency			R	R	R		R	P*	R		P		R	R			P		Risk	39	78

Perceived Likelihood of Being Caught			B		P	R			P	P	B	P		R	P				Mixed	—	—
Age Left Home	—	—	—	—	—	—	—	—	—	—	—	—			R		R		Risk	33	—
									Family Functioning												
Persistence of Discipline	P		R			P								P	—	—	—	—	Promotive	21	75
Physical Punishment	P			P	P	P			R						—	—	P		Promotive	31	83
Child Maltreatment by 12	—	—	R	R	R	R	R	R	—	—	—	—		R		R		R	Risk (d)	—	—
Parent Reinforcement					P		R				R	R	P		—	—			Mixed	—	—
Supervision			B	R	P	P	P		P		P		B		—	—	P	P	Promotive	39	70
Youth Involvement	P	P		R				P	P		R		P	P	—	—	P		Promotive	50	78
									Parent Characteristics												
Parent Antisocial Attitude		R							R					P	—	—			Mixed	—	—
Parent Aspirations for Child						P								R	—	—		P	Mixed	—	—
Parent Stress	P							R		R			P	P	—	—	P		Mixed (Y)		
																			Promotive (O)	75	100
Parent Alcohol Problem														R	—	—			Risk (d)	—	—
Father Behavior Problems	R		—	—	—	—		R	R	R				R	—	—			Risk (d)	—	—
Parent Police Contact						R				R		R							Risk (d)	—	—
									Peers												
Peer Delinquency	P*	B	R*	B	B	B	P	P	P		P		R	R*	R	R*	R		Mixed (Y)	—	—
																			Risk (O)	83	100

Table 7.1 Results of Initial Analyses to Identify Promotive, Risk, and Mixed Predictors of Violence and Theft (Youngest and Oldest Cohorts); (continued)

Predictor-Outcome Interval	Youngest Cohort						Oldest Cohort			Risk, Promotive, or Mixed Effect	% Pervasive	% Consistent
	From Middle Childhood to Late Childhood	From Late Childhood to Early Adolescence	From Early Adolescence to Late Adolescence	From Middle Childhood to Early Adolescence	From Middle Childhood to Late Adolescence	From Late Childhood to Late Adolescence	From Early Adolescence to Late Adolescence	From Late Adolescence to Early Adulthood	From Early Adolescence to Early Adulthood			
Relationship with Peers	P P	B P	R	P*	R	R	B P	— —	P	Mixed	—	—
Gets Along with Siblings	R						R	R		Risk	11	—
SCHOOL												
Academic Achievement/Educational Level	P P	P* P*	R	R R	P		B R	Rx	P	Mixed	—	—
Attitude Toward School		R	R R		P	P	P	—	P	Mixed	—	—
Repeated a Grade	R	R	R	R	R	R	R	R	R	Risk (d)	—	—
NEIGHBORHOOD												
Neighborhood Impression	P P		P	P	P	P	P	P*	P	Promotive	44	100
Neighborhood (Census)	33	— —	—	P P	—		R R	—	—	Promotive (Y) / Risk (O)	33 / 100	— / —
Victim of Violence	— —	R	R R	—	—		R	R		Risk (d)	—	—
Victim of Theft		R	R	R R			R			Risk (d)	—	—
Serious Injuries		R	R				R			Risk (d)	—	—

SOCIODEMOGRAPHICS

																		Classification		
Ethnicity	R	R	R	R	R	R	R	R		R	R	R	R	R		R	R	Risk (d)	—	—
Number of Biological Parents	R	—	R	R	R	R	R	R		R	R	R				R		Risk (d)	—	—
Two or More Caretaker Changes by Age 10	—	R	R			R	R											Risk (d)	—	—
Age of Mother at Birth of First Child	P	R	P		P	P	P	P		P		P	P	P	P		P	Promotive	50	90
Family Socioeconomic Status/Participant Socioeconomic Status	P	P	P		P	P			R				Rx					Mixed	—	—
Family on Welfare/Participant on Welfare	R	R	R		R	R	R			R	R	R	Rx	R		R	R	Risk (d)	—	—
Family Size		R	R			R				R			—	—			P	Risk	19	75
House Size		R	R							R			—	—				Risk (d)	—	—
Housing Quality	P	B	B	P*	—	R		R		R		R	—	—	R	R	R	Mixed (Y) / Risk (O)	50	50
Max Total Tests	45	45	49	49	49	46	46	44	44	48	48	52	52	33	33	50	50			
No. Significant	19	14	24	25	18	18	16	17	5	21	10	20	24	15	7	20	6			
% Significant	50.0	36.8	58.5	59.5	42.9	43.6	41.0	44.7	13.2	51.2	24.4	45.5	54.5	57.7	26.9	47.6	14.3	Average = 42.6		
Total, Promotive	12	6	5	9	8	6	5	9	2	7	6	7	9	4	2	8	3			
Total, Risk	6	7	14	14	9	11	11	8	3	12	4	9	15	10	5	10	2			
Total, Promotive and Risk	1	1	5	2	1	0	0	0	0	2	0	4	0	1	0	1	1			
% Promotive/Total	63.2	42.9	20.8	36.0	44.4	35.3	31.2	52.9	40.0	33.3	60.0	35.0	37.5	26.7	28.6	40.0	50.0	Average = 39.2		

Table 7.1 Results of Initial Analyses to Identify Promotive, Risk, and Mixed Predictors of Violence and Theft (Youngest and Oldest Cohorts); (continued)

Notes:
Approximate age range for each period: middle childhood (ages 7–9); late childhood (ages 10–12); early adolescence (ages 13–16); late adolescence (ages 17–19); early adulthood (ages 20–25).
V = Violence.
T = Theft.
− = Predictor not measured.
P = Promotive effect.
R = Risk effect.
B = Risk and promotive effect about equal.
P* = Risk and promotive effect, but promotive effect is significantly larger than risk effect.
Rx =Risk factor in the participant version.
R* = Risk and promotive effect, but risk effect is significantly larger than promotive effect.
d = Factor could not be trichotomized and, consequently, was dichotomized.
⊠ = Index not computed.
Pervasiveness index: % significant effects/total; this was not computed for dichotomous factors and for fewer than three significant effects.
Consistency index: % promotive or risk effects out of total significant effects; this was not computed for dichotomous factors, for mixed effects, and for fewer than three significant effects.

the significant 5 effects were promotive (100% consistency [C]). There were no significant risk effects. Further, the results show that low ADHD symptoms predicted a low probability of violence better than a low probability of theft (67% pervasiveness for violence vs. 17% for theft). Other forms of psychopathology that were more promotive than risk were low anxiety (17% P; 100% C) and low shy/withdrawn behavior (17% P; 100% C). Low psychopathic features were promotive of a later low probability of theft (63% P; 93% C), but not a low probability of violence. Of the child competence variables, only prosocial behavior was a promotive factor (33% P; 80% C).

Several of the family functioning factors, especially those dealing with childrearing practices, were mainly promotive, including high persistence of discipline (21% P; 75% C), low physical punishment (31% P; 83% C), and good supervision (39% P; 70% C). The boy's involvement in family activities was also a promotive factor (50% P; 80% C), reinforcing the notion that engagement with the family predicted low rates of serious offending. Of the parent characteristics, only low parent stress in the oldest cohort was a promotive factor (75% P; 100% C). None of the peer or school factors proved to be promotive. However, among the neighborhood factors, the parents' rating of the neighborhood as good was a promotive factor (44% P; 100% C). In addition, a good neighborhood according to census data was a modest promotive factor for the youngest cohort only. Of the demographic factors, only one, an older mother, proved to be a promotive factor (50% P; 89% C).

In summary, most domains contributed one or more promotive factors. Of these, the pervasiveness index shows that they occurred at a rate greater than could be expected by chance alone. Further, the high consistency index indicated that almost all of the promotive factors rarely if ever operated as risk factors (in all 10 instances of promotive factors, the consistency index was 70% or greater). These results, we think, have a direct bearing on prevention and, possibly, intervention, which we will discuss in Chapter 10.

It is possible that our conclusions about whether risk or promotive effects are stronger are affected by our use of the odds ratio as a measure of strength of effect. This is discussed further in the afterword to this chapter, but the results of analyses in the afterword do not contradict conclusions drawn from Table 7.1.

Aggravating Risk Factors

Table 7.1 also shows the pervasiveness and consistency indexes for risk factors (indicated only when factors could be trichotomized, and thus not indicated for dichotomized factors). Several variables had predominantly a risk effect, such as low self-aspirations (25% P; 75% C), a positive attitude toward delinquency (39% P; 78% C), peer delinquency for the oldest cohort (83% P; 100% C), and a large family (19% P; 75% C). Some other factors had very few significant risk effects (e.g., the pervasiveness was below 12% when the child left home at a young age, and getting along poorly with siblings).

Mixed Effects

Table 7.1 also shows that several factors had about equal proportions of promotive and risk effects (indicated by mixed effects in Table 7.1). These included the following variables: psychopathic features in the prediction of violence, depressed mood, interaction with the interviewer, perceived likelihood of being caught, parental reinforcement, parent antisocial attitude, parent aspirations for the child, parent stress (youngest cohort), peer delinquency (youngest cohort), relationship with peers, academic achievement, attitude toward school, family socioeconomic status, and housing quality (youngest cohort).

Predictors of Violence

As mentioned, analyses in Table 7.1 used trichotomization to contrast the worst and best 25% with the middle 50% of the distribution. This strategy, when applied to regression analyses, would have had one important limitation in that it reduced the number on which analyses would be based (75% instead of the normal 100% of the distribution). To optimize the use of the full cohort we repeated the prediction analyses using a 25% versus 75% dichotomy. However, we used knowledge of the prior analyses to contrast for risk factors the worst 25% versus the remaining 75%, while for promotive factors we contrasted the best 25% versus the remaining 75%. In the case of mixed risk factors, we had two contrasts: the best 25% versus the remainder, and the worst 25% versus the remainder.

Risk Factors Predicting a High Likelihood of Violence

To what extent do the number of significant risk factors that predict violence change with age? There are several possibilities to consider. First, the origins of violence may lie in early childhood, which means that the majority of the predictors of violence are already in place by then. According to another perspective, predictors of violence gradually emerge from middle to late childhood (as does violence itself) with increasing numbers of risk factors becoming significant predictors of violence with age. In a third scenario, the number of predictors of violence peaks sometime in late childhood or in early adolescence and declines afterward.

Table 7.2 shows the results for the bivariate prediction of violence in the youngest cohort, both for adjacent age blocks (middle to late childhood; late childhood to early adolescence; early to late adolescence) and for longer-term prediction (middle childhood to late adolescence). In the interests of reducing the complexity of the tables, we do not show the other two longitudinal comparisons (middle childhood to early adolescence, and late childhood to late adolescence). To facilitate comparisons of the magnitude of risk and

Table 7.2 Risk, Promotive, and Mixed Predictors (Youngest Cohort)

	Prediction (OR)							
	From Middle to Late Childhood		From Late Childhood to Early Adolescence		From Early to Late Adolescence		From Middle Childhood to Late Adolescence	
	Violence	Theft	Violence	Theft	Violence	Theft	Violence	Theft
Risk Factors								
PARTICIPANT PSYCHOPATHOLOGY								
High Truancy	3.9***	3.1***	2.4***	2.3***	2.6**	3.1**	3.0***	0.9
Running Away	2.7**	2.3*	3.0***	3.6***	2.6**	1.6	1.6	1.7
PARTICIPANT COMPETENCE								
Low Self-Aspirations	—	—	0.9	0.8	1.5	2.0	—	1.0
Positive Attitude toward Delinquency	1.9*	1.8	2.9***	2.6***	3.6***	4.1***	1.3	1.0
FAMILY FUNCTIONING								
Child Maltreatment by 12	1.6	2.6**	2.0**	2.6***	2.2*	2.7*	2.2*	2.7*
PARENTAL CHARACTERISTICS								
Father Behavior Problems	2.2*	1.6	—	—	—	—	2.5*	3.8***
Parent Police Contact	1.3	1.3	1.0	1.5	1.6	2.7**	1.6	2.7**
PEERS								
Getting along Poorly with Siblings	1.4	1.6	1.1	1.1	1.1	1.4	1.0	0.7
SCHOOL								
Repeating a Grade	2.7***	1.6	2.5***	2.3***	4.1***	1.3	4.1***	1.3

Table 7.2 Risk, Promotive, and Mixed Predictors (Youngest Cohort) (continued)

	Prediction (OR)							
	From Middle to Late Childhood		From Late Childhood to Early Adolescence		From Early to Late Adolescence		From Middle Childhood to Late Adolescence	
	Violence	Theft	Violence	Theft	Violence	Theft	Violence	Theft
NEIGHBORHOOD								
High Violence Victimization	—	—	1.5	1.6	3.7***	2.4*	—	—
High Theft Victimization	—	—	1.8**	1.7*	1.8	3.0**	—	—
High Number of Serious Injuries	0.9	1.2	1.8**	1.0	1.0	1.3	1.5	1.4
SOCIODEMOGRAPHICS								
African American	3.2**	1.7	2.4***	1.2	2.3*	0.4*	2.3*	0.4*
One or No Biological Parents	4.2***	5.1***	3.7***	2.6**	4.6**	1.6	2.6*	1.8
Two or More Changes in Caretaker by Age 10	2.8***	2.0*	2.2***	2.1**	1.3	1.6	1.3	1.6
Family on Welfare	1.3	1.8	2.8***	1.9*	1.4	0.7	2.9	0.6
Large Family	0.9	0.9	1.7*	1.5	1.5	1.0	1.4	1.1
Small House	1.6	2.6**	1.8*	1.5	1.2	1.1	1.2	1.2
Promotive Factors								
PARTICIPANT PSYCHOPATHOLOGY								
Low ADHD Symptoms	2.4	2.0	—	—	3.5*	1.3	1.9	0.8
Low Anxiety	2.0	1.4	2.0*	1.5	6.5**	1.2	0.6	0.7
PARTICIPANT COMPETENCE								

FAMILY FUNCTIONING								
High Persistence of Discipline	1.1	1.1	1.6	0.9	1.0	2.7	1.5	1.1
Low Physical Punishment	2.4*	1.5	1.9*	1.9*	1.5	1.1	1.0	0.9
Good Supervision	2.1	2.4	3.0***	1.6	2.4	1.8	2.3	1.7
Youth Involved in Family Activities	2.2	4.5**	1.4	1.8	1.3	1.0	2.4	1.2
NEIGHBORHOOD								
Good Neighborhood Impression	3.0*	4.0*	2.2**	1.8	3.7*	1.6	2.5	0.7
Good Neighborhood (Census)	1.4	1.2	1.7*	0.8	1.0	0.3**	1.0	0.3**
SOCIODEMOGRAPHICS								
Older Mother	4.2*	2.5	4.3***	2.2*	1.2	1.1	1.2	1.1
Mixed Factors								
PARTICIPANT PSYCHOPATHOLOGY								
High Psychopathic Features	2.7***	2.5**	3.6***	2.5***	4.3*	1.7	1.8	1.3
Low Psychopathic Features	18.9***	7.0**	4.0***	7.4***	6.3**	2.3	3.1*	1.1
High Depressed Mood	2.6**	3.2***	1.5	1.9*	2.7**	1.4	1.3	0.9
No Depressed Mood	3.0*	2.9*	1.9*	2.0*	2.0	3.0	3.0*	1.4
PARTICIPANT COMPETENCE								
Negative Interaction with Interviewer	—	—	1.8*	1.3	2.6**	1.3	—	—
Positive Interaction with Interviewer	—	—	2.8**	1.6	1.8	2.4	—	—
Low Perceived Likelihood of Being Caught	0.9	1.0	2.4***	1.9	2.3*	2.5*	1.3	0.6
High Likelihood of Being Caught	1.1	1.5	2.5**	1.6	2.9*	1.7	2.3	1.7

Table 7.2 Risk, Promotive, and Mixed Predictors (Youngest Cohort) (continued)

	Prediction (OR)							
	From Middle to Late Childhood		From Late Childhood to Early Adolescence		From Early to Late Adolescence		From Middle Childhood to Late Adolescence	
	Violence	*Theft*	*Violence*	*Theft*	*Violence*	*Theft*	*Violence*	*Theft*
FAMILY FUNCTIONING								
Low Parental Reinforcement	1.2	1.3	1.6	1.8*	1.1	2.2*	0.7	0.7
High Parental Reinforcement	1.5	1.3	1.0	1.5	2.1	2.1	1.1	0.9
PARENTAL CHARACTERISTICS								
Parents' High Antisocial Attitude	1.0	1.2	1.2	0.9	1.0	1.8	1.9	0.9
Parents' Low Antisocial Attitude	0.9	0.6	1.0	1.2	1.1	1.2	1.0	0.9
Parents' Low Aspirations for Child		—	0.9	0.9	0.6	1.1		—
Parents' High Aspirations for Child		—	0.7	0.9	0.9	3.1		—
High Parental Stress	1.4	1.8	1.8*	1.7	1.1	1.3	1.7	2.2*
Low Parental Stress	2.4*	1.1	2.0*	1.7	1.4	1.7	1.7	1.6
PEERS								
High Peer Delinquency	3.6***	3.0***	5.3***	4.2***	8.4***	3.3***	2.5**	1.1
Low Peer Delinquency	6.4***	3.5*	4.6***	4.7***	12.6**	4.9*	4.8**	1.3
Poor Relationship with Peers	2.1*	1.9	3.2**	2.3***	3.0***	1.6	2.6**	0.5
Good Relationship with Peers	4.2**	3.2*	3.9***	5.2***	2.7	0.9	1.8	1.4
SCHOOL								
Low Academic Achievement	1.9*	2.2*	2.8***	2.8***	2.7**	1.4	1.8	1.2

High Academic Achievement	9.0***	4.4**	7.9***	7.4***	2.2	1.5	1.6	0.6
Negative Attitude toward School	1.6	0.9	1.8*	1.9*	3.4***	3.8***	1.0	1.5
Positive Attitude toward School	1.2	0.9	1.7	1.5	2.8*	10.7***	1.0	1.3
SOCIODEMOGRAPHICS								
Low Family Socioeconomic Status	1.0	1.4	1.6	2.3***	1.1	1.2	0.8	0.8
High Family Socioeconomic Status	1.3	2.3	2.7**	1.9*	0.9	1.3	2.8*	1.6
Poor Housing Quality	1.6	1.1	2.2**	2.1**	2.9**	1.1	2.0*	1.6
Good Housing Quality	5.4**	1.3	2.5**	4.3***	6.4**	1.1	2.3	1.1

Notes: Approximate age range for each period: *middle childhood* (ages 7–9); *late childhood* (ages 10–12); *early adolescence* (ages 13–16); *late adolescence* (ages 17–19); $*p < .05$; $**p < .01$; $***p < .001$; OR = odds ratio. To facilitate comparisons of the magnitude of risk and promotive factors, the odds ratios for promotive factors, normally ranging in value from 0 to 1, were inverted to be larger than 1.

promotive factors, the odds ratios for promotive factors, normally ranging in value from 0 to 1, were inverted to be larger than 1.

The results (in Table 7.2) show that the number of significant risk factors predicting violence was higher in the prediction from late than from middle childhood (13/17, 76% vs. 8/15, 53%), or from early adolescence (8/17, 47%); numbers in the denominator vary because of measurement availability). As can be expected, the long-term prediction of violence was less good (only 6 predictors significant out of 15, or 40%).

Several aggravating risk factors were consistent across the three short-term predictions (middle to late childhood; late childhood to early adolescence; early adolescence to late adolescence), including high truancy, running away, a positive attitude toward delinquency, child maltreatment by age 12, repeating a grade, African American ethnicity, one or no biological parents at home, and two or more changes in caretaker by age 10. Less consistent results were found for father behavior problems, violence victimization, theft victimization, large family, and small house. Among the predictors at middle childhood that best predicted violence during late adolescence were high truancy, child maltreatment by age 12, father behavior problems, repeating a grade, African American ethnicity, and one or no biological parents at home. In summary, youth, family demographics and problems, and academic factors predicted early-onset violence in late childhood, and the same factors predicted violence even in late adolescence. Note that none of the child-rearing practices, peer delinquency, or neighborhood factors consistently predicted later violence.

How do these results compare with those for the oldest cohort? Note that the number of aggravating risk factors was greater for the oldest than for the youngest cohort. Table 7.3 shows that the number of aggravating risk factors significantly predicting later violence was higher for risk factors measured in late compared to early adolescence (8/13, 62% vs. 9/23, 39%), but the comparison is limited by the fact that several risk factors known from early adolescence could not be measured in late adolescence because parents and teachers were no longer informants at that time. Only a few aggravating risk factors were consistently predictive across the age blocks, including high peer delinquency, violence victimization, African American ethnicity, and one or no biological parents at home. Less consistent predictors of violence were high truancy, running away, low self-aspirations, an early age upon which the youth left home, getting along poorly with siblings, repeating a grade, low educational level, bad neighborhood (census), and family/participant on welfare. About the same number of aggravating risk factors measured in early adolescence predicted violence in late adolescence and early adulthood (high truancy, running away, low self-aspirations, high peer delinquency, violence victimization, African American ethnicity, one or no biological parents at home, and family/participant on welfare). This shows the far reach of these aggravating risk factors in predicting violence later.

Table 7.3 Risk, Promotive, and Mixed Predictors (Oldest Cohort)

	Prediction (OR)					
	From Early to Late Adolescence		From Late Adolescence to Early Adulthood		From Early Adolescence to Early Adulthood	
Risk Factors	Violence	Theft	Violence	Theft	Violence	Theft
PARTICIPANT PSYCHOPATHOLOGY						
High Truancy	2.3***	2.6***	—	—	2.3***	2.3*
Running Away	4.0***	4.2***	—	—	2.6***	1.7
PARTICIPANT COMPETENCE						
Low Self-Aspirations	1.7*	2.8***	1.2	1.3	2.2**	1.6
Early Age Left Home	1.8	1.6	2.2*	0.6	2.2*	0.6
FAMILY FUNCTIONING						
Child Maltreatment by Age 12	1.7	2.0	1.9	3.8***	1.9	3.8***
PARENTAL CHARACTERISTICS						
Parent Alcohol Problem	1.0	1.4	—	—	0.9	0.7
Father Behavior Problems	1.5	2.5**	—	—	1.8	1.0
Parent Police Contact	1.3	1.7	—	1.6	1.4	1.6
PEERS						
High Peer Delinquency	5.0***	2.8***	5.8***	2.3*	5.8***	2.3*
Getting along Poorly with Siblings	1.0	1.3	1.9*	3.1**	1.2	2.6**

Table 7.3 Risk, Promotive, and Mixed Predictors (Oldest Cohort) (continued)

| | Prediction (OR) | | | | | |
| | From Early to Late Adolescence | | From Late Adolescence to Early Adulthood | | From Early Adolescence to Early Adulthood | |
	Violence	Theft	Violence	Theft	Violence	Theft
SCHOOL						
Repeating a Grade	1.4	1.1	1.9**	1.3	1.9**	1.3
Low Educational Level	—	—	2.0**	1.3	—	—
NEIGHBORHOOD						
Bad Neighborhood (Census)	2.0***	1.5	—	—	—	1.9
High Violence Victimization	2.8***	1.1	5.4***	2.3*	1.9*	0.6
High Theft Victimization	1.4	2.1**	1.5	1.6	1.3	1.2
High Number of Serious Injuries	1.6	2.0*	1.5	1.6	1.4	1.8
SOCIODEMOGRAPHICS						
African American	1.9**	0.8	2.8***	0.7	2.8***	0.7
One or No Biological Parents	2.1**	1.5	1.9*	1.3	2.3**	1.4
Two or More Changes in Caretaker by Age 10	1.6	1.5	1.0	1.4	1.0	1.4
Family on Welfare	3.3***	1.7	—	—	3.6***	2.1*
Large Family	1.1	1.0	—	—	1.5	0.9
Small House	1.5	1.5	—	—	1.1	0.7
Poor Housing Quality	1.5	2.1**	—	—	2.3***	1.4

Promotive Factors

PARTICIPANT PSYCHOPATHOLOGY						
Low ADHD Symptoms	3.0***	3.4**	—	—	1.5	1
Low Anxiety	1.4	1.3	1.2	1.8	1.1	1.3
Low Shyness/Withdrawal	1.5	1.3	1.9*	2.3	1.4	1.1
PARTICIPANT COMPETENCE						
High Prosocial Behavior	1.4	2.0*	2.3*	1.1	1.3	0.8
Negative Attitude toward Delinquency	5.0***	2.4*	2.2*	1.3	2.7**	3.6*
FAMILY FUNCTIONING						
High Persistence of Discipline	1.6	2.8**	—	—	1.5	0.9
Low Physical Punishment	1.3	1.2	—	—	2.4**	0.7
Good Supervision	2.8***	2.4*	—	—	2.7**	1.3
Boy Involved in Family Activities	2.3**	2.9**	—	—	2.1*	2.2
Low Parental Stress	3.1***	3.2**	—	—	3.7***	1.6
NEIGHBORHOOD						
Good Neighborhood Impression	2.1**	1.7	5.1***	1.0	2.9**	1.2
SOCIODEMOGRAPHICS						
Older Mother	3.7***	2.6*	3.3***	1.8	3.3***	1.8
Mixed Factors						
PARTICIPANT PSYCHOPATHOLOGY						
High Psychopathic Features	3.4***	1.9*	—	—	2.6***	2.5*
Low Psychopathic Features	3.6***	3.4**	—	—	3.3***	2.7

Table 7.3 Risk, Promotive, and Mixed Predictors (Oldest Cohort) (continued)

| | Prediction (OR) | | | | | |
| | From Early to Late Adolescence | | From Late Adolescence to Early Adulthood | | From Early Adolescence to Early Adulthood | |
	Violence	Theft	Violence	Theft	Violence	Theft
High Depressed Mood	2.1***	1.9*	2.2**	1.8	1.6	1.4
Low Depressed Mood	1.4	1.7	1.1	1.2	1.1	0.9
PARTICIPANT COMPETENCE						
Negative Interaction with Interviewer	—	—	3.4***	2.2*	—	—
Positive Interaction with Interviewer	—	—	4.2***	4.5*	—	—
Low Likelihood of Getting Caught	1.8**	2.4**	0.9	0.6	1.4	0.8
High Likelihood of Getting Caught	1.8*	2.4*	1.8	1.3	0.9	1.6
FAMILY FUNCTIONING						
Low Parental Reinforcement	1.1	1.4	1.4	—	0.9	1.7
High Parental Reinforcement	2.2**	1.3	—	—	1.3	4.0*
Parent High Antisocial Attitude	1.4	1.5	—	—	1.1	1.8
Parent Low Antisocial Attitude	1.7	1.4	—	—	1.2	1.3
Parent Low Aspirations for Child	1.2	2.0*	—	—	0.9	1.1
Parent High Aspirations for Child	1.0	1.1	—	—	0.9	1.9

PEERS

Poor Relationship with Peers	2.1**	1.1	—	1.6	2.1*
Good Relationship with Peers	2.4**	2.1*	—	11.5***	2.1

SCHOOL

Low Academic Achievement	2.1***	2.4***	—	1.3	0.8
High Academic Achievement	2.7***	1.1	—	2.9**	1.4
Negative Attitude toward School	1.4	1.8*	—	1.3	2.1*
Positive Attitude toward School	1.3	2.7**	—	1.2	1.3

SOCIODEMOGRAPHICS

Low Family/Participant Socioeconomic Status	1.6*	1.4	2.3***	1.2	1.2
High Family/Participant Socioeconomic Status	1.8*	1.3	1.3	1.7	0.9

Notes: Approximate age range for each period: *early adolescence* (ages 13–16); *late adolescence* (ages 17–19); *early adulthood* (ages 20–25); *p* < .05; **p* < .01; ***p* < .001; OR = odds ratio. To facilitate comparisons of the magnitude of risk and promotive factors, the odds ratios for promotive factors, normally ranging in value from 0 to 1, were rescaled to be larger than 1.

Preventive Promotive Factors

The study of risk factors only reflects half of the picture in that the prediction of a high or low probability of violence is strengthened by knowledge of preventive promotive factors. Table 7.2 shows which preventive promotive factors were associated with a low probability of violence in the youngest cohort. The number of preventive promotive factors that significantly predicted a low probability of violence was fewer than the number of aggravating risk factors that predicted a high probability of violence. For preventive promotive factors we found a similar age effect as for aggravating risk factors: the number of promotive factors peaked when measured in late childhood compared to either early childhood or early adolescence (3/9, 33% vs. 6/9, 67% vs. 4/10, 40%, respectively).

The age effect for preventive promotive factors corresponded with the age effect for aggravating risk factors (summarized in Figure 7.4) indicating that the number of significant predictors of each peaked in middle childhood. This may suggest that a developmental split takes place during that period leading to a high probability of violence for some boys and a low probability of violence for others.

Which preventive promotive factors were most consistently predictive of a low probability of violence later? The consistency of findings for the youngest cohort across the comparisons was modest, but was clearest (counting two to three out of the three comparisons) for low anxiety, low physical punishment, good neighborhood impression, and older mother. Less consistent preventive promotive effects were found for low ADHD symptoms, high prosocial behavior, good supervision, and good neighborhood (census). As to long-term prediction, none of the preventive promotive factors measured in middle

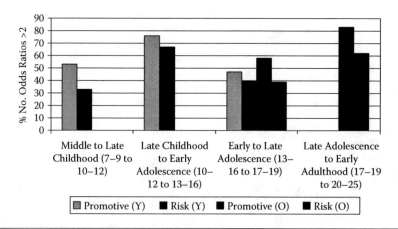

Figure 7.4 The Proportion of Promotive and Risk Factors Predicting Violence from Middle Childhood to Early Adulthood (Youngest [Y] and Oldest [O] Cohorts)

childhood predicted a low probability of violence in late adolescence. This is in sharp contrast to the aggravating risk factors in middle childhood, which had a much longer predictive reach than the preventive promotive factors. We will revisit this issue when discussing mixed risk and promotive factors.

Turning to the oldest cohort (Table 7.3), the number of preventive promotive factors predicting a low probability of violence was higher when measured during late compared to early adolescence (5/6, 83% vs. 7/12, 58%), but this finding is limited by the fact that fewer promotive factors were measured in late than in early adolescence. A few preventive promotive factors were consistent across the two measurements, including negative attitude toward delinquency, good neighborhood impression, and older mother. Less consistent preventive promotive factors were low ADHD symptoms, low shyness/withdrawal, and high prosocial behavior. The results show that good neighborhood impression and older mother were preventive promotive factors shared across the youngest and oldest cohorts.

How long over time was the reach of preventive promotive factors predicting a low probability of violence in the oldest cohort? Table 7.3 shows that seven preventive promotive factors measured in early adolescence significantly predicted a low probability of violence in early adulthood: negative attitude toward delinquency, low physical punishment, good supervision, youth involved in family activities, low parental stress, good neighborhood impression, and older mother. These findings are in sharp contrast to the previous result that none of the preventive promotive factors measured in middle childhood (i.e., about six years earlier than early adolescence) in the youngest cohort predicted a low probability of violence in late adolescence.

Mixed Risk and Promotive Factors Predicting a High or Low Likelihood of Violence

As pointed out earlier in this chapter, several factors had both risk and promotive effects. Tables 7.2 and 7.3 show that the number of mixed factors was larger than the number of solely risk or solely promotive factors predicting a high or low probability of violence. In the youngest cohort, the number of mixed factors significantly predicting a high probability of violence peaked when the factors were measured in late childhood, compared to middle childhood or early adolescence (21/32, 66% vs. 12/28, 43% vs. 14/32, 44%, respectively). Several of the mixed factors significantly predicted both high and low violence across two or three measurement intervals: psychopathic features, depressed mood, interaction with the interviewer, perceived likelihood of being caught, peer delinquency, relationship with peers, academic achievement, and quality of house. Less consistent were parental stress, negative attitude toward school, and family/participant socioeconomic status (SES). Several of the mixed factors measured in middle childhood had long-term effects on later violence, including low psychopathic features, no depressed mood, high/low peer delinquency, poor relationship with peers, high family/participant SES, and poor housing quality. Thus, although several factors operated as mixed factors, the positive side of such factors (such as low psychopathic features, no depressed mood, low peer delinquency, and high family/participant SES) predicted a low probability of violence over a period of about ten years (contrary to the lack of long-term effects of promotive factors that we reported above). Conversely, several of the mixed factors showed risk effects that had a similarly long reach: this applied to high peer delinquency, poor relationship with peers, and poor housing quality.

To what extent were the results on mixed factors in the youngest cohort replicated for the oldest cohort (Table 7.3)? A major problem was that many of the mixed factors in the oldest cohort that were measured in early adolescence were not measured in late adolescence, which severely restricts comparisons. Several mixed factors that predicted a high or low probability of violence in the youngest cohort also predicted in the oldest cohort, including psychopathic features, interaction with the interviewer, perceived likelihood of being caught, relationship with peers, academic achievement, and family SES. In addition, a few factors had specific effects in the oldest cohort. For instance, high depressed mood predicted a high probability of violence (but low depressed mood did not predict a low probability of violence), and high parental reinforcement predicted a low probability of violence (but low parental reinforcement did not predict a high probability of violence).

Which of the mixed factors had the longest reach in predicting high or low probability of violence? Table 7.3 shows that only a few factors spanned the seven years between early adolescence and early adulthood, and these included high or low psychopathic features, good relationship with peers, and high academic achievement. Again, we see that some promotive factors present in early adolescence predicted a low probability of violence over long time periods.

Consistency of Results Across Age

The extent to which results at different ages were consistent was investigated by comparing odds ratios. The natural logarithm of the odds ratio (LOR) was used to convert this ratio variable into a linear scale. For the youngest cohort, the correlation between LORs from middle childhood to late childhood and LORs from late childhood to early adolescence was .67 ($p < .0001$). The correlation between LORs from late childhood to early adolescence and LORs from early adolescence to late adolescence was .58 ($p < .0001$). The correlation between LORs from middle childhood to late childhood and LORs from early adolescence to late adolescence was .61 ($p < .0001$). Turning to the oldest cohort, the correlation between LORs from early adolescence to late adolescence and LORs from late adolescence to early adulthood was .62 ($p = .002$). The fact that these correlations were substantial and significant means that, to a considerable extent, the strongest risk and promotive factors in one age range tended to be similar to the strongest risk and promotive factors in another age range.

Logistic Regression Analyses Predicting Violence

The results so far have focused on bivariate associations between specific factors and a later high or low probability of violence. Which of the factors predicted later violence independently of other factors? Do preventive promotive factors contribute to the prediction of a low probability of violence once risk factors are taken into account? And do promotive and risk factors predict later violence once earlier deviance is included in the analyses (such as different forms of substance use, gun carrying, drug dealing, and gang membership)?

To answer these questions, we executed multivariate logistic regression analyses so that we would be able to gauge whether promotive factors had independent effects when placed "in competition" with risk and mixed factors. For that reason, a series of logistic regression analyses were undertaken: (1) first, we analyzed which aggravating risk factors out of all risk factors independently predicted a high probability of violence; (2) second, we analyzed which preventive promotive factors out of all promotive factors independently predicted a low probability of violence; (3) third, we established which mixed factors out of all mixed factors independently predicted a high or low probability of violence. In the next step (4) we examined the independent "explanatory" predictors resulting from analyses (1), (2), and (3). In the final step (5) we introduced the set of risk factors that were reviewed in Chapter 6—namely, different forms of substance use (alcohol, marijuana, and hard drug use), and several aspects of an antisocial lifestyle, including gun carrying, drug dealing, and gang membership. In order to control for earlier antisocial behavior, earlier violence was introduced wherever applicable. This final regression analysis (5) established the most important predictors out of all possible variables. In steps (4) and (5) we also examined interaction effects between aggravating risk and preventive promotive factors, to establish the extent to which protective effects might counteract risk effects. The series of regression analyses were run for each adjacent, short-term prediction from one age block to the next, and separately for long-term prediction from the first to the last age block (middle childhood to late adolescence for the youngest cohort, early adolescence to early adulthood for the oldest cohort).

We show the results separately for explanatory predictors because of our interest in drawing implications for intervention. Explanatory predictors such as poor supervision by the parents can, in principle, be targeted in intervention programs. In contrast, the results for all variables are more relevant to the development of risk assessment instruments and the identification of children at risk. However, our analyses go beyond previous research on risk assessment by including both risk and promotive factors in summary scores. Table 7.4

shows the results of the final regression analyses (4) and (5) across the various age blocks to predict violence.

Prediction from Middle to Late Childhood in the Youngest Cohort   Starting with the prediction of violence in late childhood in the youngest cohort from explanatory predictors measured in middle childhood (ages 7–9), the final regression analysis shows that two aggravating risk factors (two or more care-taker changes by age 10 and high peer delinquency) and two preventive pro-motive factors (low psychopathic features and high academic achievement) independently predicted violence. The partial odds ratio (POR) for high aca-demic achievement (9.70) shows the extent to which this predicted a low prob-ability of violence. For ease of comparison, PORs for preventive promotive factors refer to the prediction of a low probability of violence, while PORs for aggravating risk factors refer to the prediction of a high probability of violence. When earlier deviance was included in the analysis, high truancy entered the equation as a predictor in place of low psychopathic features.

Prediction from Late Childhood to Early Adolescence in the Youngest Cohort   Ta-ble 7.4 shows that the best independent predictors measured in late child-hood of violence in early adolescence were five aggravating risk factors (theft victimization, family on welfare, high psychopathic features, low perceived likelihood of being caught, and high peer delinquency), and two preventive promotive factors (good relationship with peers and high academic achieve-ment). When earlier deviance was included in the analysis, prior violence and marijuana use entered the equation in place of theft victimization and a good relationship with peers.

Prediction from Early to Late Adolescence in the Youngest Cohort   Only aggra-vating risk factors measured in early adolescence were predictors of violence in late adolescence—namely, repeating a grade, high peer delinquency, mari-juana use, and gun carrying. Thus, no promotive factors measured during early adolescence predicted a low probability of violence once risk factors had been into account.

Prediction from Middle Childhood to Late Adolescence in the Youngest Cohort   In the long-term prediction of violence from middle childhood to late adoles-cence, we found that repeating a grade, high peer delinquency, and high truancy were the best independent predictors of violence over that 10-year period.

Prediction from Early to Late Adolescence in the Oldest Cohort   For the oldest cohort, four aggravating risk factors (high peer delinquency, high psycho-pathic features, violence victimization, and family/participant on welfare), and two preventive promotive factors (low parental stress and older mother),

Table 7.4 Multivariate Logistic Regression Analyses for Violence (Youngest and Oldest Cohorts)

	Explanatory POR	p	All Variables POR	p
Youngest Cohort				
PREDICTION FROM MIDDLE CHILDHOOD TO LATE CHILDHOOD				
Two or More Changes in Caretaker by Age 10	2.5	.008	2.4	.010
Low Psychopathic Features	7.9	.045	—	—
High Peer Delinquency	3.1	.001	3.2	.0005
High Academic Achievement	9.7	.027	11.6	.017
High Truancy	—	—	2.5	.007
PREDICTION FROM LATE CHILDHOOD TO EARLY ADOLESCENCE				
High Theft Victimization	1.8	.044	—	—
Family on Welfare	2.1	.009	2.0	.014
High Psychopathic Features	1.8	.038	2.1	.008
Low Perceived Likelihood of Being Caught	1.8	.040	1.9	.023
High Peer Delinquency	3.5	.0001	2.7	.0005
Good Relationship with Peers	2.5	.025	—	—
High Academic Achievement	4.0	.012	3.8	.009
Prior Violence	—	—	3.2	.002
Marijuana Use	—	—	2.3	.016
PREDICTION FROM EARLY TO LATE ADOLESCENCE				
Repeating a Grade	4.1	.0006	3.3	.004
High Peer Delinquency	7.2	.0001	2.8	.026
Marijuana Use	—	—	3.8	.006
Gun Carrying	—	—	3.8	.003
PREDICTION FROM MIDDLE CHILDHOOD TO LATE ADOLESCENCE				
Repeating a Grade	3.9	.0003	3.3	.002
High Peer Delinquency	2.3	.02	2.1	.042
High Truancy	—	—	2.1	.043
Oldest Cohort				
PREDICTION FROM EARLY TO LATE ADOLESCENCE				
High Peer Delinquency	3.1	.0002	2.3	.008
High Violence Victimization	2.2	.022	2.3	.018

Table 7.4 Multivariate Logistic Regression Analyses for Violence (Youngest and Oldest Cohorts) (continued)

	Explanatory POR	p	All Variables POR	p
Family on Welfare	2.4	.004	2.9	.0003
Low Parental Stress	3.1	.010	2.3	.041
Older Mother	2.6	.021	—	—
High Psychopathic Features	2.0	.026	—	—
Drug Selling	—	—	3.5	.0001
Running Away	—	—	2.4	.008
PREDICTION FROM LATE ADOLESCENCE TO EARLY ADULTHOOD				
High Peer Delinquency	4.5	.0001	2.6	.005
High Violence Victimization	3.7	.0001	3.0	.0006
Negative Interaction with Interviewer	2.6	.003	2.2	.016
Older Mother	3.5	.006	—	—
Gang Membership	—	—	2.2	.044
Gun Carrying	—	—	2.3	.024
PREDICTION FROM EARLY ADOLESCENCE TO EARLY ADULTHOOD				
High Peer Delinquency	5.4	.0001	3.8	.0001
Family on Welfare	2.8	.001	2.5	.002
Low Physical Punishment	3.0	.020	—	—
Good Relationship with Peers	4.8	.012	7.8	.0008
Gun Carrying	—	—	2.0	.040

Note: Approximate age range for each period: *middle childhood* (ages 7–9); *late childhood* (ages 10–12); *early adolescence* (ages 13–16); *late adolescence* (ages 17–19); *early adulthood* (ages 20–25); POR = partial odds ratio; promotive factors in **boldface**. To facilitate comparisons of the magnitude of risk and promotive factors, the odds ratios for promotive factors, normally ranging in value from 0 to 1, were inverted to be larger than 1.

predicted violence from early adolescence to late adolescence. When earlier deviance was included in the analysis, drug selling and running away entered the equation in place of older mother and high psychopathic features. In addition, there was a significant interaction effect between peer delinquency and parental stress (likelihood ratio chi-squared = 7.88, $p <$ .005). When high peer delinquency coincided with high parental stress, 52% of boys became violent. However, when high peer delinquency coincided with low parental stress, only 17% became violent. Similarly, 17% of boys with low peer delinquency and high parental stress became violent, and 9% of boys with low peer delinquency and low parental stress.

Prediction from Late Adolescence to Early Adulthood in the Oldest Cohort   For the oldest cohort, three aggravating risk factors (high peer delinquency, violence victimization, and negative interaction with the interviewer) and one preventive promotive factor (older mother) predicted violence from late adolescence to early adulthood. When earlier deviance was included in the analysis, gang membership and gun carrying entered the equation in place of older mother.

Prediction from Early Adolescence to Early Adulthood in the Oldest Cohort   Two aggravating risk factors (high peer delinquency and family/participant on welfare), and two preventive promotive factors (low physical punishment and good relationship with peers) predicted violence from early adolescence to early adulthood. When earlier deviance was included in the analysis, gun carrying entered the equation in place of low physical punishment.

In addition, there was a significant interaction effect between peer delinquency and good relationship with peers (likelihood ratio chi-squared = 5.78, $p < .016$). When high peer delinquency coincided with a poor relationship with peers, 44% of boys became violent. However, when high peer delinquency coincided with a good relationship with peers, only 18% of boys became violent. When low peer delinquency coincided with a poor relationship with peers, 14% of boys became violent. Remarkably, none out of 103 boys with low peer delinquency and a good relationship with peers became violent.

Summary of Logistic Regression Results for Violence   Summarizing the results of the regression analyses for violence, Table 7.4 shows that one single aggravating risk factor, high peer delinquency, independently contributed to the prediction of violence in every one of the seven regression analyses. No other factor was so consistently and independently predictive of violence. The next most important aggravating risk factors were family on welfare and gun carrying, which each predicted violence in three regression analyses. The most important preventive promotive factors were high academic achievement, an older mother, and a good relationship with peers, which predicted a low probability of violence in two regression analyses. Disappointingly, most of the promotive factors that were independently predictive in the explanatory analyses did not predict when measures of prior deviance were added to the equation.

The results underscore the fact that independent predictors of violence were present in all known domains of influences, including child (also called *individual*) factors, peer factors, school (also called *academic*), and family factors. However, none of the neighborhood factors independently contributed to the prediction of violence. Therefore, neighborhood factors may have only indirect effects on violence through their effects on individual, family, and peer factors. Also, note that African American ethnicity, which significantly predicted violence in the seven bivariate analyses across the youngest and oldest cohorts (Tables 7.2 and 7.3), no longer contributed to the prediction of violence in any of the seven regression analyses (Table 7.4). Thus, there is overwhelming evidence that the association between African American ethnicity and violence could be accounted for by the presence of several other, nonethnic factors that were associated with ethnicity (especially high peer delinquency, low academic achievement, family/participant on welfare, and repeating a grade).

The Dose-Response Relationship between Risk and Promotive Factors and Later Violence

Sometimes it is good to reexamine data in a simple way. This is particularly important when the information needs to be communicated to practitioners and policy makers who as a rule are less interested or keen on interpreting statistics. Studies agree that the higher the number of aggravating risk factors, the greater the likelihood that individuals will be affected by a disease or other deviant behavior such as serious offending (Loeber, Slot, & Stouthamer-Loeber, 2006). This association is usually called a dose-response relationship and has been demonstrated for the full range of indicators of antisocial behavior: sociopathy (Robins, 1966), externalizing problems (Deater-Deckard, Dodge, Bates, & Pettit, 1998), conduct problems (Fergusson & Woodward, 2000; Sameroff, Bartko, Baldwin, Baldwin, & Seifer, 1998), delinquency (Pollard et al., 1999; Smith, Lizotte, Thornberry, & Krohn, 1995), and violence (Farrington, 1997; Loeber et al., 2006).

Virtually no studies, however, have investigated whether the dose-response relationship also applies when the best preventive promotive and aggravating risk factors are summed, thus addressing the question, "Does the sum of promotive and risk factors incrementally predict later violence?" For these analyses, each of the promotive factors in the final regression analyses was given a weighting of -1 and each of the risk factors was given a weighting of +1. We supplemented the dose-response analyses with receiver operating curves (ROCs), which indicate the degree to which the total prediction is accurate; the maximum value of the area under the ROC (AUC) = 1, and the chance value is 0.5.

Figure 7.5 shows the dose-response curve for the prediction of violence in the youngest cohort in different age ranges. As an example, the net presence of one to three promotive factors in late childhood (ages 10–12) predicted that only 3% of the boys became violent in early adolescence (ages 13–16). This percentage was similar at 6% when there was a balance between promotive and aggravating risk factors (indicated by the 0 on the x-axis in Figure 7.5). Once the number of risk factors exceeded the number of promotive factors, the probability of later violence accelerated, to 11% for one risk factor, 33% for

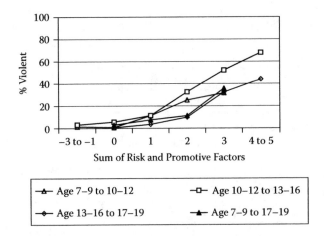

Figure 7.5 The Prediction of Violence (Youngest Cohort)

two risk factors, 52% for three risk factors, and 68% for four to five risk factors (AUC = .819; this value of AUC and all others mentioned below were statistically significant at least at the $p < .05$ level). Note that, for example, a score of 2 can stand for different combinations of promotive and risk factors (e.g., no promotive factors plus two risk factors, or one promotive factor plus three risk factors, etc.).

The four lines in Figure 7.5 each support the notion of a dose-response relationship between the sum of preventive promotive and aggravating risk factors and the probability of later violence. The AUC analyses suggest that the overall predictive efficiency for violence increased with age, especially when the predictors were measured in early adolescence (AUC for predictors at ages 7–9 to violence at ages 10–12 = .811; AUC for predictors at ages 13–16 to violence at ages 17–19 = .873). As expected, the long-term prediction from ages 7–9 to violence at ages 17–19 was the weakest (AUC = .732).

Figure 7.6 shows the results for the oldest cohort. The results again show a slightly higher prediction with age—that is, the predictive efficiency was slightly higher for the prediction from late adolescence to early adulthood (AUC = .831) compared to the prediction from early adolescence to late adolescence (AUC = .804). Again, long-term prediction (from early adolescence to early adulthood) was slightly lower (AUC = .770).

In summary, the results show that across the two cohorts and across different age blocks (a total of seven comparisons) there is a dose-response relationship between the sum of promotive and risk factors in the prediction of later violence. The magnitude of AUCs observed in the analyses is higher than those reported by Mossman (1994), who found an average AUC of .73 across studies, with only three studies having an AUC that was higher than .8.

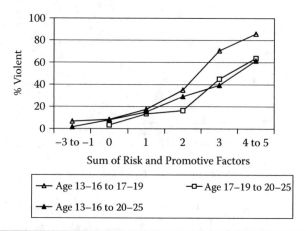

Figure 7.6 The Prediction of Violence (Oldest Cohort)

Our ROC analyses also indicate that the strength of association between this sum and later violence increased somewhat with age, with the best predictors being measured in early adolescence (youngest cohort) and late adolescence (oldest cohort), respectively. This suggests that violence processes in the youngest cohort became stronger from childhood to early adolescence, and stronger from early to late adolescence in the oldest cohort.

Generalized Estimating Equations Predicting Violence

In order to determine which explanatory variables were the most robust predictors of violence within each cohort across all age blocks, we undertook a final set of analyses using generalized estimating equations (GEE), which were developed as an extension of generalized linear models (Hardin & Hilbe, 2003; Liang & Zeger, 1986) and allow for the efficient estimation of model parameters for repeated observations in longitudinal data that are correlated. For this analysis, a logistic transition (Markov) model for binary outcomes was used to identify the explanatory variables measured in one age range that predicted violence measured in a later age range, after controlling for prior violence. Time was included in each model to account for linear decreases in the probability of violence across age blocks. Because this model explicitly characterizes the association among the violence outcomes across age blocks as a first-order binary Markov chain, an independent correlation structure for the outcomes was specified. However, robust standard errors were estimated in all analyses because they provide valid convergence in large samples even when the explicitly modeled correlation of the outcome across time is incorrect (Diggle, Liang, & Zeger, 1994; Hardin & Hilbe, 2003). These analyses are different from those previously run because the estimated parameters represent the overall pooled association between the explanatory variables and violence across all age ranges.

GEE analyses could only be performed on a subset of explanatory variables that met certain conditions. First, in order to include all waves in the analysis, the variable had to be measured across all waves within the cohort. Second, only predictors that significantly predicted violence were included (Tables 7.2 and 7.3). Once the eligible risk, promotive, and mixed variables were identified, these variables were further reduced into an explanatory model of violence for each cohort using procedures identical to those outlined for the regression analyses. The significant explanatory factors that emerged in this GEE model for the youngest and oldest cohorts are presented in Table 7.5. To determine if the explanatory variables continued to predict violence significantly after accounting for indicators of earlier deviance, a final GEE model was run adding several indicators of prior deviance to the model (including different forms of substance use, gun carrying, drug dealing, gang membership, and prior theft). The significant predictors that emerged in this final GEE model (including all variables) predicting violence for the youngest and oldest cohorts are also presented in Table 7.5. As before, the POR for promotive factors refers to the prediction of a low probability of violence, while the POR for risk factors refers to the prediction of a high probability of violence.

For the youngest cohort, a mix of both aggravating risk and preventive promotive factors predicted violence across all age blocks in the explanatory GEE analysis. The risk factors of one or no biological parent at home, high psychopathic features, and high peer delinquency, as well as the promotive factors of low psychopathic features, low peer delinquency, high academic achievement, and good housing quality emerged as significant predictors of violence. When variables measuring various forms of prior deviance were added to the model, good housing quality was reduced to nonsignificance. Of the prior deviance variables, only alcohol use and prior theft significantly predicted future violence in the final model.

The explanatory factors predicting violence in the GEE analysis with the oldest cohort also consisted of a mix of risk and promotive factors. Specifically, the risk factors of high peer delinquency and violence victimization, as well as the promotive factors of a negative attitude toward delinquency and older mother, significantly predicted violence. All of these factors remained significant when variables measuring prior deviance were added to the model. The prior deviance measures of gun carrying and gang membership emerged as significant predictors of violence in the oldest cohort in the final model.

In summary, the GEE results for both cohorts agree with the earlier age block analyses in that both risk and promotive factors predicted violence in both cohorts, but aggravating risk factors outweighed promotive factors in the GEE analyses.

Table 7.5 GEE Models Predicting Violence (Youngest and Oldest Cohorts)

Predictors	Explanatory POR	All Variables POR
YOUNGEST COHORT		
Prior Violence	1.3	1.2
Time	0.9	0.7**
One or No Biological Parents at Home	1.9**	2.1**
High Psychopathic Features	1.6*	1.5*
Low Psychopathic Features	2.1*	2.2*
High Peer Delinquency	2.8***	2.2***
Low Peer Delinquency	2.2*	2.0*
High Academic Achievement	2.9**	2.6**
Good Housing Quality	1.7*	—
Alcohol Use	—	2.0***
Prior Theft	—	2.0*
OLDEST COHORT		
Prior Violence	2.6***	2.0**
Time	0.6*	0.5**
High Peer Delinquency	3.0***	2.3**
High Violence Victimization	2.4***	2.1**
Negative Attitude toward Delinquency	2.1*	2.0*
Older Mother	3.0***	2.7**
Gun Carrying	—	2.2**
Gang Membership	—	2.1*

Notes: POR = partial odds ratio; *$p < .05$; **$p < .01$; ***$p < .001$; promotive factors in **boldface**. Confidence intervals are available from the authors. To facilitate comparisons of the magnitude of risk and promotive factors, the odds ratios for promotive factors, normally ranging in value from 0 to 1, were rescaled to be larger than 1.

Predictors of Theft

We now turn to risk, promotive, and mixed factors predictive of theft.

Risk Factors Predicting High Likelihood of Theft

The first question raised is, to what extent does the number of significant aggravating risk factors that predict theft change with age? Table 7.2 shows that, in the youngest cohort, the number of significant risk factors that predicted theft was similar in the prediction from middle and late childhood, and from early adolescence (6/15, 40%; 8/17, 47%; and 7/17, 41%, respectively; numbers in the denominator vary because of measurement availability). As might be expected, the long-term prediction of theft, from middle childhood to late adolescence, was comparatively poor (4/15, 27%).

Several aggravating risk factors were consistent across the three short-term predictions (using as a criterion two to three significant findings), including high truancy, running away, a positive attitude toward delinquency, child maltreatment by age 12, theft victimization, one or no biological parent at home, and two or more changes in caretaker by age 10. Less consistent results were found for repeating a grade, Caucasian ethnicity, and family on welfare. Among the predictors in middle childhood that best predicted long-term theft during late adolescence were child maltreatment by age 12, father behavior problems, parent police contact, and Caucasian ethnicity. In summary, youth, family, and academic factors predicted early-onset theft in late childhood, and the same factors predicted late-onset theft in late adolescence. Note that none of the child-rearing practices or even peer delinquency predicted later theft.

How do these results compare with those of the oldest cohort? Note that the array of possible aggravating risk factors was larger for the oldest than for the youngest cohort. Table 7.3 shows that the number of aggravating risk factors significantly predicting later theft was slightly higher for aggravating risk factors measured in early compared to late adolescence (8/22, 36% vs. 4/14, 29%), but the comparison is limited because several aggravating risk factors known from early adolescence could not be measured in late adolescence because parents and teachers were no longer used as informants.

Only one aggravating risk factor, high peer delinquency, consistently predicted a high probability of theft across all age blocks. Less consistent predictors of theft were high truancy, running away, low self-aspirations, child maltreatment by age 12, father behavior problems, getting along poorly with siblings, violence victimization, theft victimization, high serious injuries, and poor housing quality. Two of the aggravating risk factors measured in early adolescence that predicted theft in late adolescence also predicted theft in early adulthood (high truancy and high peer delinquency). This shows that few of the early adolescent aggravating risk factors for theft had a long 'reach' in influencing theft in adulthood.

Promotive Factors Predicting Low Likelihood of Theft

Table 7.2 shows the preventive promotive factors associated with later low probability of theft in the youngest cohort. The number of promotive effects that significantly predicted a low probability of theft was modest in number and was similar when measured in middle childhood, late childhood, or early adolescence (2/9, 22% vs. 2/9, 22% vs. 2/10, 20%). There was no consistency of preventive promotive effects across the comparisons. Among the single predictors were high prosocial behavior, low physical punishment, boy involved in family activities, good neighborhood impression, and older mother. As to long-term prediction, only one of the preventive promotive factors measured in middle childhood (good neighborhood as measured by census) predicted a low probability of theft in late adolescence. Thus, few of the preventive promotive factors measured in middle childhood had a long reach to theft in late adolescence. We will revisit this issue when discussing mixed risk and promotive factors.

Table 7.3 shows the preventive promotive factors associated with later low probability of theft in the oldest cohort. The number of preventive promotive effects that significantly predicted a low probability of theft was higher in early adolescence than in late adolescence (8/12; 67% vs. 0/6; 0%). There was no consistency of promotive effects across the comparisons because none of the effects were statistically significant in the prediction from late adolescence to early adulthood. Significant preventive promotive effects in early adolescence were low ADHD symptoms, high prosocial behavior, a negative attitude toward delinquency, persistence of discipline, good supervision, boy involved in family activities, low parental stress, and older mother. As to long-term prediction, only one of the preventive promotive factors measured in early adolescence predicted a low probability of theft in early adulthood (a negative attitude toward delinquency). This is in sharp contrast to risk factors, which we showed had a much longer reach than the promotive factors. We will revisit this issue when discussing mixed risk and promotive factors.

Mixed Risk and Promotive Factors Predicting Theft

As we showed with violence, several factors had both risk and promotive effects, which also applied to the prediction of theft (Tables 7.2 and 7.3). In the youngest cohort, the number of mixed factors significantly predicting high or low probability of theft peaked when the factors were measured in late childhood, compared to middle childhood or early adolescence (18/32, 56% vs. 10/28, 36% vs. 7/32, 22%). Several of the mixed factors significantly predicted high or low probability of theft across the two to three measurement intervals: psychopathic features, depressed mood, parental reinforcement, peer delinquency, relationship with peers, academic achievement, and attitude toward school. Less consistent was perceived likelihood of being caught. Only one of the "mixed" factors measured in middle childhood had long-term effects on the prediction of theft—namely, high parental stress. This was in contrast to the findings on mixed predictors of high or low probability of violence, where we found that several factors predicted high or low probability of violence over a period of about ten years.

To what extent were the results on mixed factors predictive of theft replicated for the oldest cohort? Recall that many of the mixed factors in the oldest cohort that were measured in early adolescence could not be measured in late adolescence, which severely restricts comparisons. With this limitation in mind, several of the mixed factors that predicted high or low probability of theft in the youngest cohort also predicted in the oldest cohort, including psychopathic features, depressed mood, interaction with the interviewer, perceived likelihood of being caught, relationship with peers, academic achievement, family SES, and housing quality (however, the effects were not always consistent across the promotive and risk sides of each factor). Which of the factors had the longest reach in predicting high or low probability of theft? Table 7.3 shows that only a few factors spanned the seven years between early adolescence and early adulthood, and these included high psychopathic features, high parental reinforcement, poor relationship with peers, and a negative attitude toward school.

Consistency of Results across Age

As before, the consistency of predictors of theft across different age blocks was investigated by correlating LORs. For the youngest cohort, the correlation between LORs from middle childhood to late childhood and LORs from late childhood to early adolescence was .57 ($p < .0001$). However, the correlation between LORs from late childhood to early adolescence and LORs from early adolescence to late adolescence was only .09 (n.s.). Also, the correlation between LORs from middle childhood to late childhood and LORs from early adolescence to late adolescence was -.09 (n.s.). For the oldest cohort, the correlation between LORs from early adolescence to late adolescence and LORs from late adolescence to early adulthood was .06 (n.s.). Therefore, except at the youngest ages, there was little tendency for the strongest aggravating risk and preventive promotive factors for theft in one age block to be similar to the strongest risk and promotive factors in another age block.

The same method was used to study the consistency between predictors of violence and theft. For the youngest cohort, the LORs from middle childhood to late childhood correlated .63 ($p < .0001$); from late childhood to early adolescence correlated .75 ($p < .0001$); and from early adolescence to late adolescence correlated .36 ($p = .006$). For the oldest cohort, the LORs from early adolescence to late adolescence correlated .53 ($p < .0001$); and from late adolescence to early adulthood correlated .34 (n.s.). We can conclude that the predictors of violence and theft are more similar at younger ages than at older ages. However, this may be because of the introduction of "new" risk factors, such as gun carrying and hard drug use, at older ages.

Logistic Regression Analyses to Predict Theft

We executed multivariate logistic regression analyses to investigate which variables independently predicted a high or low probability of theft in each of the age blocks. The same regression procedure was used as described earlier in the section on regression analyses for violence.

Prediction from Middle to Late Childhood in the Youngest Cohort   Table 7.6 shows that the best predictors measured in middle childhood that predicted theft in late childhood were three aggravating risk factors (child maltreatment by age 12, small house, and high depressed mood) and two preventive promotive factors (low psychopathic features and high involvement of the youth in family activities). When earlier deviance was included in the analysis, high truancy entered the equation in place of child maltreatment by age 12 and high youth involvement.

Prediction from Late Childhood to Early Adolescence in the Youngest Cohort Table 7.6 also shows that some predictors came in when the prediction of theft took place from late childhood to early adolescence: low psychopathic features, high peer delinquency, good relationship with peers, high academic achievement, good housing quality, and low family SES. Again, we found that preventive promotive effects (good relationship with peers, low psychopathic features, high academic achievement, and good housing quality) contributed to the prediction even when aggravating risk factors (high peer delinquency and low family SES) were taken into account. When earlier deviance was included in the analysis, prior theft entered the equation in place of a good relationship with peers and low family SES.

Prediction from Early to Late Adolescence in the Youngest Cohort   Yet another set of predictors came into play when the prediction of theft took place from early to late adolescence. Four factors increased the probability of theft (a positive attitude toward delinquency, parent police contact, theft victimization, and Caucasian ethnicity). When earlier deviance was included in the analysis, prior theft entered the equation in place of a positive attitude toward delinquency.

Prediction from Middle Childhood to Late Adolescence in the Youngest Cohort Table 7.6 shows that three factors measured in middle childhood predicted theft in late adolescence: child maltreatment by age 12, father behavior problems, and Caucasian ethnicity. The contribution of Caucasian ethnicity in two out of the four regression analyses is noteworthy, indicating that young Caucasian males were more likely to commit theft than were young African American males.

Prediction from Early to Late Adolescence in the Oldest Cohort   Turning to the oldest cohort, Table 7.6 shows that the best predictors measured in early adolescence of theft during late adolescence were low self-aspirations, theft victimization, low ADHD symptoms, persistence of discipline, and a low perceived likelihood of being caught. Thus, a combination of preventive promotive factors (low ADHD symptoms, and persistence of discipline) and aggravating risk factors (low self-aspirations, theft victimization, and low perceived likelihood

Table 7.6 Results of Multivariate Logistic Regression Analyses for Theft (Youngest and Oldest Cohorts)

Predictors	Explanatory POR	p	All Variables POR	p
Youngest Cohort				
PREDICTION FROM MIDDLE TO LATE CHILDHOOD				
Child Maltreatment by Age 12	2.1	046	—	—
Small House	2.2	.027	2.4	.016
Low Psychopathic Features	5.2	.026	5.0	.030
High Youth Involvement	3.4	.050	—	—
High Depressed Mood	2.7	.005	2.6	.008
High Truancy	—	—	2.4	.012
PREDICTION FROM LATE CHILDHOOD TO EARLY ADOLESCENCE				
Low Psychopathic Features	3.1	.043	4.5	.007
High Peer Delinquency	3.5	.0001	2.1	.016
Good Relationship with Peers	3.3	.012	—	—
High Academic Achievement	4.1	.023	5.0	.010
Low Family Socioeconomic Status	1.9	.040	—	—
Good Housing Quality	2.9	.014	2.8	.018
Prior Theft	—	—	6.7	.0001
PREDICTION FROM EARLY TO LATE ADOLESCENCE				
Positive Attitude toward Delinquency	4.2	.0005	—	—
Parent Police Contact	2.4	.035	2.6	.034
High Theft Victimization	3.3	.044	3.5	.005
Caucasian Ethnicity	3.7	.002	4.0	.003
Prior Theft	—	—	14.8	.0001
PREDICTION FROM MIDDLE CHILDHOOD TO LATE ADOLESCENCE				
Child Maltreatment by Age 12	2.9	.022	2.7	.030
Father Behavior Problems	3.0	.021	3.7	.003
Caucasian Ethnicity	3.2	.009	3.0	.011
Oldest Cohort				
PREDICTION FROM EARLY TO LATE ADOLESCENCE				
Low Self-Aspirations	2.1	.047	2.0	.048
High Theft Victimization	2.1	.041	2.2	.024
Low ADHD Symptoms	5.9	.019	5.7	.022
High Persistence of Discipline	12.3	.015	10.8	.021

Table 7.6 Results of Multivariate Logistic Regression Analyses for Theft (Youngest and Oldest Cohorts) (continued)

Predictors	Explanatory POR	p	All Variables POR	p
Low Perceived Likelihood of Being Caught	2.9	.005	2.1	.048
PREDICTION FROM LATE ADOLESCENCE TO EARLY ADULTHOOD				
Child Maltreatment by Age 12	4.2	.002	4.0	.003
High Peer Delinquency	2.6	.011	—	—
Hard Drug Use	—	—	2.9	.016
Gun Carrying	—	—	2.8	.006
PREDICTION FROM EARLY ADOLESCENCE TO EARLY ADULTHOOD				
Child Maltreatment by Age 12	3.3	.008	—	—
Poor Relationship with Siblings	2.5	.015	2.5	.016
Prior Theft	—	—	4.7	.0001

Notes: Approximate age range for each period: *middle childhood* (ages 7–9); *late childhood* (ages 10–12); *early adolescence* (age 13–16); *late adolescence* (ages 17–19); *early adulthood* (ages 20–25); POR = partial odds ratio; promotive factors in **boldface**. To facilitate comparisons of the magnitude of risk and promotive factors, the odds ratios for promotive factors, normally ranging in value from 0 to 1, were rescaled to be larger than 1.

of being caught) all contributed to the prediction of theft in late adolescence. In addition, there was a significant interaction effect between theft victimization and persistence of discipline (likelihood ratio chi-squared = 4.07, $p = .044$). Persistence of discipline acted as a protective factor in nullifying the effect of the risk factor of theft victimization. Of those receiving persistent discipline, 3% of those who had suffered theft victimization committed theft in late adolescence, compared with 3% of those who had not suffered theft victimization. Of those not receiving persistent discipline, 23% of those who had suffered theft victimization committed theft in late adolescence, compared with 13% of those who had not suffered theft victimization. This was the only significant interaction effect between risk and promotive factors in Table 7.6. However, the actual probability of finding an interaction effect among all interaction tests was lower than chance (p. 226).

Prediction from Late Adolescence to Early Adulthood in the Oldest Cohort Turning to the prediction of theft from late adolescence to early adulthood, Table 7.6 shows that two aggravating risk factors (child maltreatment, high peer delinquency) predicted a high probability of theft, but no preventive promotive factors independently contributed to the prediction of a low probability of theft. When earlier deviance was included in the analysis, hard drug use and gun carrying entered the equation in place of high peer delinquency. Finally, in terms of long-term prediction from early adolescence to early adulthood, Table 7.6 shows that only two aggravating risk factors (getting along poorly with siblings, and child maltreatment by age 12), predicted later theft in adulthood. When earlier deviance was included in the analysis, prior theft entered the equation in place of child maltreatment by age 12.

Summary of Logistic Regression Results   Summarizing the results of the regression analyses for theft, only one factor, child maltreatment by age 12, was replicated four times across the seven regression analyses. Prior theft appeared in three analyses. A few aggravating risk factors (theft victimization, high peer delinquency, and Caucasian ethnicity) were replicated in two out of the seven regression analyses. The analyses suggest a change in the pattern of the independent predictors with age: low psychopathic features were more important early in life than later (replicated in two analyses). Theft was predicted by prior theft victimization (but not violent victimization) in early adolescence in both cohorts. Very few parenting factors independently predicted theft (i.e., persistence of discipline in early adolescence, but in the oldest cohort only).

Summary of Interaction Effects for Violence and Theft   We systematically searched for significant interactions between risk and promotive factors in the regression analyses for violence and theft. However, we only discovered three significant interactions (independent of main effects) in 48 tests. This prevalence of significant results (6%) was similar to the chance expectation of 5%. Therefore, we cannot confidently conclude that there are any protective effects in our models predicting violence and theft.

The Dose-Response Relationship Between Risk and Promotive Factors and Later Theft
Figure 7.7 shows the ability of aggravating risk scores, derived from the regression analyses, to predict theft in the youngest cohort in different age blocks. As an example, of boys with one to three promotive factors in early adolescence (ages 13–16) only 1% committed theft in late adolescence (ages 17–19). This percentage was similar at 2% when there was a balance between promotive and risk factors (indicated by the 0 on the x-axis in Figure 7.8). Once the number of risk factors exceeded that of promotive factors, the probability of later theft accelerated to 11% for one risk factor, 42% for two risk factors, and 67% for three risk factors (AUC = .853; this AUC and all others mentioned below were statistically significant at least at the $p < .05$ level).

The four lines in Figure 7.7 each support the notion of a dose-response relationship between the sum of preventive promotive and aggravating risk factors and the probability of later theft. The ROC analyses suggest that the overall predictive efficiency for theft increased with age, especially when the

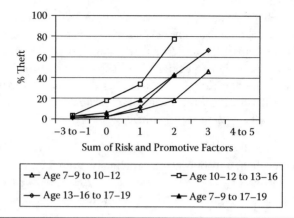

Figure 7.7 The Prediction of Theft (Youngest Cohort)

predictors were measured in late adolescence (AUC for predictors at ages 7–9 to theft at ages 10–12 = .756; AUC for predictors at ages 10–12 to theft at ages 13–16 = .819; and, as mentioned above, AUC for predictors at ages 13–16 to theft at ages 17–19 = .853). In comparison, the long-term prediction from ages 7–9 to theft at ages 17–19 was the weakest (AUC = .737).

Figure 7.8 shows the results for the oldest cohort, which do not show better prediction with age (as was found for theft in the youngest cohort). Instead, the predictive efficiency was slightly lower for the prediction from late adolescence to early adulthood (AUC = .761) compared to the prediction from early adolescence to late adolescence (AUC = .838). Note that the dose-response relationship in these two comparisons is nonlinear, but positively accelerating. Again, long-term prediction (from early adolescence to early adulthood) was the lowest (AUC = .634). In this case, there were only three scores (0, 1, and 2), whereas the percentage committing theft increased dramatically for higher scores (3, 4, and 5) in the other two comparisons (early adolescence to late adolescence, and late adolescence to early adulthood).

In summary, the results show that across the two cohorts and across different age blocks (a total of seven comparisons) there is a dose-response relationship between the sum of promotive and risk factors in the prediction of later theft. The AUC analyses do not consistently indicate an association between the magnitude of AUC and age (as we had observed for violence).

Generalized Estimating Equations Predicting Theft

GEE analyses were performed to determine which explanatory variables were the most robust predictors of theft within each cohort across all developmental age ranges. The procedures for selecting potential explanatory variables and specifying the predictive model for theft were identical to those described

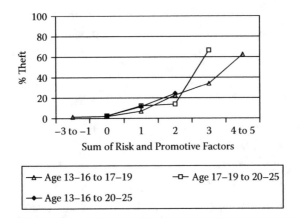

Figure 7.8 The Prediction of Theft (Oldest Cohort)

for the GEE analysis predicting violence. The significant risk, promotive, and mixed explanatory factors that emerged in the GEE model for the youngest and oldest cohorts are presented in Table 7.7. To determine if the explanatory variables identified in this model continued to predict theft significantly after accounting for indicators of earlier deviance (such as different forms of substance use, gun carrying, drug dealing, gang membership, and prior violence), a final GEE model was run adding these variables. The significant predictors that emerged in this final GEE model predicting theft for the youngest and oldest cohorts are also presented in Table 7.7.

Similar to the prediction of violence, the explanatory factors that predicted theft in the youngest cohort included a mixture of risk and promotive variables. Specifically, the aggravating risk factors of child maltreatment, low parental reinforcement, and high peer delinquency, as well as the preventive promotive factors of low psychopathic features, high academic achievement, and low peer delinquency, significantly predicted theft in the youngest cohort. Interestingly, none of the indicators of early deviance significantly contributed to the prediction of theft above and beyond these risk and promotive factors in the final model.

For the oldest cohort, the predictors of theft consisted solely of aggravating risk factors, including child maltreatment, high peer delinquency, and theft victimization. When prior deviance variables were added to the model, drug selling emerged as an additional predictor of theft in the oldest cohort. The risk factor of high peer delinquency was reduced to nonsignificance in the final model.

In summary, the GEE analyses confirmed that aggravating risk and preventive promotive factors predicted theft in the youngest cohort, but the results

Table 7.7 GEE Models Predicting Theft (Youngest and Oldest Cohorts)

Predictors	Explanatory POR	All variables POR
YOUNGEST COHORT		
Prior Theft	5.2***	5.2***
Time	0.7**	0.7**
Child Maltreatment by 12	1.7**	1.9**
Low Parental Reinforcement	1.7*	1.7*
Low Psychopathic Features	2.8**	2.8**
High Academic Achievement	1.9*	1.9*
High Peer Delinquency	1.6*	1.6*
Low Peer Delinquency	2.2*	2.1*
OLDEST COHORT		
Prior Theft	3.8***	3.4***
Time	0.6	0.5*
Child Maltreatment by 12	2.2**	2.3**
High Peer Delinquency	1.7*	—
High Theft Victimization	1.8*	1.8*
Drug Selling	—	2.3**

Notes: *$p < .05$; **$p < .01$; ***$p < .001$; POR = partial odds ratio; promotive factors in **boldface**. Confidence intervals are available from the authors. To facilitate comparisons of the magnitude of risk and promotive factors, the odds ratios for promotive factors, normally ranging in value from 0 to 1, were rescaled to be larger than 1.

indicated only risk factors for theft in the oldest cohort. Thus, the GEE analyses are largely in agreement with analyses based on age blocks.

Summary of Key Findings

Most prior research has focused on risk factors rather than promotive factors. We investigated promotive and risk factors and reached the following conclusions.

Promotive and Risk Factors

- Several factors formerly thought of as risk factors mainly operated as preventive promotive factors, including low ADHD, high persistence of discipline, low physical punishment, good supervision, boy involved in family activities, low parental stress, and living in a good neighborhood. These results held across the two cohorts and across violence and theft.

- Several factors had a predominantly aggravating risk effect (and less a promotive effect), and these included low self-aspirations, a positive attitude toward delinquency, peer delinquency, and a large family. These results applied across the two cohorts, with the exception that peer delinquency was a more consistent risk factor in the oldest than youngest cohort.
- Many factors had mixed promotive and risk effects, and these included psychopathic features, depressed mood, interaction with the interviewer, perceived likelihood of being caught, parental reinforcement, parent antisocial attitude, parent aspirations for the child, parent stress, peer delinquency, relationship with peers, academic achievement, attitude toward school, family SES, and housing quality. Most of these effects applied to the two cohorts (the exceptions were parental stress, peer delinquency, and housing quality, which applied to the youngest cohort only) and applied across violence and theft (the exception was that psychopathic features were more a risk factor for violence than for theft).
- In the explanatory regression analyses, there were twice as many significant aggravating risk factors as preventive promotive factors (20 compared with 9 for violence and 17 compared with 8 for theft). Nevertheless, preventive promotive factors predicted independently of aggravating risk factors and, hence, added to predictive efficiency.
- Preventive promotive factors had greater effects at younger ages.
- Preventive promotive factors, compared to risk factors, had a shorter reach in predicting serious offending, but mixed factors (i.e., factors with both risk and promotive effects) had a long reach in predicting serious offending.
- There was little evidence of protective effects based on interactions between risk and promotive factors.
- We found evidence of dose-response relationships in that the likelihood of violence and theft increased to the extent that the number of aggravating risk factors exceeded the number of preventive promotive factors.

Violence and Theft

- The strongest preventive promotive factors predicting a low probability of violence were high academic achievement (at younger ages), an older mother, and a good relationship with peers (at older ages).
- The strongest preventive promotive factors predicting a low probability of theft were low psychopathic features (at younger ages), high academic achievement (at younger ages), and high persistence of discipline (at older ages).

- The strongest aggravating risk factors predicting a high probability of violence were prior violence, high peer delinquency, followed by marijuana use and gun carrying.
- The strongest aggravating risk factors predicting a high probability of theft were child maltreatment and prior theft, followed by theft victimization, high peer delinquency, and Caucasian ethnicity.
- Many of the above prediction results based on regression analyses were replicated in GEE analyses.
- The strongest predictors of violence were generally similar at different ages, but the strongest predictors of theft were generally different at different ages. The strongest predictors of violence were generally similar to the strongest predictors of theft at younger ages, but not at older ages.
- Neighborhood factors did not predict violence or theft in the regression analyses, suggesting that their effects are indirect and mediated by other variables.

Ethnicity

- African American ethnicity predicted violence in zero-order relationships but did not predict in logistic regressions after controlling for other variables. Hence, it can be concluded that the relation between African American ethnicity and violence is indirect, and mediated by other risk factors such as high peer delinquency, low academic achievement, family on welfare, and repeating a grade. Caucasian ethnicity predicted theft in regression analyses even with controls for other variables, showing that Caucasian boys were more likely to steal.

The implications of the above findings for interventions will be discussed in Chapter 10.

Afterword to Chapter 7: Measuring Risk and Promotive Effects

In our analyses, we use odds ratios (ORs) to measure the strength of risk and promotive effects. The promotive OR compares the low and middle categories of a variable, whereas the risk OR compares the middle and high categories. For example, of 112 boys whose mother was old (ages 23–37) at her first birth, 9% were violent at ages 17–19, compared with 25% of 199 boys whose mother was between 18 and 22 years of age and 29% of 112 boys whose mother was young (ages 12–17). The promotive OR was 3.42 (95% confidence interval [CI] = 1.66 to 7.06, $z = 3.33$, $p = .0009$), while the risk OR was 1.19 (n.s.). Hence, we concluded that age of the mother at the birth of her first child was a promotive factor but not a risk factor for violence at age 17–19, as it was in eight out of nine other significant comparisons (Table 7.1).

To what extent, however, are our conclusions about risk and promotive effects influenced by our use of the odds ratio as the measure of strength of relationship? Table 7.8a shows the example that we began with in this chapter. We examined this using simulated data. On average, there are about 120 boys in the low (promotive) category of each trichotomized variable, 240 boys in the middle category, and 120 boys in the high (risk) category.

Tests of Nonlinear Effects

Table 7.8a shows the figures that are needed, with a prevalence of offending (violence or theft) of 50% in the middle category, for the nonlinear trend to be statistically significant (chi-squared = 3.84, p = .05). This is based on the Cochran-Armitage linear trend test (Agresti, 1990, pp. 100–102). The first line shows the promotive effect seen in Figure 7.3 (32%, 50%, and 50% delinquent in the low, middle, and high categories, respectively; OR = 2.11, z = 3.18, p = .0015). The second line shows the risk effect seen in Figure 7.2 (50%, 50%, and 68% delinquent, respectively; OR = 2.11, z = 3.18, p = .0015). With a prevalence of 50%, ORs of promotive and risk effects are equal.

The prevalence of violence and theft, however, is not 50%, but is usually between 10% and 25%. What happens as prevalence decreases? Table 7.8b shows that, in order to have significant nonlinearity with a prevalence of 25% in the middle category, the promotive OR must increase to 2.89 (z = 3.17, p = .0015). However, the corresponding risk OR would only have to be 2.11 (z = 3.13, p = .002). Table 7.8c shows that, with a prevalence of 10% in the middle category, the promotive OR would have to be an enormous 21.9 (z = 2.36, p = .018) in order to achieve a significant test of nonlinearity. However, the corresponding risk OR would only have to be 2.54 (z = 3.03, p = .002).

The implication of this analysis is that, as prevalence decreases, risk ORs are much more likely to be significant on the test of nonlinearity than promotive ORs. In order to investigate this further, sections d, e, and f of Table 7.8 show what happens when the promotive OR and the risk OR are both 2.5; in other words, when risk and promotive effects are equal according to the OR.

Table 7.8d again shows that promotive and risk effects are equal when the prevalence of offending in the middle category is 50%. The promotive OR of 2.5 has z = 3.82 (p = .001) and the nonlinear chi-squared value = 5.57 (p = .018), exactly the same as for the risk OR of 2.5. However, as prevalence decreases, the promotive ORs become less significant and their nonlinear effects also become less significant, compared to the risk ORs. Table 7.8e shows that, with a prevalence in the middle category of 25%, the promotive OR of 2.5 has z = 2.86 (p = .0042) and the nonlinear chi-squared = 3.09 (p = .079). In contrast, the risk OR of 2.5 has z = 3.84 (p = .0001) and the nonlinear chi-squared = 5.96 (p = .015). Table 7.8f shows that, with a prevalence in the middle category of 10%, the promotive OR of 2.5 has z = 1.83 (p = .067) and the nonlinear chi-squared = 1.27 (n.s.). In contrast, the risk OR of 2.5 has z = 2.97 (p = .0030) and the nonlinear

Table 7.8 Measuring Risk and Promotive Effects for Different Levels of Prevalence of Offending

Effect	% Delinquent			Promotive Factors		Risk Factors		Chi-Square Linear
	Low (120)	*Middle (240)*	*High (120)*	*OR*	*z*	*OR*	*z*	
(a) Promotive	32.18	50	50	2.11	3.18	1	0	3.84
Risk	50	50	67.82	1	0	2.11	3.18	3.84
(b) Promotive	10.34	25	25	2.89	3.17	1	0	3.84
Risk	25	25	41.25	1	0	2.11	3.13	3.84
(c) Promotive	.50	10	10	21.93	2.36	1	0	3.84
Risk	10	10	22.04	1	0	2.54	3.03	3.84
(d) Promotive	28.57	50	50	2.5	3.82	1	0	5.57
Risk	50	50	71.43	1	0	2.5	3.82	5.57
(e) Promotive	11.77	25	25	2.5	2.86	1	0	3.09
Risk	25	25	45.45	1	0	2.5	3.88	5.96
(f) Promotive	4.25	10	10	2.5	1.83	1	0	1.27
Risk	10	10	21.75	1	0	2.5	2.97	3.68
(g) Promotive	12.5	50	50	7.0	6.39	1	0	17.49
Risk	50	50	87.5	1	0	7.0	6.39	17.49
(h) Promotive	6.25	25	25	5.0	3.97	1	0	6.52
Risk	25	25	43.75	1	0	2.33	3.58	5.05
(i) Promotive	2.5	10	10	4.33	2.35	1	0	2.26
Risk	10	10	17.5	1	0	1.91	2.00	1.61

Notes: OR = odds ratio.

chi-squared = 3.68 ($p = .055$). Hence, promotive effects are less likely than risk effects to achieve statistical significance on the test of nonlinearity.

What happens to risk and promotive ORs when there is a linear relationship between the explanatory variable and the outcome? Table 7.8g shows results when 13% of the lowest 25%, 50% of the middle 50%, and 87% of the highest 25% of boys are delinquent. The promotive and risk ORs are exactly equal at 7.0 ($z = 6.39$, $p < .0001$), and the nonlinear effects are highly significant (chi-squared = 17.49, $p < .0001$).

As prevalence decreases, however, the promotive OR becomes greater than the risk OR, although their significance levels are less disparate. Table 7.8h shows that, with a prevalence of 25% and a linear relationship, the promotive OR is 5.0 ($z = 3.97$, $p < .0001$), while the risk OR is 2.33 ($z = 3.58$, $p = .0003$). Table 7.8i shows that, with a prevalence of 10% and a linear relationship, the promotive OR is 4.33 ($z = 2.35$, $p = .019$), while the risk OR is 1.91 ($z = 2.00$, $p = .046$). In general, therefore, promotive ORs will be greater than risk ORs when relationships between explanatory variables and outcomes are linear. This raises the possibility that the importance of promotive effects may have been overestimated by the use of the OR in Table 7.1 to measure strength of effect.

In order to investigate this, it would be desirable to use a measure of strength of effect that produced equal risk and promotive effects for the examples shown in Tables 7.8h and 7.8i. Most measures of association in 2 x 2 tables, for example those based on chi-square, the product-moment correlation, or Relative Improvement Over Chance (RIOC), behave like the OR. Therefore, a measure based on the binomial distribution was used. In Table 7.8h, if we assume that the true probability of offending is $p = .25$ (the middle category value), the expected number of delinquents in the low and high categories is 30 ($120^*.25$), with a standard deviation of $\sqrt{120^*.25^*.75} = 4.74$. Hence, any number of delinquents deviating from 30 by at least 9.30 ($4.74^*1.96$) is statistically significant. A number in the low category of 7.5 (6%), as in Table 7.8h, corresponds to $z = 4.74$, $p < .0001$. Similarly, a number in the high category of 52.5 (44%) corresponds to $z = 4.74$, $p < .0001$. Therefore, this binomial test produces equal risk and promotive effects with linear relationships.

How do results based on the OR compare with results based on this binomial test? In order to investigate this systematically, we focused on the 12 trichotomized variables with the most significant effects in Table 7.1:

1. Psychopathic features.
2. Depressed mood.
3. Academic achievement.
4. Attitude toward delinquency.
5. Perceived likelihood of being caught.
6. Parental supervision.
7. Involvement of youth in family activities.
8. Peer delinquency.
9. Relationship with peers.
10. Neighborhood impression.
11. Housing quality.
12. Age of the mother at birth of her first child.

Each of these variables had at least eight significant effects in Table 7.7; no other trichotomized variable had more than six significant effects.

Table 7.9 shows ORs relating the 12 key variables in different age ranges to violence in the next age range, and Table 7.10 shows corresponding ORs for theft. Each risk OR is based on the highest quarter versus the middle half on the explanatory variable, whereas each promotive OR is based on the middle half versus the lowest quarter. For example, for age of the mother at the birth of her first child predicting violence at ages 17–19, note the promotive OR of

Table 7.9 Strength of Association of Key Risk and Promotive Factors Predicting Violence (Odds Ratios)

	Youngest Cohort				Oldest Cohort			
	Middle Childhood to Late Childhood	Late Childhood to Early Adolescence	Early Adolescence to Late Adolescence	Middle Childhood to Late Adolescence	Early Adolescence to Late Adolescence	Late Childhood to Early Adulthood	Early Adolescence to Early Adulthood	Number Significant
RISK FACTORS								
High Psychopathic Features	1.8	2.8*	3.2*	1.4	2.6*	N/A	2.0*	4
High Depressed Mood	2.1*	1.3	2.5*	1.0	2.0*	2.3*	1.6	3
Low Academic Achievement	1.3	2.0*	2.4*	1.6	1.7*	N/A	1.0	3
Positive Attitude toward Delinquency	1.9	2.9*	3.4*	1.2	1.8*	1.9*	1.6	4
Low Perceived Likelihood of Being Caught	0.8	2.0*	1.9	1.1	1.6	0.7	1.5	1
Low Supervision	1.4	1.8*	1.4	0.8	1.6*	N/A	1.5	2
Low Boy Involvement in Family Activities	1.2	1.5	1.0	1.2	1.3	N/A	.08	0
High Peer Delinquency	2.6*	4.1*	6.1*	1.8	4.6*	5.3*	5.5*	6
Poor Relationship with Peers	1.5	2.5*	2.6*	2.4*	1.7*	N/A	1.0	4
Bad Neighborhood Impression	1.3	1.6*	1.8	1.9	1.6	2.2*	1.2	2
Poor Housing Quality	1.2	1.7*	2.1*	1.7	1.3	N/A	2.0*	3
Younger Mother	1.7	1.6	1.0	R	1.2	1.6	R	0
Total								**32**

Table 7.9 Strength of Association of Key Risk and Promotive Factors Predicting Violence (Odds Ratios) (continued)

	Youngest Cohort				Oldest Cohort			Number Significant
	Middle Childhood to Late Childhood	Late Childhood to Early Adolescence	Early Adolescence to Late Adolescence	Middle Childhood to Late Adolescence	Early Adolescence to Late Adolescence	Late Childhood to Early Adulthood	Early Adolescence to Early Adulthood	
PROMOTIVE FACTORS								
Low Psychopathic Features	15.1*	2.7*	3.8	2.7	2.5*	N/A	2.5*	4
Low Depressed Mood	2.2	1.7	1.4	3.0*	1.1	0.8	0.9	2
High Academic Achievement	8.3*	6.2*	1.5	1.3	2.2*	N/A	2.9*	4
Negative Attitude toward Delinquency	1.0	1.0	1.3	1.4	4.1*	1.7	2.3*	2
High Perceived Likelihood of Being Caught	1.2	2.0*	2.3	2.3	1.5	2.1*	0.8	2
High Supervision	1.9	2.4*	2.1	2.4	2.4*	N/A	2.3*	3
High Boy Involvement in Family Activities	2.0	1.2	1.3	2.3	2.1*	N/A	2.3*	2
Low Peer Delinquency	4.4*	2.6*	5.1	3.9*	1.3	1.9	1.2	3
Good Relationship with Peers	3.6*	2.7*	1.8	1.4	2.0*	N/A	11.5	4
Good Neighborhood Impression	2.7*	1.9	3.0	2.0	1.8*	3.7*	2.8*	4
Good Housing Quality	5.2*	2.0*	4.8*	1.9	1.7	N/A	1.8	3
Older Mother	3.5*	3.6*	1.2	R	3.4*	2.7*	R	4
Total								**38**

Notes: *$p < .05$; N/A = not available; R = repetitious with previous (Older Mother is the same variable in middle childhood and early adolescence).

Table 7.10 Strength of Association of Key Risk and Promotive Factors Predicting Theft (Odds Ratios)

	Youngest Cohort					Oldest Cohort		Number Significant
	Middle Childhood to Late Childhood	Late Childhood to Early Adolescence	Early Adolescence to Late Adolescence	Middle Childhood to Late Adolescence	Early Adolescence to Late Adolescence	Late Childhood to Early Adulthood	Early Adolescence to Early Adulthood	
RISK FACTORS								
High Psychopathic Features	1.8	1.7*	1.4	1.3	1.4	N/A	2.0	1
High Depressed Mood	2.8*	1.7	1.1	0.8	1.7	1.8	1.5	1
Low Academic Achievement	1.7	1.9*	1.3	1.6	2.6*	N/A	0.7	2
Positive Attitude toward Delinquency	1.9	2.5*	3.8*	0.9	2.0*	1.7	0.9	3
Low Perceived Likelihood of Being Caught	0.9	1.7	2.3*	0.5	2.0*	0.5	0.7	2
Low Supervision	1.8	1.9*	0.7	1.0	1.7	N/A	2.4*	2
Low Boy Involvement in Family Activities	0.8	1.9*	1.8	1.13	1.3	N/A	1.7	1
High Peer Delinquency	2.4*	3.3*	2.5*	1.0	2.4*	2.0	2.0	4
Poor Relationship with Peers	1.5	1.6	1.8	0.4	0.9	N/A	1.8	0
Bad Neighborhood Impression	0.8	0.9	0.8	1.1	0.9	1.9	0.9	0
Poor Housing Quality	1.0	1.5	1.1	1.6	1.9*	N/A	1.2	1
Younger Mother	2.2*	1.3	0.5	R	1.1	1.7	R	1
Total								**18**
PROMOTIVE FACTORS								
Low psychopathic features	5.6*	6.1*	2.0	1.0	3.0*	N/A	2.1	3

Table 7.10 Strength of Association of Key Risk and Promotive Factors Predicting Theft (Odds Ratios) (continued)

	Youngest Cohort					Oldest Cohort		Number Significant
	Middle Childhood to Late Childhood	Late Childhood to Early Adolescence	Early Adolescence to Late Adolescence	Middle Childhood to Late Adolescence	Early Adolescence to Late Adolescence	Late Childhood to Early Adulthood	Early Adolescence to Early Adulthood	
Low Depressed Mood	1.9	1.7	2.9	1.4	1.4	1.0	0.8	0
High Academic Achievement	3.6*	5.8*	1.2	0.5	0.8	N/A	1.5	2
Negative Attitude Toward Delinquency	0.8	1.2	1.2	1.1	1.9	1.1	3.8*	1
High Perceived Likelihood of Being Caught	1.5	1.4	1.3	2.0	1.8	1.5	1.8	0
High Supervision	1.9	1.2	2.0	1.7	1.9	N/A	0.9	0
High Boy Involvement in Family Activities	4.7*	1.4	0.8	1.1	2.7*	N/A	1.8	2
Low Peer Delinquency	2.5	3.0*	3.3	1.3	1.7	3.9	1.6	1
Good Relationship with Peers	2.8	4.3*	0.7	1.7	2.2*	N/A	1.7	2
Good Neighborhood Impression	4.3*	1.8	1.8	0.8	1.8	0.8	1.2	1
Good Housing Quality	1.3	3.8*	1.1	1.0	1.4	N/A	1.5	1
Older Mother	1.9	2.0	1.3	R	2.5*	1.4	R	1
Total								14

Notes: *$p < .05$; N/A = not available; R = repetitious (Older Mother is the same variable in early adolescence and middle childhood).

3.4 and the risk OR of 1.2 (see p. 218). Briefly, there were 38 significant promotive effects and 32 significant risk effects for violence, and 14 significant promotive effects and 18 significant risk effects for theft. Relationships with violence were stronger than relationships with theft.

For violence, the clearest risk factor was peer delinquency (six significant risk effects, three significant promotive effects). In five out of seven comparisons, the risk ORs were greater than the promotive ORs. For theft, peer delinquency had four significant risk effects and one significant promotive effect. However, in four out of seven comparisons, the promotive ORs were greater than the risk ORs. For violence, the clearest promotive factor was age of the mother at the birth of her first child (four significant promotive effects, no significant risk effects). This was only measured once, so in the youngest cohort the middle childhood–late adolescence comparison would be the same as the early adolescence–late adolescence comparison, while in the oldest cohort the early adolescence–early adulthood comparison would be the same as the late adolescence–early adulthood comparison. In all five comparisons, the promotive ORs were greater than the risk ORs. For theft, the age of the mother at the birth of her first child had one significant promotive effect and one significant risk effect.

For theft, the clearest risk factor was again peer delinquency. The clearest promotive factor for theft was psychopathic features (three significant promotive effects and one significant risk effect).

Reassuringly, results obtained with the OR were highly correlated with results obtained using the binomial test. For violence, z-values from the risk ORs correlated .987 with z-values from the risk binomial test; z-values from the promotive ORs correlated .997 with z-values from the promotive binomial test. For theft, z-values from the risk ORs correlated .996 with z-values from the risk binomial test; z-values from the promotive ORs correlated .999 with z-values from the promotive binomial test. The slightly lower correlation for violence risk ORs was a function of some very high z-values from the risk binomial test.

In general, z-values from the binomial test were greater than z-values from ORs. In every case where the OR was statistically significant, the binomial test also gave a significant result. Hence, we conclude that, despite the problems identified earlier in this Note, risk and promotive ORs give valid indications about the significance of risk and promotive effects.

Finally, Table 7.11 summarizes the nonlinear relationships that were significant or nearly significant. There were 76 tests for violence and 76 tests for theft. For violence, the number of significant results (10) was considerably in excess of the chance expectation of 3.8, but this was not true for theft (only two significant). Table 7.11 shows the percentage of violence or theft in each category, the significance of the nonlinear relationship, and the significance of

Table 7.11 Nonlinear Relationships

Predicting Violence	Block	% Violent			Nonlinear		Difference		Effect
		Low	Mid	High	Chi-Squared	p	z	p(z)	
YOUNGEST COHORT									
Attitude toward Delinquency	LC–EA	15.8	15.8	35.0	6.72	.010	-2.22	.026	Risk
Peer Delinquency	LC–EA	6.8	16.3	44.3	6.26	.012	-0.82	n.s.	Mixed
Attitude toward Delinquency	EA–LA	4.5	5.8	11.3	3.69	.055	-1.23	n.s.	Risk
Peer Delinquency	EA–LA	0.9	4.5	22.3	7.51	.006	-0.15	n.s.	Mixed
Peer Delinquency	EA–LA	12.8	16.2	46.8	12.77	.0004	-2.61	.009	Risk
OLDEST COHORT									
Depressed Mood	LA–A	16.2	13.5	26.8	5.26	.022	-2.14	.032	Risk
Perceived Likelihood of Being Caught	LA–A	11.5	21.0	15.7	4.29	.038	2.09	.037	Neither
Peer Delinquency	LA–A	6.3	11.5	40.5	11.64	.0007	-1.68	.093	Risk
Academic Achievement	EA–A	8.2	20.5	20.7	3.04	.081	2.04	.041	Promotive
Boy Involvement in Family Activities	EA–A	10.6	21.3	16.9	4.67	.031	2.23	.026	Neither
Peer Delinquency	EA–A	9.2	10.6	39.5	15.57	.0001	-2.77	.006	Risk
Relationship with Peers	EA–A	2.5	22.4	22.8	7.92	.005	3.46	.0005	Promotive

Predicting Theft	% Theft	Nonlinear			Difference				Effect
	Block	Low	Mid	High	Chi-Squared	p	z	p(z)	
YOUNGEST COHORT									
Boy Involvement in Family Activities	MC–LC	2.4	10.5	9.0	3.69	.055	2.18	.029	Promotive
Neighborhood Impression	MC–LC	2.7	10.4	8.8	3.37	.066	2.05	.040	Promotive
Attitude toward Delinquency	LC–EA	11.4	13.3	27.5	3.23	.072	-1.39	n.s.	Risk
Peer Delinquency	LC–EA	5.1	13.8	34.2	2.98	.084	-0.17	n.s.	Mixed
Attitude toward Delinquency	EA–LA	3.6	4.4	15.1	4.26	.039	-1.32	n.s.	Risk
Perceived Likelihood of Being Caught	MC–LA	4.4	8.6	4.5	3.12	.077	1.74	.082	Neither
Relationship with Peers	MC–LA	5.0	8.7	3.8	3.16	.075	1.76	.078	Neither
OLDEST COHORT									
Academic Achievement	EA–LA	12.9	10.0	22.7	6.21	.013	-2.29	.022	Risk
Relationship with Peers	EA–LA	8.1	16.4	14.4	2.75	.097	1.77	0.77	Promotive

Notes: Nonlinear = results of nonlinear test; Difference = test of difference between promotive and risk ORs; LC = late childhood; EA = early adolescence; LA = late adolescence; A = adulthood; MC = middle childhood.

the difference between the promotive and risk ORs. Where the z-value is negative, this means that the risk OR was greater than the promotive OR.

The result showed that peer delinquency was consistently a risk factor for violence. Attitude toward delinquency showed risk effects for both violence and theft. The perceived likelihood of being caught showed unexpected effects, with the greatest probability of violence or theft in the middle category. Relationship with peers had promotive effects in two comparisons. Academic achievement had one promotive effect for violence but one risk effect for theft. Depressed mood had one risk effect for violence, while neighborhood impression and involvement of the boy in family activities had promotive effects for theft.

None of these results contradict our original classification of these variables—as risk factors, promotive factors, or a mix of both—that guided the inclusion of variables in regression analyses. Depressed mood, academic achievement, perceived likelihood of being caught, and relationship with peers were classified as mixed variables, and thus were included in the analyses as both risk and promotive factors. Attitude toward delinquency was identified as a risk factor, while parental supervision, involvement of the youth in family activities, neighborhood impression, and age of the mother at the birth of her first child were identified as promotive factors. Peer delinquency and housing quality were considered mixed variables for the youngest cohort and risk factors for the oldest cohort. Psychopathic features were considered mixed for violence and promotive for theft. The present analyses do not indicate that any changes in this classification are needed (e.g., that a variable originally classified as a promotive factor should have been included in our analyses as a risk factor, or vice versa).

Eight

Developmental Trajectories
of Violence and Theft

ERIC LACOURSE, VÉRONIQUE DUPÉRÉ, AND ROLF LOEBER

For a long time research on typologies of delinquents was either based on pre-conceived notions with little empirical support (e.g., Lombroso, 1912) or was derived from cross-sectional data only (Clinard & Quinney, 1973; Roebuck, 1966). Delinquent types based on cross-sectional data have many disadvantages in that they fail to capture changes in offending that take place with age, and that differentially affect some youth more than others (Gibbons, 1975). With the increased availability of multiwave longitudinal data over the past decade using self-reports and official records, it has proven more feasible to investigate the dynamic aspects of developmental typologies of delinquents. Buttressed by major improvements in statistical software to analyze such developmental trajectories, a new generation of findings has emerged showing that some categories of delinquents develop offending in different ways from other categories of offenders (Barker et al., 2007; Lacourse et al., 2002; Nagin, Farrington, & Moffitt, 1995; Nagin & Land, 1993, White, Bates, & Buyske, 2001).

Using such improved statistical techniques, this chapter has three general objectives. First, on the basis of prevalence data, we investigate developmental trajectories of violence and theft in terms of onset, rate of change, and duration. This constitutes a dynamic classification of youth offending from middle childhood through adolescence (youngest cohort) and from early adolescence to early adulthood (oldest cohort). Second, we explore the co-occurrence of the developmental trajectories of violence and theft in these periods. Third, we examine which factors, measured early in the study, predict why some young men have low, high, or changing trajectories of violence and theft.

In this chapter we use a statistical technique developed in the mid-1990s by Daniel Nagin and his colleagues (Nagin, 1999, 2005; Nagin & Land, 1993; Nagin & Tremblay, 2001b) that empirically identifies subgroups of individuals with different patterns of development in their criminal behaviors over time. This methodology has been very influential in developmental criminology and follows the theoretical work of Moffitt (1993), who describes the development of antisocial behaviors using a taxonomy defined by two groups—one that will tend to exhibit problem behaviors during early childhood that turn into criminal behavior during adolescence and adulthood, and another whose antisocial behaviors are limited to adolescence, with risk factors being different for these two developmental pathways. This statistical technique will help us investigate the same kind of research questions that we addressed in earlier chapters, but in a more probabilistic fashion.

In this chapter, we also investigate the topic of versatility versus specialization of criminal offending by modeling the joint distribution of violence and theft over time. Thus, we are able to describe the developmental trajectories of theft behaviors conditional on violent behaviors, and vice versa. The co-occurrence of these developmental trajectories during adolescence and adulthood is often related to a common set of risk factors that are already present in childhood (see Chapter 7). Therefore, we will try to predict specific patterns of violent and theft offending using hypotheses derived from theoretical models that try to integrate multilevel aggravating risk and preventive promotive factors from the individual, school, neighborhood, and sociodemographic domains.

This chapter addresses the following questions:

What is the yearly prevalence of the all-source measure of serious violence and serious theft from ages 10 to 25? (This is in contrast to Chapter 5, in which we reviewed the prevalence of the all-source measure of serious offending by age block.)

What number and types of developmental trajectories best describe young men's violence and theft, and what can we learn about individual differences in the onset, duration, and desistance of violence and theft?

To what extent do the developmental trajectories documented in this chapter reflect cohort differences in young men who, during their adolescence, lived in community contexts with very different rates of crime? (That is, are there cohort differences in developmental trajectories of violence and theft?)

To what extent do the young men display versatility versus specialization in their developmental trajectories of violence and theft?

Which types of factors predict membership in particular offending trajectories? How similar are factors predicting violence and theft trajectories?

Developmental Trajectories: The Nonparametric Random-Effects Model

In the past decade, many studies have tried to describe individual trajectories and pathways of criminal offending using different statistical models (Horney, Osgood, & Marshall, 1995; Nagin & Farrington, 1992; Nagin & Land, 1993; Osgood & Rowe, 1994, White et al., 2001). In addition, a great deal of work has been carried out on aggression and violence from early childhood to adolescence (Brame, Nagin, & Tremblay, 2001; Broidy et al., 2003; Lacourse et al., 2002; Nagin & Tremblay, 1999; Tremblay et al., 2004). Few studies, however, have investigated the developmental trajectories of violence from childhood to adulthood and even fewer have undertaken the investigation of theft trajectories (Brame, Bushway, Paternoster, & Thornberry, 2005; Laub & Sampson, 2003; Piquero, Paternoster, Mazerolle, Brame, & Dean, 1999). Further, most of the trajectory analyses of physical aggression have not included serious violent behaviors and usually have been based on a few repeatedly measured indicators of disruptive behavior.

During the past 25 years, there have been two major advances in the study of individual developmental trajectories. Random-effects growth modeling (Bryk & Raudenbush, 1987; Meredith & Tisak, 1990; Nagin & Farrington, 1992; Rogosa & Willet, 1985) has been a very popular analytical technique in developmental criminology and psychology. It provides tools that favor the combination of static and dynamic explanations of repeated measures data compared to more traditional approaches, such as cross-lagged regression or Markov chain models that focus mainly on dynamic aspects of crime without considering unobserved population heterogeneity (Brame, Bushway, & Paternoster, 1999; Bushway, Brame, & Paternoster, 1999). One main limitation of applying these random-effects growth models in individual trajectories is their inadequacy in testing theories that postulate a qualitatively different development of criminal behaviors resulting from possibly distinct etiological processes (Moffitt, 1993; Patterson & Yoerger, 1993, 1997).

Alternatively, nonparametric statistical models have been developed to identify clusters of similar developmental trajectories in the population that are often described as latent trajectory classes (Jones, Nagin, & Roeder, 2001; Muthén, 2001; Nagin, 1999; Nagin & Land, 1993). Nonparametric analyses of developmental trajectories usually has led to the identification of four trajectories: individuals whose antisocial behavior remains high over time, individuals who do not offend, and individuals whose antisocial behavior increases or decreases during adolescence or adulthood (see, e.g., Brame, Nagin et al., 2001; Broidy et al., 2003; Fergusson & Horwood, 1995; Lacourse et al., 2002; Nagin & Tremblay, 1999). One key feature of group-based trajectory analyses is that a statistical estimation procedure using mixture modeling identifies the shape of the trajectory and prevalence of each group (Nagin, 1999, 2005). However, few studies using trajectory analyses have shed light on the co-occurrence of different problem behaviors as they unfold over time (Nagin & Tremblay, 2001a) or have investigated specific predictors that could distinguish among trajectories of both theft and violence (Piquero, 2000).

What Have We Learned from Nonparametric Developmental Trajectory Analyses?

This section summarizes several research findings on physical aggression and other problem behaviors by Nagin and Tremblay over the past decade (Nagin & Tremblay, 2005). It also summarizes some of the findings on serious offending by other researchers in the field that used the same statistical procedure. Results from these studies suggest that (1) late-onset trajectories are far less common than originally expected by theory (Moffitt, 1993); (2) the number of trajectory groups is far greater than originally expected by theory (Brame, Nagin, et al., 2001; Bushway, Thornberry, & Krohn, 2003; Lacourse et al., 2002); and (3) predictors and outcomes often differ for specific developmental patterns or longitudinal sequences of behaviors (Chung, Hill, Hawkins, Gilchrist, & Nagin, 2002; Côté, Vaillancourt, Le Blanc, Nagin, & Tremblay, 2006; Nagin, Barker, Lacourse, & Tremblay, in press; Nagin & Tremblay, 1999; Nagin & Tremblay, 2001b; Oldgers et al., in press).

Late-onset developmental trajectories have been postulated to explain the peak of the age-crime curve around the age of 18 (Moffitt, 1993). Based on two research reports from scientific committees that were published in the 1990s, the U.S. National Research Council has concluded that violence is mainly a response learned by observing models of these behaviors in the family, the peer group, or the media. This cumulative exposure to violent models is the main explanation for the rise in serious violence during adolescence. Recently, compelling evidence from many longitudinal studies all over the world has shown that aggression peaks at an early age and declines afterward (Loeber & Hay, 1997; Nagin & Tremblay, 2001b; Tremblay et al., 1999). In fact, the research program mainly promoted by Nagin and Tremblay (2005) has provided evidence that physical aggression peaks around age 2 and is not necessarily a learned behavior. Therefore, the developmental challenge for parents of young children is to learn to control aggressive impulses in a warm and noncoercive family environment. Although this research described the developmental pattern of aggression for the whole population, it could still be possible that a subgroup of the population increases in aggression and antisocial behavior later in childhood or during adolescence.

Brame, Nagin, et al. (2001) were among the first to explore the link between trajectories of physical aggression in childhood (ages 6–13) and trajectories of violent offending in adolescence (ages 13–17) based on data from the Montreal Longitudinal and Experimental Study. Results were derived from dual-trajectory analysis, which is designed to investigate the linkage between two distinct measurement series (Nagin, 2005; Nagin & Tremblay, 2001a). Brame, Nagin et al. (2001) have found only one group that might be characterized as a late-onset violence group. This group was estimated to comprise 10% of the population. The remaining 90% followed trajectories of steady or declining physical aggression from ages 6 to 17. A similar dual trajectory analytic strategy has been used by Nagin (2005) and has led to the same conclusion. A nontrivial group of boys appears to increase their level of violence during adolescence, although the majority is either on a steady or declining trajectory. Similar results have been found for general delinquency (Bushway et al., 2003) and more specifically for vandalism and theft (Lacourse et al., 2002).

Prevalence of Violence and Theft in the Youngest and Oldest Cohorts

The results presented in this chapter are based on the all-source measure of serious violence and theft scales combining reported delinquency and official records data (see chapters 3 and 5). Because of the nature of the nonparametric random-effects model, it was more appropriate to use annual data instead of the age blocks as described in chapters 4 and 5. In the youngest cohort, offense measures were used from ages 10 to 19, whereas in the oldest cohort, the observation window was from ages 13 to 25.

Figure 8.1 reports the annual prevalence of the all-source measure of offending for both violence and theft in the youngest and oldest cohorts. Not surprisingly, prevalence for the combined scales parallel those reported in Chapter 5. For violence, the results show higher levels in the oldest cohort at all ages where comparisons were possible (ages 13–19). Also, the total prevalence is about 1.5 times higher in the oldest cohort, if we compare the total prevalence or only the prevalence for the age window overlapping in both cohorts (ages 13–19). Finally, prevalence peaked earlier in the youngest cohort (ages 13–16 years) as compared to the oldest cohort (ages 18–19), suggesting a

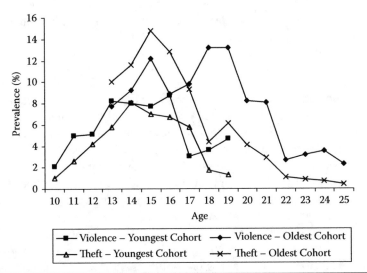

Figure 8.1 Prevalence of the All-Source Measure of Violence and Theft (Youngest and Oldest Cohorts)

delay in the desistance process in the oldest cohort. For theft, the results were generally similar, with higher prevalence at all ages in the oldest cohort. The total prevalence was again more than 1.5 times higher in the oldest cohort regardless of whether the comparisons were made across all measurement occasions or for the shared ages only. It appears that theft peaked at about the same age in both cohorts (around ages 14–16), but that its annual prevalence decreased much more rapidly in the youngest cohort. Indeed, a prevalence of theft consistently below 2% occurred four years later in the oldest cohort (about age 22) compared to the youngest one (about age 18).

Developmental Trajectories of Violence and Theft

As explained above, the nonparametric random-effects models (Nagin, 1999) identify groups of individuals following similar developmental trajectories over time. The method also provides estimates of the proportion of the population in each trajectory group. The number of groups and the shape of the associated trajectories are statistically informed with the goodness of fit indexes. In this chapter, the Bayesian Information Criterion was used to select the final models presented. Before starting to compare the results obtained in both cohorts, it is important to mention that as the number of measurement occasions increases it is possible that the number of groups increases as well, because individuals initially following similar patterns of evolution might diverge into distinct pathways only at later stages (see Nagin, 2004). Thus, because the measurement of the youngest cohort did not extend into the 20s, it is not surprising that fewer groups were found in this cohort. However, the small number of groups found in the youngest cohort was probably due not only to differences in the measurement window, but also to the fact that there was less variability in violence and theft in this cohort (see Chapter 5).

Violence Trajectories

Prevalence of Violence Trajectory Group Membership   Figures 8.2 and 8.3 show the developmental trajectories of violence for the youngest and oldest cohorts. Figure 8.2 shows three trajectories pertaining to violence: *no/low, minor stable,* and *high declining,* while Figure 8.3 shows four violence trajectories for the oldest cohort: *no/low, moderate declining, high declining,* and *late-onset.*

The results show that most boys in both cohorts belong to the no/low trajectory groups (59% and 52% for the youngest and oldest cohorts, respectively) with a practically zero probability of their committing violence throughout adolescence. Second, a substantial proportion of the boys show a low to moderate probability of engaging in violence during adolescence. In the youngest cohort, 30% of the boys were included in a minor-stable trajectory group, showing a constant, relatively low probability (below .10) of violence. In the oldest cohort, over 40% of the boys belonged to either the moderate declining

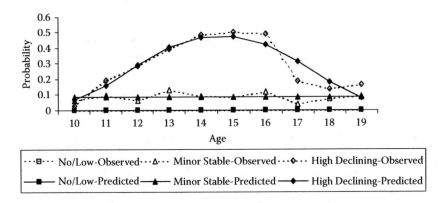

Figure 8.2 Trajectories of Violence (Youngest Cohort)

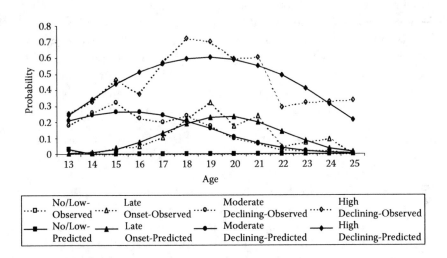

Figure 8.3 Trajectories of Violence (Oldest Cohort)

or high declining trajectory groups. In those two groups, the probability of the boys committing violence varied between 0 and 0.60. On average, the probability of offending in those two groups is higher than in the moderate group found in the youngest cohort, suggesting that higher levels of community crime under which the boys in the oldest cohort grew up might have increased their probability of committing serious violent acts. Finally, both cohorts show a small high declining trajectory group of boys with very frequent violence. In the youngest cohort, this group represented a little more than 10% of the boys. Their trajectory started with a probability near 0 by age 10, and then the probability of violence rose steadily until ages 14–15, when it became close to .50 and then declined at age 19, when it reached the same level as the minor-stable group (.10). In the oldest cohort, this group represented a little more than 5% of the boys. For this group, the probability of violence rose steadily until it reached about 0.60 at ages 18–20, and then slowly declined to 0.20 by age 25.

Onset   In the youngest cohort, there were no obvious early- or adolescent-onset trajectory groups. Indeed, the three trajectory groups started at similarly low probability levels by age 10 and became distinguished from each other very rapidly. The absence of an early-onset trajectory might be explained by the possibility that at age 10 violence is not yet expressed through its most serious forms. Of course, this does not mean that other forms of violence (or aggression) were absent before that age. The lack of an adolescent-onset group might be due to restraints in the observation window or to the lower levels of community crime in the youngest cohort. In the oldest cohort, high declining trajectory groups were more readily apparent, and a rising group was found, which more clearly corresponds to the adolescence-limited trajectory. Indeed, the probability of violence for this group remained low before ages 17 and 18, and then peaked by age 20 and thereafter declined until it became practically zero by age 25. This sort of late-onset pattern may be linked to the higher levels of crime present in the community when this cohort reached adolescence.

Rate of Change   In terms of rate of change, the most interesting observation concerns the high declining trajectory groups. The figures (and the underlying parameters) show that the rising slope and the declining slope were both steeper in the youngest cohort. This means that the emergence of violence was faster in the youngest cohort, but that desistance was also faster. In contrast, the peak of violent offending was flatter in the oldest cohort, which means that it took longer to reach the highest level of violence but also that the high level of violence lasted longer in that cohort.

Duration   Table 8.1 compares the average durations of violence depending on trajectory-group membership. Both total duration and durations for ages shared across the two cohorts (from ages 13 to 19) are shown, because of the different observation windows in the two cohorts. Not surprisingly, the general pattern is that the no/low trajectory groups showed practically zero durations, whereas the other trajectory groups (minor stable, late-onset, moderate declining, and high declining) showed longer durations. Also, even if only the overlapping period for the two cohorts (13–19 years) is considered, the average duration of violence was much longer in the oldest cohort. Again, we think that community crime might be an important factor in explaining these cohort differences, not only for the moderate trajectories but also for boys showing more persistent patterns of offending. For these more persistent boys,

Table 8.1 Mean Duration (in Years) of Violence and Theft Trajectories (Youngest and Oldest Cohorts)

Trajectory Group	Mean Duration, All Ages	Mean Duration, Ages 13–19
Violence		
YOUNGEST COHORT		
No/Low	0.00	0.00
Moderate	1.31	0.97
High Declining	3.02	2.48
Total	**0.50**	**0.39**
OLDEST COHORT		
No/Low	0.03	0.03
Late-Onset	1.56	0.75
Moderate Declining	1.93	1.76
High Declining	5.24	3.08
Total	**0.90**	**0.66**
Theft		
YOUNGEST COHORT		
No/Low	0.06	0.04
High Declining	2.23	1.88
Total	**0.40**	**0.33**
OLDEST COHORT		
No/Low	0.00	0.00
Late-Onset	1.62	1.62
Moderate Declining	1.83	1.56
High Declining	5.07	4.27
Total	**0.71**	**0.62**

Note: Standard deviations are available from the senior author of this chapter.

the level of crime in the community might have a strong effect on whether they will exhibit violence, and on how long they will persist in that pathway.

Theft Trajectories

Prevalence of Theft Trajectory Group Membership Figures 8.4 and 8.5 graph the results of the nonparametric models for theft in the youngest and oldest cohorts, respectively. We identified two trajectory groups for the youngest cohort: *no/low* and *high declining*. For the oldest cohort, we identified four trajectory groups: *no/low, moderate declining, high declining,* and *late-onset.* Again, a majority of boys in both cohorts followed a no/low trajectory with probabilities of theft near zero throughout adolescence. The prevalence of membership in the no/low theft trajectory was much higher in the youngest cohort (83%) as compared to the oldest cohort (58%). In the youngest cohort, the remaining boys (17%) followed a high declining trajectory starting with an almost zero probability by age 10 and then rising steadily until ages 14 and 15 years and then declining to return to a very low probability by age 19. In the oldest cohort, the picture was somewhat different. First, there was much greater heterogeneity in developmental trajectories with three groups of offenders. One group peaked in early adolescence, with a steady decline

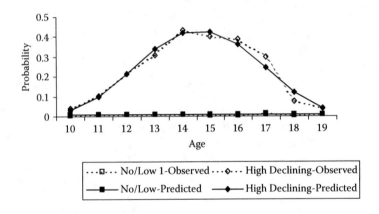

Figure 8.4 Trajectories of Theft (Youngest Cohort)

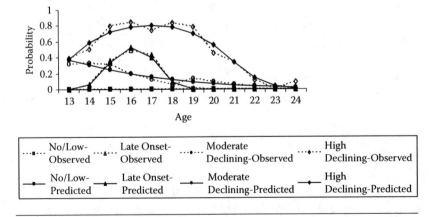

Figure 8.5 Trajectories of Theft (Oldest Cohort)

thereafter, which is similar to the high declining trajectory group in the youngest cohort. This group comprised nearly 30% of the boys, which is almost twice as many as in the youngest cohort. Second, there was a group that started stealing later in adolescence and peaked by age 16, but rapidly desisted by age 19. This late-onset group comprises a little less than 10% of the cohort. Finally, there was also a small trajectory group (3%) that had a much higher probability of theft during the whole observation window. This high declining trajectory group peaked around age 17 (with a probability of committing theft of more than 0.80 by that age) and then declined around age 23.

Onset   We did not find evidence for a clear early-onset theft trajectory group in the youngest cohort. This replicated our findings for violence for that cohort, and is probably caused by the fact that serious delinquent acts only emerge after middle childhood (ages 7–9). Given what we know about developmental pathways from minor offending to more serious forms of offending (Loeber, Keenan, Lahey, Green, & Thomas, 1993; Loeber, Wung et al., 1993), it is likely that less serious forms of theft during childhood precede the onset of serious forms of theft in late childhood or early adolescence (see also Chapter 4).

Rate of Change   Comparing the theft trajectories for the two cohorts, it is evident that, with the exception of the late-onset trajectory, desistance took longer in the oldest cohort. In fact, for the moderate and high declining trajectories, there were 6-year and 10-year intervals, respectively, between the peak age and the return to an almost zero probability of theft. In the youngest cohort this interval was 4–5 years. Thus, more boys in the oldest cohort belonged to the higher theft trajectories, which lasted longer and reached higher probabilities.

Duration   Table 8.1 shows similar patterns for theft as those reported above for violence. Indeed, the low groups show no theft during the whole observation window, whereas the other trajectory groups (late-onset, moderate declining, and high declining) show longer durations, representing significant portions of adolescence. Also, the average duration was much longer in the oldest cohort. Again, the higher prevalence of community crime seemed to have boosted the probabilities of boys in the oldest cohort being part of more serious theft trajectory groups with an extended duration of committing theft.

The Joint Modeling of Violence and Theft

So far we have presented the results for violence and theft separately. What is the relationship between violence offending trajectories and theft offending trajectories? This question can be addressed by means of an extension of the group-based, nonparametric trajectory model to jointly model the development of violence and theft (Nagin & Tremblay, 2001a). This modeling strategy allows the examination of the co-occurrence of the two behaviors' patterns of evolution over time by (1) estimating the probability of belonging to a particular violence trajectory group conditional on membership in a given theft trajectory group, and vice versa; and (2) estimating the joint probabilities of trajectory group membership.

Overlap of Violence and Theft Trajectories in the Youngest Cohort

The upper part of Table 8.2 shows probabilities of boys belonging to each violence trajectory groups conditional on membership in a given theft trajectory group. The middle part of the table shows the converse set of probabilities— that is, conditional probabilities for membership in each of the two theft trajectory groups given membership in a particular violence trajectory group. Both sets of conditional probabilities indicate substantial overlap between the two behaviors. The majority of boys in the youngest cohort, who followed the high declining theft trajectory, were also in the high declining violence trajectory (60%), or in the moderate violence trajectory (40%). In contrast, most boys in the no/low theft trajectory were also in the no/low violence trajectory (72%), few were in the moderate violence trajectory (24%), and very few were in the

Table 8.2 Overlap of Violence and Theft Trajectory Groups (Youngest Cohort)

Probability of Violence Conditional on Theft Trajectory Group			
Trajectory Group—Theft	Trajectory Group—Violence		
	No/Low	*Minor Stable*	*High Declining*
No/Low	0.72	0.24	0.04
High Declining	0.00	0.40	0.60

Probability of Theft Conditional on Violence Trajectory Group		
Trajectory Group—Violence	Trajectory Group—Theft	
	No/Low	*High Declining*
No/Low	1.00	0.00
Minor Stable	0.70	0.30
High Declining	0.20	0.80

Probability Estimates for Joint Violence and Theft		
Trajectory Group—Violence	Trajectory Group—Theft	
	No/Low	*High Declining*
No/Low	0.58	0.00
Minor Stable	0.19	0.08
High Declining	0.03	0.12

high declining violence trajectory (4%). As shown in the middle of Table 8.2, most of the boys in the high declining violence trajectory were also members of a theft trajectory (80%). However, a sizable proportion of boys (20%) in this violence trajectory group belonged to the no/low theft trajectory.

The joint probabilities of violence and theft trajectories for the youngest cohort are shown in the lower part of Table 8.2. The results show that the majority of the youngest cohort (58%) was low on both violence and theft (or engaged in no serious violence or theft) throughout adolescence. The remainder of the boys were divided into two groups that were about equal in terms of proportions; one showed only violence (moderate or high declining trajectories) and no/low theft trajectory (22%), and the other was characterized by both violence (moderate or high declining) and high declining theft trajectories (20%).

Altogether, results from the conditional and joint probabilities suggest that in the youngest cohort there was a significant amount of co-occurrence between violence and theft over time. It appears that individuals who followed a theft trajectory almost never did so without following a violence trajectory. However, the reverse was not necessarily true, because about half the boys who showed at least moderate levels of violence did not seem to engage in theft. Thus, serious theft in the youngest cohort tended to be exclusively committed by a subgroup of violent boys.

Overlap of Violence and Theft Trajectories in the Oldest Cohort

Table 8.3 presents the results obtained from the joint modeling of violence and theft in the oldest cohort. Given the similarity in terms of the number and shapes of the trajectory groups for both forms of offending, the links are easily evident. The upper part of the table reveals substantial co-occurrence between theft and violence trajectories. Indeed, the correspondence between the late-onset and moderate declining and high declining trajectories is almost perfect, meaning that knowing membership in each of the three groups for theft is a very good clue for identifying violence group membership. However, in the case of the no/low theft group the picture is a little more complex and resembles what was found in the youngest cohort. Although most boys in the no/low theft group also belonged to the no/low violence group, a substantial proportion of those in a no/low theft group belonged either to the late-onset (30%), moderate declining (8%), or high declining (5%) violence trajectory groups. This parallels the aforementioned results suggesting that no/low theft is not automatically synonymous with no/low violence.

The middle part of Table 8.3 also shows the probability of theft trajectory membership given membership in one of the violence trajectories for the oldest cohort, but the links are not as direct as in the upper part of the table. Similar to findings for the youngest cohort, boys in the oldest cohort who belonged to the no/low trajectory group for violence almost always belonged to the no/

Table 8.3 Overlap of Violence and Theft Trajectory Groups (Oldest Cohort)

Probability of Violence Conditional on Theft Trajectory Group

Trajectory Group—Theft	Trajectory Group—Violence			
	No/Low	Late-Onset	Moderate Declining	High Declining
No/Low	0.57	0.30	0.08	0.05
Late-Onset	0.00	1.00	0.00	0.00
Moderate Declining	0.00	0.00	1.00	0.00
High Declining	0.00	0.00	0.00	1.00

Probability of Theft Conditional on Violence Trajectory Group

Trajectory Group—Violence	Trajectory Group—Theft			
	No/Low	Late-Onset	Moderate Declining	High Declining
No/Low	1.00	0.00	0.00	0.00
Late-Onset	0.62	0.38	0.00	0.00
Moderate Declining	0.15	0.00	0.85	0.00
High Declining	0.30	0.00	0.00	0.70

Probability Estimates for Joint Violence and Theft

Trajectory Group—Violence	Trajectory Group—Theft			
	No/Low	Late-Onset	Moderate Declining	High Declining
No/Low	0.33	0.00	0.00	0.00
Late-Onset	0.17	0.10	0.00	0.00
Moderate Declining	0.04	0.00	0.26	0.00
High Declining	0.03	0.00	0.00	0.07

low trajectory group for theft. However, belonging to the late-onset, moderate declining, or high declining violence group did not equate with membership to the corresponding theft trajectory group. Indeed, despite good overlap in each case, there were still substantial proportions of boys who belonged to the moderate or high declining violence groups who also belonged to the no/low theft trajectory. This finding again suggests that serious violence without serious theft was not a rare phenomenon, but that serious theft without serious violence rarely occurred.

Not surprisingly, the joint probability results shown in the lower part of Table 8.3 point in the same direction. The most frequent combination was for boys to belong to the no/low trajectory groups for both forms of offending (33%). However, this percentage is much lower than what we reported for the youngest cohort. A substantial proportion of boys displayed either a late-onset, moderate declining, or high declining violence trajectory without theft (24%). The remaining boys belonged to the late-onset (10%), moderate declining (26%), or high declining (7%) groups for both violence and theft.

Results based on the conditional and joint probabilities in the oldest cohort point in the same direction as those for the youngest cohort, despite the fact that the number and shapes of trajectory groups were not perfectly matching across the cohorts. In the oldest cohort, results again indicate that co-occurrence of violence and theft was substantial. Moreover, the patterns of association were pretty similar across the two cohorts, since serious theft almost never happened without the presence of a certain amount of violence, but that the reverse was not necessarily true. Thus, results from the oldest cohort also suggest that serious theft tended to be exclusively committed by violent boys.

Prediction of Violence and Theft Trajectories

Predictors of criminal offending in early childhood or early adolescence have been extensively documented over the past 50 years. Recent reviews suggest that a cumulative effect of multiple risk factors best explains violence and theft during adolescence and adulthood (Lipsey & Derzon, 1998; Resnick, Ireland, & Borowsky, 2004; U.S. Department of Health and Human Services, 2001), which was also confirmed in Chapter 7.

Recent longitudinal studies have provided the data to test hypotheses about predictors of onset (Bartusch, Lynam, Moffitt, & Silva, 1997; Thornberry, 2005), duration (Espiritu, Huizinga, Loeber, & Crawford, 2001; Farrington, Loeber, & Van Kammen, 1990) and desistance (Laub & Sampson, 2001) of individual criminal careers. Although these three components of the criminal career have been conceived as belonging to a continuous distribution by some major developmental or life course criminologists (Blumstein & Cohen, 1979; Laub & Sampson, 2003; Thornberry, 2005), many researchers have also proposed taxonomic theories that particular developmental trajectories are related to specific etiologies or putative risk factors (Moffitt, 1993; Nagin & Tremblay, 2001b; Patterson, DeBaryshe, & Ramsey, 1989). Generally, developmental trajectories are identified using a priori criteria. One pitfall of this procedure is overlooking important developmental trajectories that could only be identified using a statistical criterion as a decision rule (Nagin, 1999).

As mentioned earlier, exploratory empirical research using the nonparametric random-effects model generally finds between four and six developmental trajectories of antisocial behaviors, more than hypothesized by Moffitt's and Patterson's original theories. There is one main advantage of the nonparametric random-effects model over other kind of analyses. It is well suited to distinguish specific sets of risk and protective factors by using a multinomial logit function to link different predictors to the trajectory groups. Thus, hypotheses derived from theories that suggest either quantitative or qualitative differences can be tested since the multinomial distribution can approximate any continuous distributions.

Nagin and Land (1993) and Nagin, Farrington, and Moffitt (1995) have pioneered studies testing the main assumptions of Moffitt's (1993) two-group taxonomic theory. Using a nonparametric random-effects model, Nagin et al. (1995) have identified four trajectories based on convictions data from ages 10 to 32 in a sample of 400 males from a poor neighborhood in London (the Cambridge Study in Delinquent Development; see Farrington, 2003). One trajectory, which peaked around age 16, closely matched the adolescence-limited group predicted by Moffitt's theory. Another inverse U-shaped trajectory that peaked around age 18, labeled *high chronics*, was similar to the life course persistent group. This group already reported antisocial activities by age 10. It is important to note that the frequency of antisocial behavior is age dependent for all trajectory groups. By age 30, the rate of conviction for all the trajectory groups was close to zero. A host of predictors from the individual, peer, and family domains measured by age 10 were included in the analysis to distinguish the four developmental trajectories. However, the results showed that overall the predictors measured by age 10 did not discriminate among the four offense trajectories. The only trajectory that was consistently identified by predictors by age 10 was the life course persistent trajectory.

Over the past decades, several other studies (Fergusson, Horwood, & Nagin, 2000; Sampson & Laub, 2003; White et al., 2001) have also identified four offense trajectory groups. Fergusson et al. (2000) have found that there were common etiological risk factors for these different trajectories related to family functioning (maternal education, marital conflict, and parental drug use) and early adjustment (conduct problems and attention problems by age 8). This study partially confirms both Patterson's and Moffitt's theories. On the other hand, White et al. (2001) have found that few of the childhood risk factors proposed by Moffitt's theory could account for the differences between adolescence-limited and life course persistent antisocial behavior. Sampson and Laub (2003) have identified six developmental trajectories based on criminal records from ages 7 to 70. With a set of 20 individual and family risk factors similar to those used in the Nagin et al. (1995) study, they have found no significant effect of childhood risk factors on offending trajectories. They have concluded that early population heterogeneity was less important than turning points during the life course in accounting for long-term and desisting criminal careers.

The present study departs in many ways from past studies that used the nonparametric random-effects model to identify predictors of specific developmental trajectories. Here we address the following questions:

Which types of factors predict membership of particular offending trajectories?

How similar are factors predicting violence and theft trajectories?

First, we investigate predictors of developmental trajectories of serious violence and theft separately. Second, we investigate preventive promotive factors in addition to aggravating risk factors in multiple domains measured at ages 7 and 13 (for the youngest and oldest cohorts, respectively) *prior to* the identification of offense trajectories (calculated over ages 10–19 for the youngest cohort, and ages 13–15 for the oldest cohort). As in Chapter 7, aggravating risk and preventive promotive factors that were significant at $p < .05$ or had an odds ratio greater than 2 were highlighted in the bivariate analyses and a level of significance of .10 was used in the multivariate analyses. We first review the results of bivariate analyses, after which we will report the results of regression analyses.

Risk and Promotive Factors Predicting Violence Trajectories

The first set of analyses examined the bivariate associations that significantly discriminated between risk and protective factors for the different developmental trajectories.

No/Low Versus Minor Stable Violence Trajectories (Youngest Cohort)

Table 8.4 shows the predictors that discriminated between the no/low and the minor stable violence trajectories. Aggravating risk factors were mainly neighborhood and sociodemographic characteristics, such as bad neighborhood, African American ethnicity, one or no biological parent at home, and family on welfare. At the individual level, depressed mood was the only significant risk factor. There were only two preventive promotive factors: having an older mother and low peer delinquency.

No/Low Versus Late-Onset Violence Trajectories (Oldest Cohort)

As shown in Table 8.5, few aggravating risk and preventive promotive factors differentiated the late-onset trajectory from the no/low violence trajectory. It is important to note, however, that some predictors here were similar to predictors that had the greatest odds ratios for the moderate and high declining trajectories in contrast to the no/low trajectory. The four aggravating risk factors that distinguished the late-onset group from the no/low group were high psychopathic features, low academic achievement, African American ethnicity, and family on welfare. The five preventive promotive factors were low psychopathic features, low parental stress, high academic achievement, having an older mother, and high family socioeconomic status (SES). Overall, these aggravating risk and promotive factors had similar odds ratios to those found for the moderate declining trajectory in contrast to the no/low trajectory.

Table 8.4 Aggravating Risk and Preventive Promotive Factors at Age 7 Predicting Violence and Theft Trajectories at Ages 10–19 (Youngest Cohort, Odds Ratios)

	Violence Trajectories		Theft Trajectories
	No/Low vs. Minor Stable Trajectories	No/Low vs. High Declining Trajectories	No/Low vs. High Declining Trajectories
Aggravating Risk Factors			
PARTICIPANT PSYCHOPATHOLOGY			
High Truancy	—	2.5*	—
Running Away	—	4.0*	—
High Psychopathic Features	—	1.9*	1.6†
Depressed Mood	1.6*	2.1*	—
PARENTAL CHARACTERISTICS			
High Parental Stress	—	1.7†	1.9**
Father Behavioral Problems	—	—	1.7†
Parent Police Contact	—	—	1.6†
PEERS			
High Peer Delinquency	—	—	—
Poor Relationship with Peers	—	2.0*	—
Gettting along Poorly with Siblings	—	—	—
SCHOOL			
Low Academic Achievement	1.5†	2.3**	1.7*
Negative Attitude toward School	—	—	—
Repeating a Grade	—	2.2**	—
NEIGHBORHOOD			
Bad Neighborhood (Census)	1.5*	2.0*	—
SOCIODEMOGRAPHICS			
African American Ethnicity	1.5*	2.5**	—
One or No Biological Parent at Home	1.8**	2.9**	2.4**
Low Family Socioeconomic Status	1.4†	1.7*	1.6*
Family on Welfare	1.6*	2.6**	1.6*
Large Family	—	—	2.1**
Small House	—	1.8*	1.6†

Table 8.4 Aggravating Risk and Preventive Promotive Factors at Age 7 Predicting Violence and Theft Trajectories at Ages 10–19 (Youngest Cohort, Odds Ratios) (continued)

| | Violence Trajectories | | Theft Trajectories |
	No/Low vs. Minor Stable Trajectories	No/Low vs. High Declining Trajectories	No/Low vs. High Declining Trajectories
Preventive Promotive Factors			
PARTICIPANT PSYCHOPATHOLOGY			
Low ADHD Symptoms	—	3.1*	—
Low Psychopathic Features	—	—	—
PEERS			
Low Peer Delinquency	1.6*	1.8†	—
SCHOOL			
High Academic Achievement	—	2.8*	1.9*
NEIGHBORHOOD			
Good Neighborhood (Census)	—	4.1*	3.4*
Good Neighborhood Impression	—	—	1.8*
SOCIODEMOGRAPHIC			
Older Mother	1.6*	2.5**	2.4**
High Family Socioeconomic Status	—	—	1.5**

Notes: †$p < .10$; *$p < .05$; **$p < .01$; ***$p <.001$. Promotive factors in **boldface**. To facilitate comparisons of the magnitude of risk and promotive factors, the odds ratios for promotive factors, normally ranging in value from 0 to 1, were rescaled to be larger than 1. *Nonsignificant risk factors:* positive attitude toward delinquency, low perceived likelihood of getting caught, parental reinforcement, parent antisocial attitude, number of serious injuries, and housing quality. *Nonsignificant promotive factors:* low depressed mood, low anxiety, high likelihood of getting caught, high persistence of discipline, physical punishment, high parental reinforcement, high supervision, boy involved in family activities, parent low antisocial attitude, low parental stress, good relationship with peers, positive attitude toward school, and good housing quality.

No/Low Versus Moderate Declining Violence Trajectories (Oldest Cohort)

Again, as shown in Table 8.5, the moderate declining trajectory group in the oldest cohort presents a similar constellation of aggravating risk and preventive promotive factors as the high declining trajectory group. Both were predicted by 15 out of 27 aggravating risk factors and 13 out of 22 preventive promotive factors. One striking difference was mainly related to the strength

Table 8.5 Aggravating Risk and Preventive Promotive Factors at Age 13 Predicting Violence Trajectories at Ages 13–25 (Oldest Cohort, Odds Ratios)

	No/Low Trajectory vs. Late-Onset Trajectory	No/Low Trajectory vs. Moderate Declining Trajectory	No/Low Trajectory vs. High Declining Trajectory
Aggravating Risk Factors			
PARTICIPANT PSYCHOPATHOLOGY			
High Truancy	—	2.5***	5.3***
Running Away	—	2.2*	4.3**
High Psychopathic Features	2.1*	2.9***	4.7***
Depressed Mood	—	—	2.3*
PARTICIPANT COMPETENCE			
Low Perceived Likelihood of Getting Caught	—	1.9**	—
FAMILY FUNCTIONING			
Child Maltreatment by Age 12	—	—	—
Low Parental Reinforcement	—	—	2.5*
PARENTAL CHARACTERISTICS			
Parent Alcohol Problem	—	—	—
Father Behavioral Problems	—	—	3.4**
PEERS			
High Peer Delinquency	—	2.9****	4.8***
Poor Relationship with Peers	—	1.7**	3.2**
SCHOOL			
Low Academic Achievement	2.0*	2.0**	2.5*
Negative Attitude toward School	—	1.9**	2.6*
Repeating a Grade	1.6†	1.7**	2.6*
NEIGHBORHOOD			
Bad Neighborhood (Census)	1.6†	1.8**	6.8***
SOCIODEMOGRAPHICS			
African American Ethnicity	1.9*	2.0**	4.8†
One or No Biological Parent at Home	—	1.8*	8.0*
Two or More Changes in Caretaker by Age 10	—	1.9**	—
Low Family Socioeconomic Status	1.4†	1.4*	—
Family on Welfare	1.8*	2.3***	4.5**

Table 8.5 Aggravating Risk and Preventive Promotive Factors at Age 13 Predicting Violence Trajectories at Ages 13–25 (Oldest Cohort, Odds Ratios) (continued)

	No/Low Trajectory vs. Late-Onset Trajectory	No/Low Trajectory vs. Moderate Declining Trajectory	No/Low Trajectory vs. High Declining Trajectory
Small House	—	—	2.3*
Bad Housing Quality	—	—	2.0*
Preventive Promotive Factors			
PARTICIPANT PSYCHOPATHOLOGY			
Low ADHD Symptoms	—	2.1**	—
Low Psychopathic Features	2.3**	2.9***	3.1*
PARTICIPANT COMPETENCE			
High Prosocial Behavior	—	1.8*	3.0†
Negative Attitude toward Delinquency	1.7†	1.8*	4.6*
FAMILY FUNCTIONING			
High Persistence of Discipline	—	1.9*	—
Good Supervision	2.0†	1.9*	6.1*
Youth Involved in Family Activities	—	2.1*	—
PARENTAL CHARACTERISTICS			
Low Parental Stress	1.9*	1.8*	2.6†
PEERS			
Good Relationship with Peers	—	1.6*	3.4*
SCHOOL			
High Academic Achievement	2.1*	2.6***	7.7*
NEIGHBORHOOD			
Good Neighborhood (Census)	—	2.2**	3.6†
SOCIODEMOGRAPHICS			
Older Mother	2.0**	1.6*	2.5*
High Family Socioeconomic Status	1.6**	1.5**	—

Notes: †$p < .10$; *$p < .05$; **$p < .01$; ***$p < .001$. Promotive factors in **boldface**. To facilitate comparisons of the magnitude of risk and promotive factors, the odds ratios for promotive factors, normally ranging in value from 0 to 1, were rescaled to be larger than 1. *Nonsignificant risk factors:* parent antisocial attitude, parent police contact, getting along with siblings, number of serious injuries, and large family. Nonsignificant promotive factors: low depressed mood, low anxiety, and low shyness/withdrawal.

of association among the aggravating risk and preventive promotive factors. Here, we highlight the risk and promotive factors for which the odds ratio is at least two times smaller for the moderate declining trajectory group than for the high declining trajectory group in contrast with the no/low group. Aggravating risk factors were one or no biological parent at home, bad neighborhood, father behavioral problems, African American ethnicity, and high truancy. Preventive promotive factors were high academic achievement, good parental supervision, and negative attitude toward delinquency. Predictors appeared to have a linear effect in discriminating this specific trajectory group.

No/Low versus High Declining Violence Trajectories (Youngest and Oldest Cohorts)

In the youngest cohort, 14 out of 26 aggravating risk factors and 5 out of 21 preventive promotive factors distinguished boys in the violence high declining trajectory group from the ones in the no/low trajectory (Table 8.4). In the oldest cohort, 17 out of 27 aggravating risk factors and 9 out of 22 preventive promotive factors were significant (Table 8.5). Many risk and promotive factors were shared between the two cohorts. Among the aggravating risk factors were high truancy, running away, psychopathic features, poor relationship with peers, low academic achievement, repeating a grade, bad neighborhood, African American ethnicity, one or no biological parent at home, and family on welfare. Shared preventive promotive factors were high academic achievement, good neighborhood (census), and having an older mother. In the youngest cohort, running away and one or no biological parent at home were the strongest aggravating risk factors; and good neighborhood and having few ADHD symptoms were the strongest preventive promotive factors. In the oldest cohort, the most important aggravating risk factors were one or no biological parent at home, bad neighborhood, and high truancy. The most important preventive promotive factors were high academic achievement, good parental supervision, and a negative attitude toward delinquency. Overall, odds ratios were much smaller in the youngest cohort. Some factors suggested nonlinear relationships. For example, in the youngest cohort, neighborhood had a stronger effect as a preventive promotive factor. In the oldest cohort, neighborhood had a stronger effect as a aggravating risk factor and academic achievement as a preventive promotive factor.

Multivariate Analyses of Risk and Promotive Factors Predicting Violence Trajectories

Multivariate multinomial regressions (weighted by the posterior probabilities of group membership) were used to assess the independent contribution of each aggravating risk and promotive factor for each cohort. In a first step, each risk and promotive factor that was significant within each domain in Tables 8.4 and 8.5 was introduced in the regressions shown in Tables 8.6 and 8.7. In a second step, all the significant risk and promotive factors identified in

Table 8.6 Multivariate Multinomial Regressions of Aggravating Risk and Preventive Promotive Factors at Age 7 Predicting Violence Trajectories at Ages 10–19 (Youngest Cohort, Odds Ratios)

	No/Low vs. Minor Stable		No/Low vs. High Declining	
	Multivariate Analysis by Age Block[a]	*Final Multivariate Analysis[b]*	*Multivariate Analysis by Age Block[a]*	*Final Multivariate Analysis[b]*
PARTICIPANT PSYCHOPATHOLOGY				
High Truancy	—	—	2.3*	—
Running Away	—	—	3.7*	3.2†
Depressed Mood	1.6*	—	—	—
Low ADHD Symptoms	—	—	3.0**	—
PARENTAL CHARACTERISTICS				
High Parental Stress	—	—	1.7†	—
PEERS				
Poor Relationship with Peers	—	—	2.0*	—
Low Peer Delinquency	1.6*	1.5†	—	—
SCHOOL				
High Academic Achievement	—	—	2.4*	2.3*
Repeating a Grade	—	—	1.9*	—
Low Academic Achievement	1.5†	—	—	—
NEIGHBORHOOD				
Bad Neighborhood (Census)	1.5*	—	—	—
Good Neighborhood (Census)	—	—	4.1*	—
SOCIODEMOGRAPHICS				
One or No Biological Parent at Home	1.8**	1.7*	2.4*	2.1*
Older Mother	—	—	2.0*	2.1*

Notes: †$p < .10$; *$p < .05$; **$p < .01$; ***$p < .001$. [a]Only the variables significant at the $p < .05$ level in the bivariate analysis are included; then, nonsignificant variables are gradually removed, starting with the least significant one, until all the variables are at least marginally significant at the $p < .10$ level. [b]Only the variables significant at the $p < .10$ level in the multivariate analysis by age block are included; then, the nonsignificant variables are gradually removed, starting with the least significant one, until all the variables are at least marginally significant at the $p < .10$ level. Promote factors in **boldface**. To facilitate comparisons of the magnitude of risk and promotive factors, the odds ratios for promotive factors, normally ranging in value from 0 to 1, were rescaled to be larger than 1. Confidence intervals are available from the senior author of this chapter.

the first multivariate regressions were introduced in the final model. In each of the models we will only list the aggravating risk and preventive promotive factors that were significant in each domain, and then we will describe the final model.

No/Low versus High Declining Violence Trajectories (Youngest Cohort)

Significant aggravating risk and preventive promotive factors in each age block were depressed mood, low peer delinquency, low academic achievement, bad neighborhood, and one or no biological parent at home. In the final model, the two predictors were low peer delinquency and one or no biological parent at home.

No/Low versus Late-Onset Violence Trajectories (Oldest Cohort)

As shown in Table 8.7, fewer aggravating risk and preventive promotive factors were significant for this specific developmental trajectory. African American ethnicity and bad neighborhood (census) were the only significant risk factors. Low psychopathic features, good parental supervision, low parental stress, high academic achievement, negative attitude toward delinquency, high family SES, and having an older mother were the preventive promotive factors. In the final model, African American ethnicity was an aggravating risk factor, while low psychopathic features, high family SES, and having an older mother were preventive promotive factors.

No/Low versus Moderate Declining Violence Trajectories (Oldest Cohort)

For this contrast, we expected to find some similar predictors as for the high declining trajectory. The significant aggravating risk factors were high truancy, high psychopathic features, low perceived likelihood of getting caught, high peer delinquency, negative attitude toward school, African American ethnicity, two or more changes in caretaker by age 10, and family on welfare. The preventive promotive factors were low psychopathic features, high prosocial behavior, negative attitude toward delinquency, high persistence of discipline, good parental supervision, high involvement of the youth in family activities, low parental stress, good relationship with peers, high academic achievement, good neighborhood, and high family SES. In the final model, high truancy, high and low psychopathic features, high persistence of discipline, high peer delinquency, negative attitude toward school, African American ethnicity, two or more changes in caretaker by age 10, and high family SES were the significant aggravating risk and preventive promotive factors.

No/Low versus High Declining Violence Trajectories (Youngest and Oldest Cohorts)

For the youngest cohort (Table 8.6), high truancy, running away, repeating a grade, poor relationship with peers, one or no biological parent at home, and high parental stress were the significant aggravating risk factors; while

Table 8.7 Multivariate Multinomial Regressions of Aggravating Risk and Preventive Promotive Factors at Age 13 Predicting Violence Trajectories at Ages 13–25 (Oldest Cohort, Odds Ratios)

	No/Low vs. Late-Onset Trajectory		No/Low vs. Moderate Declining Trajectory		No/Low vs. High Declining Trajectory	
	Multivariate Analysis by Age Block[a]	Final Multivariate Analysis[b]	Multivariate Analysis by Age Block[a]	Final Multivariate Analysis[b]	Multivariate Analysis by Age Block[a]	Final Multivariate Analysis[b]
PARTICIPANT PSYCHOPATHOLOGY						
High Truancy	—	—	1.9**	1.6†	4.0**	3.3*
High Psychopathic Features	—	—	1.9*	1.8*	3.1**	3.0*
Low Psychopathic Features	2.3**	2.3	2.0*	1.9*	—	—
PARTICIPANT COMPETENCE						
High Prosocial Behavior	—	—	1.7†	—	—	—
Negative Attitude toward Delinquency	1.7†	—	1.6†	—	4.6*	3.2†
Low Perceived Likelihood of Getting Caught	—	—	1.6*	—	—	—
FAMILY FUNCTIONING						
High Persistence of Discipline	—	—	1.8*	1.6†	—	—
Good Supervision	2.0†	—	1.7*	—	5.5*	5.6***
Youth Involved in Family Activities	—	—	1.8*	—	—	—
Low Parental Reinforcement	—	—	—	—	2.2*	—
PARENTAL CHARACTERISTICS						
Low Parental Stress	1.9*	—	1.8*	—	2.6†	—
Father Behavioral Problems	—	—	—	—	3.5**	—

Table 8.7 Multivariate Multinomial Regressions of Aggravating Risk and Preventive Promotive Factors at Age 13 Predicting Violence Trajectories at Ages 13-25 (Oldest Cohort, Odds Ratios) (continued)

	No/Low vs. Late-Onset Trajectory		No/Low vs. Moderate Declining Trajectory		No/Low vs. High Declining Trajectory	
	Multivariate Analysis by Age Block[a]	Final Multivariate Analysis[b]	Multivariate Analysis by Age Block[a]	Final Multivariate Analysis[b]	Multivariate Analysis by Age Block[a]	Final Multivariate Analysis[b]
PEERS						
High Peer Delinquency	—	—	2.8***	1.9*	4.4***	—
Poor Relationship with Peers	—	—	—	—	2.8*	—
Good Relationship with Peers	—	—	1.5†	—	—	—
SCHOOL						
High Academic Achievement	2.1*	—	2.4***	—	6.8*	—
Negative Attitude toward School	—	—	1.6*	1.6†	2.2†	—
NEIGHBORHOOD						
Bad Neighborhood (Census)	1.6†	—	1.5†	—	6.8***	—
Good Neighborhood (Census)	—	—	1.8†	—	—	—
SOCIODEMOGRAPHICS						
African American Ethnicity	1.8*	1.9*	1.6*	1.9**	2.5†	—
One or No Biological Parent at Home	—	—	—	—	4.6*	4.3*
Two or More Changes in Caretaker by Age 10	—	—	1.8*	1.7*	—	—
High Family Socioeconomic Status	1.5*	1.5*	1.4†	1.5*	—	—

| Family on Welfare | — | — | 1.7* | — | 2.5* | — |
| **Older Mother** | 1.8* | 1.7* | — | — | — | — |

Notes: †$p < .10$; *$p < .05$; **$p < .01$; ***$p < .001$. [a]Only the variables significant at the $p < .05$ level in the bivariate analysis are included; then, nonsignificant variables are gradually removed, starting with the least significant one, until all the variables are at least marginally significant at the $p < .10$ level. [b]Only the variables significant at the $p < .10$ level in the multivariate analysis by age block are included; then, the nonsignificant variables are gradually removed, starting with the least significant one, until all the variables are at least marginally significant at the $p < .10$ level. Promotive factors in **boldface**. To facilitate comparisons of the magnitude of risk and promotive factors, the odds ratios for promotive factors, normally ranging in value from 0 to 1, were rescaled to be larger than 1. Confidence intervals are available from the senior author of this chapter.

low ADHD symptoms, high academic achievement, good neighborhood (census), and having an older mother were the preventive promotive factors in the analyses for each domain. In the final model, running away and one or no biological parent at home came out as aggravating risk factors, while high academic achievement and having an older mother came out as preventive promotive factors.

The results of the regression analyses for the oldest cohort are shown in Table 8.7. The ten significant aggravating risk factors were high truancy, high psychopathic features, low parental reinforcement, father behavioral problems, high peer delinquency, poor relationship with peers, bad neighborhood, African American ethnicity, family on welfare, and one or no biological parent at home. The four significant preventive promotive factors were negative attitude toward delinquency, good parental supervision, low parental stress, and high academic achievement. In the final model, high truancy, high psychopathic features, and one or no biological parent at home were the significant aggravating risk factors. The only preventive promotive factor was a negative attitude toward delinquency.

Overall, it was more difficult to predict developmental trajectories of violence from aggravating risk and preventive promotive factors at age 7 for the youngest cohort than at age 13 for the oldest cohort. There could be three reasons for this finding: (1) the factors are more distal to the outcome in the youngest cohort; (2) there is greater heterogeneity in the developmental trajectories of violence in the oldest cohort due to the level of crime in the community; and (3) time-varying covariates could be more important than early individual differences. At the bivariate level, there are risk and promotive factors in many domains although the number of risk factors was always greater than the number of promotive factors. Since these risk and promotive factors tend to cluster together within individuals, and also because of the sample size in the separate cohorts, few factors came out significant in the multivariate regression analyses.

Risk and Promotive Factors Predicting Theft Trajectories

The first set of analyses examined the bivariate associations that significantly discriminated between risk and protective factors and different theft trajectories.

No/Low versus High Declining Theft Trajectories (Youngest and Oldest Cohorts)

Analyses on the youngest cohort (Table 8.4) were limited because of low sample size. However, ten aggravating risk factors and five preventive promotive factors discriminated between the two trajectories. In the oldest cohort (Table 8.8), we identified 11 out of 27 aggravating risk factors and two preventive promotive factors. Odds ratios were very large for high truancy, repeating a grade, running away, low academic achievement, and having one or no biological parent at home. For promotive factors, high academic achievement

Table 8.8 Aggravating Risk and Preventive Promotive Factors at Age 13 Predicting Theft Trajectories at Ages 13–25 (Oldest Cohort, Odds Ratios)

	No/Low Trajectory vs. Late-Onset Trajectory	No/Low Trajectory vs. Moderate Declining Trajectory	No/Low Trajectory vs. High Declining Trajectory
Aggravating Risk Factors			
PARTICIPANT PSYCHOPATHOLOGY			
High Truancy	1.7†	3.5***	8.4***
Running Away	—	2.3**	9.1***
High Psychopathic Features	—	1.9**	—
PARTICIPANT COMPETENCE			
Low Perceived Likelihood of Getting Caught	—	1.6†	—
FAMILY FUNCTIONING			
Child Maltreatment by Age 12	—	1.8†	3.5*
Low Parental Reinforcement	2.0*	1.9**	—
PEERS			
High Peer Delinquency	—	2.6***	3.8*
Poor Relationship with Peers	—	2.3***	—
SCHOOL			
Low Academic Achievement	—	2.4***	5.0**
Negative Attitude toward School	—	2.1***	2.8†
Repeating a Grade	—	1.6*	6.6**
NEIGHBORHOOD			
Bad Neighborhood (Census)	—	—	2.7†
SOCIODEMOGRAPHICS			
One or No Biological Parent at Home	—	2.1**	4.0*
Two or More Changes in Caretaker by Age 10	2.0*	1.5†	—
Low Family Socioeconomic Status	—	1.5**	—
Family on Welfare	—	1.9**	3.5*
Large Family	—	1.5†	2.3†
Bad Housing Quality	—	—	—

Table 8.8 Aggravating Risk and Preventive Promotive Factors at Age 13 Predicting Theft Trajectories at Ages 13–25 (Oldest Cohort, Odds Ratios) (continued)

	No/Low Trajectory vs. Late-Onset Trajectory	No/Low Trajectory vs. Moderate Declining Trajectory	No/Low Trajectory vs. High Declining Trajectory
Preventive Promotive Factors			
PARTICIPANT PSYCHOPATHOLOGY			
Low ADHD Symptoms	—	1.6†	—
Low Psychopathic Features	—	2.0**	—
Low Shyness/Withdrawal	—	1.5†	—
PARTICIPANT COMPETENCE			
Negative Attitude toward Delinquency	—	1.8*	3.7†
FAMILY FUNCTIONING			
High Persistence of Discipline	—	1.7*	—
High Parental Reinforcement	—	2.0**	—
Good Supervision	—	1.9*	—
Youth Involved in Family Activities	—	2.0**	—
PEERS			
Good Relationship with Peers	—	1.7*	—
SCHOOL			
High Academic Achievement	—	2.2**	11.7†
Positive Attitude toward School	—	—	—
SOCIODEMOGRAPHICS			
Older Mother	1.9*	1.5†	—
High Family Socioeconomic Status	—	1.3†	—

Notes: †$p < .10$; *$p < .05$; **$p < .01$; ***$p < .001$. Promotive factors in **boldface**. To facilitate comparisons of the magnitude of risk and promotive factors, the odds ratios for promotive factors, normally ranging in value from 0 to 1, were rescaled to be larger than 1.

had the largest odds ratio. Again, none of the relationships appeared to be nonlinear.

No/Low versus Late-Onset Theft Trajectories (Oldest Cohort)

As was the case with violence, relatively few aggravating risk and promotive factors predicted the late-onset trajectory in the oldest cohort. The three risk factors were high truancy, low parental reinforcement, and two or more caretaker changes by age 10. The only preventive promotive factor was having an older mother.

No/Low versus Moderate Declining Theft Trajectories (Oldest Cohort)

Similar to the violence trajectories, the moderate declining trajectory group presented a constellation of risk and promotive factors that resembled the factors predictive of the high declining trajectory in contrast to the no/low trajectory. Sixteen out of 27 aggravating risk factors and 12 out of 22 preventive promotive factors were associated with the moderate declining theft trajectory. Aggravating risk factors with the largest odds ratios were, in order of magnitude, high truancy and high peer delinquency. Among the preventive promotive factors, high academic achievement, low psychopathic features, high parental reinforcement, and youth involved in family activities had the largest odds ratios. Predictors also appeared to have linear effects.

Multivariate Analyses of Risk and Promotive Factors Predicting Theft Trajectories

The next step was multivariate multinomial regressions to ascertain the independent contributions of each aggravating risk and preventive promotive factor in predicting theft trajectories.

No/Low versus High Declining Theft Trajectories (Youngest and Oldest Cohorts)

As shown in Table 8.9 for the youngest cohort, there were two aggravating risk factors (high parental stress and one or no biological parent at home) and three preventive promotive factors (high academic achievement, good neighborhood [census], and having an older mother) predicting membership in the high declining trajectory. In the final model, only one predictor became nonsignificant: high academic achievement.

In the oldest cohort, the significant aggravating risk factors for this specific contrast were (Table 8.10): high truancy, running away, child maltreatment, high peer delinquency, low academic achievement, repeating a grade, and family on welfare. Negative attitude toward delinquency was the only preventive promotive factor that was significant. In the final model, high truancy, low academic achievement, and repeating a grade were identified as aggravating risk factors.

Table 8.9 Multivariate Multinomial Regressions of Aggravating Risk and Preventive Promotive Factors at Age 7 Predicting Theft Trajectories at Ages 10–19 (Youngest Cohort, Odds Ratios)

	No/Low vs. High Declining Trajectories	
	Multivariate Analysis by Age Block[a]	Final Multivariate Analysis[b]
PARENTAL CHARACTERISTICS		
High Parental Stress	1.9***	1.8**
SCHOOL		
High Academic Achievement	1.9**	—
NEIGHBORHOOD		
Good Neighborhood (Census)	3.4**	2.5*
SOCIODEMOGRAPHICS		
One or No Biological Parent at Home	2.0**	1.7*
Older Mother	2.0**	1.9**

Notes: †$p < .10$; *$p < .05$. [a]Only the variables significant at the $p < .05$ level in the bivariate analysis are included; then, nonsignificant variables are gradually removed, starting with the least significant one, until all the variables are at least marginally significant at the $p < .10$ level. [b]Only the variables significant at the $p < .10$ level in the multivariate analysis by age block are included; then, the nonsignificant variables are gradually removed, starting with the least significant one, until all the variables are at least marginally significant at the $p < .10$ level. Promotive factors in **boldface**. To facilitate comparisons of the magnitude of risk and promotive factors, the odds ratios for promotive factors, normally ranging in value from 0 to 1, were rescaled to be larger than 1. Confidence intervals are available from the senior author of this chapter.

No/Low versus Late-Onset Theft Trajectories (Oldest Cohort)

The significant aggravating risk factors for the oldest cohort (Table 8.10) were high truancy and two or more changes in caretaker by age 10. High parental reinforcement and having an older mother were the two preventive promotive factors. In the final model, the same variables were significant with the exception of high truancy.

No/Low versus Moderate Declining Theft Trajectories (Oldest Cohort)

The significant aggravating risk factors for the oldest cohort (Table 8.10) were high truancy, high peer delinquency, poor relationship with peers, low academic achievement, negative attitude toward school, one or no biological parent at home, and low family SES. Preventive promotive factors were negative attitude toward delinquency, high parental reinforcement, high persistence of discipline, good supervision, high involvement of the boy in family activities, and high academic achievement. In the final model, high truancy, high

Table 8.10 Multivariate Multinomial Regressions of Aggravating Risk and Preventive Promotive Factors at Age 13 Predicting Theft Trajectories at Ages 13–25 (Oldest Cohort, Odds Ratios)

	No/Low vs. Late-Onset Trajectories		No/Low vs. Moderate Declining Trajectories		No/Low vs. High Declining Trajectories	
	Multivariate Analysis by Age Block[a]	Final Multivariate Analysis[b]	Multivariate analysis by Age Block[a]	Final Multivariate Analysis	Multivariate analysis by Age Block[a]	Final Multivariate Analysis[b]
PARTICIPANT PSYCHOPATHOLOGY						
High Truancy	1.7*	—	3.5****	2.5****	5.9***	5.5***
Running Away	—	—	—	—	5.3***	—
PARTICIPANT COMPETENCE						
Negative Attitude toward Delinquency	—	—	1.8**	—	3.7*	—
FAMILY FUNCTIONING						
High Parental Reinforcement	2.0**	1.9*	1.6**	1.5*	—	—
Persistence of Discipline	—	—	1.6*	—	—	—
Good Supervision	—	—	1.6*	—	—	—
Child Maltreatment	—	—	—	—	3.5**	—
Youth Involved in Family Activities	—	—	1.7*	—	—	—
PEERS						
High Peer Delinquency	—	—	2.4****	1.8**	3.8**	—
Poor Relationship with Peers	—	—	2.2****	1.6**	—	—
Good Relationship with Peers	—	—	—	—	—	—

Table 8.10 Multivariate Multinomial Regressions of Aggravating Risk and Preventive Promotive Factors at Age 13 Predicting Theft Trajectories at Ages 13–25 (Oldest Cohort, Odds Ratios) (continued)

	No/Low vs. Late-Onset Trajectories		No/Low vs. Moderate Declining Trajectories		No/Low vs. High Declining Trajectories	
	Multivariate Analysis by Age Block[a]	Final Multivariate Analysis[b]	Multivariate analysis by Age Block[a]	Final Multivariate Analysis	Multivariate analysis by Age Block[a]	Final Multivariate Analysis[b]
SCHOOL						
Low Academic Achievement	—	—	1.8**	1.6**	3.1**	2.6*
High Academic Achievement	—	—	1.7*	—	—	—
Negative Attitude toward School	—	—	1.8**	—	—	—
Repeating a Grade	—	—	—	—	4.7**	3.4*
SOCIODEMOGRAPHICS						
Two or More Changes in Caretaker by Age 10	2.1**	2.0**	—	—	—	—
One or No Biological Parent at Home	—	—	1.9***	1.6**	—	—
Low Family Socioeconomic Status	—	—	1.4**	—	—	—
Family on Welfare	—	—	—	—	3.5**	—
Older Mother	2.0**	1.9*	—	—	—	—

Notes: †$p < .10$; *$p < .05$; [a]Only the variables significant at the $p < .05$ level in the bivariate analysis are included; then, nonsignificant variables are gradually removed, starting with the least significant one, until all the variables are at least marginally significant at the $p < .10$ level. [b]Only the variables significant at the $p < .10$ level in the multivariate analysis by age block are included; then, the nonsignificant variables are gradually removed, starting with the least significant one, until all the variables are at least marginally significant at the $p < .10$ level. Promotive factors in **boldface**. To facilitate comparisons of the magnitude of risk and promotive factors, the odds ratios for promotive factors, normally ranging in value from 0 to 1, were rescaled to be larger than 1. Confidence intervals are available from the senior author of this chapter.

parental reinforcement, high peer delinquency, poor relationship with peers, low academic achievement, and one or no biological parent at home were the significant predictors.

Summary of Key Findings

By using a nonparametric random-effects model, we identified different groups of individuals whose development varied in terms of onset, rate of change, and duration of offending. We found two to four developmental trajectories for violence and theft in the two cohorts.[1]

Trajectories

- We found the same trajectories (e.g., early versus later onset) that have been hypothesized by developmental theorists such as Moffitt (1993) and Patterson and Yoerger (1993, 1997). Trajectories varied mostly by their peak age, and all of them eventually were declining trajectories. These findings were similar to those of Laub and Sampson (2003).
- We found one trajectory (moderate declining) that differed from the adolescence-limited group proposed by Moffitt (1993). The young men in this trajectory started at the same level as the high declining trajectory, but the cessation of offending occurred close to five years earlier than for the young men in the high declining trajectory group.
- Desistance from theft happened earlier than desistance from violence.
- The moderate declining trajectory group had about the same duration of offending as the late-onset group.
- Joint trajectory modeling of violence and theft suggests that boys who follow a specific trajectory in one serious form of delinquency tend also to follow a similar trajectory in the other serious form of delinquency.
- The results indicate violence specialization but not theft specialization. In both cohorts, there were groups of violent offenders who were low in theft, but the counterpart of serious theft offenders not engaging in violence was rare or nonexistent. This means that serious theft offenders were also in most cases violent offenders. These results differed from results reported in Chapter 5, where with simpler analyses we found that specialized offenders made up half of the serious violent offenders, compared to one-third of the serious theft offenders in both cohorts.

Shared Predictors of Violent and Theft Trajectories

- We found several shared factors measured at age 7 (youngest cohort) and age 13 (oldest cohort) which predicted individuals' trajectories of offending of violence *and* theft between ages 10 and 19 (youngest cohort) and ages 14 and 25 (oldest cohort), respectively.

- Bivariate analyses revealed that more aggravating risk factors than preventive promotive factors were predictive of both violence and theft trajectories in each of the cohorts.
- Although the moderate declining trajectory of violence and theft groups in the oldest cohort were predicted by a similar constellation of aggravating risk and preventive promotive factors, they were weaker in predictive efficiency compared to predictors of the high declining trajectory violence and theft groups.
- In the youngest cohort, shared aggravating risk factors for the high declining trajectories of violence and theft were neighborhood and sociodemographic characteristics, while a shared preventive promotive factor was high academic achievement. In the oldest cohort, most of the aggravating risk and preventive promotive factors were common to both violence and theft trajectories.
- The final regression model for the youngest cohort showed one or no biological parent at home as the only shared aggravating risk factor across the high declining violence and theft trajectories.
- For the youngest cohort, having an older mother was the only shared preventive promotive factors in the final regression model for high declining violence *and* theft trajectories.
- In the final regression model for the oldest cohort, high truancy was the only shared aggravating risk factor for the high declining violence and theft trajectories.

In summary, we found several shared predictors of violence and theft trajectories, with some predictors of violence and theft trajectories operating as aggravating risk factors and other predictors operating as preventive promotive factors.

Specific Predictors of Violence and Theft Trajectories

- In the youngest cohort, at the bivariate level there were more aggravating risk factors pertaining to participant psychopathology associated with the high declining violence trajectory, while there were more aggravating risk factors pertaining to parental characteristic associated with the theft trajectories.
- For the oldest cohort, preventive promotive factors did not distinguish well between the high declining theft trajectory and the high violence trajectory (but they were distinguished by mixed factors). In addition, family functioning was more related to moderate declining theft trajectory than to the moderate declining violence trajectory.

- The final regression model for the youngest cohort showed that high academic achievement was a preventive promotive factor uniquely predictive of the no/low violence trajectory (in contrast to the high declining violence trajectory), while good neighborhood was a unique marginal promotive factor predictive of the no/low theft trajectory (in contrast to the high declining theft trajectory).
- In the final regression model for the oldest cohort, negative attitude toward delinquency (marginal effect) and good supervision were preventive promotive factors predictive of no/low violence trajectory (in contrast to the high declining violence trajectory), while good neighborhood was a marginal promotive factor predictive of the no/low theft trajectory (in contrast to the high declining theft trajectory).
- High psychopathic features and one or no biological parent at home were unique aggravating risk factors for violence, while low academic achievement and repeating a grade were unique aggravating risk factors for theft.
- Overall, late-onset violence and theft trajectories were poorly predicted by the aggravating risk and preventive promotive factors and the strongest predictors of the high and moderate declining trajectories were the same as for the late-onset trajectories, but they had weaker effects. Risk and promotive factors that are more proximal to the outcome might better explain stability and change for this specific trajectory (considered in Chapter 9).

In summary, we documented several aggravating risk and preventive promotive factors that appeared uniquely predictive of violence compared to theft trajectories. However, our models predicting late-onset violence and theft trajectories were uniformly poor.

To what extent did the prediction results of trajectories concur with results reported in Chapter 7 for the prediction of violence and theft by age blocks? In the youngest cohort, the best predictors (measured at middle childhood, ages 7–9) of offending during late adolescence (ages 17–19) were compared with the best predictors at age 7 of the high declining trajectories between ages 10 and 19 (Tables 7.4 and 8.6 for violence, and Tables 7.4 and 8.9 for theft). For the oldest cohort the comparison was between the best predictors (measured during early adolescence, ages 13–16) of offending in early adulthood (ages 20–25) and the best predictors at age 13 of the high declining trajectories between ages 13 and 25 (Tables 7.4 and 8.7 for violence and Tables 7.6 and 7.10 for theft). The results were more different than similar, and this applied to the prediction of violence and theft. We concluded that early predictors of long-term trajectory membership have unique information that is not necessarily captured by early predictors of offending at specific developmental stages, including late adolescence for the youngest cohort, and early adulthood of the oldest cohort. It is also remarkable that several preventive promotive factors predicted group trajectory membership, but only aggravating risk factors predicted offending during later life stages. This finding buttresses the notion that preventive promotive factors early in life contribute to long term trajectories of offending that originate early as well.

Note

1. The higher prevalence of offending in the oldest cohort and the difference in the window of observation into adulthood for the older cohort are possible explanations for the larger number of trajectories that we found for the oldest cohort.

Nine

Desistance from and Persistence in Offending

MAGDA STOUTHAMER-LOEBER, ROLF LOEBER, REBECCA STALLINGS, AND ERIC LACOURSE

Scholars in criminology consider desistance from offending and antisocial behavior and the causes of desistance as key topics (Ayers et al., 1999; Farrington, 2007; Gilliom, 2004; Kazemian, 2007, Laub, & Sampson, 2001; Lösel & Bender, 2003; Loeber & Le Blanc, 1990; Masten, Best, & Garmezy, 1990; Morizot & Le Blanc, 2007; Mulvey et al., 2004; Stouthamer-Loeber, Farrington, Zhang, Van Kammen, & Maguin, 1993; Stouthamer-Loeber, Loeber, Wei, Farrington, & Wikström, 2002; Stouthamer-Loeber, Wei, Loeber, & Masten, 2004; Werner, 2005). However, there are only few empirical studies assessing when desistance takes place and which factors predict it (e.g., Haapasalo & Tremblay, 1994; Hussong, Curran, Moffitt, Caspi, & Carrig, 2004; Laub & Sampson, 2001; Peersen, Sigurdsson, Gudjonsson, & Gretarssson, 2004; Stouthamer-Loeber et al., 2002, 2004).

Most desistance studies have focused on desistance during late adolescence or early adulthood, which is logical because that is the period of the downslope of the age-crime curve (Farrington, 1986). In the Pittsburgh Youth Study (PYS), the age-crime curves based on the all-source measure of offending (Figure 8.1) show that the prevalence of serious violence was decreasing between ages 15 and 17 for the youngest cohort, and between ages 19 and 22 for the oldest cohort. For the youngest cohort the key period for offenders to decrease committing theft of all levels was ages 14 through 18, while this period occurred from ages 15 through 23 for the oldest cohort. These aggregate data, however, do not clearly indicate the distribution of desistance within individuals across adolescence and early adulthood.

The age-crime curve, because it primarily reflects prevalence, does not preclude the possibility of desistance taking place prior to the downslope of the curve. Actually, a proportion of offenders already desist from serious offending prior to late adolescence. Desistance in this period is particularly important because it concerns early onset offenders, who are at risk to become tomorrow's serious and violent offenders (Loeber & Farrington, 2001).

Age-crime curves are not fixed, and vary between cohorts. In chapters 4 and 5 we found that the age-crime curve started decreasing much earlier for the youngest cohort, which probably means that the timing of the desistance processes was earlier for the youngest cohort. Therefore, it is important to establish which factors predict desistance by early adolescence and whether such factors differ from those predicting desistance later.

Most of the explanatory models on desistance bring into play positive or promotive factors that can explain why individuals decrease in their offending with time. Recall that in chapters 1 and 7 we defined preventive promotive factors as factors that predict desistance from offending in populations of known delinquents. In this chapter we are particularly interested in the study of main effects of remedial promotive factors in explaining a juvenile's desistance from moderate and serious offending (i.e., the combination of violence and theft). Because of low numbers in the desistance analyses, we will not be able to investigate interactions between protective and risk factors.

In Laub and Sampson's (2001) review of the desistance literature, they summarize six plausible explanations of desistance from offending:

1. Individuals mature and desistance takes place because of physical and mental changes (e.g., Glueck & Glueck, 1940).
2. Individuals tend to mature out of crime and, accordingly, crime naturally declines with age (following the age-crime curve)—that is, it is normative in adolescence and normally decreases from late adolescence to adulthood (e.g., Gottfredson & Hirshi, 1990).
3. Individuals undergo developmental changes, such as identity changes, that accompany aging (e.g. Neugarten, 1996), or neurocognitive, physiological or sociological changes. Moffitt's (1993) developmental model of early and late onset offenders falls under this category.
4. In studies with a life course focus, a decrease in offending is attributed to changes in informal social controls or bonds with others, and continuity and change in historical and other contextual features of life, independent of age. For instance, the emerging developmental tasks of romantic relationships and work in adolescence and early adulthood may lead young people away from crime (Sampson & Laub, 1993).
5. Rational-choice theories consider the cessation of crime to be a result of a decision by the person based on perceived costs and benefits (e.g., Cusson & Pinsonneault, 1986). Although it is stressed that this decision can be made at any time, it should be clear that the capacity for such a decision is developmentally based.
6. Social learning approaches consider that the basic variables that explain initiation (i.e., social interactions among individuals that shape behavior) also account for desistance (e.g., Akers, 1990). Thus,

if a high score on a variable (e.g., lack of caretaker supervision) is related to initiation, a low score (i.e., good supervision) may be related to desistance.

Gilliom (2004) has recast the above explanations into three main models of desistance: (1) a *dimensional model* that posits that desisters are more likely to come from those who in childhood scored moderately high on antisocial behavior and not extremely low or extremely high; (2) a *person-environment interaction model* that emphasizes that the probability of desistance is dependent on the early characteristics of the child and the child's environment; this model is a conditional one in that whether antisocial behavior persists or not partly depends on the nature of the social environment; and (3) a *life course model* that emphasizes the impact of life events on the course of antisocial behavior; this model suggests that desisters tend to have high levels of early risk but are exposed to a favorable family context and social transitions later.

We would qualify Laub and Sampson's (2001) and Gilliom's (2004) conceptualizations by adding that there probably is no single "silver bullet" that explains desistance from serious offending, and that desistance is a product of both proximal processes (e.g., life events that take place close in time prior to desistance) and longer-term factors from early life such as antisocial tendency, caretaker environment, academic performance in school, and desirable peer interaction. This is in contrast to Laub and Sampson's (2001) claim that factors that predict desistance inherently are more likely to be life events that sharply reduce individuals' offending (see also Roisman, Aguilar, & Egeland, 2004). We agree that life events can be important, but propose that there are also other factors that predict desistance from high-rate offending trajectories (see also Blokland & Nieuwbeerta, 2005). Further we propose that, for a proportion of young delinquents, desistance in offending often occurs years prior to the normal age range in which life events such as marriage or joining the military take place.

Sampson and Laub have concluded that "trajectories of desistance could not be prospectively identified based on typological accounts rooted in childhood and individual differences" and that "group membership is not easily, if at all, predictable from individual, childhood, and adolescent risk factors" (2003, p. 585). In contrast, based on earlier research on the PYS (Stouthamer-Loeber et al., 2002) and the current results, we propose that some of the foundations for eventual desistance are laid in childhood and adolescence.

We have noted that desistance can take place prior to the downslope of the age-crime curve (see also Ayers et al., 1999). It seems likely that explanatory processes will differ depending on the timing of desistance. For example, late desistance may be supported or facilitated by the person marrying a prosocial partner, although this obviously will not account for desistance occurring early in adolescence.

Earlier work in the PYS (Stouthamer-Loeber et al., 1993, 2002, 2004) has shown that the synergistic effects of promotive and risk factors explain desistance processes better than the study of either risk or promotive factors alone. Here *synergistic* means that promotive and risk factors jointly predict serious offending, and that remedial promotive factors, once hindering risk factors are taken into account, contribute unique variance in those analyses. The synergistic effects should be investigated in different age periods associated with life transitions, such as the change from middle school to high school during the transition from early to late adolescence, or the shift to independent living often taking place between late adolescence and early adulthood.

We will consider the following scenarios all leading to desistance. In one scenario, desistance is more likely to take place for those with lower levels of hindering risk factors, while desistance is less likely to take place (and persistence is more likely to occur) in the presence of multiple risk factors, both proximal and more distal, and that there is no material role for remedial promotive factors. In another scenario, desistance takes place because of a shift in the balance between hindering risk and remedial promotive factors, with the latter becoming more prominent. In that scenario, an individual may still be exposed to hindering risk factors, but the presence of remedial promotive factors increases the probability that the person will desist from further offending. Therefore, it is the combination of certain hindering risk and remedial promotive factors that matters.

Conceptualizations of the long-term antecedents to desistance may imply that both hindering risk and remedial promotive factors may have a long "reach" in predicting who will desist from offending. Yet, empirical research in this area is wanting. In Chapter 7 we mentioned that more factors that occurred during late childhood, compared to middle childhood or early adolescence, were predictive of serious offending over many years. It is unclear whether similarly the foundations for desistance processes are already laid down in late childhood rather than earlier in middle childhood or much later, as in early adolescence. We propose that our current findings lend support to two basic assumptions of intervention efforts: first, that remedial promotive processes are present early in life fostering a low probability of offending; and second, that several specific remedial promotive factors are potentially malleable. Examples of such promotive processes in interventions are specific child-rearing practices that promote prosocial behavior (e.g. positive parenting), and the teaching of social skills to children (see, e.g., Beelmann & Lösel, 2006; Weisz, Sandler, Drulak, & Anton, 2005).

This chapter consists of four sections. First, we report on the prevalence of desistance from and persistence in serious offending. Second, we investigate the prevalence of desistance from and persistence in moderate and serious offending. Third, we report on predictors of desistance from moderate and serious offending. Fourth, we examine the extent to which the developmental trajectories shown in Chapter 8 overlap with the classification of persistence and desistance presented in this chapter.

Defining Desistance

The definition of *desistance* is not the same across desistance studies. Some studies (e.g., Sampson & Laub, 2003; Peersen et al., 2004) have relied on official records only, while others have used self-reports as a criterion (Stouthamer-Loeber et al., 2002). However, self-reports can underestimate serious offenses such as rape and homicide, while official records have the disadvantage that they underestimate the prevalence of offending in general. To counter these measurement weaknesses and to achieve a more comprehensive assessment of desistance, we use for the following analyses the all-source measure combining reported offending and official records of conviction (for details, see chapters 3 and 5).

One of the key decisions in defining desisters from serious offending is to minimize false positives (i.e., mistakenly identifying as desisters those who, with time, will commit serious delinquent acts again). Research shows that individuals' conduct problems and offending fluctuate from year to year (e.g., Lahey, Loeber, Burke, Rathouz, & McBurnett, 2002). Therefore, it is critical to identify desisters who do not reoffend over a number of years. We will examine desistance from serious offending in the best way we can, and define it as the cessation of offending over three or more years as judged from reported offending *and* the absence of convictions for serious offending. The key characteristic of desistance is that the person ceases offending, and this is quite unclear when a measure of arrests or convictions is used alone. Hence, we use the dual criterion of the absence of reported serious offenses *and* the absence of convictions for serious offenses.

To speak of desistance, a person had to have committed offenses in one developmental age period and then subsequently have ceased to commit both moderate and serious offending. The advantage of the use of the age blocks of three–five years used in the earlier chapters (explained in Chapter 2; see also Table 2.1) was that desistance had to take place over at least three years, and often longer, when more age blocks were available for measurement. Desistance by early adolescence (*early desistance*) could only be studied in the youngest cohort, and was defined as the presence of offending in late childhood (ages 10-12) followed by desistance by early adolescence (ages 13–16), and continuing desistance through late adolescence (ages 17–19). For the youngest cohort, desistance in late adolescence (*intermediate desistance*) was defined as the presence of offending in late childhood (ages 10–12) and early adolescence (ages 13–16) followed by desistance by late adolescence (ages 17–19). For the oldest cohort, intermediate desistance was defined as the presence of offending in early adolescence (ages 13–16), followed by desistance by late adolescence (ages 17–19) and continued desistance into early adulthood (ages 20–25). Finally, desistance in early adulthood (*late desistance*) could only be studied in the oldest cohort, and was defined as the presence of offending in early and late adolescence (ages 13–16 and 17–19, respectively) and desistance in early adulthood (ages 20–25).

The principal questions addressed in this section are:

- How many young males persist in or desist from serious offending between ages 10 and 25?
- How many young males persist in or desist from moderate/serious offending between ages 10 and 25?
- Is the probability of desistance from offending the same whether occurring in adolescence or in adulthood, and to what extent does desistance vary by cohort?
- Which remedial promotive factors and which hindering risk factors predict desistance from moderate/serious offending?

Persistence in and Desistance from Serious Offending

Table 9.1 summarizes the key data about persistence (and desistance) in offending across the age blocks. In the following section we first separately review short-term and long-term persistence of serious offending (i.e., total of serious violence and theft), with *short-term persistence* defined as persistence from one age block to the next and *long-term persistence* defined as persistence across multiple age blocks. Short-term desistance (based on transitions between two age blocks) is shown in the first four columns of Table 9.1. For example, the first column shows that 4 out of 11 boys (36%) showing serious theft during middle childhood (ages 7–9) persisted in their serious theft during the next age block of late childhood (ages 10–12). The last three columns of Table 9.1 show longer-term persistence (and desistance) over more than two age blocks.

Persistence in Serious Offenses

As for short-term persistence, Figure 9.1 shows that for the youngest cohort, the highest level of persistence (71%) was found for those with an onset during late childhood (10–12), compared to those with an onset during middle childhood, of whom almost half (45%) persisted, which was only marginally higher than those whose onset was in early adolescence (32%). However, it should be noted that the numbers for these comparisons were small.

We also found major cohort differences: Figure 9.1 shows that persistence of serious offending from early to late adolescence was substantially higher for the oldest cohort (47% vs. 32%). For the oldest cohort, persistence remained the same for the period from early to late adolescence, compared to the period from late adolescence to early adulthood (47% vs. 42%), but these results may be affected by the fact that the period early adulthood (20–25) was two years

Table 9.1 Persistence in and Desistance from Serious Offending (Youngest and Oldest Cohorts, based on the All-Source Measure of Offending)

Number of Adjacent Age Blocks	Short-Term Persistence/Desistance				Long-Term Persistence/Desistance		
	2	2	2	2	4	3	3
	ONSET MIDDLE CHILDHOOD (AGES 7–9) AND PERSISTENCE/ DESISTANCE TO LATE CHILDHOOD (AGES 10–12)	ONSET LATE CHILDHOOD (AGES 10–12) AND PERSISTENCE/ DESISTANCE TO EARLY ADOLESCENCE (AGES 13–16)	ONSET EARLY ADOLESCENCE (AGES 13–16) AND PERSISTENCE/ DESISTANCE TO LATE ADOLESCENCE (AGES 17–19)	ONSET LATE ADOLESCENCE (AGES 17–19) AND PERSISTENCE/ DESISTANCE TO EARLY ADULTHOOD (AGES 20–25)	ONSET MIDDLE CHILDHOOD (AGES 7–9) AND PERSISTENCE/ DESISTANCE TO LATE CHILDHOOD (AGES 10–12), EARLY ADOLESCENCE (AGES 13–16), AND LATE ADOLESCENCE (AGES 17–19)	ONSET LATE CHILDHOOD (AGES 10–12) AND PERSISTENCE/ DESISTANCE TO EARLY ADOLESCENCE (AGES 13–16) AND LATE ADOLESCENCE (AGES 17–20)	ONSET EARLY ADOLESCENCE (AGES 13–16) AND PERSISTENCE/ DESISTANCE TO LATE ADOLESCENCE (AGES 17–19) AND EARLY ADULTHOOD (AGES 20–25)
Persistence Serious Offending	Y: 5/11(45.5%)	Y: 44/62(71.0%)	Y: 24/74(32.4%)O: 90/191(47.1%)	O: 20/48(41.7%)	Y: 2/11(18.2%)	Y: 18/67(26.9%)	O: 36/191(18.8%)
Desistance Serious Offending	Y: 6/11(54.5%)	Y: 18/62(29.0%)	Y: 50/74(67.6%)O: 101/191(52.9%)	O: 28/48(58.3%)	Y: 6/11(54.5%)	Y: 16/67(23.9%)	O: 76/191(39.8%)

Table 9.1 Persistence in and Desistance from Serious Offending (Youngest and Oldest Cohorts, based on the All-Source Measure of Offending) (continued)

Number of Adjacent Age Blocks	Short-Term Persistence/Desistance				Long-Term Persistence/Desistance		
	2	2	2	2	4	3	3
Persistence Serious Violence	—	Y: 27/45(60.0%)	Y: 16/65(24.6%) O: 49/118 (41.5%)	O: 25/60(41.7%)	—	Y: 6/45 (13.3%)	O: 20/118(16.9%)
Desistance Serious Violence	—	Y: 18/45(40.0%)	Y: 49/65(75.4%) O: 69/118(58.5%)	O: 35/60(58.3%)	—	Y: 17/45(37.8%)	O: 55/118(46.6%)
Persistence Serious Theft	Y: 4/11(36.4%)	Y: 19/30(63.3%)	Y: 13/49(26.5%) O: 40/136(29.4%)	O: 5/23(21.7%)	Y: 3/11(27.3%)	Y: 6/34(17.6%)	O: 6/136(4.4%)
Desistance Serious Theft	Y: 7/11(63.6%)	Y: 11/30(36.7%)	Y: 36/49(73.5%) O: 96/136(70.6%)	O: 18/23(78.3%)	Y: 7/11(63.6%)	Y: 12/34(35.3%)	O: 81/136(59.6%)

Notes: Y = youngest cohort; O = oldest cohort; — = not applicable.

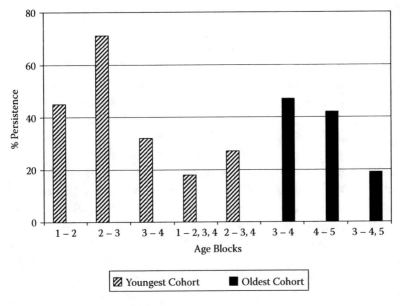

Age Block 1 = Ages 7–9; Age Block 2 = 10–12; Age Block 3 = 13–16;
Age Block 4 = 17–19; Age Block 5 = 20–25.

Figure 9.1 Persistence in Serious Offending

longer than the period of late adolescence (17–19). In summary, we docu-mented substantial persistence, but with the exception of the period from late childhood to early adolescence, the prevalence of persistence of serious offending tended to be below 50%.

It can be argued that long-term persistence is more important than short-term persistence. As expected, persistence decreased the higher the number of age blocks that were spanned (see Table 9.1 and Figure 9.1). It is particularly important to show whether there are *life course persistent offenders* (Moffitt, 1993), although this term is a bit of a misnomer because no one has ever com-prehensively examined both reported serious offending and official records of serious offending over the full life course. Table 9.1 shows that, in the youngest cohort, just under one in five (18%) of the serious offenders who had an onset during middle childhood persisted in serious offending throughout late child-hood and early and late adolescence. This percentage increased slightly to 27% for those whose onset of serious offending first occurred in late childhood. In comparison, in the oldest cohort, just under one in five (19%) of the serious offenders first documented in early adolescence continued to offend through late adolescence and early adulthood.

Desistance from Serious Offending

The short-term desistance rates (defined from age block to age block) shown in Table 9.1 were, by definition, the inverse of persistence (note that desistance is the inverse of persistence here, and that is the reason why desistance is not shown separately from persistence in Figure 9.1). About half of the boys (54%) in the youngest cohort whose serious offending was first documented in middle childhood did not commit serious acts in late childhood. Desistance was lowest for onset experienced during late childhood (29%), and substantially increased for onset experienced in early adolescence (68%). These results support the notion that early onset, compared to late onset, is associated with higher persistence and lower desistance (see also Farrington, Loeber, Elliott, 1990; Loeber, 1982; Loeber & Farrington, 2001), but qualifies this general finding in a major way. We also found that the onset of serious offending during late childhood was followed by greater continuity over time than onset during middle childhood. However, about one-fourth (24%) of the boys with an onset during late childhood subsequently did not commit serious offenses throughout adolescence (up to age 19). Hence, statements about life course offending of these boys who started offending in childhood clearly did not apply to one-fourth of the early-onset offenders.

We could not measure early onset during childhood in the oldest cohort. However, desistance rates were remarkably similar for those who were first documented to seriously offend during early compared to late adolescence (53% vs. 58%).

Differential Desistance from Violence and Theft?

Do the above results on persistence and desistance from all-source serious offending apply when serious violence and serious theft are considered separately? The answer to this question can be gleaned from Table 9.1, which shows more similarities than differences. For the youngest cohort, short-term persistence from early to late adolescence in serious violence and serious theft were very comparable (25% and 26%). In terms of long-term persistence, 60% of the serious violent offenders in the youngest cohort with an onset during late childhood persisted into early adolescence. The comparable figure for serious theft was 63%.

However, there were some notable differences between the cohorts. Short-term persistence of serious violence in the oldest cohort from early to late adolescence was higher than persistence of serious theft (41% vs. 29%). Similar results were also apparent when long-term persistence was considered. In the oldest cohort, 17% of the serious violent offenders first documented in early adolescence persisted throughout late adolescence and early adulthood, compared to 4% of the serious theft offenders. Table 9.1 also shows that in that cohort more of the serious theft offenders compared to serious violence offenders desisted over that time period (60% vs. 47%).

In summary, for those offenders with an onset in childhood, violence and theft persisted to the same degree, but for offenders with an onset during adolescence, violence persisted longer than theft. Overall, at least half of the violent offenders desisted subsequently, and this desistance was already evident from early to middle adolescence, much earlier than mentioned in most literature on desistance (e.g., Elliott, Menard, et al., 2005; Moffitt, 1993). Further, from early to late adolescence, desistance from theft was similar in the youngest (73%) compared to the oldest cohort (71%). Also, the results underscore that for the oldest cohort, a developmental trend from theft to violence may have taken place, with the proportion of theft offenders decreasing between early adolescence and early adulthood, whereas the proportion of violent offenders remained stable throughout adolescence and decreased during early adolescence to a much lesser degree than was the case for serious theft offenders. This is another view on how specialization in offending, considered in Chapter 5, may take place between adolescence and early adulthood.

Persistence in and Desistance from Moderate and Serious Offending

The criterion for desistance that we used so far was desistance from serious offending because we are interested in the group of people who perpetrate the most harm. However, it can be argued that desistance can sometimes be partial in that some people may cease serious offending but continue to offend at a lower seriousness level. Another reason to refocus on the definition of desistance is the fact that the individuals who had committed serious offending and then desisted were modest in number, which set a limit to the statistical power for the analyses. This was particularly the case since we wanted to study desistance from early adolescence onward (called *early desistance*), as distinct from desistance from late adolescence onward (*intermediate desistance*), or from early adulthood onward (*late desistance*). For these reasons, we defined desistance in this section as offenders' cessation of serious *and* moderate offending. Because the number of delinquents at ages 7–9 was small in the youngest cohort, and because their behavior needed to be traced over subsequent age blocks causing even smaller numbers, the earliest prediction analyses focused on delinquents in the 10–12 age range.

Persistence in Moderate/Serious Offending

Table 9.2 and Figure 9.2 show the prevalence of persisters when both moderate and serious offenses are included. Of those in the youngest cohort who had offended in late childhood, 37% persisted in late adolescence (20% in violence, and 30% in theft). For the oldest cohort, of those who offended in early adolescence, about half (48%) persisted into early adulthood. The respective figures for violence and theft were 35% and 39%. In summary, 3 to 4 out of 10 of the

Table 9.2 Persistence in and Desistance from Moderate/Serious Offending (Youngest and Oldest Cohorts, based on the All-Source Measure of Offending)

	Youngest Cohort				Oldest Cohort			
	N in Late Childhood (Y)	Desistance		Persistence in Late Adolescence N (%)	N in Early Adolescence (O)	Desistance		Persistence in Early Adulthood N (%)
		Early Adulthood N (%)	Late Adolescence N (%)			Late Adolescence	Early Adolescence	
Moderate/Serious Offending	163	24 (14.7)	79 (48.5)	60 (36.8)	330	66 (20.0)	105 (31.8)	159 (48.2)
Moderate/Serious Violence	111	32 (28.8)	57 (51.4)	22 (19.8)	221	80 (36.2)	64 (29.0)	77 (34.8)
Moderate/Serious Theft	109	23 (21.1)	53 (48.6)	33 (30.3)	288	80 (27.8)	96 (33.3)	112 (38.9)

Notes: N = number; Y = youngest cohort; O = oldest cohort.

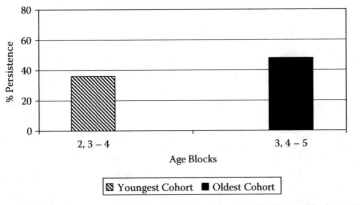

Age Block 2 = 10–12; Age Block 3 = 13–16; Age Block 4 = 17–19; Age Block 5 = 20–25.

Figure 9.2 Persistence in Moderate/Serious Offending

moderate to serious offenders early in life persisted in their offending over a period of about 6–9 years.

Desistance from Moderate/Serious Offending

For the youngest cohort, Table 9.2 shows that 163 participants had committed moderate/serious offenses in late childhood, of whom 111 committed moderate/serious violence and 109 committed moderate/serious theft. Thus, while most delinquents committed violence as well as theft, 54 (33%) of the boys committed violence only and 52 (32%) committed theft only. Desistance by early adolescence from moderate/serious offending (see Figure 9.3) took place for 15% of the delinquent boys in the youngest cohort, compared to 29% and 21% of the violence and theft delinquents, suggesting that those participants who had committed violence as well as theft were less likely to desist early than those who had committed only violence or theft. This finding agrees with the notion that early onset of offending, especially involving a pattern of varied offending (i.e., both violence and theft), compared to more specialized offending, is more persistent over time (Loeber, 1982; Loeber & Farrington, 2001).

Table 9.2 shows the results for desistance in late adolescence for the youngest cohort: 48% of the moderate/serious delinquents (i.e., violence and theft combined) in late childhood and early adolescence subsequently desisted. The comparable figures for violence and theft were 51% and 49%, respectively. Also, the results for desistance in late adolescence do not show the stark difference between desistance in both violence and theft compared to either violence or theft only that we observed for desistance by early adolescence.

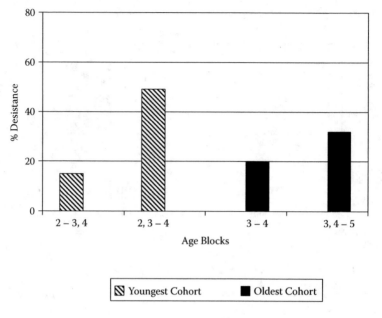

Age Block 2 = 10–12; Age Block 3 = 13–16; Age Block 4 = 17–19; Age Block 5 = 20–25.

Figure 9.3 Desistance from Moderate/Serious Offending

Turning to the oldest cohort, we found that of the 330 participants who had committed moderate/serious offending (violence and theft combined) in early adolescence, 221 committed moderate/serious violence and 288 moderate/ serious theft. Thus, again we observed that most delinquents committed violence as well as theft. There were, however, 42 (13%) who committed violence only and 109 (33%) who committed theft only. Thus, when moderate/serious offenses were the criterion, more specialization was found for theft than for violent offenders, a point to which we will return in Chapter 10.

Desistance in late adolescence took place for 20% of the moderate/serious delinquents in the oldest cohort (see Figure 9.3), compared to 36% and 28% of the violence and theft delinquents, suggesting that those participants who had committed both violence and theft were less likely to desist early than those who had committed only violence or theft. This distinction was not found for desistance in early adulthood (i.e., presence of moderate/serious offending in early and in late adolescence and desistance in early adulthood), where the percentages of those who desisted were more similar for the groups (32%, 29%, and 33% for the delinquent, violent, and theft groups, respectively).

In summary, desistance rates varied with age and by cohort. In the youngest cohort, the smallest proportion of desisters was for desistance by early adolescence, and the largest for desistance by late adolescence (about 50%). In the oldest cohort the proportion of desisters tended to be similar (about 30%) for desistance by late adolescence and desistance by early adulthood (the exception was desistance in late adolescence from moderate/serious offending, i.e., violence and theft, which was lower). It is probable that cohort differences in desistance rates reflect the age-crime curves that are wider and higher for the oldest cohort. There is another reason why information about desistance is important. It is likely that relatively low rates of desistance in adolescence for a given cohort are a foreboding that delinquents in that cohort will experience a longer and heightened delinquency career.

Observed Typology of Persisters/Desisters versus Trajectory Classification

How does the observed typology of persisters and desisters correspond to the trajectory classification of young men shown in Chapter 8? If the comparisons indicate that, for example, most of the young men in the violence trajectory are also among the persistent violent offenders across multiple age blocks (called *observed typology*) this would lend further validity to the trajectory analyses, and would provide additional information about the observed classification. The process of following the observed typology with six offender groups from Table 9.1 created too many cells with low values; for that reason, we compared the trajectory classification with those offenders who committed serious offenses in one or more age blocks irrespective of timing of the age block: (1) a single age block; (2) in two age blocks; or, (3) in three age blocks. Although not ideal, this provided an approximation of the observed typology of offenders.

The following results are presented in two types of conditional probabilities: the conditional probability of trajectory group membership given the observed typology of offending, and the reverse, the conditional probability of the observed typology given trajectory group membership.

The upper part of Table 9.3 shows the conditional probability of trajectory group membership for violence given the observed typology of violence in the youngest cohort. Because of the potentially high number of comparisons with low cell sizes, the observed classification was summarized according to the following categories: no violence across all age blocks, violence in a single age block, violence in two age blocks, and violence in three or more age blocks. The overall chi-square was highly significant ($\chi^2 = 353.21$, $p < .001$) indicating a substantial correspondence between the observed violence typology and trajectory group membership. For example, the probability of being nonoffenders in the observed typology given the membership of the no/low trajectory was 1.00, while the probability of being persistent violent offenders given membership of the high violence trajectory was .60. Table 9.4 shows the corresponding reverse probabilities: the probabilities of trajectory membership given the observed typology, which were .88 and .32 for the no/low and persistent groups, respectively. As can be seen from Tables 9.3 and 9.4, the

Table 9.3 Conditional Probability of Serious Violence and Serious Theft Trajectory Groups versus Observed Typology (Youngest Cohort)

| | Trajectory Group—Serious Violence | | | |
Observed Typology	No/Low	Minor Stable	High Declining	χ^2
Never Offenders	1.000	0.000	0.000	353.21*
One Age Block	0.349	0.542	0.108	
Two Age Blocks	0.143	0.571	0.286	
Three or More Age Blocks	0.100	0.300	0.600	

| | Trajectory Group—Serious Theft | | |
Observed Typology	No/Low	High Declining	χ^2
Never Offenders	1.000	0.000	186.17*
One Age Block	0.747	0.253	
Two Age Blocks	0.411	0.589	
Three or More Age Blocks	0.300	0.700	

Notes: *$p < .001$; χ^2 = Chi-square.

Table 9.4 Conditional Probability of Group Membership in the Observed Typology versus Serious Violence and Serious Theft Trajectory Groups (Youngest Cohort)

| Trajectory Group—Serious Violence | Observed Typology | | | | |
	Never	One Age Block	Two Age Blocks	Three or More Age Blocks	χ^2
No/Low	0.880	0.090	0.025	0.006	353.21*
Minor Stable	0.000	0.542	0.386	0.072	
High Declining	0.000	0.243	0.432	0.324	

| Trajectory Group—Serious Theft | Observed Typology | | | | |
	Never	One Age Block	Two Age Blocks	Three or More Age Blocks	χ^2
No/Low	0.758	0.165	0.061	0.016	186.17*
High Declining	0.000	0.309	0.485	0.206	

Notes: *$p < .001$; χ^2 = Chi-square.

conditional probabilities were moderately high for the comparison between the moderate trajectory and the observed typology.

Table 9.4 shows the comparison for theft in the youngest cohort. The overall chi-square was also highly significant ($\chi^2 = 186.17$, $p < .001$). Similar comparisons for violence and theft for the oldest cohort are shown in Tables 9.5 and 9.6, which again show highly significant results ($\chi^2 = 392.62$, $p < .001$, and 259.18, $p < .001$, respectively). Again the conditional probabilities were highest for the extreme categories and substantially lower for the middle categories (both according to the observed typology and the trajectories).

Overall, the conditional probabilities of the observed typology given trajectory membership were slightly higher than the conditional probabilities of trajectory membership given the observed typology. This finding suggests that the translation of trajectory membership into the observed typology was better than the reverse. In all comparisons, however, intermediate typologies and intermediate trajectories corresponded far less than the extremes. It is possible that this is partly a result of our summarizing observed types according to the persistence of serious offending, irrespective of the age dimension of successive age blocks.

Promotive and Risk Factors Predicting Desistance from Moderate/Serious Offending

As mentioned, there is a scarcity of studies that predict which youth are likely to desist from offending. Knowledge of predictors is important for the following practical reasons. First, screening instruments aimed at identifying youth at different levels of risk of reoffending often focus on the highest versus lowest risk groups, but usually do not address which youth are most likely to stop offending under which conditions. Second, knowledge of remedial promotive factors associated with desistance is potentially important for interventions that can enhance promotive factors. Third, remedial promotive factors predictive of desistance should be studied together with existing risk factors that hinder or delay desistance. In that respect we need to know much more about which remedial promotive factors are so strong that they survive even when strong, hindering risk factors are taken into account. Thus, our argument is that there is "more" value to the study of remedial promotive factors over and above knowledge based on hindering risk factors only.

The following analyses will compare, for each cohort, each group of desisters (early adolescence and late adolescence desisters for the youngest cohort, and late adolescence and early adulthood desisters for the oldest cohort) against the persisters in Table 9.2. The results concentrate on desistance from moderate/serious offending.

An argument could be made that some participants could show "false" desistance because of the fact that they were in prison for the whole age block. However, the amount of prison time was not related to desistance. For that

Table 9.5 Conditional Probability of Serious Violence and Serious Theft Trajectory Groups versus Observed Typology (Oldest Cohort)

Observed Typology	Trajectory Group—Serious Violence				χ^2
	No/Low	Late-Onset	Moderate Declining	High Declining	
Never Offenders	1.000	0.000	0.000	0.000	392.62*
One Age Block	0.438	0.198	0.355	0.008	
Two Age Blocks	0.172	0.232	0.535	0.061	
Three or More Age Blocks	0.028	0.194	0.333	0.444	

Observed Typology	Trajectory Group—Serious Theft				χ^2
	No/Low	Late-Onset	Moderate Declining	High Declining	
Never Offenders	1.000	0.000	0.000	0.000	259.18*
One Age Block	0.529	0.165	0.306	0.000	
Two Age Blocks	0.263	0.131	0.515	0.091	
Three or More Age Blocks	0.167	0.139	0.528	0.167	

Notes: *p <.001; χ^2 = Chi-square.

reason we did not remove participants from the analyses who had been in prison over the time of the prediction block. Most of these turned out to be persisters, showing that being in prison does not necessarily stop criminal activities.

This section addresses the following questions:

Which remedial promotive factors predict desistance from moderate/serious offending?

Which hindering risk factors are negatively predictive of desistance in moderate/serious offending?

Are there key developmental periods in which remedial predictors of desistance operate? And are hindering risk factors more important at later, compared to earlier, stages of desistance?

Is desistance after early adolescence more dominated by hindering risk factors, while desistance by early adolescence is more dominated by a mixture of remedial promotive and hindering risk factors?

To what extent are preventive promotive factors predicting nonoffending the same as remedial promotive factors predicting desistance?

Table 9.6 Conditional Probability of Group Membership in the Observed Typology versus Serious Violence and Serious Theft Trajectory Groups (Oldest Cohort)

Trajectory Group— Serious Violence	Observed Typology				χ^2
	Never	*One Age Block*	*Two Age Blocks*	*Three or More Age Blocks*	
No/Low	0.756	0.182	0.058	0.003	392.62*
Late-Onset	0.000	0.444	0.426	0.130	
Moderate Declining	0.000	0.398	0.491	0.111	
High Declining	0.000	0.043	0.261	0.696	

Trajectory Group— Serious Theft	Observed Typology				χ^2
	Never	*One Age Block*	*Two Age Blocks*	*Three or More Age Blocks*	
No/Low	0.696	0.203	0.082	0.019	259.18*
Late-Onset	0.000	0.526	0.342	0.132	
Moderate Declining	0.000	0.346	0.477	0.178	
High Declining	0.000	0.000	0.400	0.600	

Note: *p <.001; χ^2 = Chi-square.

Similarly, is there an overlap between aggravating risk factors predicting serious offending and risk factors that hinder desistance?

Analyses

The analyses of remedial promotive factors and hindering risk factors are accomplished in the format used for analyses on preventive promotive factors and aggravating risk factors explained in Chapter 7. Briefly, the first step in the analyses was to calculate odds ratios (ORs) comparing the best 25% of an independent variable against the middle 50%, and then repeat this for the worst 25% versus the middle 50%. Variables with ORs greater than 2 were then dichotomized in such a manner as to combine the middle 50% with the 25% that had originally been left out of the analysis. As an example, if a variable was found to be remedial promotive, then for the next set of analyses the middle 50% was combined with the worst 25%. Chi-squares were then rerun with the 25% versus 75% variables.

In analyzing the predictors of desistance, we faced problems of modest statistical power because of low cell sizes for some outcomes (see Table 9.2). For that reason, we report on factors that significantly discriminate between desisters and persisters, using chi-square as the criterion. However, we also report on findings that are more exploratory in that they are based on a minimum odds ratio of >2 (irrespective of statistical significance).

Table 9.7 Remedial Promotive Factors as Predictors of Desistance from Moderate/Serious Offending (Youngest and Oldest Cohorts, Odds Ratios)

	Youngest Cohort				Oldest Cohort	
	Early Desistance (Desistance by Early Adolescence)		Intermediate Desistance (Desistance by Late Adolescence)	Intermediate Desistance (Desistance by Late Adolescence Persisting through Early Adulthood)	Late Desistance (Desistance by Early Adulthood)	
Predictors Measured at	Middle Childhood	Late Childhood	Early Adolescence	Early Adolescence	Early Adolescence	Late Adolescence
PARTICIPANT PSYCHOPATHOLOGY						
Not Running Away	—	—	2.1	—	—	N/A
Low ADHD Symptoms	2.5	—	2.1	—	—	N/A
No Depressed Mood	—	—	2.2	—	—	—
Low Anxiety	—	2.4	—	—	—	—
Low Shyness/Withdrawal	—	3.3	2.2	—	—	—
PARTICIPANT COMPETENCE						
High Perceived Likelihood of Getting Caught	—	—	2.6	2.6**	—	—
High Prosocial Behavior	N/A	2.5	—	—	—	—
Positive Interaction with Interviewer	N/A	2.7	—	—	—	—
FAMILY FUNCTIONING						
Good Supervision	4.9**	4.0*	—	2.7**	—	N/A
High Parental Reinforcement	—	—	2.5*	—	—	N/A
Low Physical Punishment	—	—	2.1*	—	—	N/A

PARENTAL CHARACTERISTICS

Parent Low Antisocial Attitude	—	2.9*	—	—	N/A
Low Parental Stress	5.7**	4.2**	—	2.9**	N/A
Two Biological Parents in Home	—	—	—	—	2.3*
PEERS					
Low Peer Delinquency	—	—	5.1	—	N/A
Good Relationship with Peers	—	—	2.1	2.3	N/A
SCHOOL					
Positive Attitude toward School	—	—	4.0*	—	N/A
High Academic Achievement	—	5.7*	—	—	N/A
NEIGHBORHOOD					
Good Neighborhood Impression	—	4.1*	2.5	—	—
SOCIODEMOGRAPHICS					
Good Housing Quality	—	6.1**	—	—	N/A
High Family/Participant Socioeconomic Status	—	—	—	2.6**	N/A

Notes: $*p < .05$; $**p < .01$; N/A = not available; — = nonsignificant. To facilitate comparisons of the magnitude of risk and promotive factors, the odds ratios for promotive factors, normally ranging in value from 0 to 1, were rescaled to be larger than 1. The following constructs were nonsignificant: low physical aggression, low psychopathic features, low truancy, high self-aspirations, negative attitude toward delinquency, leaving home at a late age, good life skills, high liking of adults, high job skills, negative attitude toward substance use, late pubertal development, high persistence of discipline, youth involved in family activities, parent high aspirations for participant, getting along well with siblings, not repeating a grade, high educational level, Caucasian ethnicity, fewer than two changes in caretaker by age 10, having a wife/girlfriend, being in the military, having an older mother, small family, family not on welfare, and large house.

Table 9.8 Hindering Risk Factors Negatively Predicting Desistance from Moderate/Serious Offending (Oldest and Youngest Cohorts, Odds Ratios)

Predictors Measured at	Youngest Cohort			Oldest Cohort		
	Early Desistance (Desistance by Early Adolescence)		Intermediate Desistance (Desistance by Late Adolescence)	Intermediate Desistance (Desistance by Late Adolescence Persisting through Early Adulthood)	Late Desistance (Desistance by Early Adulthood)	
	Middle Childhood	Late Childhood	Early Adolescence	Early Adolescence	Early Adolescence	Late Adolescence
SUBSTANCE USE AND OFFENDING						
High Tobacco Use	—	2.8	2.6**	—	—	—
High Alcohol Use	—	—	2.5*	4.0***	1.9*	1.8*
High Marijuana Use	—	5.9	—	2.2*	—	—
High Drug Dealing	—	#	—	8.1***	2.0*	2.0**
Gang Membership	—	4.2	—	3.5*	2.4*	2.5**
Gun Carrying	—	—	—	3.8**	2.7**	3.4***
PARTICIPANT PSYCHOPATHOLOGY						
Truancy	—	2.8	—	—	—	—
Running Away	—	6.0*	—	—	—	—
Depressed Mood	—	—	—	—	2.0*	2.3**
High Anxiety	—	—	—	—	—	2.9***
High Shyness/Withdrawal	7.6	—	—	—	—	—

		PARTICIPANT COMPETENCE				
High Psychopathic Features	—	3.2*	—	2.7**	—	—
Low Perceived Likelihood of Getting Caught	—	3.0*	—	—	—	—
Low Prosocial Behavior	N/A	—	2.0	—	—	—
Negative Interaction with Interviewer	N/A	3.3	—	—	—	—
Early Age Left Home	N/A	N/A	N/A	2.2	N/A	N/A
High Violence Victimization	N/A	—	—	2.4*	—	2.2**
High Level of Serious Injuries	—	3.3*	—	—	—	—
Positive Attitude toward Delinquency	—	2.4	—	—	—	—
FAMILY FUNCTIONING						
High Physical Punishment	—	2.7	—	—	—	—
Low Persistence of Discipline	—	2.2	—	—	—	—
Two or More Changes of Caretaker by Age 10	—	N/A	N/A	—	—	—

Table 9.8 Hindering Risk Factors Negatively Predicting Desistance from Moderate/Serious Offending (Oldest and Youngest Cohorts, Odds Ratios) (continued)

	Youngest Cohort			Oldest Cohort		
	Early Desistance (Desistance by Early Adolescence)		Intermediate Desistance (Desistance by Late Adolescence)	Intermediate Desistance (Desistance by Late Adolescence Persisting through Early Adulthood)	Late Desistance (Desistance by Early Adulthood)	
Predictors Measured at	Middle childhood	Late Childhood	Early Adolescence	Early Adolescence	Early Adolescence	Late Adolescence
One or No Biological Parents at Home	—	—	—	2.0	2.3**	—
High Parental Stress	3.8*	6.0*	—	—	—	—
Mother Smoking during Pregnancy	2.4	N/A	N/A	—	—	—
Father Behavioral Problems	2.7	N/A	N/A	—	2.0*	—
PEERS						
High Peer Delinquency	—	—	2.5*	4.6***	3.0***	2.4**
Poor Relationship with Peers	—	3.3*	—	—	—	—
SCHOOL						
Repeating a Grade	NM	2.6	—	—	—	—

	NEIGHBORHOOD				
	SOCIODEMOGRAPHICS				
Bad Neighborhood Impression	2.6	—	—	—	—	2.3**
Low Family Socioeconomic Status	0.3*	—	—	—	—	—
Small House	3.5	2.1	—	—	—	—
Young Mother	N/A	—	—	—	2.5**	—
Family on Welfare	2.4	—	3.1***	—	3.4***	—

Notes: $*p < .05$; $**p < .01$; $***p < .001$; # = could not be calculated; N/A = not available; NM = not measured; — = nonsignificant. The following constructs were nonsignificant across all comparisons and, therefore, are not listed in the table: high ADHD symptoms, high physical aggression, low life skills, low liking of adults, low job skills, positive perception of problem behavior, positive attitude toward substance use, high perinatal problems, high prenatal problems, mother consuming alcohol during pregnancy, early pubertal development, high theft victimization, child maltreatment by age 12, poor supervision, youth not involved in family, low parental reinforcement, parent high antisocial attitude, parent low aspirations for participant, parent alcohol problem, parent police contact, getting along poorly with siblings, low academic achievement, negative attitude toward school, low educational level, not having a wife/girlfriend, not being in the military, African American ethnicity, large family, and poor housing quality.

The results for remedial promotive factors and for hindering risk factors are presented in Tables 9.7 and 9.8, respectively. Because of the large numbers of comparisons, we first established whether findings could have been produced by chance alone across all tests in Tables 9.7 and 9.8. To be conservative, we required a minimum p-value of .10 (e.g., if less than 10 out of 100 tests were significant, then we did not include that whole set of tests). The number of predictors measured in middle and late childhood predicting desistance by early adolescence in the youngest cohort (p = .12 and .32, respectively) was somewhat better than our preestablished p value of .10. Also, the number of predictors measured during early adolescence predicting desistance by late adolescence (intermediate desistance) was better than the chance (p = .16 and .16 for the youngest and oldest cohorts, respectively), but this was not the case for predictors measured during middle or late childhood in the youngest cohort predicting intermediate desistance (p = .06 and .06, respectively). Thus, there was no evidence that hindering risk or remedial promotive factors in childhood could account for desistance from moderate/serious offending by late adolescence in the youngest cohort. Therefore, the columns in Table 9.7 and 9.8 that would have reported these odds ratios were not included. Finally, in the oldest cohort, the number of predictors measured during early or late adolescence predicting desistance by early adulthood (late desistance) approached significance for early adolescence and were better than chance for late adolescence (p = .10 and .19, respectively). Taking these results into account, we will review the bivariate results first for the youngest and then for the oldest cohort (for each column in Tables 9.7 and 9.8 with better than chance results), after which we will summarize the findings of logistic regressions to predict desistance.

Promotive Factors Predictive of Desistance

To facilitate comparisons of the magnitude of risk and promotive factors, the odds ratios for promotive factors, normally ranging in value from 0 to 1, were rescaled to be larger than 1. Table 9.7 shows that the following remedial promotive factors in the individual domain predicted early desistance in the youngest cohort: low ADHD symptoms, low anxiety, and low shyness/withdrawal. Among the competence factors were high prosocial behavior and positive interaction with the interviewer. Among the family factors, good supervision was a predictor of desistance. In addition, low antisocial attitude of parent and low parental stress were related to desistance. Finally, the three remaining remedial promotive factors were high academic achievement, good neighborhood impression, and good housing quality. The strongest predictors were good housing quality (OR = 6.1) and high academic achievement (OR = 5.7). Among the remedial promotive factors replicated across the two prediction periods (middle and late childhood) were good supervision and low parental stress. In summary, remedial promotive processes were present in individual factors, family factors, school factors, demographics, and neighborhood factors, but not among the peer factors.

To what extent do the remedial promotive factors relevant for early desistance also predict intermediate desistance by late adolescence? Earlier we had already concluded that factors in childhood did not predict desistance by late adolescence, and, therefore, these factors were not included in Tables 9.7 and 9.8. Instead, several factors measured during early adolescence predicted desistance by late adolescence. Taking into account predictors of desistance by late adolescence in the youngest and oldest cohorts, the following remedial promotive factors emerged: not running away (oldest cohort), low ADHD (youngest cohort), no depressed mood (youngest cohort), low shyness/withdrawal (youngest cohort), high perceived likelihood of getting caught (youngest and oldest cohorts), good supervision (oldest cohort), high parental reinforcement (youngest cohort), low physical punishment (youngest cohort), low parental stress (oldest cohort), low peer delinquency (youngest cohort), good relations with peers (youngest and oldest cohorts), a positive attitude toward school (youngest cohort), good neighborhood impression (youngest cohort), and high family/participant socioeconomic status, or SES (oldest cohort). In summary, remedial promotive processes were represented among individual, family, peer, school, neighborhood, and sociodemographic domains. The only remedial promotive factors that were shared across the youngest and oldest cohorts were high perceived likelihood of getting caught and good relationship with peers. The strongest predictors were low peer delinquency (OR = 5.1) and a positive attitude toward school (OR = 4.0). Compared to desistance at an earlier period (i.e., by early adolescence) a slightly higher variety of remedial promotive factors emerged (such as high parental reinforcement, low physical punishment, low incidence of running away, low depressed mood, low peer delinquency, good relationship with peers, and a positive attitude toward school). In contrast to these positive results, Table 9.7 shows that for the oldest cohort only one remedial promotive factor (two biological parents in the home) could be documented for late desistance—that is, desistance by early adulthood.

We were interested in examining the effects of marrying or living with a partner and of joining the military (Sampson & Laub, 2003) However, we could only examine these in the oldest cohort for late desistance. The predictor constructs are derived from ages 17–19 when few participants were living with a partner or had joined the military. These constructs were not significantly related to desistance.

Hindering Risk Factors Negatively Predictive of Desistance

Table 9.8 shows which hindering risk factors negatively predicted early, intermediate, and late desistance from moderate/serious offending. Risk factors measured during middle or late childhood that negatively predicted early desistance in the youngest cohort included several deviant behaviors such as high tobacco use, high marijuana use, and gang membership. In addition, several individual variables were hindering risk factors, including high truancy, running away, high shyness/withdrawal, high psychopathic features, low perceived likelihood of getting caught, negative interaction with the interviewer, high number of serious injuries, and a positive attitude toward delinquency. Among the family factors that hindered later desistance were high physical punishment, low persistence of discipline, high parental stress, mother smoking during pregnancy, and father behavioral problems. Finally, the remaining hindering risk factors that predicted a low probability of desistance were poor relationship with peers, repeating a grade, bad neighborhood impression, small house, and family on welfare. The strongest hindering risk factors were high marijuana use (OR = 5.9), running away (OR = 6.0), and high parental stress (OR = 6.0). Only two risk factors were replicated across middle and late childhood: high parental stress and living in a small house.

For all the hindering risk factors, higher scores predicted lower desistance. The one exception was family SES. When measured in middle childhood for the youngest cohort, the lowest level of desistance occurred for those youth who came from the middle 50% of the distribution of SES. In other words, the highest level of desistance occurred in the extreme highest 25% and the extreme lowest 25%. This is reminiscent of regression toward the mean, but the fact is that we did not find this for any other risk or mixed factor. It may be that high SES boys who become offenders are more persistent than medium SES boys who become offenders, even though high SES boys are less likely to offend in the first place.

We noted before that we did not find remedial promotive factors measured during middle and late childhood that were predictive of desistance by late adolescence for the youngest cohort. This also was true for hindering risk factors measured during childhood. Instead, several hindering risk factors measured later—that is, during early adolescence—were negatively predictive of desistance by late adolescence in either the youngest or the oldest cohort: several forms of substance use (high tobacco use, alcohol use, and marijuana use), and several forms of law breaking (high drug dealing, gang membership, and gun carrying). In addition, the following hindering risk factors were negatively predictive of desistance by late adolescence: high psychopathic features, low prosocial behavior, leaving home at an early age, and violence victimization. Among the family and peer factors, the following hindering risk factors predicted a low probability of desistance: one or no biological parents at home, high peer delinquency, and family on welfare. In summary, individual factors, two family factors, and one peer factor hindered desistance. However, none of the possible hindering risk factors among the school, parental child-rearing, or neighborhood variables significantly predicted desistance by late adolescence. Among the strongest predictors were high drug dealing (oldest cohort, OR = 8.1) and high peer delinquency (oldest cohort, OR = 4.6). Among the hindering risk factors that were replicated across the youngest and oldest cohorts were high alcohol use and high peer delinquency.

The final set of columns in Table 9.8 addresses hindering risk factors measured during early or late adolescence that were negatively predictive of desistance by early adulthood for the oldest cohort. Among the hindering risk factors in the form of deviant behavior were high alcohol use, high drug dealing, gang membership, and gun carrying. Among the individual factors were depressed mood, high anxiety, and violence victimization. Risk factors among the family conditions were one or no biological parents at home and father behavioral problems. High peer delinquency, bad neighborhood impression, young mother, and family/participant on welfare were also hindering risk factors. Thus, as for hindering risk factors negatively predictive of desistance in late adolescence, hindering risk factors predicting a low probability of desistance in adulthood were concentrated among individual factors, a few family factors, and peer factors. Again, none of the possible risk factors among the school variables and parental childrearing variables were significantly predictive of a low probability of desistance. Among the strongest predictors were gun carrying (OR = 3.4) and family on welfare (OR = 3.4). Several factors measured during early and late adolescence were replicated: high alcohol use, high drug dealing, gang membership, gun carrying, depressed mood, and high peer delinquency.

Are Promotive Factors More Common than Hindering
Risk Factors in Particular Age Blocks?
The results in Tables 9.7 and 9.8 show that almost twice as many hindering risk factors compared to remedial promotive factors measured during middle and late childhood predicted desistance in early adolescence in the youngest cohort (24 vs. 13). However, 13 out of the 24 factors were dichotomous, and for that reason were inherently defined as risk factors. Therefore, excluding dichotomous factors, there were as many protective factors as risk factors.

With regard to the prediction of desistance in late adolescence in the youngest and oldest cohorts, the results show that about an equal number of hindering risk and remedial promotive factors predicted desistance by late adolescence (15 vs. 16). In contrast, hindering risk factors outnumbered remedial promotive factors in the prediction of desistance by early adulthood in the oldest cohort (19 vs. 1). Thus, major shifts took place in the proportion and types of hindering risk and remedial promotive factors associated with later desistance between childhood and adulthood with combined remedial promotive and hindering risk factors being more common early in life and hindering risk factors predominating later.

How Far Is the Reach of Promotive and Risk Factors?

Do remedial promotive factors influence desistance over multiple age blocks of time rather than from one time period to the next? We define a "short reach" predictor as a predictor from one block to the next, but not over longer periods of time, while a "long reach" is defined as a predictor from one age block to the age block after the next age block. For the prediction of desistance in early adolescence for the youngest cohort, we found that the majority of all remedial promotive factors came from the immediately preceding age block (10) and fewer were long-reach predictors (3). Among the remedial promotive factors with a long reach, the following factors measured in middle childhood predicted desistance by early adolescence in the youngest cohort: low ADHD symptoms, good supervision, and low parental stress. Good supervision stood out in that it was the only predictor of desistance in early adolescence which was significant when measured during in middle childhood *and* late childhood.

Turning to the prediction of desistance by late adolescence, only proximal remedial promotive factors were predictive of desistance (results apply to the youngest cohort only). Finally, the reach of remedial promotive factors measured during early vesus late adolescence in the prediction of desistance by early adulthood could not be calculated because of the low number of remedial promotive factors during these periods.

In reviewing the risk factors, a similar question can be raised whether there were any risk factors that influenced desistance over multiple age blocks of time rather than from the preceding time period. For the youngest cohort, the majority of all hindering risk factors negatively predicting desistance in early adolescence came from the immediately preceding age block (17) and fewer (7) were long reach predictors of two age blocks. Among the risk factors with a long reach, the following factors measured in middle childhood predicted reduced desistance by early adolescence in the youngest cohort: high shyness/withdrawal, high parental stress, mother smoking during pregnancy, father behavioral problems, bad neighborhood (census), low family SES (in the inverse direction, which we discussed earlier), and small house. High parental stress stood out in that it was the only predictor of desistance in early adolescence over two age blocks: middle childhood and early adolescence.

Turning to the prediction of desistance in late adolescence for the youngest cohort, risk factors became manifest in the immediately preceding time window rather than earlier. For the oldest cohort, nine of the risk factors measured during early adolescence had a long reach in predicting reduced desistance by early adulthood. This compares to eight risk factors in late adolescence. Thus, as a general rule, proximal predictors of desistance prevailed, but we noted a few exceptions in which predictors of desistance operated over a longer time window.

How Do Factors Predicting Desistance Compare to Factors Predicting Offending?

We cannot assume that processes that predict desistance are just the inverse of processes predicting offending. Specifically, we need to know whether remedial promotive factors that predict desistance are the same as preventive promotive factors predicting low or nonserious offending. In the same way, we need to know whether hindering risk factors that predict a low probability of desistance are similar to aggravating risk factors predicting serious offending.

In Chapter 7 we examined which factors were mostly preventive promotive factors (i.e., predicting a low probability of violence or theft), aggravating risk factors (predicting a high probability of violence or theft), or mixed factors (i.e., predicting a low probability of violence or theft or a high probability of violence or theft). A comparison between preventive promotive factors predicting a low probability of serious offending in the general population and remedial promotive factors predictive of desistance from moderate and serious offending among known delinquents (Tables 7.1 and 9.7) shows that low ADHD was a dual promotive factor (with *dual* defined as predicting both a low probability of offending and desistance from offending), while high ADHD was never a risk factor. Other forms of low psychopathology that were dual promotive factors were low anxiety and low shyness/withdrawal behavior. Of the child competence variables, prosocial behavior was a dual promotive factor.

Among the family functioning factors, good supervision and low parental stress were both dual promotive factors. The results for parental stress were particularly strong with replication across different age blocks. Youths' involvement in family activities predicted a low probability of serious offending but was not a promotive factor predicting desistance. In contrast, good relationship with peers was a remedial promotive factor predicting desistance among known delinquents but was not a preventive promotive factor predicting a low probability of serious offending in the general population. Good neighborhood impression was a dual promotive factor.

In summary, there was substantial overlap between preventive promotive factors predicting a low probability of serious offending and remedial promotive factors predicting desistance from moderate/serious offending. This was remarkable for the following reasons: preventive promotive factors predicting a low probability of serious delinquency were investigated separately for serious violence and theft (Table 7.1), while remedial promotive factors predicting desistance were investigated for moderate to serious offending (combining violence and theft) because of the smaller group sizes. Statistical power was lower for the analyses predicting desistance than for the analyses predicting a low probability of serious delinquency. Also, preventive promotive factors predicting a low probability of serious offenses were examined in their ability to predict behavior in the next age block, and only maximally over three to four age blocks (oldest and youngest cohorts, respectively). In contrast, remedial promotive factors predicting desistance were examined against the criterion that the individual had to have committed either moderate or serious violence or theft, and had to desist from moderate to serious offending usually over one or two age blocks.

To what extent are aggravating risk factors that predict serious offending in the general population the same as risk factors hindering desistance? We will use the term *dual* to indicate those risk factors that predict both offending and lack of desistance. A comparison between Tables 7.1 and 9.8 shows that high truancy and running away were dual risk factors. All of the factors that we had defined a priori as risk factors (such as various forms of substance use, drug dealing, gang membership, and gun carrying) served the dual function of increasing the risk of serious offending and hindering desistance from moderate/serious forms of offending.

In summary, there were major shared features between promotive processes that promoted nondeviance early and desistance later in the delinquency career. Similarly, there were similarities between aggravating risk factors associated with increased serious offending later, and hindering risk factors that reduced desistance in moderate and serious offending.

Regression Analyses to Predict Desistance

Regression analyses were undertaken to address both proximal and more distal predictors of desistance from moderate/serious offending. For that reason, we included all factors that were statistically significant in the bivariate analyses irrespective of whether they were measured in the prior age block or in the previous age block. In the oldest cohort, we predicted intermediate desistance separately from late desistance (desistance during adulthood). The first step in the regression analyses was to run a regression separately for risk factors, followed by a separate regression analysis of remedial promotive factors. After that the regression analyses were rerun with hindering risk variables entered first, followed by remedial promotive variables (this allowed us to examine whether remedial promotive factors were strong enough to survive in the regression analyses once risk factors had been taken into account). Tobacco, alcohol, and marijuana use; drug dealing; gang membership; and gun carrying were considered correlates of offending and were run in a separate regression. The final regression combined the significant variables from the risk and promotive regression and from the regression of the correlates of offending. The first column in Tables 9.9 and 9.10 lists the significant values of the explanatory variables before the correlates were added. The last column gives the values after the correlates were added. We were unable to study interaction effects because of the small numbers of the groups to be analyzed.

Table 9.9 Logistic Regression of Hindering Risk and Remedial Promotive Factors Predicting Desistance from Moderate/Serious Offending (Youngest Cohort)

	Explanatory		*All Variables*	
	POR	*p*	*POR*	*p*
FACTORS PREDICTING DESISTANCE IN EARLY ADOLESCENCE*				
High Psychopathic Features (LC)	4.12	.043	4.12	.043
Low Perceived Likelihood of Getting Caught (LC)	5.32	.024	5.32	.024
Low Family Socioeconomic Status (MC)	0.14	.004	0.14	.004
Low Parental Stress (MC)	4.75	.026	4.75	.026
Good Housing Quality (LC)	6.07	.032	6.07	.032
FACTORS PREDICTING DESISTANCE IN LATE ADOLESCENCE				
High Peer Delinquency (EA)	2.40	.019	2.30	.029
High Tobacco Use (EA)			2.40	.019

Notes: POR = partial odds ratio; MC = middle childhood; LC = late childhood; EA = early adolescence. Promotive factors in **boldface**. To facilitate comparisons of the magnitude of risk and promotive factors, the odds ratios for promotive factors, normally ranging in value from 0 to 1, were rescaled to be larger than 1. *Values in columns 1 and 2 for desistance in early adolescence are the same as those in columns 3 and 4 because explanatory factors (such as gang membership, and gun carrying) were not measured in childhood, as they were highly uncommon.

Table 9.9 shows the logistic regression of factors predicting desistance from moderate and serious offending for the youngest cohort. Two remedial promotive factors predicted early desistance of moderate/serious offending—that is, desistance by early adolescence: low parental stress and good housing quality. Note, however, that medium family SES was associated with a decreased probability of desistance. Desistance by early adolescence was best predicted by several factors measured during middle childhood (low family SES and low parental stress) and several factors measured during late childhood (high psychopathic features, low perceived likelihood of getting caught, and good housing quality). None of the correlates (i.e., tobacco, alcohol, and marijuana use; drug dealing; gang membership; and gun carrying) entered the equation.

The number of predictors for the youngest cohort measured during middle and late childhood that predicted desistance by late adolescence with a significant OR or an OR at 2 or larger was lower than could be expected by our preestablished level of chance ($p = .10$). For that reason, we do not further report on these analyses and no regression analyses were undertaken for factors measured during middle and late childhood predicting desistance during early adolescence.

Table 9.10 Logistic Regression of Hindering Risk and Remedial Promotive Factors Predicting Desistance from Moderate/Serious Offending (Oldest Cohort)

	Explanatory		All Variables	
	POR	p	POR	p
FACTORS PREDICTING DESISTANCE IN LATE ADOLESCENCE				
High Peer Delinquency (EA)	4.18	.000	2.61	.015
Family on Welfare (EA)	2.79	.006	2.47	.022
High Drug Dealing (EA)	—	—	4.24	.007
High Alcohol Use (EA)	—	—	2.35	.044
FACTORS PREDICTING DESISTANCE IN EARLY ADULTHOOD				
Depression (EA)	2.44	.010	2.25	.022
Young Mother (EA)	2.11	.038	—	—
Family on Welfare (EA)	3.17	.001	3.00	.002
Gang Member (EA)	—	—	2.78	.028
Gun Carrying (LA)	—	—	2.50	.005

Notes: POR = partial odds ratio; EA = early adolescence; LA = late adolescence.

Of the variables measured in early adolescence that predicted desistance by late adolescence in the youngest cohort, high peer delinquency and high tobacco use stayed in the regression and predicted low probability of desistance.

In the oldest cohort (Table 9.10), logistic regression of risk and remedial promotive factors predicting desistance from moderate/serious offending in late adolescence showed that the following risk factors remained in the model: high peer delinquency, family on welfare, high drug dealing, and high alcohol use. Thus, for the oldest cohort, none of the remedial promotive factors predicted later desistance when risk factors were taken into account. In the same way, desistance in early adulthood was predicted by risk factors only: depression, family/participant on welfare, gang membership, and gun carrying. Again, no promotive factor contributed to the prediction.

In summary, the regression results partly reflect the bivariate results in that remedial promotive factors in combination with risk factors predicted early desistance, but intermediate and late desistance were predicted solely negatively by risk factors. The results probably reflect a developmental pattern in that with age and with the development of offending, risk factors are the most prominent influences on desistance from moderate and serious offending, with remedial promotive factors operating earlier in the developmental sequence, and not later. The results may also mean that the most crucial events that fosters desistance in late adolescence and early adulthood is the removal or decrease of risk factors. Examples are terminating contact with delinquent peers, cessation of drug dealing, quitting a gang, and stopping the carrying of a gun. In contrast, the enhancement of promotive factors together with the removal or reduction of risk factors may be the most optimal strategy for desistance at an earlier age. Admittedly, these speculations can only be buttressed by replication in other longitudinal studies and by systematic manipulation of promotive and risk processes in intervention studies.

Summary of Key Findings

To our knowledge this is the first study that has examined persistence in and desistance from moderate and serious offending from childhood through early adolescence.[1] The following is a brief summary of our key findings.

Persistence

- Almost one in five of the young serious offenders in each of the two cohorts became persistent serious offenders over a period of six or more years.
- A higher level of persistence of serious offending was found for those with an onset during late childhood, compared to those with an onset during middle childhood or those with an onset during early adolescence. Across the two cohorts, about one in five of the serious offenders with an onset early in life persisted in serious offending over the next 7–9 years.
- Four to five out of ten of the moderate-to-serious offenders early in life persisted in their offending over a period of about 7–9 years.

Desistance from Serious Offending

- One-fourth of the early-onset offenders who had committed serious offenses desisted in serious offending later on.
- Desistance processes operated from at least childhood onward and were documented throughout adolescence and early adulthood.
- Persistence in serious violence and theft was similar in the youngest cohort, but in the oldest cohort a higher percent of serious violent compared to serious theft offenders persisted in their offending.
- Across the two cohorts, however, at least half of the violent offenders desisted in their violence over time.

Desistance from Moderate Serious Offending

- The desistance rate was highest when offending was present in late childhood and desistance took place in late adolescence (48%), lower for desistance in early adolescence (15%), and slightly higher after onset in early adolescence in the oldest cohort (20% for desistance in late adolescence and 32% for desistance in early adulthood).

- Those youth who had committed both violence and theft were less likely to desist than those who had committed violence or theft only.
- Desistance rates varied between the youngest and oldest cohorts.
- A low rate of desistance during adolescence for a given cohort may be a foreboding that delinquents in that cohort will experience a longer and heightened delinquency career.

General Predictors of Desistance

In the introduction to this chapter we reviewed several models of desistance. The *dimensional model* posits that desisters are more likely to be those who in childhood scored moderately high on risk factors (including early antisocial behavior) and are not those youth who scored either very low or very high on risk factors (including early antisocial behavior). The *person-environment interaction model* emphasizes that the probability of desistance is dependent on the early characteristics of the child and the child's environment. The *life course model* emphasizes the impact of life events on the course of antisocial behavior, and posits that desisters tend to have high levels of early risk but are exposed to a favorable family context and social transitions later. Starting with the life events model, we could only test this in the oldest cohort. We did not find that living with a wife or a girlfriend or being in the military predicted desistance in offending. In addition, high job skills were also not predictive of desistance. Further, related characteristics such as good life skills, high family/participant SES, and family/participant not being on welfare were similarly not predictive of desistance. It should be noted, however, that the PYS is based on an enriched community sample of African American and Caucasian youth, with fewer of the African American than the Caucasian men getting married. In fact, ethnicity and population representativeness in the PYS sample differed in major ways from the sample of Caucasian delinquents and nondelinquent controls studied by Sampson and Laub (2001). Further, we have documented desistance from offending at a young age often years prior to the typical timing of life events such as marriage, employment, and military service, and our findings support the notion that factors other than life events are relevant to desistance occurring at a young age.

Given the remaining positive findings about predictors of desistance (Tables 8.7 and 8.8), the results lend more support to a dimensional and a person-environmental interaction model than to a life course model of desistance (see also Blokland & Nieuwbeerta, 2005 showing that life events such as marriage did not significantly decrease the conviction rate in a large Dutch sample; in addition, see Massoglia & Uggen, 2007). It is possible, however, that in later follow up assessments we may find more evidence of life events playing an important role.

Specific Predictors of Desistance

- Among the replicated remedial promotive factors were good supervision and low parental stress.
- Among the replicated risk factors that hinder desistance were high parental stress, living in a small house, high alcohol use, high drug dealing, gang membership, gun carrying, depressed mood, and high peer delinquency.
- Among the strongest hindering risk factors negatively predictive of desistance from offending at a young age were high psychopathic features and low perceived likelihood of getting caught, while at an older age this was high drug dealing.
- Among the strongest remedial promotive factors predictive of desistance at a young age were low parental stress and good housing quality. It still remains to be seen what the factors may be that connect good housing quality to desistance.

Factors Not Associated with Desistance

- Low levels of early misbehavior did not foster desistance. This applied to low physical aggression, low psychopathic features, and low truancy.
- Several forms of social competence (good life skills, high liking of adults, and high job skills) and social cognitions (high self-aspirations, negative attitude toward delinquency, and negative attitude toward substance use) did not predict desistance. This does not necessarily mean that social competence and skills are irrelevant to desistance, because we know from the intervention literature that social skills training can be effective in decreasing antisocial behavior and delinquency (Beelmann & Lösel, 2006). It is possible that our measurements did not capture those aspects of social skills and competence that are probably relevant for desistance from offending.
- Other variables that were not associated with desistance were ethnicity, fewer than two changes in caretaker before age 10, high parental aspirations for the youth, having an older mother, and the family not being on welfare.

General Findings on Predictors of Desistance

- There was a negative age gradient for remedial promotive factors: we found a larger number of remedial promotive factors measured during middle and late childhood (ages 7–12) predicting early desistance (by early adolescence, ages 13–16) than for the prediction of intermediate desistance (by late adolescence, ages 17–19) or late desistance (by early adulthood, ages 20–25).

- Hindering risk factors that negatively predicted desistance were found for early, intermediate, and late desistance.
- Regression analyses showed that remedial promotive factors contributed unique variance in the prediction of desistance from offending by late adolescence even when hindering risk factors in early adolescence were taken into account.
- Predictors measured during childhood were stronger for early desistance (i.e., by early adolescence) than for intermediate desistance (by late adolescence). Thus, desistance in the downslope of the age-crime curve was more difficult to predict on the basis of childhood factors than desistance occurring at earlier ages.
- There was considerable overlap between remedial promotive factors predicting desistance from moderate/serious offending and preventive promotive factors predicting a low probability of serious offending.
- There was also considerable overlap between hindering risk factors negatively associated with later desistance from moderate/serious offending and aggravating risk factors positively predicting serious offending.

Note

1. The results vary somewhat from an earlier report on desistance by Stouthamer-Loeber et al. (2004). The principal reason is that desistance in that study was defined differently. Desisters were classified as offenders who had been persistent serious offenders for more than 2 years in adolescence (ages 13–19), but who committed no delinquent acts during adulthood (ages 20–25).

Part IV
Conclusions

Ten
Conclusions and Policy Implications

ROLF LOEBER, DAVID P. FARRINGTON, MAGDA
STOUTHAMER-LOEBER, AND HELENE RASKIN WHITE

This volume has presented findings that are unique in the annals of criminology and clarify many delinquency career and explanatory parameters (see
Table 1.1 definitions in Chapter 1). We are not aware of any other longitudinal study that prospectively covers—with regular, uninterrupted measurements and low attrition—the age span 7–25 using two sizable cohorts of young
males. Thus, this study avoids potential bias resulting from often faulty retrospective recall, and instead uses biannual to annual reporting periods with
higher reliability of recall. Outcome measures included self-reports, reports
from caretakers and teachers, and official records of offending, which have
been combined into a measure of all-source offending, thereby compensat-
ing for the weaknesses of each source and also capitalizing on the strengths
of each. Predictor constructs in this study have been based mostly on multiple measurements from multiple informants (the youths, the parents, and,
where possible, teachers) thereby increasing their measurement and predictive validity. The longitudinal analyses have been undertaken in several complementary ways, thereby strengthening the overall results. The availability
of two age cohorts with a six-year age difference, together with the peaking of
community crime in Pittsburgh in the early 1990s, has allowed us to examine cohort differences in offending, a topic that has rarely been considered in
longitudinal studies on crime. Further, this study contributes to the literature on differences in delinquency career parameters depending on whether
reported delinquency, arrest, or conviction data are the foci of study. Also
for the first time, analyses that focus on the prediction of serious offending
have been based on an empirical demonstration of promotive, protective, and
risk factors as they operate from childhood through late adolescence. Notably,
this study's features make it possible to examine the extent to which several
current theories of crime apply to the two inner-city cohorts of young males
in this study. Finally, a great advantage of the study is that we could replicate
many of the findings between the youngest and oldest cohorts for the developmental period that they shared (ages 13–19) when serious offending increased

alongside gang membership, gun carrying, drug dealing, and various forms of substance use.

Examples of Linkages of the Present Results to Theories

The principal aim of this volume is to use longitudinal data to address important questions about offending and its putative causes from childhood to early adulthood. Thus, this volume does not aim to test particular theories or to develop a new theory of crime. However, the findings presented herein have direct bearing on many existing theories (see overviews in Cullen, Wright, & Blevins, 2006; Farrington, 2005; Thornberry & Krohn, 2003). To present a few examples:

- We did not find clear evidence for two separate life-course persistent and adolescent-limited groups of delinquents (Moffitt, 1993).
- In contrast to Laub and Sampson (2001), we found that early factors predicted desistance, and we did not find that life events such as having a wife or a girlfriend or being in the military predicted desistance from offending.
- Our results are concordant with bonding theories like those proposed by Hawkins's social development theory (Hawkins et al., 2003), which also emphasizes promotive factors.
- Our results are also concordant with Thornberry and Krohn's (2003) focus on bonding, and the importance of parenting, school problems, and peer delinquency.

Limitations

We will briefly discuss the limitations of this study and its analyses. Although we measured a very wide range of variables, there were several restrictions on the available measurements: (1) a measure of intelligence was available only for a portion of the participants (Koolhof et al., in press) and only academic achievement could be used as a proxy for intelligence; (2) we did not have a measure of moral reasoning or empathy, factors that are known to be associated with offending (Jolliffe & Farrington, 2004; Raaijmakers, Engels, & Van Hoof, 2005), but used several proxy measures such as attitude toward delinquency, attitude toward substance use, lack of guilt, and the perceived likelihood of getting caught for delinquent acts; and (3) we were not in the position to measure individuals' legal socialization defined as their perception of the legitimacy of law and legal institutions (Piquero et al., 2005).

The analyses for this book did not include biological factors. In a substudy on the youngest cohort undertaken in collaboration with Adrian Raine, we have measured cortisol, heart rate, electrodermal arousal, and EEG (Fung et al., 2005; Gatzke-Kopp, Raine, Loeber, Stouthamer-Loeber, & Steinhauer, 2002; Loeber, Pardini, Stouthamer-Loeber, & Raine, in press; McBurnett et al., 2005; Raine et al., 2005), but these measures could not be included in this volume because they are based on a reduced number of participants and would have decreased statistical power to study serious offending. Personality measures were taken in the middle cohort only (Caspi et al., 1992, 1994; John, Caspi, Robins, Moffitt, & Stouthamer-Loeber, 1994; Krueger, Caspi, Moffitt, White, & Stouthamer-Loeber, 1996), but since that cohort, with its relatively short and irregular follow-up, could not be included in this volume, personality constructs could not be covered here. This study does not attempt to clarify which "underlying" factors—such as impulsivity, sensation seeking, or neuro-cognitive impairments—could best explain serious offending. We agree with Rutter (2003) that there probably is no single temperamental or behavioral trait that can explain all forms of antisocial behavior. We should mention that a substudy to the middle cohort of the Pittsburgh Youth Study (PYS), initiated by Terrie Moffitt, focuses on an intensive assessment of neuropsychological aspects of impulsivity relevant to offending (Lynam et al., 2000; White, Moffitt et al., 1994). Also, recent analyses of the PYS data indicate that anxiety decreases especially between ages 10 and 15 (Hughes & Loeber, 2007; see also Muris, 2006), which can help to account for increases in daring, delinquent-type behaviors. In addition, episodic irritability in another, large sample tends to increase between ages 9 and 21 (Leibenluft, Cohen, Gorrindo, Brook, & Pine, 2006), which is likely to negatively affect interpersonal relations with parents and peers. Also, we were not in a position to measure social-cognitive mediators, which have been mostly related to aggression rather than nonaggressive forms of antisocial and delinquent behavior (Dodge & Pettit, 2003; Lochman & Wells, 2002; Loeber & Coie, 2001). Social-cognitive mediators often operate in certain settings where opportunities for the commission of offending are available. Because the assessments in the PYS were done with a large sample at biannual and annual intervals, we were not in a good position to study the situational and opportunity aspects of offending.

Molecular genetic factors (Rhee & Waldman, 2002) were not included in this volume, but we anticipate collecting such information in the near future. On the other hand, we included several indicators of family burden (some of which could be genetically based), such as parental alcohol problems, fathers' behavioral problems, and parent police contact. In addition, we are of the opinion that the present study is a necessary step to define the developmental aspects of the phenotype essential for future genetic studies that potentially can shed light on gene-environmental interactions (Moffitt, 2005). Further, brain imaging studies comparing violent individuals with controls in this study are currently underway (Pardini, 2007).

The impact of neighborhoods on individuals' lives and offending was measured through reports of parents' and later participants' perceptions of neighborhood quality, while we also used a neighborhood index of social disadvantage based on census information (Wikström & Loeber, 2000). Although later, as part of the Pittsburgh Girls Study, we used direct observations of neighborhood qualities (Wei, Hipwell, Pardini, Beyers, & Loeber, 2005), these were not available for the present study in time to be included in the present volume. We cannot claim that the set of neighborhood constructs used in this volume approximates collective community efficacy as measured, for example, by Sampson, Raudenbush, and Earls (1997). On the other hand, our measure of neighborhood advantage is predictive of a low probability of serious offending.

We would be the last ones to state that we know enough about the direction of causal effects over time. This book does not claim to differentiate between risk factors as markers and those risk factors that have a causal status (however, see our discussion below of African American ethnicity as a marker rather than as a risk factor). The differentiation between these categories of factors, as much as it is needed (Bunge, 2004; Gottlieb & Halpern, 2002; Hinshaw, 2002; Loeber & Farrington, in press; Rutter, 2003), would have made this volume very unwieldy. In addition, increasing evidence has been forthcoming about the reciprocal nature of disruptive (including probably delinquent) behavior and parent child-rearing practices (Patrick, Snyder, Schrepferman, & Snyder, 2005; Stattin & Kerr, 2000), and the reciprocity among victimization, exposure to violence, and delinquent offending (Bingenheimer, Brennan, & Earls, 2005; Lauritsen, 2003). Knowledge of the reciprocal processes would necessitate different analytic strategies, including tests of transactional models (Sameroff & MacKenzie, 2003), and cascade models of sequences of temporally related risk factors (Masten et al., 2005). Instead, our strategy to examine predictors of serious offending, including family processes, measured by age block had the advantage of aggregating measurements of, for example, parental supervision and physical punishment over several years, but precluded more fine-grained analyses of their reciprocal effects over time. However, the study data are enormously extensive and make it possible to address many of these issues in the future.

The study analyses can be criticized for focusing on trichotomized and dichotomized constructs (Preacher, Rucker, MacCallum, & Nicewander, 2005), but these types of analyses allowed us to concentrate on serious offenders, did not materially affect the results of regression analyses (Farrington & Loeber, 2000), and dealt with nonlinear effects for the identification of risk, promotive, and protective factors.

The time window of the study design restricted the analyses in that no prospective data were available prior to age 7 for the youngest cohort and prior to age 13 for the oldest cohort. Thus, we could not address the important question raised by Tremblay and Nagin (2005) about whether all aggression has its origins in the preschool period. For that reason, we could not investigate whether, among the delinquents emerging after the preschool period, there were relatively late starters in aggression or violence (Vitaro, Brengden, & Barker, 2006). Instead, our study makes a contribution by showing the course of aggression and violence from middle childhood through early adulthood. Another restriction of our study is right-hand censoring beyond age 25. Studies with longer follow-ups, such as the Cambridge Study on Delinquent Development, show that a proportion of offenders continue to offend after age 25 (the terminal date for the oldest cohort in this volume) and that desistance processes continue throughout the next decades (see recent trajectory analyses in Piquero, Farrington, & Blumstein 2007; see also Laub & Sampson, 2003). An extended follow-up of the youngest cohort is currently under way, while the further follow-up of the oldest cohort is being planned. Future analyses can benefit from studying desistance and deceleration in offense severity as processes rather than as dichotomies (Bushway, Piquero, Broidy, Cauffman, & Mazerolle, 2001; Bushway, Thornberry, & Krohn, 2003; Le Blanc & Loeber, 1998).

This volume focuses on the development of offending in young males and does not deal with young females. Our initial strategy with the PYS was to study large samples of males because we reasoned that we would need even larger sample sizes to study serious offending in females. About eight years ago we were able to start the Pittsburgh Girls Study (Hipwell et al., 2002). Its sample size of 2,451 girls and their parents makes this one of the largest studies on girls in the U.S. We plan to continue to assess them throughout adolescence and into early adulthood.

Key Findings

We now return to the key questions raised in Chapter 1.

Outcomes and Development

How High is the Prevalence and Frequency of Reported Violence and Theft in Inner-City Young Males? (Addressed in Chapters 4 and 5) A surprisingly high proportion of boys in the study committed homicide (about 2%) during the study period, and another 2% have been killed (Farrington, Loeber, Homish, & Stallings, in press; Loeber et al., 2005; Loeber, Lacourse & Homish, 2005). Homicide, however, is the tip of a much broader swell of violence. One in four boys in the youngest cohort and two out of five in the oldest cohort had committed serious violence by age 19. Similar figures apply to serious theft.

As expected, a higher proportion of young men committed less serious forms of violence and theft. Less serious forms of offending tended to occur prior to the onset of more serious forms, which supports the notion of escalation models of development of offending and the notion of developmental pathways (e.g., Loeber, Wung, et al. 1993). The probability of young men's escalation to more serious forms of offending was highest for the lower compared to the intermediate seriousness levels. About half of the young men who had committed minor theft progressed to moderate theft, in contrast to one-fifth to one-fourth of the men who had committed moderate theft or violence progressing to serious theft or violence. Thus, the probability of progression is inversely related to seriousness. The results lend support to the notion that a higher prevalence of moderately serious offending over time forewarns that more youth will escalate to serious offending.

The age-crime curve (prevalence and frequency) could be studied in both cohorts, albeit with some limitations due to different time windows of measurement. Our study is the first investigation of age-crime curves using complete prospective survey data. The onset of offending was gradual rather than in a dichotomized fashion as suggested by Moffitt's (1993) theory. The age-crime curve applied to both violence and theft (the exception was minor theft, which was already high during middle and late childhood). An early onset of offending was associated with persistence of offending. Unexpectedly, we also found that an onset of offending in late childhood, compared to an onset in middle childhood, was predictive of persistent offending.

How Common Are Arrest and Conviction for Violence and Theft for These Males? *(Addressed in Chapter 5)* One-fourth to one-third of the young men had been arrested for violence, but only one in seven was convicted for violence. One in three had been arrested for serious theft, and one in five was convicted for serious theft. Thus, the young men's arrests for delinquent acts imposed a considerable burden on the police, and a smaller—albeit still significant—burden on the justice system that processed offenders through conviction and later disposition (not detailed here). In the section on policy implications below, we will discuss the cost of offending during the juvenile years.

How Does Self-Reported Offending Compare with Arrest and Conviction Data? *(Addressed in Chapter 5)* The prevalence and duration of self-reported violence and arrest were very similar. However, the annual self-reported frequency of violence was three times higher that that of arrests for violence, indicating that two out of three incidents of violence escape the notice of the police.

The proportion of violence or theft that did not lead to either arrest or conviction was high. During early adolescence, proportionally more of the serious delinquent youth got away with these acts without arrest, but this proportion decreased in late adolescence.

How Common Is Persistent Serious Offending when Based on a Combination of Reported Offending and Conviction for Delinquent Acts? *(Addressed in Chapter 5)* We found that self-reported offending underestimated actual offending when conviction was also known. For that reason, we combined measures of reported offending and conviction in an all-source measure of offending. For the youngest cohort, just more than one-fourth (27%) committed serious violence/theft offenses during early adolescence (ages 13–16), after which the prevalence dropped to 13% during late adolescence (ages 17–19). In comparison, the results for the oldest cohort show that 40% of the boys were identified on the measure of all-source violence/theft during early adolescence, which decreased by half to 21% during early adulthood (ages 20–25).

How High Is the Persistence in Serious Offending? (Addressed in Chapter 8)   About one in five serious offenders who had an onset early in life persisted in offending over the next 7–9 years. Four to five out of ten of the moderate to serious offenders early in life persisted in their offending over a period of about 7–9 years. Thus, although the data identify a small group of persistent offenders over time, many of the early-onset offenders desisted at an early age (see more about desistance below).

How Common Are Substance Use, Drug Dealing, Gang Membership, and Gun Carrying, and How Do They Relate to Violence and Theft? (Addressed in Chapter 6)   There were major developmental differences between violence and theft compared to different forms of substance use. The inverted U-shape of the age-crime curve was not found for substance use, which tended to increase during the period in which violence and theft tended to decrease. This probably means that with age the number of substance users who did not engage in serious forms of offending increased (see also Loeber, 1988). The developmental pattern of drug dealing, gang membership, and gun carrying largely followed the developmental pattern of violence and theft, but gun carrying and drug dealing persisted longer and did not decrease in line with the age-crime curve for serious offending.

Hard drug use was more strongly related to theft than violence, suggesting that economic forms of crime to obtain goods and money to purchase drugs were more common than the notion that drug use creates more violence in exposed than nonexposed individuals. In contrast, drug dealing was related to violence but not to theft (see also Bennett, Holloway, & Farrington, in press).

To What Extent Are There Cohort Differences in Offending? (Addressed in Chapters 4, 5, and 6)   For the comparable age period 13–19, the oldest cohort had a higher prevalence and frequency of serious and less serious forms of offending than did the youngest cohort. The oldest cohort also had a longer onset window for serious offending, resulting in twice as many late-onset offenders. In terms of rate of change, the emergence of violence in the youngest cohort was faster, but the desistance from violence was also faster. The latter meant that the youngest cohort, appeared to outgrow offending at a faster rate.

When the all-source measure of offending was used as a criterion, the results showed that the oldest cohort had a higher persistence of offending than did the youngest cohort. More of the oldest cohort reported alcohol and hard drug use, but more of the youngest cohort reported marijuana use. In summary, more young males in the oldest cohort were involved in serious offending and related problem behaviors, but more of the youngest cohort engaged in marijuana use. There are additional cohort differences in developmental trajectories and in desistance, which we will review below.

How Much Are Gang Membership, Gun Carrying, Drug Dealing, and Substance Use Interrelated, and How Are They Related to Violence and Theft? (Addressed in Chapter 6) The different forms of problem behaviors were intercorrelated, but several specific associations stand out. Tobacco use predicted serious offending, but only at a young age. Alcohol and marijuana use predicted later violence, but alcohol rather than marijuana use appears to be more critical element in the explanation of violence (White, Loeber, Stouthamer-Loeber, & Farrington, 1999). Hard drug use was related to theft but not to violence, while drug dealing was related to violence and not to theft. Substance use, especially tobacco use in late childhood and early adolescence, predicted serious offending.

Are There Developmental Sequences among Substance Use, Drug Dealing, Gang Membership, Gun Carrying, and Violence and Theft? (Addressed in Chapter 6) The study shed light on several developmental sequences between problem behaviors and delinquent acts. Violent offending tended to precede rather than follow illegal drug use. Gang membership preceded the commission of serious offenses, which is also known from other studies (e.g., Battin-Pearson, Thornberry, Hawkins, & Krohn, 1998; Gordon et al, 2004; Thornberry, Krohn, Lizotte, Smith, & Tobin, 2003), but we found that the effect was stronger for the youngest compared to the oldest cohort.

The onset of gun carrying tended to follow rather than precede the onset of violence and theft for the oldest cohort, but this was not the case for boys in the youngest cohort, many of whom carried a gun prior to their first serious offense. The latter results fit a preemptive model in which carrying a gun creates protection but eventually increases offending for gang members. Overall, a higher proportion of the young males in the oldest cohort engaged in drug dealing and gun carrying in late adolescence, while a higher proportion of young males in the youngest cohort engaged in gun carrying and gang membership at a younger age. It appears that in the course of this study more boys armed themselves and formed gangs, possibly in anticipation of having to defend themselves from victimization by delinquent peers. This process was taking place at an earlier age for the youngest compared to the oldest cohort.

Are Violence and Theft Developmentally Distinct Offenses? (Addressed in Chapters 4, 5, 7, and 9) We found differences in the age-crime curve of reported violence and theft. The cumulative onset of theft tended to precede the onset of violence, but the decrease of violence and theft in the downslope of the age-crime curve tended to be more synchronous. Further, developmental sequences between the two showed that theft tended to precede violence, but the effect was larger for the youngest cohort than for the oldest cohort. For most periods, the frequency of theft was much higher than the frequency of violence. However, frequent theft was more common in the early part of criminal careers, where frequent violence became more common in the later part of criminal careers. We also found (using the all-source measure of offending) that the persistence of violence was higher in the younger cohort than that of theft in the oldest cohort, which as a group had a higher level of serious offending than did the youngest cohort. This agrees with the results of our trajectory analyses showing that desistance from theft tends to occur earlier than desistance from violence.

Persistence of violence and theft did not operate exactly in the same way. Whereas offenders with a childhood onset of violence and theft persisted to the same degree in violence and theft, offenders with an adolescent onset persisted longer in violence than theft.

To What Extent Is There Specialization in Violence or Serious Theft? (Addressed in Chapters 5 and 8) The topic of offense specialization continues to attract scholarly analyses, but is usually studied based on official records of offending rather than self-reports or a combination of both (Piquero, Farrington, & Blumstein, 2003, 2007). Using the all-source measure of offending based on reported delinquency and conviction, we found that whereas a substantial proportion of young offenders were versatile offenders in the sense that they committed both violence and theft, significant numbers were specialist offenders committing only theft or only violence. The results showed that one-half of the violent offenders were specialist offenders (that is, they did not commit serious theft), compared to one-third of the serious theft offenders (that is, they did not commit violent offenses). Information from the trajectory analyses also shed light on offenses specialization. Results on the co-occurrence of trajectories of violence and theft presented in Chapter 8 are in the same direction as the results on offense specialization reported in Chapter 5, showing more violence specialization than theft specialization. However, results presented in Chapter 9 on moderate/serious offending showed that compared to the violent offenders, twice as many of the theft offenders were specialized offenders. Thus, patterns of specialization in violence and theft much depended on the level of the severity of offenses.

Finally, desistance analyses on moderate/serious offenses (Chapter 9) indicated developmental trends from theft to violence for the oldest cohort, with the proportion of theft offenders decreasing between early adolescence and early adulthood, whereas the proportion of violent offenders remained stable throughout adolescence and decreased during early adolescence to a much lesser degree than was the case for serious theft offenders. These trends again support the notion that specialization may increase with age.

Can Cohort Differences Be Explained by Different Probabilities of Youths Progressing to Serious Offending? (Addressed in Chapter 4)   As noted, the oldest cohort committed more serious forms of offenses than did the youngest cohort. Since less serious forms of offending tend to precede more serious forms of offending, the key question is whether a proportion of youth involved in the earlier stages of delinquency constitutes a signal that a higher proportion of offenders will escalate to serious offending some time in the future. The results support the notion that once one cohort of young men has a higher prevalence of less serious forms of offending than another cohort, a higher proportion will progress to more serious forms of offending. This suggests that the forecasting of secular changes in serious forms of offending can in part be predicted by the volume of youth showing less serious forms of crime at an earlier age.

What Proportion of Young Males Desist from Serious Violence and Theft between Ages 10 and 25? (Addressed in Chapters 5 and 8)   The results show that desistance processes operate from at least late childhood onward, and were documented here throughout adolescence and early adulthood. The probability of desistance is inversely related to age of onset (particularly, onset in late childhood is negatively associated with later desistance). Nearly one-fourth of the early-onset offenders desisted in serious offending later, which supports the notion that early-onset offenders are a primary target group for preventive interventions (Farrington, Leober, Elliot, et al., 1990).

In Chapter 8, we identified some developmental trajectories showing desistance from violence and theft based on the all-source measure of offending for each of the cohorts. Desistance trajectories varied from desistance in late adolescence (youngest and oldest cohorts) to desistance in early adulthood (oldest cohort).

We have not yet examined life adjustment and life successes in the desister group. However, Farrington, Gallagher, Morley, St. Ledger, and West (1988), in the Cambridge Study on Delinquent Development, found that many unconvicted men from criminogenic backgrounds were isolated at age 32. At age 48, the desisters were similar to the unconvicted men in most measures of life success, but the desisters showed a higher use of alcohol and drugs (Farrington et al., 2006).

What Proportion of Young Males Desist from Moderate and Serious Offending between Ages 13 and 25? (Addressed in Chapter 9)   For reasons explained in Chapter 9, we also studied desistance from moderate *and* serious offending (based on reported offending and conviction data) after age 12. Again, we found that the desistance rate was highest when the onset of offending took place in middle childhood (55%), and lower after onset in late childhood (24%). Although based on a low number, this finding fits with increased predictability of offending in late compared to middle childhood, which we will review later. As found in many other studies (Farrington, Loeber & Elliott, et al., 1990; Loeber, 1982), the desistance rate increased (to 40%) when the onset of offending occurred in late adolescence. Those boys who had committed both violence and theft were less likely to desist than those who had committed violence or theft only. A low rate of desistance during adolescence for a given cohort may be a foreboding that delinquents in that cohort will experience a longer and heightened delinquency career.

Risk and Promotive Factors

In this volume we have made a distinction between two types of risk factors and two types of promotive factors. *Aggravating risk factors* are factors that predict a high probability of later offending and are distinguished from *hindering risk factors*, which are factors that negatively predict desistance and thus have a hindering influence on desistance from offending. *Preventive promotive factors* predict a low probability of later offending in the general population and, possibly, have a direct ameliorative effect on prosocial behavior, while *remedial promotive factors* predict desistance from offending in populations of known delinquents.

Which Variables Operate as Preventive Promotive Factors Only? (Addressed in Chapter 7) The results contradicted what we and other researchers had thought, and several factors formerly thought of as risk factors instead mainly operated as promotive factors. This means that rather than increasing the risk of serious offending, a low score on these factors was predictive of a low probability of serious offending. The following factors mostly had a promotive effect (and less of a risk effect): low ADHD, high persistence of discipline, low physical punishment, good supervision, youth involvement in family activities, and living in a good neighborhood. These results held across the two cohorts and across violence and theft.

Which Variables Operate as Aggravating Risk Factors Only? (Addressed in Chapter 7) Several factors had predominantly an aggravating risk effect (and less a preventive promotive effect), and these included low self-aspirations, a positive attitude toward delinquency, peer delinquency, and living in a large family. These results applied across the two cohorts, with the exception that peer delinquency was especially a risk factor in the oldest cohort.

Which Variables Operate as Both Risk and Promotive Factors? (Addressed in Chapter 7) Many factors had both risk and promotive effects, and these included psychopathic features, depressed mood, interaction with the interviewer, perceived likelihood of being caught, parental reinforcement, parent antisocial attitude, parent aspirations for the child, parent stress, peer delinquency, relationship with peers, academic achievement, attitude toward school, family socioeconomic status (SES), and housing quality. Most of these effects applied to the two cohorts (the exceptions were parental stress, peer delinquency, and housing quality, which applied to the youngest cohort) and applied across violence and theft (the exception was that psychopathic features were more a risk factor for violence than theft). The prediction analyses of trajectories (see Chapter 8) are important in that they illustrate the long-term predictive power of factors measured at age 7 (youngest cohort) and age 13 (oldest cohort) for delinquency trajectories over ages 10–19 (youngest cohort) and ages 13–25 (oldest cohort).

Are There Developmental Periods in Which Promotive Factors Predominate, and Are There Developmental Periods in Which Risk Factors Predominate? (Addressed in Chapter 7) Promotive effects had a greater effect at younger than at older ages. However, the number of significant predictors (both risk and promotive factors) for violence was higher when risk factors were measured during late childhood compared to middle childhood, which supports the notion that positive and negative criminogenic processes crystallize during the transition between middle and late childhood (ages 7–9 and 10–12, respectively). This finding qualifies the notion articulated by Fergusson, Horwood and Ridder (2005a, 2005b) that "show me the child at seven" forms the basis for predicting negative outcomes in adulthood. Keeping in mind the restriction in our data that the youngest cohort covered the age range 7–9, our results show that prediction is better when based on measures at ages 10–12 than at ages 7–9. It is not clear what the explanation is for this finding. The results fit with the finding we reported earlier that desistance rates are lower after onset at ages 10–12 than after onset at ages 7–9, suggesting more experimentation, and at a young age, and a higher crystallization of behavior in late childhood. However, we cannot exclude the possibility that the results reflect temperamental or personality changes (e.g., impulsivity or sensation seeking) from middle to late childhood, or an accrual of risk factors with age during that period.

Among the most consistent aggravating risk factors in bivariate analyses across age periods for both the youngest and oldest cohorts were peer delinquency, African American ethnicity (see, however, our discussion of this variable below), and having only one or no biological parents at home. In addition, the following aggravating risk factors were highly consistent across the period of childhood and early adolescence in the youngest cohort: high truancy, running away, a positive attitude toward delinquency, child maltreatment by age 12, and repeating a grade. Further, in the period of early to late adolescence, violence victimization was a consistent predictor of serious offending in the oldest cohort. Thus, the results support the notion that developmental changes in the accrual of aggravating risk factors operate in childhood and adolescence to influence the onset of serious offending (for more on this, see

Loeber, Slot, & Stouthamer-Loeber, 2006). In addition to a short-term effect, many of the risk factors have a far reach over many years.

Consistency across age periods was somewhat lower for preventive promotive factors than for aggravating risk factors. The following preventive promotive factors applied across the two age cohorts and across childhood and adolescence: good neighborhood impression and having an older mother. Low anxiety and low physical punishment during childhood and early adolescence were consistent preventive promotive factors for the youngest cohort, while a negative attitude toward delinquency was a consistent preventive promotive factor during adolescence for the oldest cohort. Thus, some changes took place over time in the unfolding of the most consistent preventive promotive factors predictive of a low probability of serious offending.

Is There an Association between Ethnicity and Offending? (Addressed in chapters 7, 8, and 9) More African American youth were involved in serious offending than were Caucasian youth. Although African American ethnicity emerged in several of the bivariate analyses predicting serious offending, none of the final regression analyses included African American ethnicity. In other words, once risk (and promotive factors) had been taken into account, African American ethnicity no longer contributed to the explanation of serious offending. Thus, in the predictions from one age block to another, African American ethnicity appears more a marker than a causal factor of serious offending (see also Huizinga et al., 2007). In fact, we found that Caucasian rather than African American ethnicity predicted theft in two out of the four regression analyses, indicating that young Caucasian males were *more* likely to commit theft than were young African American males.

The results on predictors of offense trajectories (Chapter 8), however, are somewhat contradictory with the preceding findings in that in bivariate analyses, African American ethnicity discriminated among different violent trajectories in the youngest and oldest cohorts, but not among different theft trajectories in both cohorts. Further, the logistic regression analyses showed that African American ethnicity was an independent predictor of violence trajectories in the oldest cohort only. Finally, the bivariate desistance analyses (Chapter 9) did not show that African American ethnicity was a predictor of desistance from moderate/serious offending in either the youngest or oldest cohorts.

In summary, all of the logistic regression analyses consistently showed that African American ethnicity, once other risk factors were known, did not play a role in the prediction of either violence or theft. In fact, the results show that Caucasian ethnicity was more related to theft. In addition, the desistance analyses show that African American ethnicity was not a hindering risk factor for desistance from offending. Only in the trajectory analyses did African American ethnicity remain predictive of violent trajectories, but this applied to one cohort only. Thus, overall the analyses lend meager support for the notion of African American ethnicity as a risk factor for delinquency career parameters. Instead, the results support the notion that a wide range of other risk and promotive factors collectively predict the probability of serious offending.

Are There Unique Predictors of Either Violence or Theft? (Addressed in Chapter 7) The regression analyses showed that there were only a few aggravating risk factors that were shared in the prediction of violence and theft (e.g., in the youngest cohort, high truancy in middle childhood, and peer delinquency in late childhood; in the oldest cohort, peer delinquency and gun carrying in late adolescence). The strongest predictors of violence were generally similar to the strongest predictors of theft at younger ages, but not at older ages. The results indicate many unique factors predictive of violence and unique factors predictive of theft. For example, gun carrying and the family being on welfare were the best predictors of violence, whereas child maltreatment, theft victimization, and Caucasian ethnicity were the best predictors of theft. Thus, the majority of the best predictors differentially predicted violence and theft. Among the unexpected results we found that child maltreatment predicted serious theft more strongly than violence, which contradicts some studies that found that child maltreatment was related to violence as well (see, e.g., Smith & Thornberry, 1995; Wekerle & Wolfe, 1998). However, this could be because our measure of child maltreatment included physical abuse and neglect.

We also found that different sets of promotive factors predicted a low probability of violence and theft. The most important promotive factors predicting a low probability of violence were high academic achievement, having an older mother, and a good relationship with peers. In contrast, the most important promotive factor predictive of a low probability of theft was low psychopathic features. The results from this volume lend further support to the evidence gathered by Loeber and Stouthamer-Loeber (1998) as to why a distinction should be made between violence and theft and between aggressive (overt) forms of disruptive behavior and nonaggressive (covert) forms of disruptive behavior. Since that review, several other studies have been published showing the utility of the distinction between aggressive (overt) and nonaggressive (covert) conduct problems (Barker et al., 2007; Eley, Lichtenstein, & Stevenson, 1999; Le Blanc & Bouthullier, 2003; Le Blanc & Kaspy, 1998; Patrick et al., 2005; Patterson, Shaw, Synder, & Yoerger, 2005; Sampson & Laub, 2003) and that the overlap between their trajectories between ages 9 and 16 is limited (Maughan, Pickles, Rowe, Costello, & Angold, 2000). However, not all experts are in agreement about whether different developmental pathways and differential patterns of causes apply for violence and theft, or whether a single pathway to serious delinquent behavior is the most useful assumption (e.g., Farrington, 1991; Patterson, 1982; Robins, 1966).

Which Types of Factors Predict Membership in Particular Offending Trajectories? (Addressed in Chapter 8) Factors predictive of offense trajectories were restricted to the first measurement prior to the trajectories (age 7 for the youngest cohort, and age 13 for the oldest cohort) so that the analyses could be truly predictive. The results show that risk and promotive factors each predicted offense trajectories. We will focus here on factors that were replicated across analyses. For example, having an older mother was the only shared promotive factors in the final model of multinomial regressions for high declining violence *and* theft trajectories for the youngest cohort. High academic achievement was a promotive factor uniquely predictive of a high declining violence trajectory, while good neighborhood was a unique promotive factor predictive of the high declining theft trajectory.

Turning to risk factors in the youngest cohort, the final multinomial regression model showed one or no biological parents in the household as the only shared risk factor across the high declining violence and theft trajectories. Running away was a unique risk factor for violence, while high parental stress was a risk factor for theft. In the final multinomial regression model for the oldest cohort, a negative attitude toward delinquency (marginal effect) and good supervision were promotive factors predictive of the high declining trajectory for violence, while good neighborhood was a marginal promotive factor predictive of the high declining trajectory for theft. In the oldest cohort, high truancy was the only shared risk factor for the high declining violence and theft trajectories. High psychopathic features and living with one or no biological parents were unique risk factors for violence, while low academic achievement and repeating a grade were unique risk factors for theft. In summary, a wide range of risk and promotive factors measured early life predicted subsequent offense trajectories. However, the results varied much by cohort.

Which Factors Predict Desistance from Serious Offending? (Addressed in Chapter 9) Among the replicated remedial promotive factors were good supervision and low parental stress. Among the replicated hindering risk factors that were predictive of a low probability of desistance were high parental stress, living in a small house, high alcohol use, high drug dealing, gang membership, gun carrying, depressed mood, and high peer delinquency. Thus, among the risk factors that hinder desistance from offending was high alcohol use (and to some extent, high marijuana use); this agrees with findings from several other studies (Hussong, Curran, Moffitt, Caspi, & Carrig, 2004; Schroeder, Giordano, & Cernkovich, 2007). Among our replicated findings are stressors as they affect parents and probably indirectly affect the behavioral adjustment of their children, which we will discuss below more in detail.

The results failed to show that risk or promotive factors measured in childhood predicted desistance from moderate/serious offending by late adolescence. We found also that several factors were not related to desistance.

324 • Violence and Serious Theft

For example, low forms of psychopathology (such as low physical aggression, low psychopathic features, and low truancy) did not predict desistance from offending. However, low ADHD symptoms and low shyness/withdrawn behavior predicted later desistance in two out of the three comparisons for the youngest cohort. Further, several forms of social competence (high life skills, high liking of adults, and high job skills) and social cognitions (high self-aspirations, negative attitude toward delinquency, and negative attitude toward substance use) also did not predict desistance. Other factors that were not associated with desistance were ethnicity, fewer than two changes in caretaker before age 10, high parental aspirations for the boy, having an older mother, and the family not being on welfare.

Are There Key Periods during Which Predictors of Desistance Operate? (Addressed in Chapter 9) There was a negative association between remedial protective factors and age: we found a larger number of protective factors for the prediction of early desistance (by early adolescence) than for the prediction of intermediate desistance (by late adolescence) or late desistance (by early adulthood). Regression analyses showed that remedial protective factors buffered the impact of hindering risk factors in early adolescence. Desistance in the downslope of the age-crime curve was more difficult to predict on the basis of childhood factors than desistance occurring at a younger age.

How Much Overlap Is There between Factors Positively or Negatively Predicting Later Serious Offending and Factors Predicting Desistance? (Addressed in Chapters 7 and 9) The results show that there was considerable overlap between remedial protective factors predicting desistance from moderate to serious offending and preventive promotive factors predicting nonoffending or nonserious offending. In addition, there was considerable overlap between hindering risk factors negatively associated with later desistance and aggravating risk factors positively predicting serious offending.

Other Key Issues Illustrated by the Results: Parental Child-Rearing Practices, Parental Stress, Peer Interactions, Deterrents and Constraints, and Neighborhoods

Parental Child-Rearing Practices and Youth Involvement in Family Activities

The findings shed much light on the role of parental child-rearing practices in their sons' offending. In Chapter 7 we noted that several forms of child rearing that we and other researchers formerly thought as risk factors actually operated as promotive factors. Thus, high persistence of discipline, low physical punishment, and good supervision were predictive of a low probability of serious offending rather than that these factors predicted serious offending (the only exception was parental reinforcement, which operated as a mixed factor). The finding that youth involvement in family activities mostly functioned as a promotive factor further reinforces the notion that positive parental behaviors and youth engagement with the family coalesce into a pattern of positive interactions that are probably characterized by positive problem solving and mutual bonding between parents and children.

Trajectory analyses provided further support for promotive factors in parents' child-rearing practices. In the oldest cohort, high persistence of discipline, good supervision, and youth involvement in family activities served as promotive factors negatively predicting several of the violence trajectories between ages 13 and 25 (however, results in the youngest cohort were nonsignificant). None of the risk ends of these family process factors (low persistence of discipline, poor supervision, and boy uninvolved) predicted the no/low violence trajectory in either the youngest and oldest cohorts, which strengthens the notion that promotive factors in the family are important elements to generate prosocial behavior in young people (judged as a low probability of serious offending). The results for theft, although nonsignificant and somewhat less consistent for the oldest cohort, were in the same direction. Four promotive factors—high persistence of discipline, high parental reinforcement, good supervision, and youth involvement in family activities—predicted no/low theft trajectory in the oldest cohort (compared to a single risk factor of low parental reinforcement predicting the late-onset and moderately declining trajectories).

We do not want to give the impression that only promotive factors in families matter. One of the consistent results was that child maltreatment—measured in terms of child abuse and neglect—was especially predictive of theft. Thus, these results lend further support to the notion that part of delinquency prevention consists of providing safe and nourishing family environments for children.

The importance of positive family interactions is further strengthened by findings on remedial promotive factors that predicted desistance from offending: good supervision, high parental reinforcement, and low physical punishment all "worked" in the same direction, albeit not fully consistently across all comparisons. However, in a few of the comparisons, high physical punishment and low persistence of discipline operated as risk factors hindering desistance. In summary, most of the findings lend much support for the beneficial influence of positive child-rearing practices to prevent the onset of serious delinquency and enhance desistance from offending among delinquent young men. These findings are highly relevant for optimizing interventions involving parents, a point to which we will return when discussing the policy implications of the findings.

Parental Stress

Family functioning should be viewed as being sensitive to stressors, which codetermine how children grow up. We have mentioned that parental stress was a mixed factor predictive of offending (low stress functioned as a promotive factor, while high stress functioned as a risk factor). Also we found that low parental stress was a predictor of desistance from offending.

Unfortunately, we did not gather information about the contribution of different forms of stressors that contribute to parents' feeling stressed, and instead inquired about their reactions, such as irritation, anger, coping, feeling in control, and the like. However, given the low SES of many of the parents in the study, it is likely that they experienced economic stressors. The findings lend tentative support to earlier research that economic and other forms of stressors negatively affect parents and the adjustment of their offspring (e.g., Conger et al., 1992; Conger, Conger, Matthews, & Elder, 1999; Costello, Compton, Keeler, & Angold, 2003; Hetherington, Bridges, & Insabella, 1998).

Peer Interactions

In contrast to positive parental child-rearing practices, peer interactions had a much more mixed effect on the boys' behavior, with high peer delinquency, poor relationship with peers, and poor relationship with siblings serving as risk factors for serious delinquency and low peer delinquency and good relationship with peers serving as promotive factors predicting a low probability of serious delinquency. Concentrating on the promotive factors, the results showed that low peer delinquency at age 7 predicted the no/low violence trajectory for the youngest cohort, while good relationship with peers at age 13 predicted the no/low violence and theft trajectories in the oldest cohort. Further, low peer delinquency and a good relationship with peers predicted desistance from moderate/serious offending in the youngest cohort. The higher number of peer findings for the youngest cohort at an early age, compared to the oldest cohort at a later age, suggest that positive peer influence may set the stage for the early absence of serious offending as well as early desistance from offending.

Deterrents and Constraints

One of key issues in criminology is what are deterrents and restraints toward recidivism. Although this volume does not deal directly with deterrents in the justice system, our findings shed some light on how young men perceive the probability of their being caught for offending and whether that influences future offending. The findings in this volume extend our earlier work (Zhang, Loeber, & Stouthamer-Loeber, 1997) showing that cognitions such as attitudes favorable to delinquency are among the predictors of future offending.

In Chapter 7 we found that the perception of the likelihood of being caught for offending was a mixed factor in that low perceived likelihood was predictive of future serious delinquency, while high perceived likelihood was predictive of a low probability of serious delinquency, but this was when it was measured in late childhood or early adolescence rather than late adolescence. The perceived likelihood of getting caught did not consistently predict individuals' trajectories of violence or theft. However, there was some—albeit not consistent—evidence that the perception of high likelihood of getting caught was a predictor of desistance from moderate/serious offending in both cohorts. The results lend modest support for the deterrent function of individuals' perceptions that they might be caught for delinquent acts. The process by which this takes place needs further investigation—particularly the deterrent effects of being processed in the court, the nature of sanctions, or witnessing the consequences of delinquency by peers.

Neighborhood

Delinquency and crime tends to be concentrated in disadvantaged neighborhoods, and this is also the case in Pittsburgh. What more did we learn from the results on neighborhoods in this volume? Contrary to expectations, we found that the promotive effects of neighborhoods were stronger than their risk effects in predicting future serious violence or theft. This was true for neighborhoods measured by means of census information, but also by means of parental impressions. Specifically, participants' living in a good neighborhood was a preventive promotive factor predicting a low probability of serious delinquency, and this applied across violence and theft, and across the youngest and oldest cohorts. We also know from the PYS that late-onset offenders are more common in the most disadvantaged neighborhoods than in the advantaged neighborhoods (Wikström & Loeber, 2000), which further strengthens the notion for the protective side of good neighborhoods.

We think the impact of living in a good neighborhood derives from it being correlated with other promotive factors, and that the aggregate of these positive factors constitutes a counterweight to the presence of risk factors. This agrees with our finding that neighborhood factors, once other factors were taken into account, did not contribute to the results of all the regression analyses on violence and theft. Therefore, neighborhood factors may have only indirect effects on violence through their effects on individual, family, and peer factors.

The above results need two qualifications: (1) in the violence trajectory analyses (Chapter 8), neighborhood was, for the youngest and oldest cohorts, a mixed factor having both promotive and risk effects. The same was found for theft trajectories in the youngest and oldest cohorts. Regression analyses on violence showed that once other risk factors were known, neighborhood no longer contributed to the prediction of violence. However, regression analyses on theft showed that for the youngest cohort neighborhood remained a promotive factor predicting a low likelihood of theft. Finally, the desistance analyses (Chapter 9) showed that good neighborhood impressions were a remedial promotive factor for desistance from moderate/serious delinquency by late childhood (ages 10–12) and early adolescence (ages 13–16) in the youngest cohort, but acted as an aggravating risk factor that predicted a low probability of desistance in early adulthood (ages 20–25) in the oldest cohort. In summary, the results reveal that neighborhood operated as a promotive factor predicting a low probability of violence and theft, but the trajectory and the desistance analyses showed that neighborhood factors operated more as mixed promotive and risk factors. Analyses currently underway focus on individuals' moving from one neighborhood to another so that we can better establish whether neighborhood quality has an effect on within-individual changes in offending over time.

Research Questions for the Future

The current volume cannot be all-encompassing and tackle all questions that might be addressed in the PYS data set. Examples of important questions that remain are:

- What transitions are important between middle and late childhood that influence the emergence of an early-onset group of boys who are at greatest risk to become serious delinquents later?
- What explains how risk factors work together (Kraemer, 2003), and how promotive factors work together? Relatedly, what are mediating and moderating processes that influence the accumulation of risk factors for later serious offending?
- What more needs to be learned about within-individual causes of offending?
- Which mental health problems are relevant for persistent offending, and are there mental health problems that function as preventive promotive factors predictive of a low probability of serious delinquency or remedial promotive factors predictive of desistance?
- Are there individuals whose aggression decreases during the pre-school years, but who relapse with high levels of aggression later and become violent offenders?
- Which additional predictors of desistance from serious offending should be included in future studies?
- What is the impact of moving from a low-SES or high-crime neighborhood to a high-SES or a low-crime neighborhood on individuals' rate of offending? Are some categories of offenders more sensitive to such a move than other types of offenders?
- Do later life events, such as marriage and becoming unemployed, affect individuals' subsequent offending?
- Which factors determine the residual career length (Kazemian & Farrington, 2006)?
- Which factors influence the downslope of the age-crime curve?
- What are the predictors of late-onset offending?

- What are the causes of period effects that probably contributed to cohort differences in offending (Fabio et al., 2006)?
- What are the characteristics of offenders who are least likely to outgrow age-normative offending?
- Which experimental studies best complement longitudinal studies to narrow down causes among risk factors (e.g., Loeber & Farrington, in press)?

Finally, the PYS data set has a larger number of measures than could be included in this volume. These and other measures will make it possible to undertake numerous innovative analyses in the future.

Policy Implications

The Cost of Crime

Earlier studies on the cost of offending have been based on official records only (Cohen, 1998, 2000). In contrast, Welsh et al. (in press), using data from 503 young men in the youngest cohort in the PYS, are the first to examine the costs of self-reported offending between ages 7 and 17. Juvenile delinquency by the young men in the youngest cohort caused a substantial burden of harm on citizens in our society through victim costs, with the estimate ranging from a low of $89 to a high of $110 million. Most of the costs of offending derive from violent as opposed to property offenses. The authors also found that the costs of early-onset offenders were much higher than that of later-onset offenders, while chronic offenders (those accounting for half of all self-reported offenses), compared to other offenders, caused five to eight times higher average victim costs. Given the much higher rate of offending in the oldest cohort of the PYS, the cost for society must have been much higher than that caused by the youngest cohort. Data presented in this volume make it clear that offending for a proportion of young men was not limited to the juvenile years, but extended into early adulthood, which undoubtedly further increased the total cost of their offending. In summary, the cost data from the PYS, even when based on the youngest cohort who were least involved in offending, is highly relevant for policy makers, because the costs of offending are often hidden, and for that reason its implications for policy are not sufficiently drawn. Both early-onset and chronic offenders are target groups that deserve more attention by policy makers and experts in the justice system.

Interventions

Many of the PYS participants with behavioral and mental health problems did not receive services or only had contact once or twice with service providers (Stouthamer-Loeber & Loeber, 2002). For these reasons, we need to examine the relevance of the findings for future interventions. One of the best integrated statements about crime, its causes, and interventions is

Howell and Wilson's Comprehensive Strategy (Howell, 2003). Developed at the U.S. Office of Juvenile Justice and Delinquency Prevention in the 1990s, the Comprehensive Strategy has the following principles: (1) strengthen the family in its primary responsibility to instill moral values and provide guidance and support for children; (2) support "core" social institutions, schools, religious institutions, and community organizations in their role of developing capable, mature, and responsible youth; (3) promote delinquency prevention as the most cost-effective approach to reducing juvenile delinquency; (4) intervene immediately and effectively when delinquent behavior occurs to successfully prevent delinquent offenders from becoming chronic offenders committing more serious and violent offenses; and (5) identify and control the small group of serious, violent and chronic juvenile offenders who have committed felony offenses or have failed to respond to intervention with non-secure, community-based treatment and rehabilitation services offered by the juvenile justice system (Howell, 2003, pp. 220–221).

Among the many findings in this volume, the following aspects mentioned in the Comprehensive Strategy warrant attention:

1. *Strengthen the family in its primary responsibility to instill moral values and provide guidance and support for children.* The present study provides strong support for factors in the family that can stimulate serious offending, promote a low probability of serious offending, and promote desistance from offending. Particularly, good supervision, no physical punishment, and high persistence of discipline emerged as important factors predicting a low probability of serious offending. Of these family child-rearing processes, good supervision was also predictive of desistance from serious offending. Probably, the key to all of this is the maintenance of positive contacts between parents and children, even if misbehavior and delinquency occurs. This is supported by the finding that youth's high involvement in family activities predicts a low probability of serious offending. Our results are in line with findings from several studies (see, e.g., Crosnoe, Erickson, & Dornbusch, 2002; Gorman-Smith, Henry, & Tolan, 2004). For example, Gorman-Smith et al. (2004) have shown that youth exposed to high levels of community violence but living in families that functioned well in terms of parenting and family relationships committed less violence than similarly exposed youth from less-well functioning families. Our results thus strengthen the rationale for family interventions aimed at improving parents' child-rearing practices and positive interchanges between parents and children (see, e.g., Farrington & Welsh, 2003, 2007; Patterson, 1982). Another finding from the current study—that low family stress predicts a low probability of serious offending and that high family stress predicts

a low probability of desistance—supports the notion that parents' child-rearing practices (and family functioning as whole) can be impaired in the face of the stressors of everyday life. Thus, strengthening of families in the spirit of the Comprehensive Strategy may also be achieved by reducing stressors or, possibly, by improvements in coping skills to better deal with stressors.

2. *Support "core" social institutions, schools, religious institutions, and community organizations in their role of developing capable, mature, and responsible youth.* The present study does not address how religious and community organizations encourage positive, nondelinquent development. However, our results lend considerable support to school experiences that can fuel or discourage serious offending. Specifically, academic achievement and boys' attitude toward school functioned as mixed factors—that is, low academic performance and a negative attitude toward school increased the risk of serious offending while high academic performance and a positive attitude toward school predicted a low probability of serious offending. Creating environments in schools that encourage academic competence and success (especially for those youth with ADHD problems or those with low intelligence) is known to be effective in reducing aggression (Kellam, Rebok, Ialongo, & Mayer, 1994) and is likely to reduce truancy and co-offending with peers.

Our study results indirectly lend support to community and neighborhood approaches (in contrast to individual approaches) to crime reduction. Our results show that theft victimization was predictive of serious theft later. Reduction of victimization in the community is certainly a key aspect of reducing both individual offending as well as reducing community levels of crime, improving the safety of people and goods, enhancing the livability of neighborhoods, and laying the foundation for economic enterprise. Along that line, the study supports the notion that living in an advantaged neighborhood inhibits the development of serious offending. From other analyses on the PYS data, we also know that late-onset serious offenders tend to emerge more in disadvantaged neighborhoods (Wikström & Loeber, 2000).

3. *Promote delinquency prevention as the most cost-effective approach to reducing juvenile offending.* The present study could not directly ascertain the cost-effectiveness of prevention approaches. However, the study results lend considerable support to preventive interventions, and provide "new ammunition" for such approaches. The increased probability of later serious offending for problem boys in late (ages 10–12) as compared to middle childhood (7–9) indicates that preventive efforts should especially focus on the former group.

This notion is reinforced by the finding that predictors of serious offending appear stronger in late compared to middle childhood. Although there are sophisticated screening instruments to identify youth at risk (e.g., Augimeri et al., 2001), there is a need for the next generation of screening instruments to be based on knowledge of risk and promotive factors, to better articulate strengths and deficiencies in youth behavior, and promotive and risk factors that youth are exposed to in their social environment. Because of the evolving risk patterns with development, screening needs to be done at multiple time points between childhood and adolescence rather than at a single point in time.

4. *Intervene immediately and effectively when delinquent behavior occurs to successfully prevent delinquent offenders from becoming chronic offenders and perhaps progressively committing more serious and violent offenses.* This volume and a report by Farrington, Jolliffe, Loeber, & Homish (2007) shed new light on the proportion of offenses that lead to contact with the police and the court. Comparisons between reported offending and arrest showed that the probability of arrest following offending in early adolescence is lower than in late adolescence. This study did not reveal whether young offenders were caught more by the police and let go without arrest, but the question needs to be raised as to whether changes in police response to early offenders would curtail individuals' criminal careers and reduce community levels of crime. We certainly do not advocate increasing arrest and conviction. This study has documented the relatively high prevalence of gun carrying among the young men in the PYS. For the youngest cohort, gun carrying peaked at 8% at age 16, and was as high as 6.5% at age 17. Gun carrying was twice as common in the oldest cohort, with the annual prevalence rate of gun carrying by age 17 at 11%. Gun ownership by minors is clearly illegal, and since gun-carrying juveniles, especially those engaged in illegal activities, are a threat to public safety, this poses a major challenge to policy makers and to the police. How do we get guns out of the hands of minors, and can we manage to reduce violent crime through gun reduction programs?

5. *Identify and control the small group of serious, violent and chronic juvenile offenders who have committed felony offenses or have failed to respond to intervention and nonsecure, community-based treatment and rehabilitation services offered by the juvenile justice system.* Earlier reviews of this topic have focused on, among others, early-onset offenders who appear at highest risk for serious offending (see, e.g., Farrington, Loeber, Elliott, et al., 1990; Loeber & Farrington, 2001). This study supports such a focus, but also provides evidence

that a substantial proportion of late-onset offenders become serious offenders.

The present study results are also relevant to policy in several other ways:

- The study illustrates that developmental trajectories can start at approximately the same level, but subsequently unfold in different directions (see, e.g., Figure 8.3). The results show very imperfect predictions of which offense trajectory individuals will follow over time. We agree with Piquero (in press) that, nevertheless, there is a danger that policy makers will start to use less than good predictions as a rationale for harsh punishment and severe legal sanctions. The data presented in this volume in no way support such a policy.

- The finding that violence and theft differ in their development and in terms of risk and promotive factors has implications for optimizing interventions, because we cannot assume that all causes of violence are also causes of theft. This is particularly important in light of the evidence presented in this book about the large proportion of offenders who specialize either in violence or theft.

- This volume is a major departure from most of the current literature and makes a case that knowledge of promotive factors in addition to risk factors adds substantially to the prediction of serious offending. The results show that many of the identified promotive factors are potentially modifiable. Currently, many interventions already use techniques to enhance positive factors in youth's lives. The introduction of empirically based promotive factors into interventions and optimizing intervention efficacy has high urgency.

- Often, discussions about desistance processes have focused on adolescence-limited offenders (Moffitt, 1993). This volume shows that desistance processes operate from childhood onward. A major policy implication is to focus more on factors that promote desistance from childhood onward.

- The higher rate of violence in the oldest cohort, compared to the youngest cohort, can in part be explained by the higher rate of moderate violence earlier in the life of the young men in that cohort. Thus, one of the entry points for controlling the level of community crime is a focus on precursor stages of violence as known from earlier steps in the overt pathway leading to violence (Loeber, Wung, et al., 1993).

- Finally, the time is ripe to implement the next generation of prevention initiatives based on a larger range of risk *and* promotive factors than currently included in intervention programs so that favorable outcomes will be enhanced for current and future generations of youth. In addition, the findings from this volume make a case that interventions should not just be aimed at reducing offending in individuals, but also at reducing offending in populations of youth. Particularly needed are intervention strategies that reduce the height and length of the age-crime curve for successive age cohorts and reduce offenders' residual career length (Kazemian & Farrington, 2006), because such changes are likely to reduce crime waves in communities.

Early Surveillance Systems

The results represented in this volume on developmental sequences in offending and other problem behaviors illustrate that, on the whole, individuals who commit serious offenses have also committed less serious offenses earlier in life. We also found that early onset, compared to late onset, of offending is a predictor of later serious offending and a longer delinquency career. The results also indicate that late-onset offending accounts for some cohorts becoming much more involved in offending than other age cohorts. Further, the findings support the notion that cohorts differ in their rate of outgrowing delinquency, thereby causing disproportionate harm to others and society. Relatively low rates of desistance in adolescence for a given cohort signal that delinquents in that cohort will experience a longer and heightened delinquency career. The four aspects have implications for what needs to be tracked in offense surveillance systems that are relevant for anticipating cohort changes in offending rates, and relatedly, future changes in community crime rates:

1. The proportion of the youth population that starts offending before age 12 (tracking early-onset offenders).
2. The proportion of the youth population who are late-onset offenders.
3. The proportion of the youth population who commits less serious offenses and is at risk of escalating to serious offenses.
4. The proportion of the youth population that does not outgrow delinquency at an age when other age cohorts are known to outgrow such behaviors.

In short, we advocate the need for regular, preferably yearly, surveillance systems of communities on a local level (preferably at the neighborhood level) that can help to identify and follow youth with early problem behaviors. In addition, such surveillance systems could fruitfully monitor yearly changes in known key risk and promotive factors that are positively or negatively predictive of serious offending.

Appendix:
Publications from the
Pittsburgh Youth Study

The Pittsburgh Youth Study website, at http://www.wpic.pitt.edu/research/ famhist/PYS.htm, contains many of the actual articles and chapters. The full text of publications sponsored by the U.S. Department of Justice's Office of Juvenile Justice and Delinquency Prevention can be found at http://www. ojjdp.ncjrs.org/publications/index.html.

Books

Loeber, R., Farrington, D. P., Stouthamer-Loeber, M., & Van Kammen, W. B. (1998). *Antisocial Behavior and Mental Health Problems: Explanatory Factors in Childhood and Adolescence.* Mahwah, NJ: Erlbaum.

Stouthamer-Loeber, M., & Van Kammen, W. B. (1995). *Data Collection and Management: A Practical Guide.* Newbury Park, CA: Sage.

Articles and Reports

The following articles and reports are listed by primary category; however, one article or report may in fact fit in several different categories.

General Overviews

Browning, K., Huizinga, D., Loeber, R., & Thornberry, T. P. (1999, April). *Causes and correlates of delinquency program.* (OJJDP Fact Sheet) Washington, DC: U.S. Department of Justice, Office of Juvenile Justice and Delinquency Prevention.

Browning, K., & Loeber, R. (1999, February). *Highlights of findings from the Pittsburgh Youth Study.* (OJJDP Fact Sheet No. 95.) Washington, DC: U.S. Department of Justice, Office of Juvenile Justice and Delinquency Prevention.

Loeber, R., Farrington, D. P., Stouthamer-Loeber, M., Moffitt, T. E., & Caspi, A. (1998). The development of male offending: Key findings from the first decade of the Pittsburgh Youth Study. *Studies in Crime and Crime Prevention, 7,* 141–172.

Loeber, R., Farrington, D. P., Stouthamer-Loeber, M., Moffitt, T. E., Caspi, A., & Lynam, D. (2001). Male mental health problems, psychopathy and personality traits: Key findings from the first 14 years of the Pittsburgh Youth Study. *Clinical Child and Family Psychology Review, 4,* 273–297.

Loeber, R., Farrington, D. P., Stouthamer-Loeber, M., Moffitt, T. E., Caspi, A., White, H. R., Wei, E. H., & Beyers, J. M. (2003). The development of male offending: Key findings from fourteen years of the Pittsburgh Youth Study. In T. Thornberry & M. Krohn (Eds.), *Taking stock of delinquency: An overview of findings from contemporary longitudinal studies* (pp. 93–136). New York: Kluwer/Plenum.

Loeber, R., Stouthamer-Loeber, M., Farrington, D. P., Lahey, B. B., Keenan, K., & White, H. R. (2002). Editorial introduction: Three longitudinal studies of children's development in Pittsburgh: The Developmental Trends Study, the Pittsburgh Youth Study, and the Pittsburgh Girls Study. *Criminal Behaviour and Mental Health, 12*, 1–23.

Thornberry, T. P., Huizinga, D., & Loeber, R. (2004). The Causes and Correlates Studies: Findings and policy implications. *Journal of the Office of Juvenile Justice and Delinquency Prevention, 9*(1), 3–19.

Academic Achievement

Lynam, D., Moffitt, T., & Stouthamer-Loeber, M. (1993). Explaining the relation between IQ and delinquency: Class, race, test motivation, school failure or self-control? *Journal of Abnormal Psychology, 102*, 187–196.

Maguin, E., & Loeber, R. (1996). Academic performance and delinquency. In M. Tonry (Ed.), *Crime and justice: An annual review of research, Vol. 20* (pp. 145–264). Chicago: University of Chicago Press.

Maguin, E., Loeber, R., & LeMahieu, P. (1993). Does the relationship between poor reading and delinquency hold for different age and ethnic groups? *Journal of Emotional and Behavioral Disorders, 1*, 88–100.

Maughan, B., Rowe, R., Loeber, R., & Stouthamer-Loeber, M. (2003). Reading problems and depressed mood. *Journal of Abnormal Child Psychology, 31*, 219–229.

Antisocial Personality Disorder and Psychopathy

Fabrega, H., Ulrick, R., & Loeber, R. (1996). Adolescent psychopathology as a function of informant and risk status. *Journal of Nervous and Mental Disease, 184*, 27–34.

Lynam, D. (1997). Pursuing the psychopath: Capturing the fledgling psychopath in a nomological net. *Journal of Abnormal Psychology, 106*, 425–438.

Lynam, D. R., Caspi, A., Moffitt, T. E., Loeber, R., & Stouthamer-Loeber, M. (2006). Longitudinal evidence that psychopathy scores in early adolescence predict adult psychopathy. *Journal of Abnormal Psychology, 116*, 155–165.

Lynam, D. R., Caspi, A., Moffitt, T. E., Raine, A., Loeber, R., & Stouthamer-Loeber, M. (2005). Adolescent psychopathy and the big five: Results from two samples. *Journal of Abnormal Child Psychology, 33*, 431–443.

Lynam, D. R., Derefinko, K. J., Caspi, A., Loeber, R., & Stouthamer-Loeber, M. (in press). The content validity of juvenile psychopathy: An empirical examination. *Psychological Assessment.*

Obradović, J., Pardini, D., Long, J. L., & Loeber, R. (in press). Measuring interpersonal callousness in boys from childhood to adolescence: An examination of longitudinal invariance and temporal stability. *Journal of Clinical Child and Adolescent Psychology.*

Pardini, D., & Loeber, R. (in press). Interpersonal callousness trajectories across adolescence: Early social influences and adult outcomes. *Criminal Justice and Behavior.*

Anxiety, Depression, and Internalizing Problems

Angold, A., Erklani, A., Loeber, R., Costello, E. J., Van Kammen, W., & Stouthamer-Loeber, M. (1996). Disappearing depression in a population sample of boys. *Journal of Emotional and Behavioral Disorders, 4*, 95–104.

Loeber, R., Russo, M. F., Stouthamer-Loeber, M., & Lahey, B. B. (1994). Internalizing problems and their relation to the development of disruptive behaviors in adolescence. *Journal of Research on Adolescence, 4*, 615–637. Reprinted in G. A. Adams (Ed.). (2000). *Adolescent Development: The Essential Readings* (275–298). Oxford, England: Blackwell.

Biological Factors

Fung, M. T., Raine, A., Loeber, R., Lynam, D. R., Steinhauer, S. R., Venables, P. H., & Stouthamer-Loeber, M. (2005). Reduced electrodermal activity in psychopathy-prone adolescents. *Journal of Abnormal Psychology, 114*, 187–196.

Gatzke-Kopp, L. M., Raine, A., Loeber, R., Stouthamer-Loeber, M., & Steinhauer, S. (2002). Serious delinquent behavior, sensation-seeking and electrodermal arousal. *Journal of Abnormal Child Psychology, 30*, 477–486.

McBurnett, K., Lahey, B. B., Raine, A., Stouthamer-Loeber, M., Loeber, R., Kumar, A., Kumar, M., Moffitt, T., & Caspi, A. (2005). Mood and hormone responses to psychological challenge in adolescent males with conduct problems. *Biological Psychiatry, 57*, 1109–1116.

Raine, A., Moffitt, T. E., Caspi, A., Loeber, R., Stouthamer-Loeber, M., & Lynam, D. (2005). Neurocognitive impairments in boys on the life-course persistent antisocial path. *Journal of Abnormal Psychology, 114*, 38–49.

Wakschlag, L. S., Pickett, K. E., Kasza, K. E., & Loeber, R. (2006). Is maternal smoking during pregnancy associated with a developmental pattern of conduct problems in young boys? *Journal of the American Academy of Child and Adolescent Psychiatry, 45*, 461–467.

Child Abuse

Stouthamer-Loeber, M., Loeber, R., Homish, D. L., & Wei, E. (2001). Maltreatment of boys and the development of disruptive and delinquent behavior. *Development and Psychopathology, 13*, 941–955.

Stouthamer-Loeber, M., Wei, E., Homish, D. L., & Loeber, R. (2002). Which family and demographic factors are related to both maltreatment and persistent serious delinquency? *Children's Services: Social Policy, Research, and Practice, 5*, 261–272.

Comorbidity

Huizinga, D., Loeber, R., Thornberry, T. P., & Cothern, L. (2000, November). *Co-occurrence of serious and violent juvenile offending and other problem behaviors.* (OJJDP Juvenile Justice Bulletin.) Washington, DC: U.S. Department of Justice, Office of Juvenile Justice and Delinquency Prevention.

Loeber, R., Farrington, D. P., Stouthamer-Loeber, M., & Van Kammen, W. B. (1998). Multiple risk factors for multi-problem boys: Co-occurrence of delinquency, substance use, attention deficit, conduct problems, physical aggression, covert behavior, depressed mood, and shy/withdrawn behavior. In R. Jessor (Ed.), *New Perspectives on Adolescent Risk Behavior* (pp. 90–149). Cambridge, England: Cambridge University Press.

Correlates/Prediction of Disruptive Child Behavior and Juvenile Delinquency

Farrington, D. P. (1998). Predictors, causes and correlates of male youth violence. In M. Tonry & M. H. Moore (Eds.), *Crime and justice: Vol. 24. Youth violence* (pp. 421–475). Chicago: University of Chicago Press.

Farrington, D. P., Loeber, R., Yin, Y., & Anderson, S. (2002). Are within-individual causes of delinquency the same as between-individual causes? *Criminal Behaviour and Mental Health, 12*, 53–68.

Keltner, D., Moffitt, T. E., & Stouthamer-Loeber, M. (1995). Facial expression of emotion and psychopathology in adolescent boys. *Journal of Abnormal Psychology, 104*, 644–652.

Pardini, D., Loeber, R., & Stouthamer-Loeber, M. (2005). Developmental shifts in parent and peer influences on boys' beliefs about delinquent behavior. *Journal of Research on Adolescence, 15*, 299–323.

White, J. L., Moffitt, T. E., Caspi, A., Bartusch, D. J., Needles, D. J., & Stouthamer-Loeber, M. (1994). Measuring impulsivity and examining its relationship to delinquency. *Journal of Abnormal Psychology, 103*, 192–205.

Development of Disruptive Child Behavior/Attention Problems/Hyperactivity and Delinquency

Broidy, L. M., Nagin, D. S., Tremblay, R. E., Bates, J. E., Brame, B., Dodge, K., et al. (2003). Developmental trajectories of childhood disruptive behaviors and adolescent delinquency: A six-site, cross-national replication. *Development and Psychopathology, 39*, 222–245.

Farrington, D. P. (2001). Cross-national comparative studies in criminology. In H. N. Pontell & D. Schichor (Eds.), *Contemporary Issues in Crime and Criminal Justice: Essays in Honor of Gilbert Geis* (pp. 307–320). Upper Saddle River, NJ: Prentice Hall.

Farrington, D. P., & Loeber, R. (1999). Risk factors for delinquency over time and place. *Youth Update, 17*(2), 4–5.

Farrington, D. P., & Loeber, R. (1999). Transatlantic replicability of risk factors in the development of delinquency. In P. Cohen, C. Slomkowski, & L. N. Robins (Eds.), *Historical and Geographical Influences on Psychopathology* (pp. 299–329). Mahwah, N.J.: Erlbaum.

Hartman, C. A., Hox, J., Auerbach, J. G., Erol., N., Fonseca, A. C., Mellenbergh, G. J., et al. (1999). Syndrome dimensions of the child behavior checklist and the teacher report form: A critical empirical evaluation. *Journal of Child Psychology and Psychiatry, 40*, 1095–1116.

Huizinga, D., Loeber, R., & Thornberry, T. P. (1993). Longitudinal study of delinquency, drug use, sexual activity, and pregnancy among children and youth in three cities. *Public Health Reports: Journal of the U.S. Public Health Service, 108*(Suppl. 1), 90–96.

Kalb, L., & Loeber, R. (2003). Child disobedience and noncompliance: A review. *Pediatrics, 111*, 641–652.

Koolhof, R., Loeber, R., Wei, E. H., Pardini, D., D'Escury, A. C., Moffitt, T., et al. (in press). Inhibition deficits of serious delinquent boys with low intelligence. *Criminal Behaviour and Mental Health.*

Loeber, R. (1992). Viewing emotional problems of children and adolescents from a developmental perspective. In K. Kutash, C. Liberton, A. Algarin, & R. Friedman (Eds.), *Fifth annual research conference proceedings on A System of Care for Children's Mental Health: Expanding the Research Base* (pp. 53–60). Tampa, FL: Research and Training Center for Children's Mental Health, Florida Mental Health Institute, University of South Florida.

Loeber, R., Stouthamer-Loeber, M., Van Kammen, W. B., & Farrington, D. P. (1991). Initiation, escalation and desistance in juvenile offending and their correlates. *Journal of Criminal Law and Criminology, 82,* 36–82.

Pardini, D., Obradović, J., & Loeber, R. (2006). Interpersonal callousness, hyperactivity/impulsivity, inattention, and conduct problems as precursors to delinquency persistence in boys: A comparison of three grade-based cohorts. *Journal of Clinical Child and Adolescent Psychology, 35,* 46–59.

Smith, C. A., Krohn, M. D., Lizotte, A. J., McCluskey, C. P., Stouthamer-Loeber, M., & Weiher, A. (2000). The effect of early delinquency and substance use on precocious transitions to adulthood among adolescent males. In G. L. Fox & M. L. Benson (Eds.), *Families, crime and criminal justice* (pp. 233–253). Amsterdam: JAI.

Zhang, Q., Loeber, R., & Stouthamer-Loeber, M. (1997). Developmental trends of delinquency attitudes and delinquency: Replication and synthesis across time and samples. *Journal of Quantitative Criminology, 13,* 181–216.

Developmental Pathways

Keenan, K., Loeber, R., Zhang, Q., Stouthamer-Loeber, M., & Van Kammen, W. B. (1995). The influence of deviant peers on the development of boys' disruptive and delinquency behavior: A temporal analysis. *Development and Psychopathology, 7,* 715–726.

Kelley, B. T., Loeber, R., Keenan, K., & DeLamatre, M. (1997). *Developmental pathways in disruptive and delinquent behavior.* (OJJDP Juvenile Justice Bulletin). Washington, DC: U.S. Department of Justice, Office of Juvenile Justice and Delinquency Prevention.

Loeber, R., DeLamaire, M., Keenan, K., & Zhang, Q. (1998). A prospective replication of developmental pathways in disruptive and delinquent behavior. In R. Cairns, L. Bergman, & J. Kagan (Eds.), *Methods and Models for Studying the Individual* (pp. 185–215). Thousand Oaks, CA: Sage.

Loeber, R., & Keenan, K. (1995). Developmental pathways in boys' disruptive and delinquent behavior. *Youth Update, 13,* 4–5.

Loeber, R., Keenan, K., & Zhang, Q. (1997). Boys' experimentation and persistence in developmental pathways toward serious delinquency. *Journal of Child and Family Studies, 6,* 321–357.

Loeber, R., Wei, E., Stouthamer-Loeber, M., Huizinga, D., & Thornberry, T. P. (1999). Behavioral antecedents to serious and violent juvenile offending: Joint analyses from the Denver Youth Survey, the Pittsburgh Youth Study, and the Rochester Youth Development Study. *Studies in Crime and Crime Prevention, 8,* 245–263.

Loeber, R., Wung, P., Keenan, K., Giroux, B., Stouthamer-Loeber, M., Van Kammen, W. B., et al. (1993). Developmental pathways in disruptive child behavior. *Development and Psychopathology, 5,* 101–132.

Desistance

Loeber, R., Pardini, D. A., Stouthamer-Loeber, M., & Raine, A. (2007). Do cognitive, physiological and psycho-social risk and promotive factors predict desistance from delinquency in males? *Development and Psychopathology, 19,* 867–887.

Stouthamer-Loeber, M., Wei, E., Loeber, R, & Masten, A. F. (2004). Desistance from persistent serious delinquency in the transition to adulthood. *Development and Psychopathology, 16*, 897–918.

Diagnosis

Russo, M., Loeber, R., Lahey, B. B., & Keenan, K. (1994). Oppositional defiant and conduct disorders: Validation of the DSM-III-R and an alternative option. *Journal of Clinical Child Psychology, 23*, 56–68.

Economics

Welsh, B. C., Loeber, R., Stouthamer-Loeber, M., Cohen, M. A., Farrington, F. P., & Stevens, B. R. (in press). The cost of juvenile crime in urban areas: A longitudinal perspective. *Youth Violence and Juvenile Justice*.

Family Factors

Farrington, D. P., Jolliffe, D., Loeber, R., Stouthamer-Loeber, M., & Kalb, L. (2001). The concentration of offenders in families, and family criminality in the prediction of boys' delinquency. *Journal of Adolescence, 24*, 579–596.

Hoeve, M., Blokland, A., Dubas, J. S., Loeber, R., Gerris, J. R. M., & van der Laan, P. H. (in press). Trajectories of delinquency and parenting styles. *Journal of Abnormal Child Psychology*.

Hoeve, M., Smeenk, W., Loeber, R., Stouthamer-Loeber, M., Van der Laan, P., Gerris, J., et al. (2004). Opvoeding en delinquent gedrag bij jongvolwassenen mannen [Child rearing and delinquency by young adult men]. *Tijdschrift voor Criminologie, 46*, 347–360.

Hoeve, M., Smeenk, W., Loeber, R., Stouthamer-Loeber, M., Van der Laan, P. H., Gerris, J. R. M., et al. (2007). Long term effects of parenting and family characteristics on delinquency of male young adults. *European Journal of Criminology, 4*, 161–194.

Loeber, R., Drinkwater, M., Yin, Y., Anderson, S. J., Schmidt, L. C., & Crawford, A. (2000). Stability of family interactions from ages 6 to 18. *Journal of Abnormal Child Psychology, 28*, 353–369.

Stouthamer-Loeber, M., Drinkwater, M., & Loeber, R. (1999–2000). Family functioning profiles, early onset offending, and disadvantaged neighborhoods. *International Journal of Child and Family Welfare, 4*, 247–256.

Thornberry. T. P., Smith, C. A., Rivera, C., Huizinga, D., & Stouthamer-Loeber, M. (1999, September). *Family disruption and delinquency*. (OJJDP Juvenile Justice Bulletin.) Washington, DC: U.S. Department of Justice, Office of Juvenile Justice and Delinquency Prevention.

Fatherhood and Sexual Behavior

Stouthamer-Loeber, M., & Wei, E. (1998). The precursors of young fatherhood and its effect on the delinquency career of teenage males. *Journal of Adolescent Health, 22*, 56–65.

Thornberry, T. P., Wei, E. H., Stouthamer-Loeber, M., & Van Dyke, J. (2000, January). *Teenage fatherhood and delinquent behavior.* (OJJDP Juvenile Justice Bulletin.) Washington, DC: U.S. Department of Justice, Office of Juvenile Justice and Delinquency Prevention.

Wei, E. H., Loeber, R., & Stouthamer-Loeber, M. (2002). How many of the offspring born to teenage fathers are produced by repeat serious delinquents? *Criminal Behaviour and Mental Health, 12,* 83–98.

Gangs

Gordon, R. A., Lahey, B. B., Kawai, E., Loeber, R., Stouthamer–Loeber, M., & Farrington, D. P. (2004). Antisocial behavior and youth gang membership: Selection and socialization. *Criminology, 42,* 55–87.

Lahey, B. B., Gordon, R. A., Loeber, R., Stouthamer-Loeber, M., & Farrington, D. P. (1999). Boys who join gangs: A prospective study of predictors of gang entry. *Journal of Abnormal Child Psychology, 27,* 261–276.

Homicide

Farrington, D. P., Loeber, R., Homish, D. L., & Stallings, R. (in press). Early risk factors for homicide offenders and victims. In M. J. Delisi & P. J. Conis (Eds.), *Violent Offenders: Theory, Research, Public Policy, and Practice.* Sudbury, MA: Jones and Bartlett.

Loeber, R., Lacourse, E., & Homish, D. L. (2005). Homicide, violence and developmental trajectories. In R. E. Tremblay, W. W. Hartup, & J. Archer (Eds.), *Developmental Origins of Aggression* (pp. 202–220). New York: Guilford.

Loeber, R., Pardini, D., Homish, D. L., Wei, E. H., Crawford, A. M., Farrington, D. P., et al. (2005). The prediction of violence and homicide in young men. *Journal of Consulting and Clinical Psychology, 73,* 1074–1088.

Intervention/Treatment

Loeber, R., & Stouthamer-Loeber, M. (1991). A survey of services for children with disruptive and delinquent behavior. In A. Algarin & R. M. Friedman (Eds.), *Fourth annual research conference proceedings on A System of Care for Children's Mental Health: Expanding the Research Base* (pp. 323–326). Research and Training Center for Children's Mental Health, Florida Mental Health Institute, University of South Florida, Tampa, FL.

Pajer, K., Stouthamer-Loeber, M., Gardner, W., & Loeber, R. (2006), Antisocial women: Long-term help-seeking for emotional problems and long-term health. *Criminal Behaviour and Mental Health, 16,* 29–42.

Stouthamer-Loeber, M., Loeber, R., & Thomas, C. (1992). Caretakers seeking help for boys with disruptive and delinquent child behavior. *Comprehensive Mental Health Care, 2,* 159–178.

Measurement

Farrington, D. P., Jolliffe, D., Loeber, R., & Homish, D. L. (2007). How many offenses are really committed per juvenile court offender? *Victims and Offenders, 2,* 227–249.

Farrington, D. P., Loeber, R., Stouthamer-Loeber, M., Van Kammen, W. B., & Schmidt, L. (1996). Self-reported delinquency and a combined delinquency seriousness scale based on boys, mothers, and teachers: Concurrent and predictive validity for African-Americans and Caucasians. *Criminology, 34*, 493–517.

Lizotte, A. J., Chard-Wierschem, D. J., Loeber, R., & Stern, S. B. (1992). A shortened child behavior checklist for delinquency studies. *Journal of Quantitative Criminology, 8*, 233–245.

Loeber, R., Stouthamer-Loeber, M., Van Kammen, W. B., & Farrington, D. P. (1989). Development of a new measure of self-reported antisocial behavior for young children: Prevalence and reliability. In M. Klein (Ed.), *Cross-national Research in Self-reported Crime and Delinquency* (pp. 203–225). Boston: Kluwer-Nijhoff.

Lynam, D. R., Derefinko, K. J., Caspi, A., Loeber, R., & Stouthamer-Loeber, M. (in press). The content validity of juvenile psychopathy: An empirical examination. *Psychological Assessment.*

Messer, S. C., Angold, A., Loeber, R., Costello, E. J., Van Kammen, W. B., & Stouthamer-Loeber, M. (1995). The development of a short questionnaire for use in epidemiological studies of depression in children and adolescents: Factor composition and structure across development. *International Journal of Methods in Psychiatric Research, 5*, 251–262.

Raine, A., Dodge, K., Loeber, R., Gatzke-Kopp, L., Lynam, D., Reynolds, C., Stouthamer-Loeber, M., & Liu, J. (2006). The Reactive-Proactive Aggression (RPQ) Questionnaire: Differential correlates of reactive and proactive aggression in adolescent boys. *Aggressive Behavior, 32*, 159–171.

Youngstrom, E., Loeber, R., & Stouthamer-Loeber, M. (2000). Patterns and correlates of agreement between parent, teacher, and male adolescent ratings of externalizing and internalizing problems. *Journal of Consulting and Clinical Psychology, 68*, 1038–1050.

Neighborhood Factors

Beyers, J. M., Loeber, R., Wikström, P-O. H., & Stouthamer-Loeber, M. (2001). What predicts adolescent violence in better-off neighborhoods? *Journal of Abnormal Child Psychology, 29*, 369–381.

Ireland, T. O., Thornberry, T. P., & Loeber, R. (2003). Violence among adolescents living in public housing: A two-site analysis. *Criminology and Public Policy, 3*, 3–38.

Ireland, T. O., Thornberry, T. P., & Loeber, R. (2006). Residential stability among adolescents in public housing: A risk factor for delinquent and violent behavior? In J. Flint (Ed.), *Housing, Urban Governance and Anti-social Behaviour: Perspectives, Policy, and Practice* (pp. 301–323). Bristol, England: Policy Press.

Loeber, R., & Wikström, P-O. (1993). Individual pathways to crime in different types of neighborhoods. In D. P. Farrington, R. J. Sampson, and P-O. Wikström (Eds.), *Integrating individual and ecological aspects of crime* (pp. 169–204). Stockholm, Sweden: National Council for Crime Prevention.

Lynam, D. R., Caspi, A., Moffitt, T., Wikström, P-O. H., Loeber, R., & Novak, S. (2000). The interaction between impulsivity and neighborhood context on offending: The effects of impulsivity are stronger in poorer neighborhoods. *Journal of Abnormal Psychology, 109*, 563–574.

Peeples, F., & Loeber, R. (1994). Do individual factors and neighborhood context explain ethnic differences in juvenile delinquency? *Journal of Quantitative Criminology, 10,* 141–157.

Wikström, P-O. (1998). Communities and crime. In M. Tonry (Ed.), *The Oxford Handbook of Crime and Punishment* (pp. 269–301). Oxford, England: Oxford University Press.

Wikström, P-O., & Loeber, R. (2000). Do disadvantaged neighborhoods cause well-adjusted children to become adolescent delinquents? A study of male juvenile serious offending, risk and protective factors, and neighborhood context. *Criminology, 38,* 1109–1142.

Personality

Caspi, A., Block, J., Block, J. H., Klopp, B., Lynam, D., Moffitt, T. E., et al. (1992). A "Common-Language" version of the California Q-Set for personality assessment. *Psychology Assessment, 4,* 512–523.

Caspi, A., Moffitt, T. E., Silva, P. A., Stouthamer-Loeber, M., Krueger, R. F., & Schmutte, P. (1994). Are some people crime-prone? Replications of the personality–crime relationship across countries, genders, races, and methods. *Criminology, 32,* 163–195.

John, O. P., Caspi, A., Robins, R. W., Moffitt, T. E., & Stouthamer-Loeber, M. (1994). The "Little Five": Exploring the five-factor model of personality in adolescent boys. *Child Development, 65,* 160–178.

Krueger, R., Caspi, A., Moffitt, T. E., White, J., & Stouthamer-Loeber, M. (1996). Delay of gratification, psychopathology, and personality: Is low self-control specific to externalizing problems? *Journal of Personality, 64,* 107–129.

Lynam, D. R., Caspi, A., Moffitt, T. E., Raine, A., Loeber, R., & Stouthamer-Loeber, M. (2005). Adolescent psychopathy and the Big Five: Results from two samples. *Journal of Abnormal Child Psychology, 33,* 431–443.

Moffitt, T. E., Caspi, A., Silva, P. A., & Stouthamer-Loeber, M. (1995). Individual differences in personality and intelligence are linked to crime: Cross-context evidence from nations, neighborhoods, genders, races, and age-cohorts. In J. Hagan (Ed.), *Current perspectives on aging and the life cycle: Vol. 4. Delinquency and disrepute in the life course* (pp. 1–34). Greenwich, CT: JAI.

Robins, R. W., John, O. P., Caspi, A., Moffitt, T. E., & Stouthamer-Loeber, M. (1996). Resilient, overcontrolled, and undercontrolled boys: Three replicable personality types. *Journal of Personality and Social Psychology, 70,* 157–171.

Protective Factors

Stouthamer–Loeber, M., Loeber, R., Farrington, D. P., Zhang, Q., Van Kammen, W. B., & Maguin, E. (1993). The double edge of protective and risk factors for delinquency: Interrelations and developmental patterns. *Development and Psychopathology, 5,* 683–701.

Stouthamer–Loeber, M., Loeber, R., Wei, E., Farrington, D. P., & Wikström, P-O. H. (2002). Risk and promotive effects in the explanation of persistent serious delinquency in boys. *Journal of Consulting and Clinical Psychology, 70,* 111–123.

Race

Farrington, D. P., Loeber, R., & Stouthamer–Loeber, M. (2003). How can the relationship between race and violence be explained? In D. F. Hawkins (Ed.), *Violent crime: Assessing race and ethnic differences* (pp. 213–237). New York: Cambridge University Press.

Loeber, R., & Farrington, D. P. (2004). Verschillende oorzaken van delinquentie tussen etnische en national groepen? Longitudinale analyses van criminaliteit onder jonge mannen in Pittsburgh and London [Are between-race and between-country causes of delinquency the same? Longitudinal analyses of young males in Pittsburgh and London]. *Tijdschrift voor Criminologie, 46*, 330–346.

Research Implementation

Stouthamer–Loeber, M. (1993). Optimizing data quality of individual and community sources in longitudinal research. In D. P. Farrington, R. J. Sampson, & P-O. Wikström (Eds.), *Integrating individual and ecological aspects of crime* (pp. 259–277). Stockholm, Sweden: National Council for Crime Prevention.

Stouthamer-Loeber, M., Van Kammen, W. B., & Loeber, R. (1992). The nuts and bolts of implementing large-scale longitudinal studies. *Violence and Victims, 7*, 63–78.

Van Kammen, W. B., & Stouthamer–Loeber, M. (1997). Practical aspects of interview data collection and data management. In L. Bickman & D. Rog (Eds.), *Handbook of Applied Social Research Methods* (pp. 375–398). Thousand Oaks, CA: Sage.

Service Delivery

Hirschfield, P., Maschi, T., White, H. R., Goldman-Traub, L., & Loeber, R. (2006). Mental health and juvenile arrests: Criminality, criminalization, or compassion? *Criminology, 44*, 593–630.

Loeber, R., & Stouthamer-Loeber, M. (1991). A survey of services for children with disruptive and delinquent behavior. In A. Algarin, & R. M. Friedman (Eds.), *Fourth annual research conference proceedings on A System of Care for Children's Mental Health: Expanding the Research Base* (pp. 323–326). Research and Training Center for Children's Mental Health, Florida Mental Health Institute, University of South Florida, Tampa, FL.

Stouthamer-Loeber, M., & Loeber, R. (2002). Lost opportunities for intervention: Undetected markers for the development of serious juvenile delinquency. *Criminal Behaviour and Mental Health, 12*, 69–82.

Stouthamer-Loeber, M., Loeber, R., Thomas, C. (1992). Caretakers seeking help for boys with disruptive and delinquent child behavior. *Comprehensive Mental Health Care, 2*, 159–178.

Stouthamer-Loeber, M, Loeber, R., Van Kammen, W. B., & Zhang, Q. (1995). Uninterrupted delinquent careers: The timing of parental helpseeking and juvenile court contact. *Studies on Crime and Crime Prevention, 4*, 236–251.

Sex Offenses

Van Wijk, A., Loeber, R., Ferwerda, H., Smulders, A., & Vermeiren, R. (2005). Jeugdige zedendelinquenten en geweldplegers. Een vergelijkende studie op grond van de Pittsburgh Youth Study [Juvenile sex offenders and violent delinquents: A comparative study based on data from the Pittsburgh Youth Study]. *Justitiële Verkenningen, 1*, 105–118.

Van Wijk, A., Loeber, R., Vermeiren, R., Pardini, D., Bullens, R., & Doreleijers, T. (2005). Violent juvenile sex offenders compared with violent juvenile nonsex offenders: Explorative findings from the Pittsburgh Youth Study. *Sexual Abuse: A Journal of Research and Treatment, 17*, 333–352.

Statistics

Farrington, D. P., & Loeber, R. (2000). Some benefits of dichotomization in psychiatric and criminological research. *Criminal Behaviour and Mental Health, 10*, 102–122.

Substance Use

Burke, J. D., Loeber, R., White, H. R., Stouthamer-Loeber, M., & Pardini, D. A. (in press). Inattention as a key predictor of tobacco use in adolescence. *Journal of Abnormal Psychology.*

Loeber, R., Stouthamer-Loeber, M., & White, H. R. (1999), Developmental aspects of delinquency and internalizing problems and their association with persistent juvenile substance use between ages 7 and 18. *Journal of Clinical Child Psychology, 28*, 322–332.

Loeber, R., Wei, E. H., & White, H. R. (2003). Developmental pathways to substance use and other problem behaviors. In W. L. Dewey & L. S. Harris (Eds.), *Problems of drug dependence 2002: Proceedings of the 64th annual scientific meeting. The College on Problems of Drug Dependence, Inc.* (p. 100–101). (Research Monograph Series No. 183.) Bethesda, MD: National Institute of Drug Abuse.

Pardini, D., White, H. R., & Stouthamer-Loeber, M. (2007). Early adolescent psychopathology as a predictor of alcohol use disorders by young adulthood. *Drug and Alcohol Dependence, 88*, S38–S49.

Van Kammen, W. B., & Loeber, R. (1992). Drugs, delinquency and discipline. *School Safety, 3*, 7–10.

Van Kammen, W. B., & Loeber, R. (1994). Are fluctuations in delinquent activities related to the onset and offset of juvenile illegal drug use and drug dealing? *Journal of Drug Issues, 24*, 9–24.

Van Kammen, W. B., Loeber, R., & Stouthamer-Loeber, M. (1991). Substance use and its relationship to conduct problems and delinquency in young boys. *Journal of Youth and Adolescence, 20*, 399–414.

Van Kammen, W. B., Maguin, E., & Loeber, R. (1994). Initiation of drug selling and its relationship with illicit drug use and serious delinquency in adolescent boys. In E. G. M. Weitekamp & H. J. Kerner (Eds.), *Cross-national longitudinal research on human development and criminal behavior* (pp. 229–241). Dordrecht, Netherlands: Kluwer.

Wei, E. H., Loeber, R., & White, H. R. (2004). Teasing apart the developmental associations between alcohol and marijuana use and violence. *Journal of Contemporary Criminal Justice, 20*, 166–183.

White, H. R., Jarrett, N., Valencia, E. Y., Loeber, R., & Wei, E. (2007). Stages and sequences of initiation and regular substance use in a longitudinal cohort of Black and White male adolescents. *Journal of Studies on Alcohol and Drugs, 68,* 173–181.

White, H. R., Loeber, R., Stouthamer-Loeber, M., & Farrington, D. P. (1999). Developmental associations between substance use and violence. *Development and Psychopathology, 11,* 785–803.

White, H. R., Metzger, L., Stouthamer-Loeber, M., Violette, N., & Nagin D. 2006. Racial differences in developmental risk and protective factors for cigarette smoking. In E. V. Metrosa (Ed.), *Racial and Ethnic Disparities in Health and Health Care.* New York: Nova Science Publishers.

White, H. R., Nagin, D., Repogle, E., & Stouthamer-Loeber, M. (2004). Racial differences in trajectories of cigarette use. *Drug and Alcohol Dependence, 76,* 219–227.

White, H. R., Pandina, R. J., Loeber, R., & Stouthamer-Loeber, M. (2003). Developmental patterns of drug use and crime. In W. L. Dewey & L. S. Harris (Eds.), *Problems of drug dependence 2002: Proceedings of the 64th annual scientific meeting. The College on Problems of Drug Dependence, Inc.* (pp. 107–109). (Research Monograph Series No. 183.) Bethesda, MD: National Institute of Drug Abuse.

White, H. R., Tice, P. C., Loeber, R., & Stouthamer-Loeber, M. (2002). Illegal acts committed under the influence of alcohol and drugs. *Journal of Research in Crime and Delinquency, 39,* 131–152.

White, H. R., Violette, N. M., Metzger, L., & Stouthamer-Loeber, M. (2007). Adolescent risk factors for late-onset smoking among African American young men. *Nicotine and Tobacco Research, 8,* 153–161.

White, H. R., Xie, M., Thompson, W., Loeber, R., & Stouthamer-Loeber, M. (2001). Psychopathology as a predictor of adolescent drug use trajectories. *Psychology of Addictive Behavior, 15,* 227–236.

Theory

Loeber, R., Slot, N. W., & Stouthamer–Loeber, M. (2006). A three-dimensional, cumulative developmental model of serious delinquency. In P-O. H. Wikström & R. Sampson (Eds.), *The Explanation of Crime: Contexts and Mechanisms* (pp 153–194). Cambridge, England: Cambridge University Press.

Loeber, R., & Farrington, D. P. (in press). Advancing knowledge about causes in langitudial studies: Experimental and quasi-experimental methods. A. Liberman (Ed.), *The Yield of Recent Longitudinal Research on Crime and Delinquency.* New York: Springer, in press.

Violence

Fabio, A., Loeber, R., Balasurbramani, G. K., Roth, J., & Farrington, D. P. (2006). Why some generations are more violent than others: Assessment of age, period, and cohort effects. *American Journal of Epidemiology, 164,* 151–160.

Kelley, B. T., Huizinga, D., Thornberry, T. P., & Loeber, R. (1997, June). *Epidemiology of serious violence.* (OJJDP Juvenile Justice Bulletin.) Washington, DC: U.S. Department of Justice, Office of Juvenile Justice and Delinquency Prevention.

Lahey, B. B., Loeber, R., Waldman, I. D., & Farrington, D. P. (2006). Child socioemotional dispositions at school entry that predict adolescent delinquency and violence. *Impuls. Tidsskrift for Psykologi, 3,* 40–51.

Loeber, R., DeLamaire, M., Tita, G., Cohen, J., Stouthamer-Loeber, M., & Farrington, D. P. (1999). Gun injury and mortality: The delinquent backgrounds of juvenile victims. *Violence and Victims, 14,* 339–352.

Loeber R., & Hay, D. F. (1997). Key issues in the development of aggression and violence from childhood to early adulthood. *Annual Review of Psychology, 48,* 371–410.

Loeber, R., Kalb, L., & Huizinga, D. (Aug. 2001). *Serious injury victimization.* (OJJDP Juvenile Justice Bulletin.) Washington, DC: U.S. Department of Justice, Office of Juvenile Justice and Delinquency Prevention.

Loeber, R., & Stouthamer-Loeber, M. (1998). Juvenile aggression at home and at school. In D. S. Elliott, K. R. Williams, & B. Hamburg (Eds.), *Violence in American Schools* (pp. 94–126). Cambridge, England: Cambridge University Press.

Loeber, R., & Stouthamer-Loeber, M. (1998). The development of juvenile aggression and violence: Some common misconceptions and controversies. *American Psychologist, 53,* 242–259.

Thornberry, T. P., Huizinga, D., & Loeber, R. (1995). The prevention of serious delinquency and violence: Implications from the Program of Research on the Causes and Correlates of Delinquency. In J. C. Howell, B. Krisberg, J. D. Hawkins & J. J. Wilson (Eds.), *Sourcebook on Serious, Violent and Chronic Juvenile Offenders* (pp. 213–237). Thousand Oaks, CA: Sage.

References

Achenbach, T. M. (1978). The child behavior profile. I: Boys aged 6–11. *Journal of Consulting and Clinical Psychology, 46,* 478-488.

Achenbach, T. M. (1997). *Young adult self-report.* Burlington: University of Vermont Department of Psychiatry.

Achenbach, T. M., & Edelbrock, C. S. (1979). The child behavior profile. II: Boys aged 12–16 and girls aged 6–11 and 12–16. *Journal of Consulting and Clinical Psychology, 47,* 223-233.

Achenbach, T. M., & Edelbrock, C. S. (1983). *Manual for the child behavior checklist and revised child behavior profile.* Burlington: University of Vermont Department of Psychiatry.

Achenbach, T. M., & Edelbrock, C. S. (1987). *Manual for the youth self-report and profile.* Burlington: University of Vermont Department of Psychiatry.

Agnew, R. (1992). Foundation for a general strain theory of crime and delinquency. *Criminology, 30,* 47–87.

Agresti, A. (1990). *Categorical data analysis.* New York: Wiley.

Akers, R. L. (1973). *Deviant behavior: A social learning approach.* Belmont, CA: Wadsworth.

Akers, R. L. (1990). Rational choice, deterrence, and social learning theory in criminology: The path not taken. *Journal of Criminal Law and Criminology, 81,* 653–676.

Altschuler, D. M., & Brounstein, P. J. (1991). Patterns of drug use, drug trafficking, and other delinquency among inner-city adolescent males in Washington, D.C. *Criminology, 29,* 589–622.

American Psychiatric Association. (1980). *Diagnostic and statistical manual of mental disorders* (3rd edition). Washington, DC: Author.

American Psychiatric Association (1987). *Diagnostic and statistical manual of mental disorders* (3rd ed., rev.). Washington, DC: Author.

Angold, A., Erkanli, A., Loeber, E., Costello, E. J., Van Kammen, W., & Stouthamer-Loeber, M. (1995). Disappearing depression in a population of boys. *Journal of Emotional and Behavioral Disorders, 4,* 95–104.

Arthur, M. W., Hawkins, J. D., Pollard, J. A., Catalano, R. F., & Baglioni, A. J., Jr. (2002). Measuring risk and protective factors for substance use, delinquency, and other adolescent problem behaviors: The communities that care youth survey. *Evaluation Review, 26,* 575–601.

Augimeri, L. K., Koegl, C. J., Webster, C. D., & Levene, K. S. (2001). *Early assessment risk list for boys (EARL-20B)* (version 2). Toronto, Ontario, Canada: Earlscourt Child Family Centre.

Augimeri, L. K., Farrington, D. P., Koegl, C. K., & Day, D. M. (in press). The SNAP under 12 outreach project: Effects of a community-based program for children with problems. *Journal of Child and Family Studies.*

349

Ayers, C. D., Williams, J. H., Hawkins, J. D., Peterson, P. L., Catalano, R. D., & Abbott, R. D. (1999). Assessing correlates of onset, escalation, deescalation, and desistance of delinquent behavior. *Journal of Quantitative Criminology, 15,* 277–306.

Barker, E. D., Séguin, J. R., White, H. R., Bates, M. E., Lacourse, E., Carbonneau, R., & Tremblay, R. E. (2007). Developmental trajectories of male physical violence and theft: Relation to neurocognitive performance. *Archives of General Psychiatry, 64,* 592–599.

Barnett, A., Blumstein, A., & Farrington, D. P. (1987). Probabilistic models of youthful criminal careers. *Criminology, 25,* 83–107.

Barnett, D., Manly, J. T., & Cicchetti, D. (1993). Defining child maltreatment: The interface between policy and research. In D. Cicchetti and S. L. Toth (Eds.), *Child abuse, child development, and social policy* (pp. 7–73). Norwood, NJ: Ablex.

Bartusch, D. R. J., Lynam, D. R., Moffitt, T. E., & Silva, P. A. (1997). Is age important? Testing a general versus a developmental theory of antisocial behavior. *Criminology, 35,* 13–48.

Battin-Pearson, S. R., Thornberry, T. P., Hawkins, J. D., & Krohn, M. D. (1998, October). *Gang membership, delinquent peers, and delinquent behavior.* (OJJDP Juvenile Justice Bulletin. Washington, DC: U.S. Department of Justice, Office of Juvenile Justice and Delinquency Prevention.

Beelmann, A., & Lösel, F. (2006). Child social skills training in development crime prevention: Effects on antisocial behavior and social competence. *Psicothema, 18,* 603–610.

Bell, R. Q. (1953). Convergence: An accelerated longitudinal approach. *Child Development, 24,* 145–152.

Bennett, T. H., Holloway, K., & Farrington, D. P. (in press). The statistical association between drug misuse and crime: A meta-analysis. *Aggression and Violent Behavior.*

Beyers, J., Loeber, R., Wikström, P. O. H., & Stouthamer-Loeber, S. (2001). What predicts adolescent violence in better-off neighborhoods? *Journal of Abnormal Child Psychology, 29,* 369–381.

Biglan, A., Mrazek, P. J., Carnine, D., & Fly, B. R. (2003). The integration of research and practice in the prevention of youth problem behaviors. *American Psychologist, 58,* 433–440.

Bingenheimer, J. B., Brennan, R. T., & Earls, F. J. (2005). Firearm violence exposure and serious violent behavior. *Science, 308,* 1323–1326.

Bjerregaard, B., & Lizotte, A. J. (1995). Gun ownership and gang membership. *Journal of Criminal Law and Criminology, 86,* 37–58.

Bjerregaard, B., & Smith, C. (1993). Gender differences in gang participation, delinquency, and substance use. *Journal of Quantitative Criminology, 9,* 329–355.

Blokland, A. A. J., & Nieuwbeerta, P. (2005). The effects of life circumstances on longitudinal trajectories of offending. *Criminology, 43,* 1203–1240.

Blumstein, A. (1995). Violence by young people: Why the deadly nexus? *National Institute of Justice Journal, 229,* 2–9.

Blumstein, A., & Cohen, J. (1979). Estimation of individual crime rates from arrest records. *Journal of Criminal Law and Criminology, 70,* 561–585.

Blumstein, A., Cohen, J., Roth, J. A., & Visher, C.A. (Eds.) (1986). *Criminal careers and "career criminals."* Washington D.C.: National Academy of Sciences.

Brame, R., Bushway, S., & Paternoster, R. (1999). On the use of panel research designs and random effect models to investigate static and dynamic theories of criminal offending. *Criminology, 37*, 599–641.

Brame, R., Bushway, S., Paternoster, R., & Thornberry, T. P. (2005). Temporal linkages in violent and nonviolent criminal activity. *Journal of Quantitative Criminology, 21*, 149–174.

Brame, R., Mulvey, E. P., & Piquero, A. R. (2001). On the development of different kinds of criminal activity. *Sociological Methods, 29*, 319–341.

Brame, B., Nagin, D. S., & Tremblay, R. E. (2001). Developmental trajectories of physical aggression from school entry to late adolescence. *Journal of Child Psychology and Psychiatry, 42*, 503–512.

Broidy, L. M., Nagin, D. S., Tremblay, R. E., Bates, J. E., Brame, B., Dodge, K. A., Fergusson, D., Horwood, J. L., Loeber, R., Laird, R., Lynam, D. R., Moffitt, T. E., Pettit, G. S., & Vitaro, F. (2003). Developmental trajectories of childhood disruptive behaviors and adolescent delinquency: A six-site, cross-national study. *Developmental Psychology, 39*, 222–245.

Bronfenbrenner, U. (1979). Contexts of child rearing. *American Psychologist, 34*, 844–850.

Bryk, A. S., & Raudenbush, S. W. (1987). Application of hierarchical linear-models to assessing change. *Psychological Bulletin, 101*, 147–158.

Bunge, M. (2004). How does it work? The search for explanatory mechanisms. *Philosophy of the Social Sciences, 34*, 1–29.

Bureau of Justice Statistics. (1994). *Drug offenders in federal prison.* Washington DC: U.S. Department of Justice.

Burns, B. J., Angold, A., & Magruder-Habib, K. (1990). *The Child and Adolescent Services Assessment, CASA, Child Interview, Version 2.0.* Durham, NC: Developmental Epidemiology Program, Department of Psychiatry, Duke University.

Bursik, R. J. (1988). Social disorganization and theories of crime and delinquency: Problems and prospects. *Criminology, 26*, 519–551.

Bushway, S. D., Brame, R., & Paternoster, R. (1999). Assessing stability and change in criminal offending: A comparison of random effects, semi-parametric, and fixed effects modeling strategies. *Journal of Quantitative Criminology, 15*, 23–61.

Bushway, S. D., Piquero, A. R., Broidy, L. M., Cauffman, E., & Mazerolle, P. (2001). An empirical framework for studying desistance as a process. *Criminology, 39*, 491–515.

Bushway, S. D., Thornberry, T. P., & Krohn, M. D. (2003). Desistance as a developmental process: A comparison of static and dynamic approaches. *Journal of Quantitative Criminology, 19*, 129–153.

Cairns, R. B., & Cairns, B. D. (1994). *Lifelines and risks: Pathways of youth in our time.* Cambridge, England: Cambridge University Press.

Caron, C., & Rutter, M. (1991). Comorbidity in child psychopathology: Concepts, issues and research strategies. *Journal of Child Psychology and Psychiatry, 32*, 1063–1080.

Caspi, A., Block, J., Block, J. H., Klopp, B., Lyman, D., Moffitt, T. E., & Stouthamer-Loeber, M. (1992). A "common language" version of the California Child Q-Set for personality assessment. *Psychological Assessment, 4*, 512–523.

Caspi, A., Moffitt, T. E., Silva, P. A., Stouthamer-Loeber, M., Krueger, R. F., & Sch-mutte, P. S. (1994). Are some people crime-prone? Replications of the per-sonality-crime relationship across countries genders, races, and methods. *Criminology, 32*, 163–194.

Catalano, R. F., & Hawkins, J. D. (1996). The social development model: A theory of antisocial behavior. In J. D. Hawkins (Ed.), *Delinquency and crime: Current theories* (pp. 149–197). New York: Cambridge University Press.

Catalano, R. F., & Hawkins, J. D. (2002). Response from authors to comments on "Positive youth development in the United States: Research findings on evaluation of positive youth development programs." *Prevention and Treatment, 5*, article 20.

Chung, I. J., Hill, K. G., Hawkins, J. D., Gilchrist, L. D., & Nagin, D. S. (2002). Childhood predictors of offense trajectories. *Journal of Research in Crime and Delinquency, 39*, 60–90.

Cicchetti, D. (1987). Developmental psychopathology in infancy: Illustration from the study of maltreated youngsters. *Journal of Consulting and Clinical Psychology, 55*, 837–845.

Clinard, M. B., & Quinney, R. (1973). *Criminal behavior systems: A typology* (2nd ed.). New York: Holt, Rinehart and Winston.

Cohen, P. (1996). Childhood risks for young adult symptoms of personality disorder: Method and substance. *Multivariate Behavioral Research, 31*, 121–148.

Cohen, J. (2000). *Distinguishing between effects of criminality and drug use on violent offending*, Final Report to the National Institute of Justice, Grant 92-IJ-CX-0010.

Cohen, M. A. (1998). The monetary value of saving a high-risk youth. *Journal of Quantitative Criminology, 14*, 5–33.

Coie, J., Terry, R., Lenox, K., Lochman, J., & Hyman, C. (1995). Childhood peer rejection and aggression as predictors of stable patterns of adolescent disorder. *Development and Psychopathology, 7*, 697–713.

Collins, J. J., & Messerschmidt, P. M. (1993). Epidemiology of alcohol-related violence. *Alcohol Health and Research, 17*, 93–100.

Collishaw, S., Maughan, B., Goodman, R., & Pickles, A. (2004). Time trends in adolescent mental health. *Journal of Child Psychology and Psychiatry, 45*, 1350–1362.

Conger, R. D., Conger, K. J., Elder, G. H., Lorenz, F. O., Simons, R. L., & Whitbeck, L. B. (1992). A family process model of economic hardship adjustment of early adolescent boys. *Child Development, 63*, 526–541.

Conger, R. D., Conger, K. J., Matthews, L. S., & Elder, G. H. (1999). Pathways of economic influence on adolescent adjustment. *American Journal of Community Psychology, 27*, 519–541.

Cook, P. J., & Laub, J. H. (2002). After the epidemic: Recent trends in youth violence in the United States. In M. Tonry (Ed.), *Crime and justice: A Review of Research. Vol. 29:* (pp. 117–153). Chicago: University of Chicago Press.

Costello, E. J., & Angold, A. (1988). Scales to assess child and adolescent depression: Checklists, screens and nets. *Journal of the American Academy of Child and Adolescent Psychiatry, 27*, 726–737.

Costello, E., Compton, S. N., Keeler, G., & Angold, A. (2003). Relationships between poverty and psychopathology: A natural experiment. *Journal of the American Medical Association, 290*, 2023–2029.

Costello, E. J., Edelbrock, C., & Costello, A. J. (1985). The validity of the NIMH Diagnostic Interview Schedule for Children (DISC): A comparison between pediatric and psychiatric referrals. *Journal of Abnormal Child Psychology, 13,* 579–595.

Costello, A., Edelbrock, C., Kalas, R., Kessler, R., & Klaric, S. H. (1982). *The Diagnostic Interview Schedule for Children, Parent Version* (revised). Worcester: University of Massachusetts Medical Center.

Côté, S., Vaillancourt, T., Le Blanc, J. C., Nagin, D. S., & Tremblay, R. E. (2006). The development of physical aggression from toddlerhood to pre-adolescence: A nation wide longitudinal study of Canadian children. *Journal of Abnormal Child Psychology, 34,* 71–85.

Cottle, C. C., Lee, R. J., & Heilbrun, K. (2001). The prediction of criminal recidivism in juveniles. *Criminal Justice and Behavior, 28,* 367–394.

Cronbach, L. J. (1951). Coefficient alpha and the internal structure of tests. *Psychometrika, 16,* 297–334.

Crosnoe, R., Erickson, K. G., & Dornbusch, S. M. (2002). Protective functions of family relationships and school factors on the deviant behavior of adolescent boys and girls: Reducing the impact of risky friendships. *Youth and Society, 33,* 515–544.

Cullen, F. T., Wright, J. P., & Blevins, K. R. (Eds.) (2006). *Taking stock: The status of criminological theory.* New Brunswick, NJ: Transaction.

Cusson, M., & Pinsonneault, P. (1986). The decision to give up crime. In D. B. Cornish & R. V. Clarke (Eds.), *The reasoning criminal: Rational choice perspectives on offending* (pp. 72–82). New York: Springer-Verlag.

Deane, G., Armstrong, D. P., & Felson, R. B. (2005). An examination of offense specialization using marginal logit models. *Criminology, 43,* 955–988.

Deater-Deckard, K., Dodge, K. A., Bates, J. E., & Pettit, G. S. (1998). Multiple risk factors in the development of externalizing behavior problems: Group and individual differences. *Development and Psychopathology, 10,* 469–493.

Diggle, P. J., Liang, K. Y., & Zeger, S. L. (1994). *Analysis of longitudinal data.* Oxford, England: Oxford University Press.

Dodge, K. A., Murphy, R. R., & Buchsbaum, K. (1984). The assessment of intention-cue detection skills in children: Implications for developmental psychopathology. *Child Development, 55,* 163–173.

Dodge, K. A., & Pettit, G. S. (2003). A biopsychosocial model of the development of chronic conduct problems in adolescence. *Developmental Psychology, 39,* 349–371.

Dorsey, T. L., Zawitz, M. W., & Middleton, P. (2002). *Drugs and crime facts.* Washington, DC: U.S. Department of Justice.

Edelbrock, C., & Achenbach, T. (1984). The teacher version of the child behavior profile. I: Boys aged six through eleven. *Journal of Consulting and Clinical Psychology, 52,* 207–217.

Eisner, M. (2004). Violence and the rise of modern society. *Criminology in Europe: Newsletter of the European Society of Criminology, 3,* 14–16.

Elder, G. H. (1998). The life course and human development. In R. M. Lerner (Ed.), *Handbook of child psychology: Theoretical models of human development* (pp. 939–991). New York: Wiley.

Eley, T. C., Lichtenstein, P., & Stevenson, J. (1999). Sex differences in the etiology of aggressive and nonaggressive antisocial behavior: Results from two twin studies. *Child Development, 70,* 155–168.

Elliott, D. S. (1989). Criminal justice procedures in family violence crimes. In L. Ohlin & M. Tonry (Eds.), *Family violence* (pp. 427–480). Chicago: University of Chicago Press.

Elliott, D. S., Huizinga, D., & Ageton, S. S. (1985). *Explaining delinquency and drug use.* Beverly Hills, CA: Sage.

Elliott, D. S., Huizinga, D., & Menard, S. (1989). *Multiple problem youth: Delinquency, substance use, and mental health problems.* New York: Springer-Verlag.

Elliott, D. S., Menard, S., Elliott, A., Rankin, B., Wilson, W. J., & Huizinga, D. (2005). *Good kids from bad neighborhoods.* Chicago: University of Chicago Press.

Elliott, D. S., & Morse, B. J. (1989). Delinquency and drug use as risk factors in teenage sexual activity. *Youth and Society, 21,* 32–60.

Ensminger, M. E., Anthony, J. C., & McCord, J. (1997). The inner city and drug use: Initial findings from an epidemiological study. *Drug and Alcohol Dependence, 48,* 175–184.

Espiritu, R., Huizinga, D., Loeber, R., & Crawford, A. (2001). Epidemiology of self-reported delinquency. In R. Loeber & D. Farrington (Eds.), *Child delinquents: Development, intervention, and service needs* (pp. 47–66). Thousand Oaks, CA: Sage.

Fabio, A., Loeber, R., Balasubramani, G. K., Roth, J., Fu, W., & Farrington, D. P. (2006). Why some generations are more violent than others: Assessment of age, period and cohort effects. *American Journal of Epidemiology, 164,* 151–160.

Fagan, J. (1989). The social organization of drug use and drug dealing among urban gangs. *Criminology, 27,* 633–669.

Fagan, J., & Chin, K. (1990). *Violence as regulation and social control in the distribution of crack.* (NIDA research monograph series no. 103: Drug and violence: Causes, correlates, and consequences, (pp. 8–43). Bethesda, MD: National Institute on Drug Abuse.

Fagan, J., Weis, J. G., Cheng, Y-T., & Watters, J. K. (1987). *Drug and alcohol use, violent delinquency and social bonding: Implications for theory and intervention.* San Francisco: URSA Institute.

Farrington, D. P. (1986). Age and crime. In M. Tonry and N. Morris (Eds.), *Crime and Justice* (Vol. 7, 189–250). Chicago: University of Chicago Press.

Farrington, D. P. (1991). Childhood aggression and adult violence: Early precursors and later life outcomes. In D. J. Pepler and K. H. Rubin, (Eds.) *The Development and Treatment of Childhood Aggression.* Hillsdale, NJ: Lawrence Erlbaum Associates.

Farrington, D. P. (1993). Motivations for conduct disorder and delinquency. *Development and Psychopathology, 5,* 225–241.

Farrington, D. P. (1997). Human development and criminal careers. In M. Maguire, R. Morgan, & R. Reiner (Eds.), *The Oxford Handbook of Criminology* (2nd ed., pp. 511–584). Oxford, England: Clarendon Press.

Farrington, D. P. (2003). Developmental and life-course criminology: Key theoretical and empirical issues—The 2002 Sutherland Award address. *Criminology, 41,* 201–235.

Farrington, D. P. (Ed.) (2005). *Integrated developmental and life course theories of offending.* New Brunswick, NJ: Transaction.

Farrington, D. P. (2007). Advancing knowledge about desistance. *Journal of Contemporary Criminal Justice, 23,* 125–134.

Farrington, D. P., Barnes, G. C., & Lambert, S. (1996). The concentration of offending in families. *Legal and Criminological Psychology, 1,* 47–63.

Farrington, D. P., Coid, J. W., Harnett, L., Jolliffe, D., Soteriou, N., Turner, R., & West, D. J. (2006). *Criminal careers up to age 50 and life success up to age 48: New findings from the Cambridge study in delinquent development.* London: Home Office Research Study.

Farrington, D. P., Gallagher, B., Morley, L., St. Ledger, R. J., & West, D. J. (1988). Are there any successful men from criminogenic backgrounds? *Psychiatry, 51,* 116–130.

Farrington, D. P., Gallagher, B., Morley, L., St. Ledger, R. J., & West, D. J. (1990). Minimizing attrition in longitudinal research: Methods of tracing and securing cooperation in a 24-year follow-up study. In D. Magnusson & L. Bergman (Eds.), *Data quality in longitudinal research* (pp. 122–147). Cambridge, England: Cambridge University Press.

Farrington, D. P. and Jolliffe, D. (2005) Cross-national comparisons of crime rates in four countries, 1981–1999. In Tonry, M. and Farrington, D. P. (Eds.) *Crime and Punishment in Western Countries, 1980–1999* (pp. 377–397). Chicago: University of Chicago Press.

Farrington, D. P., Jolliffe, D., Hawkins, J. D., Catalano, R. F., Hill, K. G., & Kosterman, R. (2003) Comparing delinquency careers in court records and self-reports. *Criminology, 41,* 933–958.

Farrington, D. P., Jolliffe, D., Loeber, R., & Homish, D. L. (2007), How many offenses are really committed per juvenile court offender? *Victims and Offenders: 2,* 227–249.

Farrington, D. P., Jolliffe, D., Loeber, R., Stouthamer-Loeber, M., & Kalb, L. (2001). The concentration of offenders in families, and family criminality in the prediction of boys' delinquency. *Journal of Adolescence, 24,* 579–596.

Farrington, D. P., & Loeber, R. (1999). Transatlantic replicability of risk factors in the development of delinquency. In P. Cohen, C. Slomkowski, & L. N. Robins (Eds.), *Historical and geographical influences on psychopathology* (pp. 299–329). Mahwah, NJ: Erlbaum.

Farrington, D. P., & Loeber, R. (2000). Some benefits of dichotomization in psychiatric and criminological research. *Criminal Behaviour and Mental Health, 10,* 100–122.

Farrington, D. P., Loeber, R., Elliott, D. S., Hawkins, J. D., Kandel, D. B., Klein, M. W., McCord, J., Rowe, D. C., & Tremblay, R. E. (1990). Advancing knowledge about the onset of delinquency and crime. In B. B. Lahey and A. E. Kazdin (Eds.), *Advances in clinical child psychology* (vol. 13, pp. 283–342). New York: Plenum.

Farrington, D. P., Loeber, R., Homish, D. L., & Stallings, R. (in press). Early risk factors for homicide offenders and victims. In M. J. Delisi & P. J. Conis (Eds.), *Violent Offenders: Theory, Research, Public Policy, and Practice.* Sudbury, MA: Jones and Barlett.

Farrington, D. P., Loeber, R., Stouthamer-Loeber, M., Van Kammen, W. B., & Schmidt, L. (1996). Self-reported delinquency and a combined delinquency seriousness scale based on boys, mothers, and teachers: Concurrent and predictive validity for African-Americans and Caucasians. *Criminology, 34,* 493–517.

Farrington, D. P., Loeber, R., & Van Kammen, W. B. (1990). Long-term criminal outcomes of hyperactivity—impulsivity—attention deficit and conduct problems in childhood. In L. N. Robins & M. Rutter (Eds.), *Straight and devious pathways from childhood to adulthood* (pp. 62–81). Cambridge, U.K.: Cambridge University Press.

Farrington, D. P., Loeber, R., Yin, Y., & Anderson, S. J. (2002). Are within-individual causes of delinquency the same as between-individual causes? *Criminal Behaviour and Mental Health, 12,* 53–68.

Farrington, D. P., Snyder, H. N., & Finnegan, T. A. (1988). Specialization in juvenile court careers. *Criminology, 26,* 461–487.

Farrington, D. P., & Welsh, B. C. (2002). Family-based crime prevention. In L. W. Sherman, D. P. Farrington, & B. C. Welsh (Eds.), *Evidence-based crime prevention* (pp. 62-90). London: Routledge.

Farrington, D. P., & Welsh, B. C. (2003). Family-based prevention of offending: A meta-analysis. *Australian and New Zealand Journal of Criminology, 36,* 127–151.

Farrington, D. P., & Welsh, B. C. (2007). *Saving children from a life of crime: Early risk factors and effective interventions.* Oxford, England: Oxford University Press.

Fergusson, D. M., & Horwood, L. J. (1995). Early disruptive behavior, IQ and later school achievement and delinquent behavior. *Journal of Abnormal Child Psychology, 23,* 183–199.

Fergusson, D. M., Horwood, L. J., & Nagin, D. S. (2000). Offending trajectories in a New Zealand birth cohort. *Criminology, 38,* 525–551.

Fergusson, D. M., Horwood, L. J., & Ridder, E. M. (2005a). Show me the child at seven: The consequences of conduct problems in childhood for psychosocial functioning in adulthood. *Journal of Child Psychology and Psychiatry, 46,* 837–849.

Fergusson, D. M., Horwood, L. J., & Ridder, E. M. (2005b). Show me the child at seven II: Childhood intelligence and later outcomes in adolescence and young adulthood. *Journal of Child Psychology and Psychiatry, 46,* 850–858.

Fergusson, D. M., & Woodward, L. J. (2000). Educational, psychosocial, and sexual outcomes of girls with conduct problems in early adolescence. *Journal of Child Psychology and Psychiatry, 41,* 779–792.

Frick, P. J., O'Brien, B. S., Wootton, J., & McBurnett, K. (1994). Psychopathy and conduct problems in children. *Journal of Abnormal Psychology, 103,* 700–707.

Fung, M. T., Raine, A., Loeber, R., Lynam, D. R., Steinhauer, S. R., Venables, P. H., & Stouthamer-Loeber, M. (2005). Reduced electrodermal activity in psychopathy-prone adolescents. *Journal of Abnormal Psychology, 114,* 187–196.

Gatzke-Kopp, L. M., Raine, A., Loeber, R., Stouthamer-Loeber, M., & Steinhauer, S. (2002). Serious delinquent behavior, sensation-seeking and electrodermal arousal. *Journal of Abnormal Child Psychology, 30,* 477–486.

Gershoff, E. T. (2002). Corporal punishment, physical abuse, and the burden of proof: Reply to Baumrind, Larzelere, and Cohen (2002), Holden (2002), and Parke (2002). *Psychological Bulletin, 128,* 602–611.

Gibbons, D. C. (1975). Offender typologies—Two decades later. *British Journal of Criminology, 15,* 140–156.

Gilliom, M. (2004). *Desistance from childhood physical aggression.* Unpublished doctoral dissertation, University of Pittsburgh.

Glueck, S., & Glueck, E. T. (1940). *Juvenile delinquents grown up.* New York: Commonwealth Fund.

Goldstein, P. J. (1985). The drugs/violence nexus: A tripartite conceptual framework. *Journal of Drug Issues, 15*, 493–506.

Gordon, R. A., Lahey, B. B., Kawai, E., Loeber, R., Stouthamer-Loeber, M., & Farrington, D. P. (2004). Antisocial behavior and youth gang membership: Selection and socialization. *Criminology, 42*, 55–87.

Gorman-Smith, D., Henry, D. B., & Tolan, P. H. (2004). Exposure to community violence and violence perpetration: The protective effects of family functioning. *Journal of Clinical Child and Adolescent Psychology, 33*, 439–449.

Gorman-Smith, D., & Loeber, R. (2005). Are developmental pathways in disruptive behaviors the same for girls and boys? *Journal of Child and Family Studies, 14*, 15–27.

Gorman-Smith, D., & Tolan, P. (1998). The role of exposure to community violence and developmental problems among inner-city youth. *Development and Psychopathology, 10*, 101–116.

Gottfredson, G. D., & Gottfredson, D. C. (2001). *Gang problems and gang programs in a national sample of schools.* Ellicott City, MD: Gottfredson Associates.

Gottfredson, M., & Hirschi, T. (1987). The methodological adequacy of longitudinal research on crime. *Criminology, 25*, 581–614.

Gottfredson, M. R. & Hirschi, T. (1990). *A general theory of crime.* Stanford, CA: Stanford University Press.

Gottlieb, G., & Halpern, C. T. (2002). A relational view of causality in normal and abnormal development. *Development and Psychopathology, 14*, 421–435.

Greenfeld, L. A., & Henneberg, M. A. (2001). Victims and offender self-reports of alcohol involvement in crime. *Alcohol Research and Health, 25*, 20–31.

Greenwood, P. W. (2006). *Changing lives: Delinquency prevention as crime-control policy.* Chicago: University of Chicago Press.

Haapasalo, J., & Tremblay, R. E. (1994). Physically aggressive boys from ages 6 to 12: Family background, parenting behavior, and prediction of delinquency. *Journal of Consulting Clinical Psychology, 62*, 1044–1052.

Hardin, J. W., & Hilbe, J. M. (2003). *Generalized estimating equations.* Boca Raton, FL: Chapman & Hall/CRC Press.

Harlow, C. W. (1999). Prior abuse reported by inmates and probationers. Washington, DC: *Bureau of Justice Statistics- Selected Findings*, 1–4.

Harrison, L. D. (1992). Trends in illicit drug use in the USA: Conflicting results of national surveys. *International Journal of the Addictions, 27*, 817–847.

Harrison, L., & Freeman, C. (1998, Nov.). *The drug-violence nexus among youth.* Paper presented to the American Society of Criminology, Washington, D.C.

Hawkins, J. D., Catalano, R. F., & Arthur, M. W. (2002). Promoting science-based prevention in communities. *Addictive Behaviors, 27*, 951–976.

Hawkins, J. D., Catalano, R. F., & Miller, J. Y. (1992). Risk and protective factors for alcohol and other drug problems in adolescence and early adulthood–Implications for substance abuse prevention. *Psychological Bulletin, 112*, 64–105.

Hawkins, J. D., Herrenkohl, T., Farrington, D. P., Brewer, D., Catalano, R. F., & Harachi. T. W. (1998). A review of predictors of youth violence. In R. Loeber & D. P. Farrington (Eds.), *Serious and violent juvenile offenders: Risk factors and successful interventions* (pp. 106–146). Thousand Oaks, CA: Sage.

Hawkins, J. D., Smith, B. H., Hill, K. G., Kosterman, R., Catalano, R. F., & Abbott, R. D. (2003). Understanding and preventing crime and violence findings from the Seattle social development project. In T. P. Thornberry & M. D. Krohn (Eds.), *Taking stock of delinquency: An overview of findings from contemporary longitudinal studies* (pp. 255–312). New York: Kluwer Academic/Plenum.

Hetherington, E. M., Bridges, M., & Insabella, G. M. (1998). What matters—what does not: Five perspectives on the association between marital transaction and children's adjustment. *American Psychologist, 53,* 167–184.

Hinshaw, S. P. (1992). Academic underachievement, attention deficits, and aggression: Comorbidity and implications for intervention. *Journal of Consulting and Clinical Psychology, 60,* 893–903.

Hinshaw, S. P. (2002). Process, mechanism, and explanation related to externalizing behavior in developmental psychopathology. *Journal of Abnormal Psychology, 30,* 431–446.

Hipwell, A., Loeber, R., Stouthamer-Loeber, M., Keenan, K., White, H. R., & Kroneman, L. (2002). Characteristics of girls with early onset disruptive and antisocial behaviour. *Criminal Behaviour and Mental Health, 12,* 99–118.

Hirschi, T. (1969). *Causes of delinquency.* Berkeley: University of California Press.

Hollingshead, A. B. (1975). *Four factor index of social status.* Unpublished manuscript, Yale University.

Homish, D. L. (2002). *Official record project manual.* Unpublished manuscript, University of Pittsburgh.

Horney, J., Osgood, D. W., & Marshall, I. H. (1995). Criminal careers in the short-term: Intra-individual variability in crime and its relation to local life circumstances. *American Sociological Review, 60,* 655–673.

Howell, J. C. (2003). Diffusing research into practice using the comprehensive strategy for serious, violent, and chronic juvenile offenders. *Youth Violence and Juvenile Justice, 1,* 219–245.

Howell, J. C., & Decker, S. H. (1999). *The youth gang, drugs, and violence connection.* (OJJDP Juvenile Justice Bulletin.) Washington, DC: U.S. Department of Justice, Office of Juvenile Justice and Delinquency Prevention.

Hsia, H. M. (1997). *Allegheny County, PA: Mobilizing to reduce juvenile crime.* (OJJDP Juvenile Justice Bulletin.) Washington, DC: U.S. Department of Justice, Office of Juvenile Justice and Delinquency Prevention.

Huesmann, L. R., Eron, L. D., & Dubow, E. F. (2002). Childhood predictors of adult criminality: Are all risk factors reflected in childhood aggressiveness? *Criminal Behavior and Mental Health, 12,* 185–208.

Hughes, T. L., & Loeber, R. (2007, August). Developmental trajectory analysis of self-report anxiety in children and adolescents. Paper presented at the American Psychological Association Conference in San Francisco, CA.

Huizinga, D., & Elliott, D. S. (1987). Juvenile offenders: Prevalence, offender incidence, and arrest rates by race. *Crime and Delinquency, 33,* 206–223.

Huizinga, D. H., Menard, S., & Elliot, D. S. (1989). Delinquency and drug use: Temporal and developmental patterns. *Justice Quarterly, 6,* 419–455.

Huizinga, D., Thornberry, T. P., Knight, K. E., Lovegrove, P. J., Loeber, R., Hill, K., & Farrington, D. P. (2007). *Disproportionate minority contact in the juvenile justice system: A study of differential minority arrest/referral to court in three cities.* (Report.) Washington, DC: U.S. Department of Justice, Office of Juvenile Justice and Delinquency Prevention.

Huizinga, D., Weiher, A. W., Espiritu. R., & Esbensen, F. (2003) Delinquency and crime: Some highlights from the Denver Youth Survey. In T. Thornberry and M. Krohn (Eds). *Taking stock of delinquency: An overview of findings from contemporary longitudinal studies* (pp. 47–91). New York: Kluwer Academic/Plenum.

Hunt, D. E. (1990). In M. Tonry (Ed.) Drugs and consensual crimes. *Crime and justice: Vol. 13* (pp. 159–202). Chicago: University of Chicago Press.

Hunt, G. P., & Laidler, K. J. (2001). Alcohol and violence in the lives of gang members. *Alcohol Research and Health, 25,* 66–71.

Hussong, A. M., Curran, P. J., Moffitt, T. E., Caspi, A., & Carrig, M. M. (2004). Substance abuse hinders desistance in young adults' antisocial behavior. *Developmental Psychopathology, 16,* 1029–1046.

Inciardi, J. A., & Pottieger, A. E (1991). Kids, crack, and crime. *Journal of Drug Issues, 21,* 257–270.

Inciardi, J. A., & Pottieger, A. E. (1994). Crack-cocaine use and street crime. *Journal of Drug Issues, 24,* 273–292.

Inciardi, J. A., & Pottieger, A. E. (1998). Drug use and street crime in Miami: an (almost) twenty year retrospective. *Substance Use and Misuse, 33,* 1839–1870.

Jessor, R., & Jessor, S. L. (1973). The perceived environment in behavioral science: Some conceptual issues and some illustrative data. *American Behavioral Scientist, 16,* 801–828.

John, O. P., Caspi, A., Robins, R. W., Moffitt, T. E., & Stouthamer-Loeber, M. (1994). The "little five": Exploring the five-factor model of personality in adolescent boys. *Child Development, 65,* 160–178.

Johnston, L. D., O'Malley, P. M., & Bachman, J. G. (2001). *Monitoring the future: National results on adolescent drug-use overview of key findings 2001.* Bethesda, MD: National Institute of Drug Abuse.

Jolliffe, D., & Farrington, D. P. (2004). Empathy and offending: A systematic review and meta-analysis. *Aggression and Violent Behavior, 9,* 441–476.

Jones, B. L., Nagin, D. S., & Roeder, K. (2001). An SAS procedure based on mixture models for estimating developmental trajectories. *Sociological Methods of Research, 29,* 374–393.

Juon, H. S., Ensminger, M. E., & Sydnor, K. D. (2002). A longitudinal study of developmental trajectories to young adult cigarette smoking. *Drug and Alcohol Dependency, 66,* 303–314.

Kandel, D. B., Yamaguchi, K., & Chen, K. (1992). Stages of progression in drug involvement from adolescence to adulthood—Further evidence for the gateway theory. *Journal of Studies on Alcohol, 53,* 447–458.

Kazemian, L. (2007). Desistance from crime: Theoretical, empirical, methodological, and policy considerations. *Journal of Contemporary Criminal Justice, 23,* 5–27.

Kazemian, L., & Farrington, D. P. (2005). Comparing the validity of prospective, retrospective, and official onset for different offending categories. *Journal of Quantitative Criminology 21,* 127–147.

Kazemian, L., & Farrington, D. P. (2006). Exploring residual career length and residual number of offenses for two generations of repeat offenders. *Journal of Research in Crime and Delinquency, 43,* 89–113.

Keenan, K., & Shaw, D. D. (2003). Development of conduct problems during the preschool years. In B. B. Lahey, T. E. Moffitt, & A. Caspi (Eds.), *Causes of conduct disorder and juvenile delinquency* (pp. 153–181). New York: Guilford.

Keenan, K., & Wakschlag, L. S. (2003). Psychiatric diagnosis in preschool children: Drs. Keenan and Wakschlag reply. *Journal of the American Academy of Child and Adolescent Psychiatry, 42,* 129–130.

Kellam, S. G., Rebok, G. W., Ialongo, N., & Mayer, L. S. (1994). The course and malleability of aggressive behavior from early first grade into middle school: Results of a developmental epidemiologically based preventive trial. *Journal of Child Psychology and Psychiatry, 35,* 259–281.

Kelley, B. T., Loeber, R., Keenan, K., & DeLamatre, M. (1997). *Developmental pathways in boys' delinquent behavior.* (OJJDP Juvenile Justice Bulletin.) Washington, DC: U.S. Department of Justice, Office of Juvenile Justice and Delinquency Prevention.

Kirk, D. S. (2006). Examining the divergence across self-report and official data sources on interferences about the adolescent life-course of crime. *Journal of Quantitative Criminology, 22,* 107–129.

Klein, M. W. (1984). Offense specialization and versatility among juveniles. *British Journal of Criminology, 24,* 185–194.

Klein, M. W., Maxson, C. L., & Miller, J. (1995). The modern gang reader. *Journal of Criminal Justice, 23,* 572.

Klinteberg, B. A., Andersson, T., Magnusson, D., & Stattin, H. (1993). Hyperactive behavior in childhood as related to subsequent alcohol problems and violent offending: A longitudinal study of male subjects. *Personality and Individual Differences, 15,* 381–388.

Kohlberg, L. (1969). Stage and sequence: The cognitive-developmental approach to socialization. In D. A. Goslin (Ed.), *Handbook of socialization theory and research* (pp. 347–480). Chicago: Rand McNally.

Koolhof, R., Loeber, R., Wei, E. H., Pardini, D., D'Escury, A. C., Moffitt, T., & Lynam, D. (in press). Inhibition deficits of serious delinquent boys with low intelligence. *Criminal Behaviour and Mental Health.*

Kouri, E. M., Pope, H. G., Powell, K. F., Olivia, P. S., & Campbell, C. (1997). Drug use history and criminal behavior among 133 men. *American Journal of Drug and Alcohol Abuse, 23,* 413–420.

Krueger, R., Caspi, A., Moffitt, T. E., White, J., & Stouthamer-Loeber, M. (1996). Delay of gratification, psychopathology, and personality: Is low self-control specific to externalizing problems? *Journal of Personality, 64,* 107–129.

Lacourse, E., Côté, S., Nagin, D. S., Vitaro, F., Brendgen, M., & Tremblay, R. E. (2002). Longitudinal-experimental approach to testing theories of antisocial behavior development. *Development and Psychopathology, 14,* 909–924.

Lacourse, E., Nagin, R. E., Tremblay, F., Vitaro, F., & Claes, M. (2003). Developmental trajectories of boys' delinquent group membership and facilitation of violent behaviors during adolescence. *Development and psychopathology, 15,* 183–197.

Lahey, B. B., Loeber, R., Burke, J., Rathouz, P. J., & McBurnett, K. (2002). Waxing and waning in concert: Dynamic comorbidity of conduct disorder with other disruptive and emotional problems over 7 years among clinic-referred boys. *Journal of Abnormal Psychology, 111,* 556–567.

Lahey, B. B., Moffitt, T. E., & Caspi, A. (2003). Cause of conduct disorder and juvenile delinquency. In P-O. H. Wikström, & R. J. Sampson (Eds.), *Social mechanisms of community influences on crime and pathways in criminality* (pp. 118–147). New York: Guilford.

Laub, J. H., & Sampson, R. J. (2001). Understanding desistance from crime. In M. Tonry (Ed.), *Crime and justice: An annual review of research, Vol. 18:* (pp. 1–69). Chicago: University of Chicago Press.

Laub, J. H., & Sampson, R. J. (2003). *Shared beginnings, divergent lives: Delinquent boys to age 70.* Cambridge, MA: Harvard University Press.

Lauritsen, J. L. (2003). *How families and communities influence youth victimization.* Washington, DC: U.S. Department of Justice, Office of Juvenile Justice and Delinquency Prevention.

Le Blanc, M., & Bouthillier, C. (2003). A developmental test of the general deviance syndrome with adjudicated girls and boys using hierarchical confirmatory factor analysis. *Criminal Behaviour and Mental Health, 13,* 81–105.

Le Blanc, M., Côté G., & Loeber, R. (1991). Temporal paths in delinquency: Stability, regression, and progression analyzed with panel data from an adolescent and a delinquent male sample. *Canadian Journal of Criminology, 33,* 23–44.

Le Blanc, M., & Kaspy, N. (1998). Trajectories of delinquency and problem behavior: Comparison of social and personal control characteristics of adjudicated boys on synchronous and nonsynchronous paths. *Journal of Quantitative Criminology, 14,* 181–214.

Le Blanc, M., & Loeber, R. (1998). Developmental criminology updated. In M. Tonry (Ed.), *Crime and justice: A review of research, Vol. 23* (pp. 115–197). Chicago: University of Chicago Press.

Le Blanc, M., McDuff, P., & Kaspy, N. (1998). Family and early adolescent delinquency: A comprehensive sequential family control model. *Early Child Development and Care, 142,* 63–91.

Leibenluft, E., Cohen, P., Gorrindo, T., Brook, J., & Pine, D. S. (2006). Chronic versus episodic irritability in youth: A community-based, longitudinal study of clinical and diagnostic associations. *Journal of Child and Adolescent Psychopathology, 16,* 456-466.

Levine, F., & Rosich, K. (1996). *Social causes of violence: Crafting a science agenda.* Washington D.C.: American Sociological Association.

Liang, K., & Zeger, S. I. (1986). Longitudinal data analysis using generalized linear models. *Biometricka, 73,* 13–22.

Lipsey, M. W., & Derzon, J. H. (1998). Predictors of violent or serious delinquency in adolescence and early adulthood: A synthesis of longitudinal research. In R. Loeber & D. P. Farrington (Eds.), *Serious and violent juvenile offenders: Risk factors and successful interventions* (pp. 86–105). Thousands Oaks, CA: Sage.

Lipton, D. S., & Johnson, B. D. (1998). Smack, crack, and score: Two decades of NIDA-funded drugs and crime research at NDRI 1974-1994. *Substance Use and Misuse, 33,* 1779-1815.

Lochman, J. E., & Wells, K. C. (2002). Contextual social-cognitive mediators and child outcome: A test of the theoretical model in the coping power program. *Development and Psychopathology, 14*, 945–967.

Loeber, R. (1982). The stability of antisocial and delinquent child behavior: A review. *Child Development, 53*, 1431–1446.

Loeber, R. (1988). Natural histories of conduct problems, delinquency, and associated substance use: Evidence for developmental progressions. In B. B. Lahey & A. E. Kazdin (Eds.), *Advances in Clinical Child Psychology* (Vol. 11, pp. 73–124). New York: Plenum.

Loeber, R., & Coie, J. (2001). Continuities and discontinuities of development, with particular emphasis on emotional and cognitive components of disruptive behavior. In J. Hill & B. Maughan (Eds.), *Conduct disorders in childhood and adolescence* (pp. 379–407). Cambridge, England: Cambridge University Press.

Loeber, R., DeLamaire, M., Keenan, K., & Zhang, Q. (1998). A prospective replication of developmental pathways in disruptive and delinquent behavior. In R. Cairns, L. Bergman & J. Kagan (Eds.), *Methods and models for studying the individual* (pp. 185–215). Thousand Oaks, CA: Sage.

Loeber, R., DeLamaire, M., Tita, G., Cohen, J., Stouthamer-Loeber, M., & Farrington, D. P. (1999). Gun injury and mortality: The delinquent backgrounds of juvenile victims. *Violence and Victims, 14*, 339–352.

Loeber, R., & Dishion, T. (1983). Early predictors of male delinquency: A review. *Psychological Bulletin, 94*, 68–99.

Loeber, R., Drinkwater, M., Yin, Y., Anderson, S. J., Schmidt, L. C., & Crawford, A. (2000). Stability of family interaction from ages 6 to 18. *Journal of Abnormal Child Psychology, 28*, 353–369.

Loeber, R., & Farrington, D. P. (Eds.) (1998). *Serious and violent juvenile offenders: Risk factors and successful interventions.* Thousand Oaks, CA: Sage.

Loeber, R., & Farrington, D.P. (Eds.) (2001). *Child delinquents: Development, intervention, and service needs.* Thousand Oaks, CA: Sage.

Loeber, R., & Farrington, D. P. (in press). Advancing knowledge about causes using longitudinal studies. In A. Liberman (Ed.), *The yield of recent longitudinal research on crime and delinquency.* New York: Springer.

Loeber, R., Farrington, D. P., & Petechuk, D. (May, 2003). *Child delinquency: Early intervention and prevention.* (Child Delinquency Bulletin Series no. NCJ-186162.) Washington DC: U.S. Department of Justice, Office of Juvenile Justice and Delinquency Prevention.

Loeber, R., Farrington, D. P., Stouthamer-Loeber, M., Moffitt, T. E., & Caspi, A. (1998). The development of male offending: Key findings from the first decade of the Pittsburgh Youth Study. *Studies in Crime and Crime Prevention, 7*, 141–171.

Loeber, R., Farrington, D. P., Stouthamer-Loeber, M., & Van Kammen, W. B. (1998). *Antisocial behavior and mental health problems: Explanatory factors in childhood and adolescence.* Mahwah, NJ: Erlbaum.

Loeber, R., Farrington, D. P., & Waschbusch, D. A. (1998). Serious and violent juvenile offenders. In R. Loeber, & D. P. Farrington (Eds.), *Serious and violent juvenile offenders: Risk factors and successful interventions* (pp. 13–29). Thousand Oaks, CA: Sage.

Loeber, R., Green, S. M., Lahey, B. B., & Kalb, L. (2000), Physical fighting in childhood as a mental health risk. *Journal of the American Academy of Child and Adolescent Psychiatry, 39,* 1–8.

Loeber, R., & Hay, D. (1997). Key issues in the development of aggression and violence from childhood to early adulthood. *Annual Review of Psychology, 48,* 371–410.

Loeber, R., Keenan, K., Lahey, B. B., Green, S. M., & Thomas, C. (1993). Evidence for developmentally based diagnoses of oppositional defiant disorder and conduct disorder. *Journal of Abnormal Child Psychology, 21,* 377–410.

Loeber, R., Keenan, K., Russo, M. F., Green, S. M., Lahey, B. B., & Thomas, C. (1998). Secondary data analyses for DSM-IV on the symptoms of oppositional defiant disorder and conduct disorder. In T. Widiger, A. Frances, H. A. Pincus, R. Ross, M. B. First, W. Davis, & M. Kline (Eds.), *DSM-IV sourcebook* (vol. 4, pp. 465–490). Washington, DC: American Psychiatric Association Press.

Loeber, R., Keenan, K., & Zhang, Q. (1997). Boys' experimentation and persistence in developmental pathways toward serious delinquency. *Journal of Child and Family Studies, 6,* 321–357.

Loeber, R., Lacourse, E., & Homish, D. L. (2005). Homicide, violence and developmental trajectories. In R. E. Tremblay, W. W. Hartup, & J. Archer (Eds.), *Developmental origins of aggression* (pp. 202–220). New York: Guilford.

Loeber, R., & Le Blanc, M. (1990). Toward a developmental criminology. In M. Tonry and M. Morris (Eds.), *Crime and justice: An annual review of research, Vol. 2(12)* (pp. 375–473). Chicago: University of Chicago Press.

Loeber, R., Pardini, D., Homish, D. L., Wei, E. H., Crawford, A. M., Farrington, D. P., Stouthamer-Loeber, M., Creemers, J., Koehler, S. A., & Rosenfeld, R. (2005). The prediction of violence and homicide in young men. *Journal of Consulting and Clinical Psychology, 73,* 1074–1088.

Loeber, R., Pardini, D. A., Stouthamer-Loeber, M., & Raine, A. (in press). Do cognitive, physiological and psycho-social risk and promotive factors predict desistance from delinquency in males? *Development and Psychopathology.*

Loeber, R., Slot, N. W., & Stouthamer-Loeber, M. (2006). A three-dimensional, cumulative developmental model of serious delinquency. In P-O. H. Wikström & R. Sampson (Eds.), *The explanation of crime: Contexts and mechanisms* (pp 153–194). Cambridge, England: Cambridge University Press.

Loeber, R., & Snyder, H. N. (1990). Rate of offending in juvenile careers: Findings of constancy and change in lamda. *Criminology, 28,* 97–109.

Loeber, R., & Stouthamer-Loeber, M. (1998). Development of juvenile aggression and violence. Some common misconceptions and controversies. *American Psychology, 53,* 242–259.

Loeber, R., & Stouthamer-Loeber, M. (1986). Family factors as correlates and predictors of juvenile conduct problems and delinquency. In N. Morris & M. Tonry (Eds.), *Crime and justice: An annual review of research, Vol. 7* (pp. 29–149). Chicago: University of Chicago Press.

Loeber, R., Stouthamer-Loeber, M., Van Kammen, W. B., & Farrington, D. P. (1989). Development of a new measure of self-reported antisocial behavior for young children: Prevalence and reliability. In M. Klein (Ed.), *Cross-national research in self-reported crime and delinquency* (pp. 203–225). Boston: Kluwer Academic.

Loeber, R., Wei, E., Stouthamer-Loeber, M., Huizinga, D., & Thornberry, T. (1999). Behavioral antecedents to serious and violent offending: Joint analysis from the Denver Youth Survey, Pittsburgh Youth Study, and The Rochester Youth Development Study. *Studies on Crime and Crime Prevention, 8*, 245–263.

Loeber, R., Wung, P., Keenan, K., Giroux, B., Stouthamer-Loeber, M., Van Kammen, W. B., & Maughan, B. (1993). Developmental pathways in disruptive child behavior. *Development and Psychopathology, 5*, 101–132.

Lombroso, C. (1912). Crime and insanity in the twenty-first century. *Journal of the American Institute of Criminal Law and Criminology, 3*, 57–61.

Lösel, F., & Bender, D. (2003). Protective factors and resilience. In D. P. Farrington & J. Coid (Eds.), *Early Prevention of Adult Anti-social Behaviour* (pp. 130-204). Cambridge, England: Cambridge University Press.

Lösel, F., & Bender, D. (2006). Risk factors for serious and violent antisocial behaviour in children and youth. In A. Hagell, & R. Jeyarajah-Dent (Eds.), *Children Who Commit Acts of Serious Interpersonal Violence* (pp. 42–72). London: Jessica Kingsley.

Luthar, S. S., Cicchetti, D., & Becker, B. (2000). The construct of resilience: a critical evaluation and guidelines for future work. *Child Development, 71*, 543–562.

Lynam, D. (1997). Pursuing the psychopath: Capturing the fledgling psychopath in a nomological net. *Journal of Abnormal Psychology, 106*, 425–438.

Lynam, D. R., Piquero, A. R., & Moffitt, T. E. (2004). Specialization and the propensity to violence: Support from self-reports but not official records. *Journal of Contemporary Criminal Justice, 20*, 215–228.

Magnusson, D. (1998). The person in developmental research. In J. G. Adair, D. Belanger, & K. L. Dion (Eds.), *Advances in psychological science: Social, personal and cultural aspects* (pp. 495–511). Hove, East Sussex, England: Psychology Press.

Magnusson, D. (2003). The person approach: Concepts, measurement models, and research strategy. *New Directions for Child and Adolescent Development, 101*, 3–23.

Maguin, E. (1994), *Manual for retrieving juvenile court data from the Allegheny County Juvenile Court files.* Unpublished manuscript, Western Psychiatric Institute and Clinic, University of Pittsburgh.

Massoglia, M., & Uggen, C. (2007). Subjective desistance and the transition to adulthood. *Journal of Contemporary Criminal Justice, 23*, 90–103.

Masten, A. S., Best, K. M., & Garmezy, N. (1990). Resilience and development: Contributions from the study of children who overcome adversity. *Development and Psychopathology, 2*, 425–444.

Masten, A. S., & Garmezy, N. (1985). Risk, vulnerability, and protective factors in developmental psychopathology. In B. B. Lahey & A. E. Kazdin (Eds.), *Advances in clinical child psychology* (Vol. 8, pp. 1–52). New York: Plenum.

Masten, A. S., Roisman, G. I., Long, J. D., Burt, K. B., Obradovic, J., Riley, J. R., Boelcke-Stennes, K., & Tellegen, A. (2005). Developmental cascades: Linking academic achievement and externalizing and internalizing symptoms over 20 years. *Developmental Psychology, 41*, 733–746.

Maughan, B., Pickles, A., Rowe, R., Costello, E. J., & Angold, A. (2000). Developmental trajectories of aggressive and non-aggressive conduct problems. *Journal of Quantitative Criminology, 16*, 199–221.

McBurnett, K., Lahey, B. B., Raine, A., Stouthamer-Loeber, M., Loeber, R., Kumar, A., Kumar, M., Moffitt, T., & Caspi, A. (2005). Mood and hormone responses to psychological challenge in adolescent males with conduct problems. *Biological Psychiatry, 57,* 1109–1116.

McCord, J. (1991). Family relationships, juvenile delinquency and adult criminality. *Criminology, 29,* 397–417.

McCord, J., Widom, C. S., & Crowell, N. A. (2001). *Juvenile crime, juvenile justice. (Panel on juvenile crime: Prevention, treatment, and control).* Washington D.C.: National Academy Press.

Meredith, W., & Tisak, J. (1990). Latent curve analysis. *Psychometrika, 55,* 107–122.

Messer, S. C., Angold, A., Loeber, R., Costello, E. J., Van Kammen, W. B., & Stouthamer-Loeber, M. (1995), The development of a short questionnaire for use in epidemiological studies of depression in children and adolescents: Factor composition and structure across development. *International Journal of Methods in Psychiatric Research, 5,* 251–262.

Moffitt, T. E. (1993). Adolescence-limited and life-course-persistent antisocial behavior: A developmental taxonomy. *Psychological Review, 100,* 674–701.

Moffitt, T. E. (2005). The new look of behavioral genetics in developmental psychopathology: Gene-environment interplay in antisocial behaviors. *Psychology Bulletin, 131,* 533–554.

Moffitt, T. E., Caspi, A., Rutter, M., & Silva, P. A. (2001). *Sex differences in antisocial behaviour: Conduct disorder, delinquency, and violence in the Dunedin longitudinal study.* Cambridge, England: Cambridge University Press.

Moore, J. W. (1990). *Gangs, drugs, and violence.* (NIDA Research Monograph Series no. 103: Drug and violence: Causes, correlates, and consequences, pp. 160–176). Bethesda, MD: National Institute on Drug Abuse.

Moos, R. H., & Moos, B. S. (1975). Evaluating correctional and community settings. In R. H. Moos (Ed.), *Families* (pp. 263–286). New York: Wiley.

Morizot, J. & LeBlanc, M. (2007). Behavioral, self, and social control predictors of desistance from crime, *Journal of Contemporary Criminal Justice, 23,* 50–71.

Mossman, D. (1994). Assessing predictors of violence—Being accurate about accuracy. *Journal of Consulting and Clinical Psychology, 62,* 783–792.

Mulvey, E. P., Steinberg, L., Fagan, J., Cauffman, E., Piquero, A. R., Chassin, L., Knight, G. P., Brame, R. B., Schubert, C. A., Hecker, T., & Losoya, S. H. (2004). Theory and research on desistance from antisocial activity among serious adolescent offenders. *Youth Violence and Juvenile Justice, 2,* 213–236.

Muris, P. (2006). The pathogenesis of childhood anxiety disorders: Considerations from a developmental psychopathology perspective. *International Journal of Behavioral Development,* 30, 5–11.

Muthén, B. (2001). Latent variable mixture modeling. In G. A. Marcoulides & R. E. Schumacker (Eds.), *New Developments and Techniques in Structural Equation Modeling* (pp. 1–33). Hillsdale, NJ: Erlbaum.

Nagin, D. S. (1999). Analyzing developmental trajectories: A semiparametric, group-based approach. *Psychological Methods, 4,* 139–157.

Nagin, D. S. (2004). Response to 'Methodological sensitivities to latent class analysis of long-term criminal trajectories.' *Journal of Quantitative Criminology, 20,* 27–35.

Nagin, D. S. (2005). *Group-based Modeling of Development.* Cambridge, MA: Harvard University Press.

Nagin, D. S., Barker, E. D., Lacourse, É., & Tremblay, R. E. (in press). The inter-relationship of temporally distinct risk markers and the transition from childhood physical aggression to adolescent violent delinquency. In P. Cohen, R. Pruzek, & R. Cudeck (Eds.), *Applied Data Analytic Techniques for Turning Points Research.* Mahwah, NJ: Erlbaum.

Nagin, D. S., & Farrington, D. P. (1992). The stability of criminal potential from childhood to adulthood. *Criminology, 30,* 235–260.

Nagin, D. S., Farrington, D. P., & Moffitt, T. E. (1995). Life-course trajectories of different types of offenders. *Criminology, 33,* 111–139.

Nagin, D. S., & Land, K. C. (1993). Age, criminal careers, and population heterogeneity: Specification and estimation of a nonparametric, mixed Poisson model. *Criminology, 31,* 327–362.

Nagin, D. S., & Tremblay, R. E. (1999). Trajectories of boys' physical aggression, opposition, and hyperactivity on the path to physically violent and nonviolent juvenile delinquency. *Child Development, 70,* 1181–1196.

Nagin, D. S., & Tremblay, R. E. (2001a). Analysing developmental trajectories of distinct but related behaviors: A group-based method. *Psychological Methods, 6,* 18–34.

Nagin, D. S., & Tremblay, R. E. (2001b). Parental and early childhood predictors of persistent physical aggression in boys from kindergarten to high school. *Archives of General Psychiatry, 58,* 389–394.

Nagin, D. S., & Tremblay, R. E. (2005). What has been learned from group-based trajectory modeling? Examples from physical aggression and other problem behaviors. *Annals of the American Academy of Political and Social Science, 602,* 82–117.

Neugarten, D. A. (1996). *The meaning of age: Selected papers of Bernice L. Neugarten.* Chicago: University of Chicago Press.

Odgers, C. L., Caspi, A., Broadbent, J. M., Dickson, N., Hancox, R. J., Harrington, H., Poulton, R., Sears, M. R., Thomson, W. M., & Moffitt, T. E. (in press). Conduct problems subtypes in males predict differential adult health burden. *Archives of General Psychiatry.*

Osgood, D. W., & Rowe, D. C. (1994). Bridging criminal careers, theory, and policy through latent variable models of individual offending. *Criminology, 32,* 517–554.

Patrick, M. R., Snyder, J., Schrepferman, L. M., & Snyder, J. (2005). The joint contribution of early parental warmth, communication and tracking, and early child conduct problems on monitoring in late childhood. *Child Development, 76,* 999–1014.

Patterson, G. R. (1982). *A Social Learning Approach: Vol. 3: Coercive Family Process.* Eugene, OR: Castalia.

Patterson, G. R., DeBaryshe, B. D., & Ramsey, E. (1989). A developmental perspective on antisocial behavior. *American Psychologist, 44,* 329–335.

Patterson, G. R., Dishion, T. J., & Yoerger, K. (2000). Adolescent growth in new forms of problem behavior: Macro- and micro- peer dynamics. *Prevention Science, 1,* 3–13.

Patterson, G. R., Shaw, D. S., Synder, J. J., & Yoerger, K. (2005). Changes in maternal ratings of children's overt and convert antisocial behavior. *Aggressive Behavior, 31*, 473–484.

Patterson, G. R., & Yoerger, K. (1993). Developmental models for delinquent behavior. In S. Hodgins (Ed.), *Crime and mental disorder* (pp. 140–172). Newbury Park, CA: Sage.

Patterson, G. R., & Yoerger, K. (1997). A developmental model for late onset delinquency. In R. Dienstbier & D. W. Osgood (Eds.), *The Nebraska Symposium on Motivation* (pp. 119–177). Lincoln: University of Nebraska Press.

Peersen, M., Sigurdsson, J. F., Gudjonsson, G. H., & Gretarsson, S. J. (2004). Predicting re-offending: A 5-year prospective study of Icelandic prison inmates. *Psychology, Crime and Law, 10*, 197–204.

Petersen, A. C., Crockett, L. J., Richards, M., & Boxer, A. (1988). A self-report measure of pubertal status: Reliability, validity, and initial norms. *Journal of Youth and Adolescence, 17*, 117–133.

Piquero, A. R. (2000). Frequency, specialization, and violence in offending careers. *Journal of Research in Crime and Delinquency, 37*, 392–418.

Piquero, A. R. (in press). Taking stock of developmental trajectories of criminal activity over the life course. In A. Liberman (Ed.), *The Long View of Crime: A Synthesis of Longitudinal Research.* New York: Springer.

Piquero, A. R., Blumstein, A., Brame, R., Haapanen, R., Mulvey, E. P., & Nagin, D. (2001). Assessing the impact of exposure time and incapacitation on longitudinal trajectories of criminal offending. *Journal of Adolescent Research, 16*, 54–74.

Piquero, A. R., Fagan, J., Mulvey, E. P., Steinberg, L., & Odgers, C. (2005). Developmental trajectories of legal socialization among serious adolescent offenders. *Journal of Criminal Law and Criminology, 96*, 267–298.

Piquero, A. R., Farrington, D. P., & Blumstein, A. (2003). The Criminal career paradigm. In M. Tonry, (Ed.), *Crime and justice: An annual review of research, Vol. 30* (pp. 359–506). Chicago: University of Chicago Press.

Piquero, A. R., Farrington, D. P., & Blumstein, A. (2007). *Key issues in criminal career research: New analyses of the Cambridge Study in Delinquent Development.* Cambridge, England: Cambridge University Press.

Piquero, A., Paternoster, R., Mazerolle, P., Brame, R., & Dean, C. W. (1999). Onset age and offense specialization. *Journal of Research in Crime and Delinquency, 36*, 275–299.

Pollard, J. A., Hawkins, J. D., & Arthur, M. W. (1999). Risk and protection: Are both necessary to understand diverse behavioral outcomes in adolescence? *Social Work Research, 23*, 145–158.

Preacher, K. J., Rucker, D. D., MacCallum, R. C., & Nicewander, W. A. (2005). Use of the extreme groups approach: A critical reexamination and new recommendations. *Psychological Methods, 10*, 178–192.

Raaijmakers, Q. A. W., Engels, R. C. M. E., & Van Hoof, A. (2005). Delinquency and moral reasoning in adolescence and young adulthood. *International Journal of Behavioral Development, 29*, 247–258.

Raine, A. (1993). The Psychopathology of Crime. San Diego, CA: Academic Press.

Raine, A., Moffitt, T. E., Caspi, A., Loeber, R., Stouthamer-Loeber, M., & Lynam, D. (2005). Neurocognitive impairments in boys on the life-course persistent antisocial path. *Journal of Abnormal Psychology, 114*, 38-49.

Reiss, A. J., & Farrington, D. P. (1991). Advancing knowledge about co-offending: Results from a prospective longitudinal survey of London males. *Journal of Criminal Law and Criminology, 82*, 360–395.

Reiss, A. J., & Roth, J. A. (Eds.) (1993). *Understanding and Preventing Violence.* Washington, DC: National Academy Press.

Resnick, M. D., Ireland, M., & Borowsky, I. (2004). Youth violence perpetration: What protects? What predicts? Findings from the National Longitudinal Study of Adolescent Health. *Journal of Adolescent Health, 35*, e1–e10.

Rhee, S. H., & Waldman, I. D. (2002). Genetic and environmental influences on antisocial behavior: A meta-analysis of twin and adoption studies. *Psychological Bulletin, 128*, 490–529.

Robins, L. N. (1966). *Deviant Children Grown Up: A Sociological and Psychiatric Study of Sociopathic Personality.* Baltimore: Williams and Wilkins.

Robins, L. N. (1979). Follow-up studies. In H. C. Quay, & J. S. Werry (Eds.), *Psychopathological disorders of childhood* (pp. 483–513). New York: Wiley.

Roebuck, J. B. (1966). *Criminal Typology.* Springfield, IL: Charles C. Thomas.

Rogosa, D. R., & Willett, J. B. (1985). Understanding correlates of change by modeling individual-differences in growth. *Psychometrika, 50*, 203–228.

Roisman, G. I., Aguilar, B., & Egeland, B. (2004). Antisocial behavior in the transition to adulthood: The independent and interactive roles of developmental history and emerging developmental tasks. *Developmental Psychopathology, 16*, 857–871.

Roizen, R. (1993). *Paradigm sidetracked: Explaining early resistance to the alcoholism paradigm at Yale's Laboratory of Applied Physiology, 1940–1944.* Paper presented to the International Congress on the Social History of Alcohol, Huron College, London, Ontario, Canada.

Rutter, M. (1979). Protective factors in children's responses to stress and disadvantage. *Annals of the Academy of Medicine, 8*, 324–338.

Rutter, M. (2003). Commentary: Causal processes leading to antisocial behavior. *Developmental Psychology, 39*, 372–378.

Sameroff, A. J., Bartko, W. T., Baldwin, A., Baldwin, C., & Seifer, R. (1998). Family and social influences on the development of child competence. In M. Lewis & C. Feiring (Eds.), *Families, Risk, and Competence* (pp. 161–185). Mahwah, NJ: Erlbaum.

Sameroff, A. J., & Mackenzie, M. J. (2003). Research strategies for capturing transactional models of development: The limits of the possibility. *Development and Psychopathology, 15*, 613–640.

Sampson, R. J., & Laub, J. H. (1993). *Crime in the Making: Pathways and Turning Points through Life.* Cambridge, MA: Harvard University Press.

Sampson, R. J. & Laub, J. H. (2003). Life-course desisters? Trajectories of crime among delinquent boys followed to age 70. *Criminology, 41*, 301–340.

Sampson, R. J., Raudenbush, S. W., & Earls, F. (1997). Neighborhoods and violent crime: A multilevel study of collective efficacy. *Science, 277*, 918–951.

Schroeder, R. D., Giordano, P. C., & Cernkovich, S. A. (2007). Drug use and desistance processes. *Criminology, 45*, 191–222.

Shaw, D. S., Gilliom, M., Ingoldsby, E. M., & Nagin, D. S. (2003). Trajectories leading to school-age conduct problems. *Developmental Psychology, 39*, 189–200.

Shaw, D. S., Lacourse, E., & Nagin, D. S. (2004). Developmental trajectories of conduct problems and hyperactivity from ages 2 to 10. *Journal of Child Psychology and Psychiatry, 45*, 1–12.

Skinner, H. A., Steinhauer, P. D., & Santa-Barbara, J. (1983). The family assessment measure. *Canadian Journal of Community Mental Health, 2*, 91–105.

Smart, D., Vassallo, S., Sanson, A., Richardson, N., Dussuyer, I., McKendry, W., Toumbourou, J., Prior, M., & Oberklaid, F. (2003). *Patterns and precursors of adolescent antisocial behaviour—Second report*. Melbourne, Australia: Crime Prevention Victoria.

Smith, C., Lizotte, A. J., Thornberry, T. P., & Krohn, M. D. (1995). Resilient youth: Identifying factors that prevent high-risk youth from engaging in delinquency and drug use. In J. Hagan (Ed.), *Current perspectives in aging and the life cycle: Vol. 4: Delinquency and disrepute in the life course* (pp. 217–247). Greenwich, CT: JAI.

Smith, C., & Thornberry, T. P. (1995). The relationship between childhood maltreatment and adolescent involvement in delinquency. *Criminology, 33*, 451–477.

Stander, J., Farrington, D. P., Hill, G., & Altham, P. M. E. (1989). Markov chain analysis and specialization in criminal careers. *British Journal of Criminology, 29*, 317–335.

Stattin, H., & Kerr, M. (2000). Parental monitoring: A reinterpretation. *Child Development, 71*, 1072–1085.

Stouthamer-Loeber, M., & Loeber, R. (2002). Lost opportunities for intervention: Undetected markers for the development of serious juvenile delinquency. *Criminal Behaviour and Mental Health, 12*, 69–82.

Stouthamer-Loeber, M., Loeber, R., Farrington D. P., Zhang, Q., Van Kammen, W. B., & Maguin, E. (1993). The double edge of protective and risk factors for delinquency: Inter-relations and developmental patterns. *Development and Psychopathology, 5*, 683–701.

Stouthamer-Loeber, M., Loeber, R., & Thomas, C. (1992). Caretakers seeking help for boys with disruptive delinquent behavior. *Comprehensive Mental Health Care, 2*, 159–178.

Stouthamer-Loeber, M., Loeber, R., Wei, E., Farrington, D. P., & Wikström, P-O. H. (2002). Risk and promotive effects in the explanation of persistent serious delinquency in boys. *Journal of Consulting and Clinical Psychology, 70*, 111–123.

Stouthamer-Loeber, M., & Van Kammen, W. B. (1995). *Data Collection and Management: A Practical Guide*. Newbury Park, CA: Sage.

Stouthamer-Loeber, M., Wei, E. H., Homish, D. L., & Loeber, R. (2002). Which family and demographic factors are related to both maltreatment and persistent serious juvenile delinquency? *Children's Services: Social Policy, Research, & Practice, 5*, 261–272.

Stouthamer-Loeber, M., Wei, E., Loeber, R., Masten, A. S. (2004). Desistance from persistent serious delinquency in the transition to adulthood. *Development and Psychopathology, 16*, 897–918.

Szapocznik, J., & Coatsworth, J.D. (1999). An ecodevelopmental framework for organizing the influences on drug abuse: A developmental model of risk and protection. In M. D Glantz & C. R. Hartel (Eds.), *Drug abuse: Origins and Interventions* (pp. 331–366). Washington, DC: American Psychological Association.

Thornberry, T. P. (1998). Membership in youth gangs and involvement in serious and violent offending. In R. Loeber & D. P. Farrington (Eds.), *Serious and violent juvenile offenders: Risk factors and successful interventions* (pp. 147–166). Thousand Oaks, CA: Sage.

Thornberry, T. P. (2005). Explaining multiple patterns of offending across the life course and across generations. *Annals of the American Academy of Political and Social Science, 602,* 296–298.

Thornberry, T. P., Freeman-Gallant, A., Lizotte, A. J., Krohn, M. D., & Smith, C. A. (2003). Linked lives: The intergenerational transmission of antisocial behavior. *Journal of Abnormal Child Psychology, 31,* 171–184.

Thornberry, T. P., Hops, H., Conger, R. D., & Capaldi, D. M. (2003). Replicated findings and future directions for intergenerational studies: Closing comments. *Journal of Abnormal Child Psychology, 31,* 201–203.

Thornberry, T. B., & Krohn, M. D. (Eds.) (2003). *Taking Stock of Delinquency: An Overview of Findings from Contemporary Longitudinal Studies.* New York: Kluwer Academic/Plenum.

Thornberry, T. P., Krohn, M. D., Lizotte, A. J., Smith, C. A., & Tobin, K. (2003). *Gangs and Delinquency in Developmental Perspective.* Cambridge, England: Cambridge University Press.

Tita, G. E., Cohen, J., & Engberg, J. (2005). An ecological study of the location of gang "set space." *Social Problems, 52,* 272–299.

Tolan, P. H., & Gorman-Smith, D. (1998). Development of serious and violent offending careers. In R. Loeber & D. P. Farrington (Eds.), *Serious and Violent Juvenile Offenders: Risk Factors and Successful Intervention.* Thousand Oaks, CA: Sage.

Tolan, P. H., Gorman-Smith, D., & Loeber, R. (2000). Developmental timing of onsets of disruptive behaviors and later delinquency of inner-city youth. *Journal of Child and Family Studies, 9,* 203–230.

Tolan, P. H., Guerra, N. G., & Kendall, P. C. (1995). A developmental-ecological perspective on antisocial behavior in children and adolescents: Toward a unified risk and intervention framework. *Journal of Consulting and Clinical Psychology, 63,* 579–584.

Tracy, P. E., Wolfgang, M. E., & Figlio, R. M. (1990). *Delinquency Careers in Two Birth Cohorts.* New York: Plenum.

Tremblay, R. (2003). Why socialization fails: The case of chronic physical aggression. In B. B. Lahey, T. E. Moffitt, & A. Caspi (Eds.), *Causes of Conduct Disorder and Juvenile Delinquency* (pp. 182–224). New York: Guilford.

Tremblay, R., Hartup, W. W., & Archer, J. (2005). *Developmental Origins of Aggression.* New York: Guilford.

Tremblay, R. E., Japel, C., Pérusse, D., McDuff, P., Boivin, M., Zoccolillo, M., & Montplaisir, J. (1999). The search for the age of "onset" of physical aggression: Rousseau and Bandura revisited. *Criminal Behaviour and Mental Health, 9,* 8–23.

Tremblay, R. E., Massé, B., Perron, D., Leblanc, M., Schwartzman, A. E., & Leding-ham, J. E. (1992). Early disruptive behavior, poor school achievement, delin-quent behavior, and delinquent personality: Longitudinal analysis. *Journal of Consulting and Clinical Psychology, 60,* 64–72.

Tremblay, R. E., & Nagin, D.S. (2005). The developmental origins of physical aggres-sion in humans. In R. E. Tremblay & W. W. Hartup (Eds.), *Developmental Ori-gins of Aggression* (pp. 85–106). New York: Guilford.

Tremblay, R. E., Nagin, D. S., Séguin, J. R., Zoccolillo, M., Zelazo, P. D., Boivin, M., Pérusse, D., & Japel, C. (2004). Physical aggression during early childhood: Tra-jectories and predictors. *Pediatrics, 114,* e43–e50.

Tremblay, R. E., Vitaro, F., Bertrand, L., Le Blanc, M., Beauchesne, H., Boileau, H., & David, L. (1992). Parent and child training to prevent early onset of delinquency: The Montreal longitudinal experimental study. In J. McCord & R. E. Tremblay (Eds.), *Preventing Antisocial Behavior: Interventions from Birth through Adoles-cence* (pp. 117–137). New York: Guilford.

Tremblay, R. E., Vitaro, F., Gagnon, C., Piche, C., & Royer, N. (1992). A prosocial scale for the preschool behavior questionnaire: Concurrent and predictive correlates. *International Journal of Behavioral Development, 15,* 227–245.

U.S. Department of Health and Human Services (DHHS). (2001). *Youth violence: A report of the surgeon general.* Available online at www.surgeongeneral.gov/library/youthviolence/toc.html.

Valdez, A., Yin, Z., & Kaplan, C.D. (1997). A comparison of alcohol, drugs, and aggres-sive crime among Mexican-American, black, and white male arrestees in Texas. *American Journal of Drug and Alcohol Abuse, 23,* 249–265.

Van Kammen, W. B., & Loeber, R. (1994). Are fluctuations in delinquent activities related to the onset and offset in juvenile illegal drug use and drug dealing? *Journal of Drug Issues, 24,* 9–24.

Van Wijk, A., Loeber, R., Vermeiren, R., Pardini, D., Bullens, R., & Doreleijers, T. (2005). Violent juvenile sex offenders compared with violent juvenile nonsex offenders: Explorative findings from the Pittsburgh Youth Study. *Sexual Abuse: A Journal of Research and Treatment, 17,* 333–352.

Vassallo, S., Smart, D., Sanson, S., Dussuyer, I., Bourne, M., Toumbourou, J., Prior, M., & Oberklaid, F. (2002). *Patterns and precursors of adolescent antisocial behav-iour: First report 2002.* Unpublished report.

Vitaro, F., Brengden, M., & Barker, E. D. (2006). Subtypes of aggressive behaviors: A developmental perspective. *International Journal of Behavioral Development, 31,* 11–18.

Von Eye, A., & Bergman, L. R. (2003). Research strategies in developmental psychopa-thology: Dimensional identity and the person-oriented approach. *Development and Psychopathology, 15,* 553–580.

Wei, E., Hipwell, A., Pardini, D., Beyers, J. M., & Loeber, R. (2005). Block observations of neighbourhood physical disorder are associated with neighbourhood crime, firearm injuries and deaths, and teen births. *Journal of Epidemiology and Com-munity Health, 59,* 904–908.

Wei, E. H., Loeber, R., & White, H. R. (2004). Teasing apart the developmental associa-tions between alcohol and marijuana use and violence. *Journal of Contemporary Criminal Justice, 20,* 166–183.

372 • References

Weinrott, M. (1975). Manual for retrieval of juvenile court data. Unpublished manuscript, Evaluation Research Group, Eugene, OR.

Weisz, J. R., Sandler, I. N., Drulak, J. A., & Anton, B. S. (2005). Promoting and protecting youth mental health through evidence-based prevention and treatment. *American Psychologist, 60,* 628–649.

Wekerle, C., & Wolfe, D. A. (1998). The role of child maltreatment and attachment style in adolescent relationship violence. *Development and Psychopathology, 10,* 571–586.

Welsh, B. C., Loeber, R., Stouthamer-Loeber, M., Cohen, M.A., Farrington, F. P., & Stevens, B. R. (in press). The cost of juvenile crime in urban areas: A longitudinal perspective. *Youth Violence and Juvenile Justice.*

Werner, E. E. (2005). What can we learn about resilience from large-scale longitudinal studies? In S. Goldstein & R. B. Brooks (Eds.), *Handbook of Resilience in Children* (pp. 91–106). New York: Kluwer Academic/Plenum.

West, D. J., & Farrington, D. P. (1977). *The Delinquent Way of Life.* London: Heinemann.

White, H. R., Bates, M. E., & Buyske, S. (2001). Adolescence-limited versus persistent delinquency: Extending Moffitt's hypothesis into adulthood. *Journal of Abnormal Child Psychology, 110,* 600–609.

White, H. R., & Gorman, D. M. (2000). Dynamics of the drug-crime relationships. In the nature of crime: Continuity and change. *Criminal Justice, 1,* 151–218.

White, H. R., & Hansell, S. (1998). Acute and long-term effects of drug use on aggression from adolescence into adulthood. *Journal of Drug Issues, 28,* 837–858.

White, H. R., & Labouvie, E. W. (1994). Generality versus specificity of problem behavior: Psychological and functional differences. *Journal of Drug Issues, 24,* 55–74.

White, H. R., Loeber, R., Stouthamer-Loeber, M., & Farrington, D. P. (1999). Developmental associations between substance use and violence. *Development and Psychopathology, 11,* 785–803.

White, H. R., Nagin, D., Replogle, E., & Stouthamer-Loeber, M. (2004). Racial differences in trajectories of cigarette use. *Drug and Alcohol Dependence, 76,* 219–227.

White, H. R., Pandina, R. J., & LaGrange, R. L. (1987). Longitudinal predictors of serious substance use and delinquency. *Criminology, 25,* 715–740.

White, H.R., Tice, P.C., Loeber, R., & Stouthamer-Loeber, M. (2002). Illegal acts committed by adolescents under the influence of alcohol and drugs. *Journal of Research in Crime and Delinquency, 39,* 131–152.

White, J. L., Moffitt, T. E., Caspi, A., Bartusch, D. J., Needles, D. J., & Stouthamer-Loeber, M. (1994). Measuring impulsivity and examining its relationship to delinquency. *Journal of Abnormal Psychology, 103,* 192–205.

Wiggins, J. S. (1973). *Personality and Prediction: Principles of Personality Assessment.* Reading, MA: Addison Wesley.

Wikström, P. O., & Loeber, R. (2000). Do disadvantaged neighborhoods cause well-adjusted children to become adolescent delinquents? A study of male juvenile serious offending, risk and protective factors, and neighborhood context. *Criminology, 38,* 1109–1141.

Wilson, J. Q., & Herrnstein, R. J. (1985). *Crime and Human Nature.* New York: Simon and Schuster.

Wolfgang, M. E., Figlio, R. M., & Sellin, T. (1972). *Delinquency in a Birth Cohort.* Chicago: University of Chicago Press.

Wolfgang, M. E., Figlio, R. M., Tracy, P. E., & Singer, S. I. (1985). *The National Survey of Crime Severity.* Washington, DC: U.S. Government Printing Office.

Yoshikawa, H. (1994). Prevention as cumulative protection: Effects of early family support and education on chronic delinquency and its risks. *Psychological Bulletin, 115,* 28–54.

Zhang, Q., Loeber, R., & Stouthamer-Loeber, M. (1997). Developmental trends of delinquent attitudes and behaviors: Replications and synthesis across domains, time, and samples. *Journal of Quantitative Criminology, 13,* 181–215.

Index